Lecture Notes
in Business Information Processing   42

W0090964

Daniel Dolk
Janusz Granat (Eds.)

Modeling
for Decision Support
in Network-Based Services

The Application of Quantitative Modeling
to Service Science

 Springer

Volume Editors

Daniel Dolk
Naval Postgraduate School
Department of Information Sciences
Monterey, CA, USA
E-mail: drdolk@nps.edu

Janusz Granat
Warsaw University of Technology
Institute of Control and Computation Engineering
and
National Institute of Telecommunications
Warsaw, Poland
E-mail: j.granat@itl.waw.pl

ISSN 1865-1348   e-ISSN 1865-1356
ISBN 978-3-642-27611-8   e-ISBN 978-3-642-27612-5
DOI 10.1007/978-3-642-27612-5
Springer Heidelberg Dordrecht London New York

Library of Congress Control Number: 2011944287

ACM Computing Classification (1998): J.1, H.3.5, I.2

Typesetting: Camera-ready by author, data conversion by Scientific Publishing Services, Chennai, India

Printed on acid-free paper

Springer is part of Springer Science+Business Media (www.springer.com)

Preface

The genesis of this book came from several recent workshops and related activities conducted by the IFIP Working Group 7.6 on Optimization-Based Computer-Aided Modeling and Design (see http://www.ifip.or.at/bulletin/ bulltcs/tc7_aim.htm). This group has been active for 20 years with the stated objective of developing "high-performance computer-aided systems to support modeling, decision analysis, optimization and multicriteria decision making." An equally important goal of the group is the successful solution of interesting real-world problems, which over the years has occurred largely in the four areas of network design (communications, transportation, traffic, and supply chain), planning and scheduling in transportation logistics, production planning and scheduling, and environmental planning problems.

In recent years our group, in recognition of the worldwide transition from product-oriented to service-oriented economies, has turned our attention to the application of modeling and optimization to service science, management and engineering (SSME). SSME is an initiative of the IBM Corporation to legitimize service science as a proper scientific discipline much as they did with computer science in the 1950s. SSME is by nature multidisciplinary, requiring synergies among operations research, management science, knowledge science, network science, information science and economics. SSME is also still a young research field searching for theoretical underpinnings, and one which has many opportunities for analytical modeling to not only advance our understanding, but also to actually help form the foundation of a new discipline.

This book is the result of our introductory foray into the application of quantitative modeling to the nascent field of service science with special emphasis on the network aspects of services. Our hope is that it will showcase the value of modeling in a new and timely context and, as with all scientific inquiry, we hope that it provides a seed for further exciting research.

October 2011

Daniel Dolk
Janusz Granat

Table of Contents

Introduction

Section I - Network Science

Section II - Computational and Analytical Modeling

Section III - Knowledge Science

Modeling for Decision Support
in Network-Based Services

Daniel Dolk[1] and Janusz Granat[2]

[1] Naval Postgraduate School, Dept of Information Sciences,
Faculty of Electronics, Monterey, CA USA 93943
drdolk@nps.edu
[2] Institute of Control and Computation Engineering Warsaw University
of Technology and National Institutute of Telecommunications Warsaw, Poland
J.Granat@itl.waw.pl

Abstract. In this introduction to the book, we discuss our current motivation for modeling and optimization applications involving network-based services. Our conceptual model of service science management and engineering (SSME) as the basis for better understanding network-based services embraces the confluence of network science, computational and analytical modeling, knowledge science and decision support. We segment the contributed articles into these four categories and provide a capsule summary of each paper.

Keywords: Network-based services, decision support, modeling, optimization, knowledge science.

1 Introduction

It is no secret by now that we are experiencing a worldwide shift from a product-oriented to a service-oriented global economy which has accelerated dramatically during the past decade. In concert with this transformation, there has been a strong push by industry and many universities to establish service science, management and engineering (SSME) as a legitimate field of academic study[1] [2]. Heightened interest in "service research", in particular, research into service provision and innovation is becoming progressively more important as automated service-provision via the web matures as a technology [16].

We therefore have undertaken in this book to re-examine aspects of the mature, largely product-oriented, discipline of operations research (OR) through the newer lens of SSME. Our IFIP Working Group 7.6 on Optimization-Based

---

[1] "SSME" typically signifies "Service Science Management and Engineering" in the literature. However we prefer the less heroic rendition "Service Systems Management and Engineering", believing that a systems approach to services is immediately applicable and profitable whereas it remains a stretch as to whether services can be elevated to a science. Henceforth in this article "SSME" will refer to the latter.
[2] See the IBM initiative in this regard at http://www.research.ibm.com/ssme/workuniv.shtml

D. Dolk et al. (Eds.): Decision Support Modeling in Service Networks, LNBIP 42, pp. 1–13, 2012.
© Springer-Verlag Berlin Heidelberg 2012

Computer Aided Modeling and Design has historically addressed the successful solution of interesting real world OR problems in transportation and telecommunications network design, production planning and scheduling in transportation logistics and supply chain management, and environmental planning problems. A large number of the applications dealt with have been very large-scale, complex, and highly collaborative modeling problems (e.g. [7], [10]). Four different foci provide the conceptual framework for these related research interests as shown in Fig. 1.

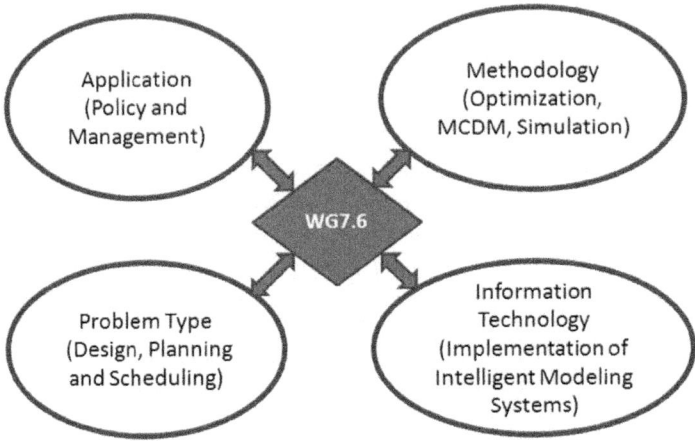

Fig. 1. Four basic focus themes of WG7.6

SSME on the other hand, being a young discipline, is still searching for basic paradigms upon which to establish its theoretical groundwork. On the application side of SSME, there has been relatively little discussion of the linkage between decision support systems (DSS) in the form of computational and analytical modeling and service science. Adopting a services systems approach has significant implications for the kinds of modeling that need to be done, but which we believe by and large have not been systematically addressed in either the OR or service science literature. This book is an initial attempt to remedy this shortcoming.

Key concepts and conceptual frameworks for SSME include service-dominant logic, co-creation of value, service systems, and service innovation. According to [17], "service-dominant logic is focused on the interaction of the producer and the consumer and other supply and value network partners as they co-create value through collaborative processes". Major characteristics of service- versus traditional economic goods-dominant logic include a shift to service processes (workflows) from goods creation, the primacy of knowledge in sustaining competitive advantage, a strong emphasis on symmetric collaborative processes of exchange for co-creating value and communications, and a shift from goals of profit maximization to optimal levels of service.

Thinking in terms of selling a flow of service as opposed to a tangible product leads to consideration of a service system. A *service system* is an integrated, value-creating configuration of service providers, clients, partners, and consumers [16]. The best-performing service systems are increasingly IT-enabled, customer-centered, relationship-focused, and knowledge-intensive. This has many implications for modeling approaches for representing service systems. From an optimization modeling perspective, this might indicate a change in focus from the objective of profit maximization / cost minimization to one of optimal configuration of goods for a particular level of service, optimal network configurations for maintaining service, and optimal payment mechanisms for providing the service [17]. Since service systems are also heavily process-oriented and collaborative in nature, simulation approaches may also be appropriate technologies for modeling these systems. Discrete event simulation systems such as Arena are well-suited for modeling processes and workflows. Given the high level of feedback that characterizes a true service relationship, system dynamics may be another profitable approach to consider in modeling such a relationship. Agent-based simulation may also be able to capture aspects of the increased social relational dynamics inherent in service relationships.

Service innovation is also a major tributary to SSME philosophy. No coherent definition of service innovation has emerged but it can be thought of usefully as the rapid, dynamic creation of new services from existing resources which provide value to multiple parties concurrently, often, but not always, facilitated by service-based information platforms. One familiar example is the proliferation of award-based purchasing of airline tickets, hotels, rental cars, etc. and the partnerships which emerge between these various purveyors. Service innovation is often closely linked to service design and to the creation of value webs or value networks that are in turn characterized in terms of the tangible and intangible benefits which they provide. The design and deployment of new services has much in common with information modeling and system design but informed by the new paradigm of dynamically configurable and executable models in the spirit of the Semantic Web.

2 Conceptual Framework of SSME

Our view of service systems management and engineering represents a confluence of three major disciplines: network science, computational / analytical modeling, and knowledge science / engineering in concert with a portfolio of large-scale, complex decision support applications (Fig. 2).

2.1 Network Science

Networks underlie our contemporary view of complexity and complex systems [1] and play an undeniable role in SSME. Value webs consist of networks of partners who collaborate at different stages of interlinked value chains enabled and coordinated by information communications technology (ICT). These technologies support both formalized inter-business and inter-personal informal processes

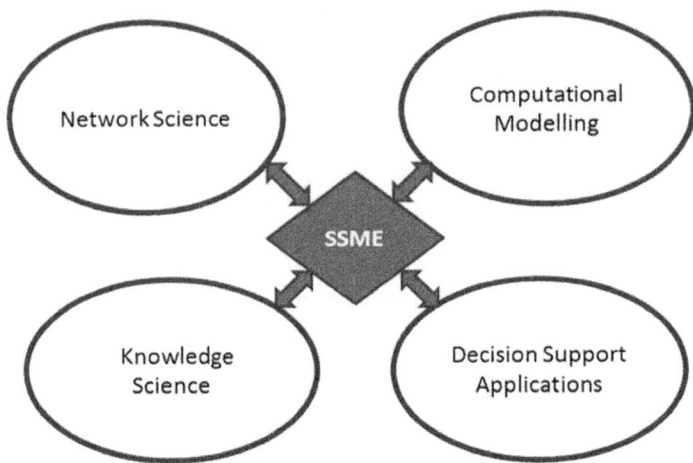

Fig. 2. Conceptual Framework for SSME

and relationships and offer ways to embed relationships into broader contexts. Collaborative decision-making in general relies upon our understanding of social networks in addition to the technological networks which deliver information and knowledge.

2.2 Computational and Analytical Modeling

Computational and analytical modeling has a key role to play in advancing the discipline of SSME. As SSME strives to establish and extend its conceptual and theoretical bases, it is critical to marshal relevant modeling techniques for the design, development, and evaluation of service systems. We make a fundamental distinction between computational and analytical modeling. Specifically, we use "analytical modeling" to refer to the modeling paradigms typically associated with operations research and management science (e.g., optimization, econometrics, discrete event simulation, Monte Carlo simulation, etc.). These modeling technologies will continue to occupy an important niche in SSME research, some of the ways of which we have indicated above. Indeed, several of the articles in this book deal with various optimization approaches to service-related applications.

"Computational modeling", on the other hand, we view primarily in the context of simulation technologies, especially agent-based simulation (ABS). Computational modeling has assumed an increasingly important role in scientific inquiry as our understanding of complexity has progressed from Simon's "top down" hierarchical decomposition perspective [15] to one of complex adaptive systems characterized by "bottom up" network-based emergent processes [11]. The effectiveness of ABS in modeling more qualitative, human-driven open system phenomena such as societies [4], organizations [9], and markets have opened the doors for combining the study of technological and social networks in tandem [3]. This is especially promising for research into service systems which often have many of the qualities of emergent systems, and which, by definition, deal with networks of players who wish to engage in collaborative activities. Supply chain management is one such collaborative example where not only ABS but also optimization modeling approaches are fruitful [8].

As shown in Fig. 3, we focus on modeling from two distinct, yet complementary, perspectives:

- The modeling of services and service-specific IT systems to include computational modeling approaches such as agent-based simulation and game theory, and analytical operations research modeling paradigms such as optimization, multi-criteria decision analysis, simulation and uncertainty-based approaches in designing service systems.
- Service-based support of modeling to facilitate the delivery of modeling support and associated environments using Web service-based principles. This includes various approaches to service-oriented architectures such as grid computing, software and models as a service, solvers as a service, Web services for modeling and optimization-based problem solving, and methodologies, techniques, and tools for automated service composition and delivery.

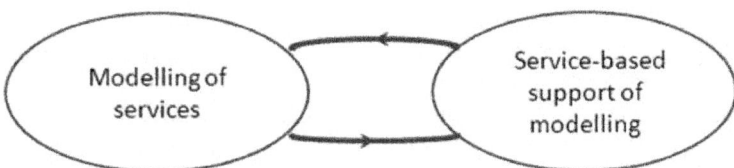

Fig. 3. Modeling services vis-à-vis Service-oriented modeling

2.3   Knowledge Science and Engineering

The evolution of knowledge management to knowledge science has been earmarked by a shift from structure and technology to processes and people. Whereas the first generation of knowledge management emphasized knowledge representation and the manipulation of knowledge bases, for example in the form of expert system technology, the second generation focuses upon knowledge dynamics, and how knowledge flows within a system [12], [13]. This contemporary view of knowledge management emphasizes people rather than technology and encompasses the interactions of four basic components: personnel, work processes, organizations, and technologies (Fig. 4).

Knowledge is a critical factor in the SSME landscape, particularly as it relates to innovation. Knowledge is typically segmented into explicit versus tacit knowledge (sometimes referred to as tangible versus intangible) where the former is quantifiable and documentable, and the latter is qualitative in nature embedded

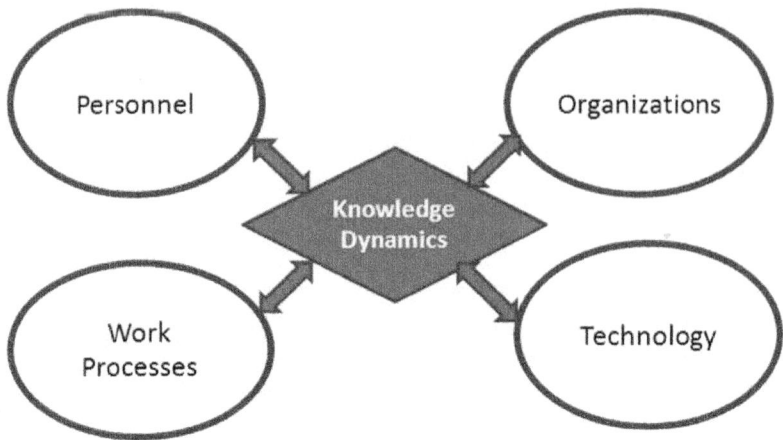

Fig. 4. Components of Knowledge Dynamics

in human experience and intuition. The flow of knowledge typically addresses how to move tacit knowledge which is often "clumped" into pockets of experts to a broader audience who can benefit from this as well. Closely related is the process of knowledge creation which is extremely important in collaborative activities which earmark services relationships, particularly in the creation of new services from existing resources.

A continuing area of interest for the modeling community is the development of knowledge-based support for modeling processes. Knowledge-based research areas relevant for SSME include knowledge science approaches to services and their modeling, Semantic Web, ontologies, business rules for modeling and services computing, knowledge-based modeling environments, and the dynamics of service evolution.

2.4   Decision Support

Decision support systems (DSS) comprise the application dimension of our confluence between modeling and SSME. DSS have perhaps enjoyed their greatest success in the field of operations research because of the basic assumption that there is a tight connection between decision-making and models [Forrester 1961]. The nature of DSS has changed dramatically over the last decade however due to a variety of factors:

– Exponential increase in sources and amounts of data: Sensor technology, for example, has made extensive technological advances, now providing data feeds encompassing multiple orders of magnitude from satellite level to nano-level phenomena. The need to squeeze information from these huge stores of data has moved data, text and Web mining to the forefront of decision analysis.

– The nature of the decision-making terrain has been transformed substantially since 9-11 and Hurricane Katrina. Crisis management, especially emergency response, has become an overriding priority, but these applications involve decision parameters of very high risk, very high uncertainty, and tightly constrained timelines, a significant departure from the more conventional view of DSS. From a network perspective, we are now forced to deal with extremely fluid networks where players enter and leave the network in unpredictable ways. From a Bayesian perspective, we are not only unable to attach probabilities to the outcomes set in these situations; we are unable even to define what all the possible outcomes may be. This marks a shift from "we know what we don't know" to what is now commonly referred to as "we don't know what we don't know". In such dynamic decision environments, there often is simply not enough time to build models to support decision-making processes. Agent-based simulation, or constructive modeling, can sometimes be helpful in illuminating such decision landscapes, emphasizing the "what might be" over the "what is", "what will be", or "what should be" perspectives of descriptive, predictive, and normative models respectively.

– As a result, the focus has shifted decidedly over the past decade from individual-based DSS to network-based collaborative decision-making [3], from single decision points to decision chains, and from relatively structured model applications and environments to dynamically configurable processes and workflows facilitated by service-oriented architectures.

It would appear then that the services system approach can be of potential benefit to the "new breed" of DSS and reciprocally that DSS can be deployed in the design and development of innovative service systems. In the next section, we discuss each of the articles in the book and how they connect back to one or more of the principles discussed above.

3   Overview of the Articles

In this book, we have collected papers which realize the confluence of network science, computational / analytical modeling, knowledge science, and decision support as applied to the emerging area of services systems management and engineering (SSME). We have assigned each article into the one of three categories: network science, computational and analytical modeling, or knowledge science, realizing full well that in many instances there will be overlap and complementarity.

3.1   Network Science and SSME

The first article in the network science section, *Supporting and optimizing interactive decision processes in grid environments with a model-driven approach* by Reichwald et al, deals with service-oriented grid computing for engineering applications. Grid computing has become an increasingly attractive option for modeling applications such as large-scale optimization, co-simulation design, and agent-based simulation where multiple processors facilitate solutions that might otherwise be prohibitively inefficient to obtain, if not infeasible. This paper describes how grid technology can serve as the vehicle for designing, optimizing and executing workflows for complex engineering processes.

The next two articles focus on optimization modeling in complex, large-scale transportation networks. Although a strong case can be made for putting these articles in the next section on modeling, the strong network nature of their respective models makes their consideration here extremely relevant. Sebastian's chapter on *Optimization approaches in the strategic and tactical planning of networks for letter, parcel and freight mail*, deftly describes how optimization modeling is applied to very large-scale network-based services. Typically, postal organizations are concerned with reducing transportation and delivery times, and minimizing costs under service quality constraints. Networks as large as the real world distribution networks for letter, parcel or freight mail are typically structured hierarchically which lends them to a general solution approach of heuristic decomposition using cut-off times and time windows in order to model service quality requirements. The article describes the models, optimization approaches and associated DSS of three real world cases of sub-networks of distribution networks: The Deutsche Post World Net (DPWN) night-airmail network for letter mail, optimal location of delivery stations within the allocated zip code areas of a letter-/ parcel mail sorting centre, and DHL's parcel and freight mail long haul transportation network using swap body containers and intermodal (rail/ road) transportation. These case studies amply show how complex and nontrivial the concept of services is in very large-scale, network-driven applications and how central they are to effective decision-making.

The third and last article on networks, Kopfer and Schnberger's *Adaptation of optimization models in volatile transport scenarios*, tackles the very interesting challenge of how to adapt online optimization to solving transport problems where the problem parameters change nontrivially in real time and render static solutions obsolete. The specific problem consists of solving a dynamic vehicle routing and scheduling problem where, at any point in time, options exist for subcontracting some of the incoming requests to external carriers in order to meet delivery service quality constraints. Clearly the decision to utilize one or more of these subcontractors immediately compromises the current optimal routing schedule. The authors generate, test, and evaluate several static as well as adaptive rules for automatically adjusting the objective functions and/or constraint sets of the emerging decision models of the online optimization problem. The results reveal that a flexible balancing between the short-term goals of the single decision problems and the long-term goal of the entire online problem is possible. What this application, in conjunction with the previous articles, demonstrates is that a very high degree of modeling sophistication is required to satisfy service-related constraints in the real world.

3.2   Computational and Analytical Modeling in SSME

Four papers directly address the intersection of computational modeling and SSME. There are two perspectives in this regard: modeling tools which facilitate the design and development of service-based systems, and conversely, service-based technological support of modeling applications. The paper by Becker, Beverungen, and Knackstedt, *Modeling languages and reference models for product-service systems*, adopts the former perspective by enumerating requirements for modeling languages which support service dominant logic in conjunction with product dominant logic. Currently such languages exist only in the product dominant domain. The development of modeling languages has been a significant advance in the promulgation of executable modeling systems, that is, systems which provide interfaces for representing models at high degrees of abstraction that bridge the gap between the technical details of their respective models and the conceptual requirements of users and decision-makers, thus allowing the latter to more easily specify and solve the former. Developing such languages for service dominant applications will eventually facilitate the design of service systems. This paper represents a first step in the evolution of such modeling tools by examining existing product-oriented languages as a basis for conceptualizing what features service-oriented counterparts must provide.

Modeling languages are also the focus of the second article in this section. *SC-CoJava: A service composition language to unify simulation and optimization of supply chains*, by Brodsky, Al-Nory, and Nash describes extensions to the Java programming language that facilitate the integration of optimization modeling and discrete event simulation in the same environment for solving certain classes of supply chain problems. Their system automatically generates and solves an optimization model of decision choice variables which are in turn plugged into a Java-based simulation engine. In addition to showing how to meld optimization and simulation, the authors have constructed an extensible library of supply-chain modeling components such as items, services and business metrics in a modular service composition framework that could in principle form the foundation of a service-oriented architecture for constructing and solving simple classes of supply chain problems. Although the user interface for the SC-CoJava system is currently programming-oriented, it is easy to see how this system could be generalized using a conceptual modeling formalism such as structured modeling [6] to provide a powerful baseline for an integrated supply chain service system environment. In this ideal case, we have a convergent synergy where SOA generates a modeling environment which in turn can be used to generate service systems that inform and refine the SOA in an iterative fashion.

The remaining two papers reverse the focus to examine how service-oriented architecture (SOA) technology can be deployed to build modeling environments. Deokar, A. and El-Gayar, O. *An ontology-based service-oriented architecture for decision support systems*, has much in common with the previous paper but deals at a much more general level with the components of an SOA for implementing "decision support models as a service". The concept of "decision support as a service" was first introduced nearly fifteen years ago in the DecisionNet architecture created by [2], in which the various components of a model-based DSS (model representation, solver, data sets, data visualization, etc) are web resources integrated and executed on demand through the mechanism of a registry and a service composition algorithm. The environment described and demonstrated in this article refines and updates this architecture by recasting it in contemporary technologies for service oriented computing, web services, and the semantic web. For example, models are represented in the more general form of ontologies using the OWL and OWL-S ontology language. This truly distributed, heterogeneous modeling environment facilitates the elusive goal of model sharing and reuse while illustrating how it can serve as an enabler for service innovation. Two case studies demonstrating model reuse and sharing in an intra-organizational setting, and model composition in an inter-organizational context, show clearly how this SOA in principle implements the "model as a service" paradigm.

The final paper by Bui, Gachet, Dolk, and Sebastian, *Virtual environments for advanced modeling: A telemedicine application* has a decidedly computational modeling slant. Although all modeling systems can be trivially characterized as virtual environments, agent-based simulations carry virtuality to a more pronounced degree. Popular agent-based virtual worlds such as SimCity, Second Life and World of Warcraft provide compelling alternate realities that attract a very large number of committed players. The potential of such virtual worlds to serve as foundations for service systems is intriguing. Second Life players, for example, form virtual communities, markets, and alliances which emulate "real world" counterparts. It is not inconceivable that service relationships with attendant service systems could be formed in virtual space. The authors characterize in general terms several dimensions of virtuality and attendant opportunities for building modeling environments which exhibit one or more of these dimensions. Increasingly, we are likely to see virtual environments proliferate in many aspects of business decision-making, and this will change dramatically the "look and feel" of modeling systems in the future. The authors conclude by describing a prototype agent-based simulation implemented in the Brahms agent environment, which provides basic telemedicine services. Health care is an area where service innovation is desperately needed and computational, constructivist models may be very useful in the design of health care service systems.

3.3   Knowledge Science and SSME

Kimbrough, Lee, and Oktem's paper, *On deriving indicators from texts*, is an intriguing treatment on text mining techniques in the service of knowledge discovery (or "knowledge discovery in texts (KDT)" in the authors' phraseology). Text mining has typically involved the retrieval of relevant documents in response to a query, the document equivalent of an SQL query to a relational database. The authors' intention, however, is to extend the scope of text mining beyond just the retrieval of existing knowledge to the actual discovery of new knowledge. This would be akin in database terms to an SQL query augmented by a logical inference engine of some sort. They introduce the C-M-A framework (Categorization/classification, Measurement, Association) as a way of generating "investigationally valid patterns of information" which interestingly may or may not have statistical validity, but which nevertheless may warrant further investigation, and which in their own right may be useful in guiding decision-making in fuzzy domains such as social science and public policy where narratives are important. Their timely and entertaining examples augmented by their portfolio of existing and new retrieval techniques open up a new way of thinking about data, text and Web mining. One could certainly conceive of their innovative approach bundled as a knowledge discovery service above and beyond the familiar search engines. And if one is willing to view "investigationally valid" patterns as possible precursors to model-building, then one can even cast "indicators from text" as a preliminary step in the traditional model formulation process of the analytical modeling life cycle.

The paper by Beulens and Scholten, *Better modeling practices: An ontological approach*, has much in common with papers from the Modeling section, but has been positioned here because of its emphasis on the intersection between knowledge and model management. The authors have taken a decidedly knowledge-based approach to modeling, relying heavily upon ontologies and meta-ontologies for representing three major dimensions of the modeling landscape: the process dimension of multidisciplinary modeling, structured knowledge about the problem dimension and knowledge about the model dimension including available models for analysis and design complete with their properties, requirements and available solvers. The main thrust of their paper is the practice of model management in the large, that is, to support the organization, execution and management of large, complex modeling projects with potentially significant social impact. Thus, they are concerned with the overall context in which models are being developed and used, with special emphasis upon the human dynamics involved in the project management processes attendant to large-scale model development. This aspect of model management has largely been ignored in the literature where the technical details of the model itself tend to take precedence. One could envision the knowledge-based modeling framework the authors propose as providing collaborative modeling services to the project participants, especially the managers of such projects. Further, the artifacts of the modeling projects themselves may provide valuable services to the eventual "consumers" whether they be nations, NGOs, or other cross-cultural agencies.

The last two papers in the knowledge section come from the Japanese paradigm of knowledge science which is considerably broader in scope and more holistic in nature than its Western counterparts. Whereas the latter focuses upon the rational, mechanistic, and technological aspects of knowledge, the Japanese tradition embraces the full spectrum of the human mind including emotions, intuition, adaptability, and open-mindedness, an approach referred to as Shinayakana [14]. Further, the universal process of knowledge creation and usage is considered within a far-reaching philosophical and sociological context [18]. The paper by Nakamori and Wierzbicki, *Knowledge pentagram system and application*, continues this tradition by describing the conceptual knowledge pentagram, consisting of Intelligence (scientific dimension), Involvement (social dimension),

Imagination (creativity dimension), Intervention (problem application dimension), and Integration (knowledge dimension), and applying this framework to construct a food management system that can be offered as a network service to sales managers. The system development methodology is a hybrid of Western scientific empiricism with Eastern dialectic thought which combines systems engineering and knowledge management to address demand forecasting problems. The result is a "model as service" application leveraging very general knowledge management principles.

The related paper by Ren, Tian, Wierzbicki, Nakamori, and Kilamasara, *Ontology construction and its applications in local research communities*, also continues the Japanese approach to knowledge creation. In this case the objective is to build a generalized research-oriented knowledge creation environment to benefit local communities, and then to tailor this environment to a specific domain, namely telecommunications. The ontologies which underlie this knowledge space are again based on the Shinayakana approach employing a two-pronged approach of bottom-up explicit knowledge and top down tacit, or intuitive and experiential knowledge. This work has led to development of a software system named adaptive hermeneutic agent (AHA), a toolkit for document gathering, keyword extraction, keyword clustering, and ontology visualization, which is described in the article. AHA can be seen as a knowledge creation service to be used by research communities. It is also interesting to compare this approach with the CMA pattern identification text mining approach described in the earlier Kimbrough et al work.

4   Summary

The chapters in this book cover a wide range of territory but with surprising cross-currents and threads of similarity. We hope that they will stimulate and motivate further research in the application of modeling, knowledge, and network science to SSME.

References

1. Barabasi, A.-L.: Linked: How everything is connected to everything else and what it means for business, science, and everyday life. Penguin Group (2002)
2. Bhargava, H.K., Krishnan, R., Muller, R.: Decision support on demand: Emerging electronic markets for decision technologies. Decision Support Systems 19, 193–214 (1997)
3. Bordetsky, A., Bourakov, E., Hutchins, S., Kemple, B.: Network aware tactical collaborative environments. In: Proceedings of 9th International Command and Control Systems and Technology Symposium, Copenhagen (2004)
4. Epstein, J.M.: Generative social science: Studies in agent-based computational modeling. Princeton University Press (2006)
5. Forrester, J.: Industrial dynamics. Productivity Press, Portland (1961)
6. Geoffrion, A.M.: An introduction to structured modeling. Management Science 33(5), 547–588 (1987)

7. Grünert, T., Sebastian, H.-J.: Planning models for long-haul operations of postal and express shipment companies. European Journal of Operational Research 122, 2 (2000)
8. Kimbrough, S.O., Wu, D.J., Zhong, F.: Computers play the beer game: can artificial agents manage supply chains? Decision Support Systems 33(3), 323–333 (2002)
9. Levitt, R.E.: Computational Modeling of Organizations Comes of Age. Journal of Computational & Mathematical Organization Theory 10(2), 127–145 (2004)
10. Makowski, M.: A structured modeling technology. European Journal of Operational Research 166(3), 615–648 (2005)
11. Miller, J.H., Page, S.E.: Complex adaptive systems: An introduction to computational models of social life. Princeton University Press (2007)
12. Nissen, M.: Harnessing knowledge dynamics: Principled organizational knowing & learning. IRM Press (2005)
13. Nonaka, I., Takeuchi, H.: The knowledge creating company. Oxford University Press, New York (1995)
14. Sawaragi, Y., Nakamori, Y.: Shinayakana systems approach in modeling and decision support. In: Proc. of 10th Int. Conf. on Multiple Criteria Decision Making, Taipei, Taiwan, July 19–24, vol. I, pp. 77–86 (1992)
15. Simon, H.: The Sciences of the Artificial , 3rd edn. MIT Press (1996)
16. Spohrer, J., Vargo, S., Caswell, N., Maglio, P.: The service system is the basic abstraction of service science. In: Proceedings of the 41st Hawaii International Conference on System Sciences (HICSS) (CD-ROM), Jan. 7-10, pages 10. Computer Society Press (2008)
17. Vargo, S.L., Lusch, R.F.: Evolving to a new dominant logic for marketing. Journal of Marketing 68, 1–17 (2004)
18. Wierzbicki, A.P., Nakamori, Y.: Creative space - Models of creative processes for the knowledge civilization age. Springer, Berlin (2006)

Supporting and Optimizing Interactive Decision Processes in Grid Environments with a Model-Driven Approach

Julian Reichwald[1], Tim Dörnemann[2], Thomas Barth[3],
Manfred Grauer[3], and Bernd Freisleben[2]

[1] Qosit Softwaretechnik GmbH Eichenhang 50 D-57076 Siegen, Germany
julian.reichwald@qosit.de,
[2] Department of Mathematics and Computer Science, University of Marburg,
Hans-Meerwein-Str. 3, D-35032 Marburg, Germany
{doernemt,freisleb}@informatik.uni-marburg.de
[3] Information Systems Institute, University of Siegen,
Hölderlinstr. 3, D-57068 Siegen, Germany
{barth,grauer}@fb5.uni-siegen.de

Abstract. Increasing the complexity of products and processes in engineering domains, accompanied by time as well as cost pressures, lead to complex decision processes comprising human expert's interaction and excessive use of sophisticated tools from computational engineering. Grid technology offers both basic concepts and tools to automate decision processes as Grid workflows and to integrate distributed resources for computational engineering. Grid computing infrastructures and service-oriented architectures commonly rely on web services as their implementation technology. This technology allows complex workflows to be designed and executed by workflow engines in either Grid or standard web service environments. Nevertheless, the integration of human intervention in Grid workflows is still a manual, therefore time-consuming and error-prone task, caused by the lack of software support for designing workflows that incorporate human tasks in Grid environments. Furthermore, service-oriented architecturess (and especially dynamic Grid infrastructures) are subject to frequent changes, influencing the workflows running on them. This fact makes a good workflow design a non-trivial task, making IT support for automatically optimizing workflows running on service-oriented architectures in Grid environments a valuable issue. In this paper, we present a model-driven approach for designing efficient Grid workflows covering both the topics of human tasks and automatic transformation and optimization of a workflow regarding the underlying infrastructure and its performance characteristics. The solution also covers the automatic creation of user interfaces for human interventions. The approach is implemented and validated by a virtual prototyping process from metal casting.

Keywords: Model-Driven, Service-orientation, Human Tasks, Workflow-Optimization, Decision.

D. Dolk et al. (Eds.): Decision Support Modeling in Service Networks, LNBIP 42, pp. 14–35, 2012.
© Springer-Verlag Berlin Heidelberg 2012

1   Introduction

Workflows are widely understood as completely or partly automated (business) processes, during which documents, information or tasks are passed from one participant to another one for action, according to a set of procedural rules [3]. In engineering domains like e.g. sheet metal forming or metal casting in the automotive supplier industry, processes in product development often comprise complex and knowledge-intensive decision processes (e.g. finding the optimal geometrical design, the optimal material, the optimal machinery). Hence, they incorporate virtual prototyping techniques (e.g. numerical simulation and optimization). The quality of such virtual prototypes highly depends on the knowledge of various experts (e.g. domain experts and computational engineers), making decisions throughout the process (e.g. adjusting optimization parameters or calibrating the prototyping model). Hence, coping with human tasks is mandatory when designing workflows in such domains. Such workflows typically span multiple institutions. On the one hand, several engineers from different domains (i.e. computational engineers, domain experts etc.) have to work in close collaboration and share their knowledge during the process. On the other hand, highly specialized resources like High Performance Computing (HPC) hardware and software for numerical simulations are required, which are typically unaffordable for the gross of the industrial landscape [15] and therefore do not reside in a single enterprise. The Grid computing paradigm [11,12] can help to overcome certain barriers which are encountered when trying to interconnect multiple institutions and coevally share computing and storage resources. Since the Grid computing paradigm adopted many concepts from Service-Oriented Architectures (SOAs) [21,26], the Business Process Execution Language (BPEL) became subject of interest for representing and executing workflows in web and Grid service based infrastructures [13]. However, the task of designing or changing workflows that incorporate human tasks in a Grid environment is lengthy and error-prone, since workflow editors either can cope with standard web services and map human tasks to a vendor-specific implementation, or can deal with Grid services, lacking human task implementations. Furthermore, a human task may require some sort of user interface (UI), depending on the task to accomplish. The UI can be realized using any technology, e.g. a web portal or a smart client. The UI needs to interface with the task (and the process, respectively). Thus, creating an adequate UI can be a time-consuming task.

Since service-oriented architectures and especially dynamic Grid infrastructures without centralized control are subject to frequent changes, workflows running on such infrastructures may be influenced by underlying changes. Workflow designers have to face the task of constantly monitoring the infrastructure and – if changes appear – adjusting the workflows to gain a maximum efficiency in the execution. But not only infrastructural changes may trigger a workflow adjustment. Also the incorporation of Grid resources according to a predefined optimization goal (e.g. workflow execution at lowest costs or highest speed) may be a reason to permanently adjust the workflows in the environment.

In this paper, a model-driven approach for designing and executing work-flows in service-oriented Grid environments that may be modeled as interactive workflows is presented. According to the Model-Driven Architecture (MDA) approach [25], a platform independent model represents the workflow model and can be enriched with additional information about the underlying infrastructure (i.e. technology information as well as the interface used to present human tasks to the user). Both the platform independent model as well as the technology information is transformed to a platform specific model, i.e. to valid code that can be deployed to a workflow engine along with necessary user interfaces. An intermediate step prior to the deployment is able to adjust the workflow by using the additional information provided. A prototypical implementation using the Globus Toolkit 4 as the Grid middleware and a GridSphere portal as the UI will be presented together with a virtual prototyping application based on a process from metal casting.

The paper is organized as follows. Section 2 gives a detailed description of the problems faced by implementing workflows with human tasks in a Grid computing environment as well as the issues appearing with workflow optimization. A conceptual solution to these problems is presented in section 3, and a prototypical implementation is described in section 4. In section 5, the implemented prototype is then used to realize an example workflow from virtual prototyping in metal casting. Related work is discussed in section 6. Section 7 concludes the paper and outlines areas for future research.

2   Problem Statement

Increasing complexity of products and processes in engineering domains, accompanied by a shortened time to market and cost pressure require efficient support of the domain experts in various complex decision support situations in the course of processes, e.g. in product planning and design. This is the reason for the increasing use of *virtual prototyping*, a collective term comprising a variety of techniques for mapping products and processes to computer models for simulating their behavior under certain circumstances. Since building real prototypes is a costly and time-consuming process, virtual prototyping can be utilized for achieving the aforementioned business goals. In engineering domains, especially numerical simulations and simulation-based optimizations are of great benefit. Single simulations are able to simulate a given model using a static parameter set, while optimization runs are able to generate model variations which are simulated and evaluated, aiming at an optimal product or process design. However, the utilization of such technologies requires the access to high performance computing (HPC) resources and highly specialized software systems, which are typically unaffordable for small and medium enterprises (SMEs).

Service-oriented Grid computing already proved to be an adequate infrastructure for supporting virtual prototyping business processes in engineering [16]. The Grid paradigm provides a way for accessing the required HPC resources without the expenses for purchasing, running and maintaining the hard- and software systems, therefore allowing SMEs to collaborate with – or maybe even compete against – large scale enterprises which are able to afford the technologies themselves. On a technical layer, resource access is realized using a Grid middleware which offers basic services like file transfers and basic job execution mechanisms and also implements security concepts like e.g. the Grid Security Infrastructure (GSI). Custom services can be implemented to support complex numerical simulations or optimization algorithms. Both basic services as well as higher level simulation and optimization services can be orchestrated according to an end user's underlying business process. Since service-oriented Grid environments often rely on web services as their implementation method, workflow engines which execute processes described in the Business Process Execution Language (BPEL) can be used.

2.1   Use Case: Metal Casting

As an example, the casting process of a turbine blade as it is used for modern aircrafts or power plants is given here. Such turbine blades are commonly produced by directional solidification or single crystals in a Bridgman furnace (s. fig. 1 and [18]). A directional heat flow is created by withdrawing the shell mould of the turbine blade out of the heating zone into a cooling zone. The strong temperature gradient at the interface between heating and cooling zone leads to a directional solidification. Despite the simplicity of the Bridgman principle, the optimization of all process parameters is complex for real blade geometries. Technically relevant casting parameters, such as a heater's temperature and withdrawal velocity, are currently determined by series of expensive experiments.

A numerical simulation code offered as a Grid service can be used to numerically predict the transient temperature response during the Bridgman casting process. It calculates transient temperature distributions in mold, core and alloy, taking into account both latent heat release as a function of fraction solid, and heat transfer resistance at material interfaces. The main criteria are temperature and heat flux field. Based on this data, temperature gradients and defect maps can be calculated for each set of input process parameters, which are the basis for the evaluation of the turbine blade. The calculations allow a simulation-based optimization run, aiming at an optimized withdrawal profile for the Bridgman process. An appropriate optimization algorithm, also provided as a Grid service, based on direct search methods creates different sets of solution candidates which are evaluated by the simulation runs (detailed information about the algorithm, the objective function and constraints can be found in [18]).

During the process, an optimization expert needs to set up the algorithm with the appropriate parameters. The optimization itself is then started on the Grid, utilizing distributed resources.

2.2   Use Case: Collision Analysis in Metal Forming

The same business goals like shortening time to market or quality improvements apply to the metal forming domain. This use case especially copes with the sheet

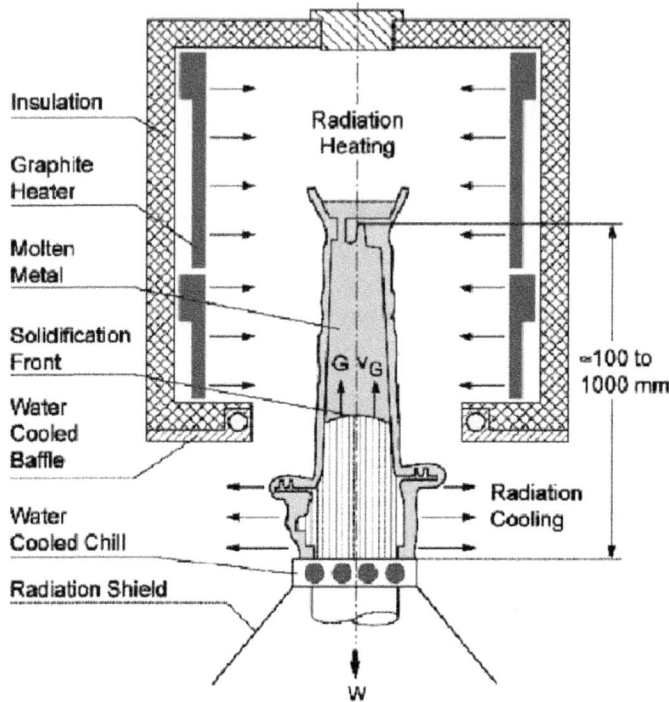

Insulation

Graphite
Heater

Molten
Metal

Solidification
Front

Water
Cooled
Baffle

Water
Cooled Chill

Radiation Shield

Radiation
Heating

G V_G

≈100 to
1000 mm

Radiation
Cooling

W

Fig. 1. Schematic description of a Bridgman furnace used for directional solidification (s.[18])

metal forming discipline of deep drawing. Press systems draw metal blanks under high pressure to their final form (e.g. a hatchback). Due to the complexity of the final product, a single stage often turns out to be insufficient, therefore multistage press systems equipped with transfer systems can be used for multistage production processes (see fig. 2). The transfer system lifts up the forming part after each stage, moves it to the next and lowers it for further processing, which is done by a press stroke. The movement of the parts throughout the processing stages is done by grippers mounted to gripper rails. A press equipped with a transfer system therefore requires the moving parts to be coordinated in a way that no collisions appear, since it would cause heavy damage to the press, the transfer system and the tools used. The parts to be coordinated are the grippers, the gripper rails and the vertical press movement itself. The final goal is the optimization of the stroke rate of the press to produce a maximum output.

A Digital Mock-Up (DMU) kinematics simulation can help to simulate the moving parts in the press (s. [8]). Again, a DMU kinematics system based on CATIA V5 which is wrapped as a Grid service is able to process appropriate data of the press and the transfer system. The computational result is either a

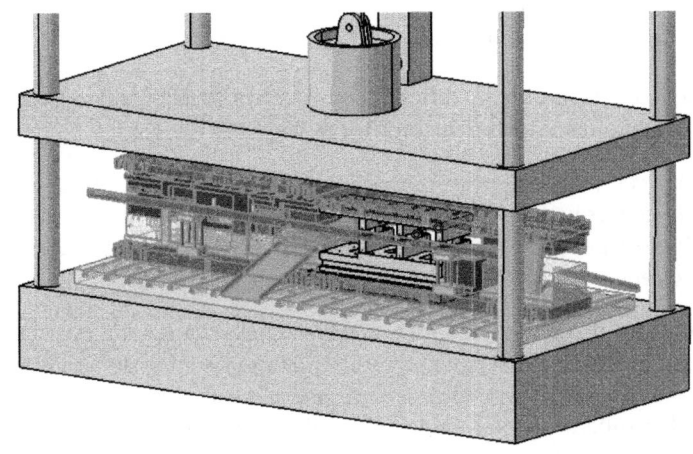

Fig. 2. Image of a press equipped with a transfer system [16]

video or a report of the possible collisions. Typially, the videos are sent back to the service consumer while the reports can be viewed as a web page.

2.3 Process Support

Supporting the mentioned use cases in service-oriented Grid computing environments is far from trivial. Due to the use of standard technologies like web services etc. which are used for calling services on remote sites, workflow support should be a manageable task.

However, there are several problems that render the workflow design process much more complicated. First, a vast knowledge of technical details is still needed. Designing a workflow means knowing the infrastructure the workflow will be executed on, incorporating the middleware and the workflow engine, coping with security issues and knowing the used workflow execution language, e.g. BPEL. Second, support for human tasks in BPEL-based workflows has been integrated into commercial products using standard web service infrastructures (and recently trying to implement the newly released specifications BPEL for People (BPEL4Pepole) [1] and Web Services Human Task (WS-HT) [2]), but the integration into service-oriented Grid computing environments is still missing. Neither applications like BPEL editors exist which are able to cope with Grid infrastructures, nor are they able to provide appropriate interfaces for humans to interact with the process. Hence, the user interface for the human task always has to be adopted by hand. Finally, the knowledge of the underlying infrastructure could lead workflow designers to modify the workflow supporting the business process in order to optimize it with respect to certain criteria:

- Bandwidth limitations between special Grid nodes or at the end user's side could lead to alternatives in the result visualization and

Knowledge about CPU speeds, architectures and prices on remote sides render a given site insufficient.

Since the execution of a workflow is often a tradeoff between execution time vs. execution costs, the optimization objective could be e.g.:

- the lowest possible price for a whole workflow, i.e. it is executed on the cheapest resources, no matter how long the workflow will run and
- the fastest possible execution, incorporating fast resources, short local scheduler queues etc. in the objective function, not regarding the costs.

The workflow designer therefore needs to keep track of every change in the underlying infrastructure and the sites connected to the middleware. All the named facts make the workflow design process a highly complex and error-prone task, and requires special knowledge of the technical details, the underlying infrastructure, the top-level business process to be supported and the way users interact with the system. In the next section, a solution approach based on Model-Driven Architectures is presented which solves this problematic issues.

3   Solution Architecture

As already pointed out in section 2, the workflow design process is highly complex and error-prone. The Grid computing value chain described in section 3.1 identifies the necessary competencies for a comprehensive workflow support in a service-oriented Grid environment. Next, a solution based on model-driven architectures is given.

3.1   Grid Computing Value Chain

In [15], different roles in a Grid environment have been identified and a value chain for service-oriented computing has been presented especially for scenarios incorporating SMEs. Grid computing therefore generates value from an economic viewpoint. From the technical perspective, service-oriented Grid computing is a layered architecture, reaching from the physical hardware to the end user. Figure 3 depicts both the economic and the technical view to service-oriented Grid technology.

Service-oriented Grid technology is divided into the basic hardware infrastructure (incorporating networks and computing resources) and the service-oriented Grid technology, i.e. standards like Web Services, the Web Services Resource Framework (WSRF) etc. The information processing point of view is a technology stack, where hardware is interconnected by a middleware, on which services are built. These services may then be orchestrated to higher-level services, representing entire workflows to be used by the end user. From the economic perspective, value is created by first providing the hardware resources and interconnecting them by utilizing a middleware. Service providers are then in charge of providing high level and coarse-grained services, which are orchestrated by integrators to support a specific business process and solve an end user's problem. According to this value chain, the integrator acts as the interface between the lower technical layers of the Grid infrastructure and the higher business requirements in the form of complex workflows the end user expects. The utilization of workflows and workflow engines – in service-oriented architectures typically compliant to the BPEL-standard mentioned before – already allows a fast adoption of complex workflows and can be a great benefit to the integrators, who are in charge of developing adequate workflows to fit the end user's needs.

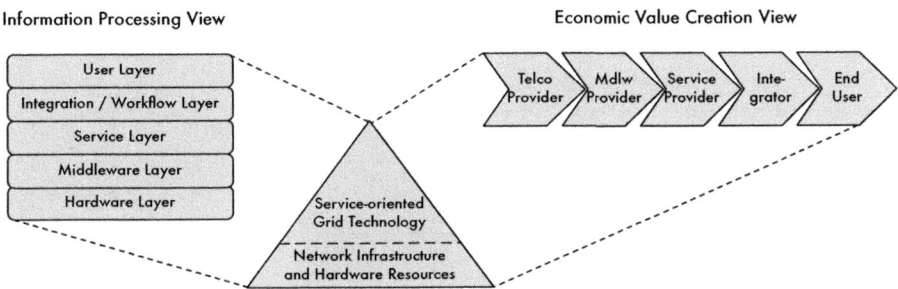

Fig. 3. Service-oriented value chain and corresponding technical layers of a service-oriented Grid computing environment

Combining section 2 and section 3.1, creating or adjusting virtual prototyping workflows in service-oriented Grid computing environments is a hard task for the integrators with lots of manual and error-prone work to do. Tools for graphical workflow design as well as workflow execution already exist, but either they do not support Grid computing environments or lack features concerning human intervention. Furthermore, no mechanisms exist to automatically transform the workflow in a way that fits well to the underlying infrastructure with their network interconnections and hardware resources. A model-driven approach for service-oriented Grid environments covering both – human tasks as well as automatic workflow transformation and optimization – will be presented next.

3.2   Supporting Human Tasks in Grid Workflows

Workflows with human intervention are different from fully automated workflows in many ways. First, the execution environment must provide some kind of user interface allowing a user to perform the required task. A typical task could be that the user has to enter some values required by subsequent workflow steps. Due to the broad variety of possible workflows and corresponding human tasks it is impossible to provide a generic user interface for arbitrary human tasks. For this reason, our solution allows to deploy custom user interface code for every workflow (s. figure 4). This goal is achieved by utilizing the process's

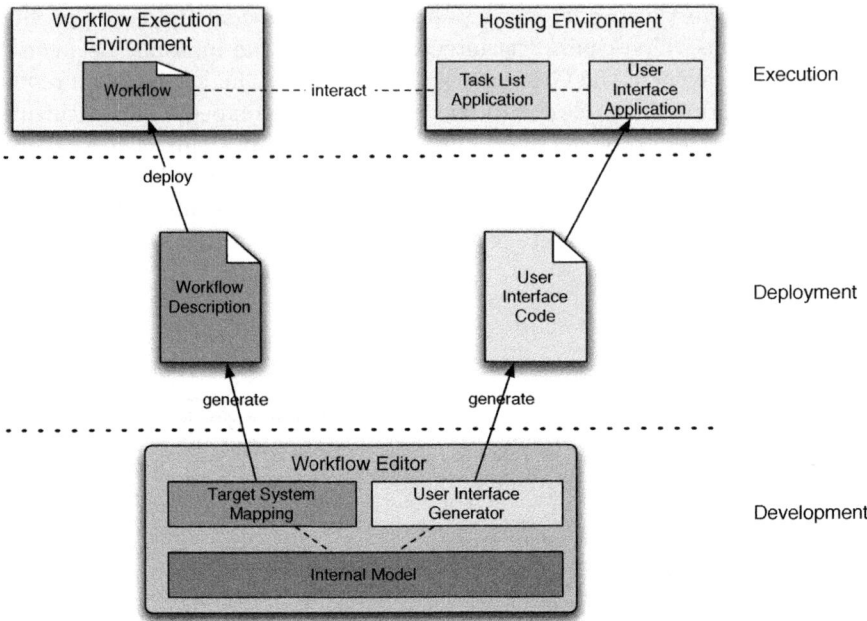

Fig. 4. Components of our solution and their interaction

external WSDL representation to determine required input data for human tasks. The WSDL document contains information on data types and names of input variables which can be used to create a custom user interface. This procedure is schematically illustrated on the right side of figure 4. The left side illustrates that platform-specific workflow code is generated using the workflow editor's internal model. In most cases, the user will not directly enter the required information since workflows often run outside business hours or higher prioritized tasks must be completed first. The workflow execution environment must be able to cope with this highly asynchronous behavior. Ideally, a workflow executing a human task should be suspended until the user's reply arrives to save hardware resources on the hosting environment. Furthermore, the execution environment should be capable of running many workflow instances in parallel. Then, a solution is needed to correlate the results of human tasks with workflow instances.

The asynchronous behavior requires a component that stores all open human tasks per user. Whenever a new human task is created by a workflow step, it is automatically added to the component's repository. A task description includes the name of the user the task is allocated to, an identifier of the corresponding workflow instance as well as information needed to render the task-specific user interface. Beyond that, the component is equipped with a user interface to display a list of open tasks.

As already stated, workflow developers should be relieved from the error-prone and time-consuming process of writing workflows by hand, especially since many workflow languages have not been designed for manual editing. For this reason, a demand for a graphical workflow modeling tool exists. Besides modeling of fully automated workflows, it should provide support for developing workflows containing human tasks. Our proposed solution satisfies this requirement and is even able to automatically generate user interfaces for human tasks as described above. The modeling tool following the MDA approach operates on an internal data model and transforms it into an executable workflow description as well as user interface code for the desired target platform. Using this model-driven approach, our solution basically remains independent of concrete technologies. Pluggable target system mapping components transform the internal model into workflow environment-specific code. User interface code is generated from pluggable generators as well.

3.3   Model-Driven Workflow Optimization

Since model-driven architectures are already a key design issue in the solution architecture for supporting human tasks, they are also a key point in automatic workflow transformation and optimization. A typical scenario for automatic workflow optimization is directly derived from the mentioned use cases. The results produced by the simulation systems are going to be viewed by the end users at the end of the process. In our use cases, the end users do not possess a high bandwidth network connection, so the transfer of the result data might lead to a lengthy task. If the process designer is aware of this situation, a visualization on a remote desktop might be more useful. The creation of the fastest possible workflow by using the most powerful resources and shortest job queues on the compute resource's scheduler (not regarding the higher price) would also be conceivable.

In both cases, the default workflow would have to be adjusted, regarding the main objective. In case of remote visualization, the result data would need to be transferred to a remote desktop server instead of a transfer back to the end user; in case of the fastest workflow, resources should be chosen by a rule according to the subject. Modeling a workflow covering all possible situations would result in unreadable, large and very difficult to handle workflows. A runtime decision would require a special workflow engine far off every standard BPEL engine. Our solution therefore optimizes the workflow at design time in a model-driven way, according to specified rules. It is important to note that not only search/replace - operations are supported. The optimizer needs full access to the whole workflow and the permission to apply arbitrary changes to it.

The workflow transformation and optimization tool also uses an internal representation of the workflow, which is generated by a graphical model from the workflow editor. Since the system is modular and flexible, every graphical editor can be used for the modeling itself. Additional information is added by using annotations for single elements (e.g. comments in BPMN-models or special annotation elements in proprietary workflow editors). The annotations are

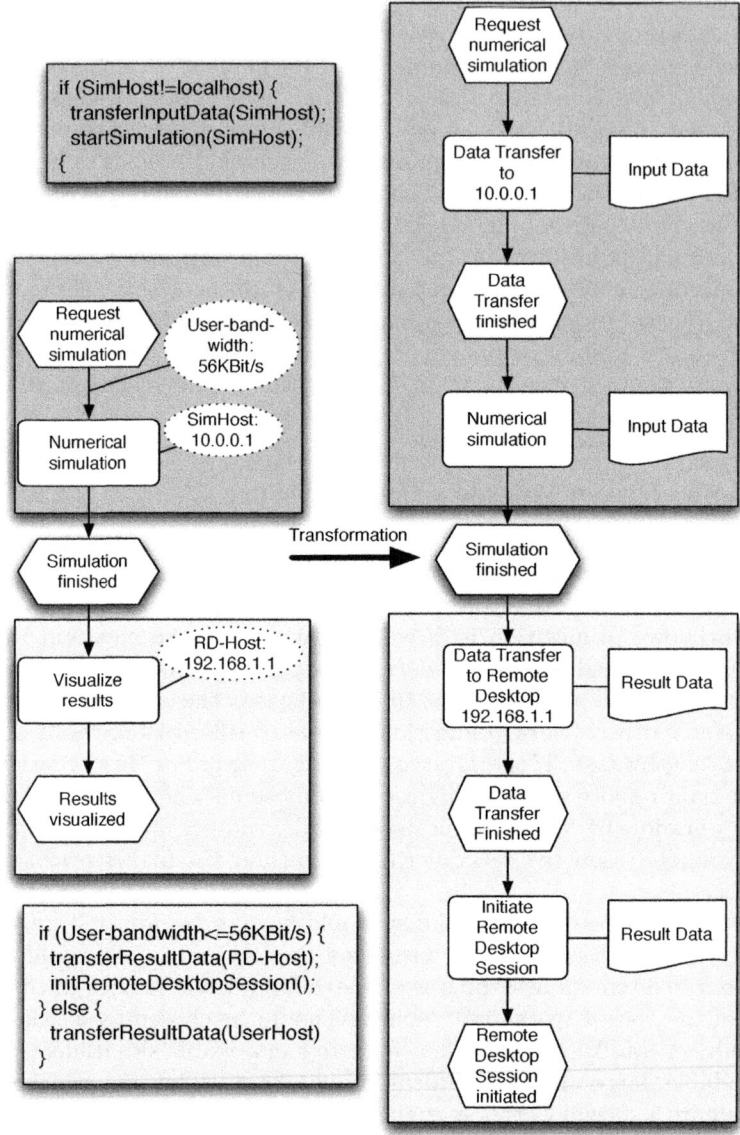

Fig. 5. Workflow transformation according to a set of rules

used to trigger the transformation and optimization engine, which modifies the workflow model according to a predefined ruleset. The optimized model can then be mapped to a target engine and deployed for direct execution. Figure 5 exemplarily describes the process of a user requesting a numerical simulation on a given Grid node. After the simulation is finished, the results should be visualized. The example stresses the fact that end users in the named use cases (see section 2) do not possess high bandwidth Internet connections. This fact is known by the workflow designer, who annotates this circumstance to the top level model (`User-bandwidth: 56KBit/s`). The Grid node providing the appropriate simulation code is annotated in the model as well (`SimHost: 10.0.0.1`). Since the simulation results can bevome quite large, a transfer to a remote desktop server with a fast Internet connection makes more sense instead of having the results transferred back to the user, so the remote desktop server is named, too (`RD-Host: 192.168.1.1`). The transformation and optimization engine now works on the internal data model and applies the given rules to it. While the first rule only replaces the numerical simulation with a data transfer to another Grid node, followed by the numerical simulation, the second rule works on the whole data model. A check is made whether the user's network connection is fast enough. If not, the results are transferred to a remote desktop server instead of directly to the user. If the user's network connection will be faster in the future, the workflow designer only has to change the annotation, and the workflow will be automatically modified according to the new situation – in this case transferring the files directly back to the user. This example only shows the basic possibilities of the approach. The model-driven approach accompanied by a set of rules are highly flexible, being also able to deal with complex rules, e.g. cost- or time-optimizing rules which react on annotations as mentioned in section 2.3.

4   Prototype Implementation

A prototype has been implemented according to the solution concept described in the previous section. The Globus Toolkit Version 4 (GT4) has been chosen as the middleware platform, since GT4 can be seen as the de-facto standard for service-oriented Grid infrastructures. Furthermore, GT4 implements the Web Services Resource Framework (WSRF), which allows the implementation of stateful web services.

4.1   Implementation of Human Task Support

A Task List Service (TLS) will store and manage human tasks and acts as an interface between the user interface and the process. GridSphere [28], a Java-based portal framework, provides the presentation layer for user interfaces. Since GT4 relies on web service techniques, the Business Process Execution Language (BPEL) is used for workflow modeling, with ActiveBPEL as the execution engine. For this special case, ActiveBPEL has been slightly modified to adequately support the GT4 environment (s. [9,10]). The prototype system and its action sequence are depicted in figure 6.

The figure shows a BPEL process, reaching an invoke-operation for a human task. In this context, invoking (1) means calling the TLS and storing all necessary task information. At this point, the BPEL process suspends itself until the human task finishes. A user can now log on to the portal (2), and the task list

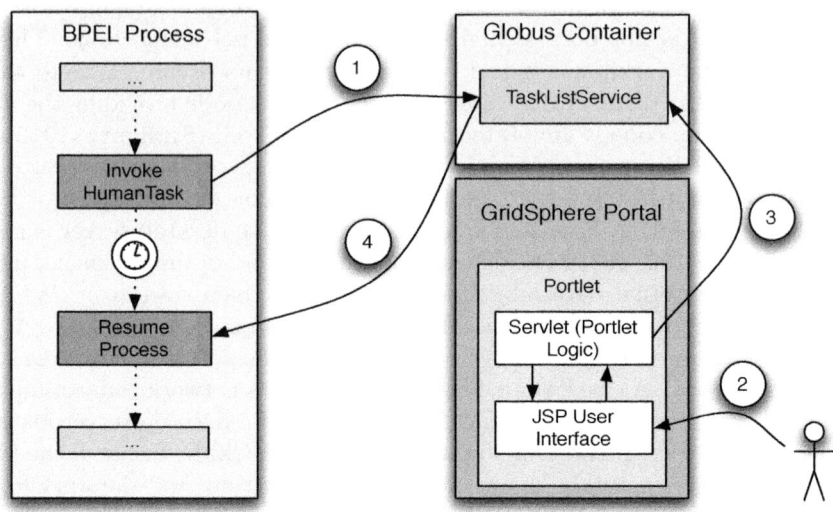

Fig. 6. Interaction between middleware components when invoking human tasks

portlet displays a list of open tasks. For each task, the portal provides a user interface. The information entered by the user is reported to the TLS by the portlet (3), which in turn calls the suspended BPEL process (4). The process then collects the entered information and resumes.

The TLS has been implemented as a GT4 service following the factory pattern, and stores each task as a resource property. Thus, the WSRF framework implemented by GT4 is utilized. Calling the createResource-operation provided by the factory service creates tasks. During the creation of a new task, a given username is automatically stored in the task object; hence it is possible to grant access to a specific task just to a predefined user. After the resource is created, the correct endpoint reference (EPR) to that resource is returned to the caller. By using this EPR for further calls to the instance service, the caller can uniquely identify the task to modify, process or delete it – necessary operations are provided by the instance service. Additionally, a short description of the task, its actual state, a unique ID, the process URL, the task's own endpoint reference as well as viewing information for the graphical user interface are saved. In this case, the viewing information is the name of a JSP, but it could also be any other information for rendering the task in a user interface. The task's own EPR is used by the user interface for calling update or delete methods on the correct endpoint. The process URL is needed by the TLS for calling back the process and transferring data when the task is accomplished. Calling back the process is triggered by the processTask operation, which takes an array of task parameters as argument, consisting of the parameter name as a generic string, the parameter's data type as a string-represented QNAME and finally the parameter's value, entered by the human and mapped to the data type Object.

A generic SOAP client then takes the parameters and transfers them to the waiting process, using the process URL stored in the task object. Due to the fact that it is possible to have multiple workflows waiting to be resumed, the correct workflow instance is identified by BPEL correlations, technically achieved by adding correlation-related code to the process' WSDL file.

The utilization of GridSphere as the portal system requires JSR-168 compliant portlets, which can be arbitrarily arranged by users inside a standard web browser. In our prototype, a portlet also takes care of displaying the human tasks to the user and also providing the possibilities to accomplish them (as far as user input is required). Each portlet consists of an implementation class that realizes the processing logic, while a JSP is responsible for rendering the user interface. In this context, the portlet implementation class calls the TLS for all open tasks for the user who is currently logged in. The information will be passed to a JSP, which is in charge of displaying the open tasks as a list, incorporating a unique task identifier, the description and a link to process the task. Since processing different tasks will result in different user interfaces, the task itself will provide the portal with the appropriate JSP that has to be shown for processing and entering data. When the user finishes the task, the data is passed to the implementation class, which in turn calls the TLS for updating the process with the corresponding data entered by the end user.

Modeling of BPEL workflows is a complex challenge, and tool support is needed to ease this error-prone and time-consuming task. Especially when correlations are involved to model asynchronous invocation behavior (as needed when human intervention is required) the process description becomes cluttered. To alleviated the workflow designer from manually writing code, extensions to an Eclipse based workflow designer [13] have been developed (figure 7 shows a screenshot of the editor).

Modeling human tasks is made as easy as dragging the human task symbol from the editor's palette to the desired location in the workflow. Then, a graphical wizard pops up and asks for required information. The user has to provide the location of the TLS, which can be selected from a dropdown box of pre-configured services or added manually. All other information like the aforementioned JSP URL, username etc. are automatically created and used in the gridInvoke operation. In the next step, the workflow designer has to decide which input should be requested by the corresponding JSP interface. The editor creates appropriate messages and variables for the BPEL process and adds them to the receive operation, which resumes the process when the required data is submitted by the user using the portlet. After finishing the design of a process, it has to be exported from the BPEL editor. In doing so, the process's internal representation is transformed into valid BPEL code. For every human task in the process, a code generator is run. It retrieves required information, namely data types, message names and JSP name, from the process's internal model and generates JSP pages with the given names for every human task. Thus, the BPEL editor can be seen as a one-stop-shop application for the creation of

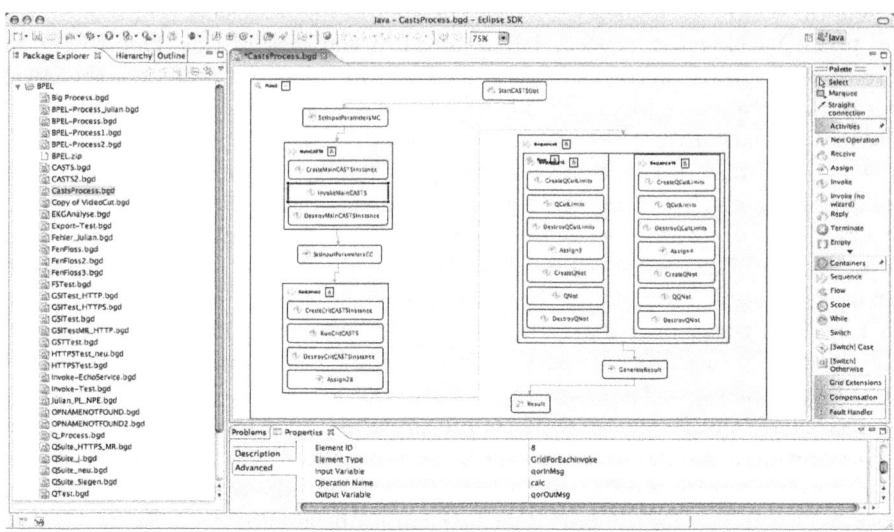

Fig. 7. Screenshot of the Eclipse-based workflow editor

workflows involving human tasks since it also automatically creates user interfaces and callback code for the GridSphere portal solution.

4.2   Implementation of the Workflow Optimization Facility

The workflow optimization facility mainly operates in the background. The UML class diagram depicted in fig. 8 shows the overall architecture of this software component (attributes and methods are omitted here). The `reader` package provides an interface for reading models created by a graphical editor. Actually, there is just an implementation for reading the model of an Eclipse based editor, but the interface may easily be implemented for other software modeling tools as well. The model reader's output is a `BPMNModel`, a class which stores `NodeElements`, `Edges` and `Annotations`. As it can be seen in the figure, all objects stored in the model are derived from the superclass `Element`, hence further extensions to the model are easily possible. At this time, gateways, start and stop elements and tasks are implemented. Due to the inheritance structure of the model, every `NodeElement` stores the incoming and outgoing edges, while every `Element` stores possible annotations (thus every object stored in the BPMNModel can be annotated).

Classes in the `analyzer` package take a BPMNModel object and walk through a set of patterns which are derived from the superclass `Pattern`. The patterns act as an implementation of the transformation triggers and rules, see e.g. the pseudo code blocks as seen in fig. 5. An abstract processing method is called by the analyzer on each pattern instance (thus implementing the processing method). The user is able to choose which patterns should be applied to a single

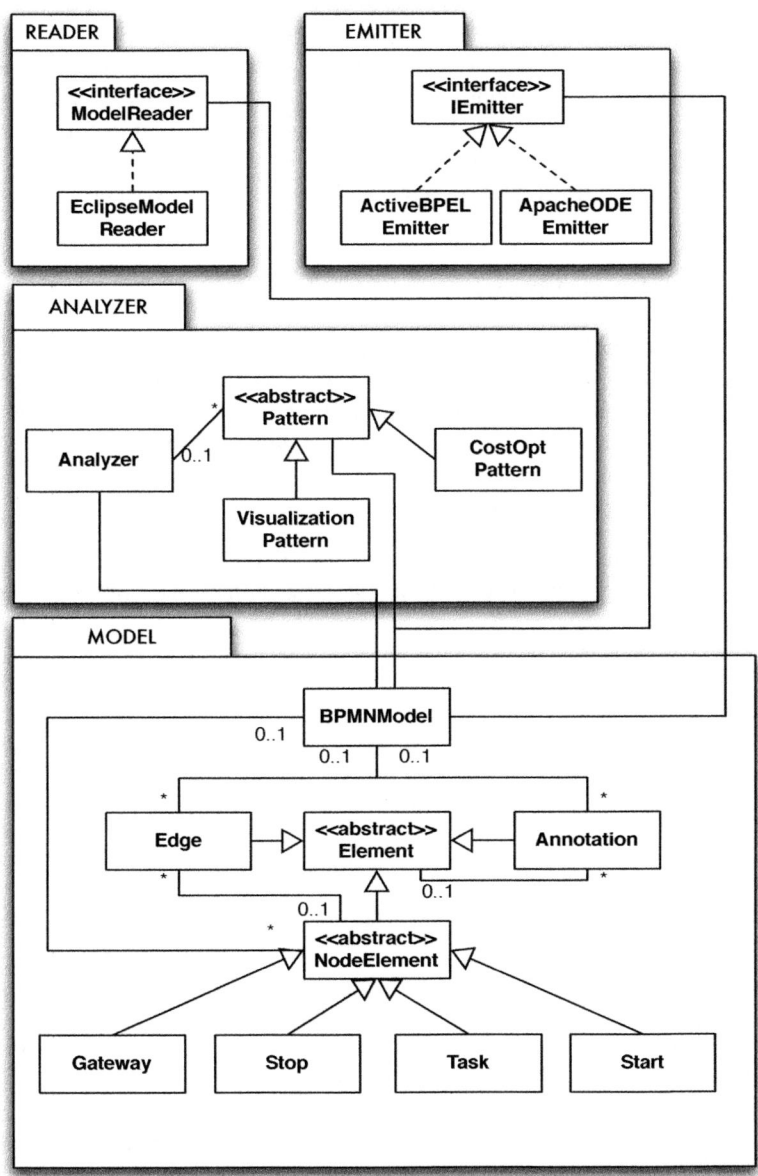

Fig. 8. UML class diagram of the optimization and transformation facilities

model analyzation run. The content of the model's annotations are evaluated by the patterns. A match results in a modification of the whole BPMNModel. By subclassing patterns from the abstract superclass Pattern, a flexible system is created, providing the ability to simply extend the pattern repository with powerful rules which may access the whole model.

Finally, the `emitter` package provides an interface to create the workflow codes and secondary documents (e.g. the deployment descriptor for a special workflow engine) from the model. At this point, code emitters for ActiveBPEL and the Apache ODE [4] engine are available. For the Grid use, the Grid-enabled ActiveBPEL Engine from section 4.1 can be used while Apache ODE works in standard web services environments.

5 Sample Application

As a sample application, a workflow from virtual prototyping in metal casting industry as already introduced in section 2.1 has been taken. Two sections of the process are taken to show exemplarily the feasibility of the implementation. Detailed information about the whole process can be found in [16].

5.1 Processing Human Tasks

The process in figure 9, displayed as an event-driven process chain (EPC), depicts a section of a virtual prototyping process. During the process, the Model

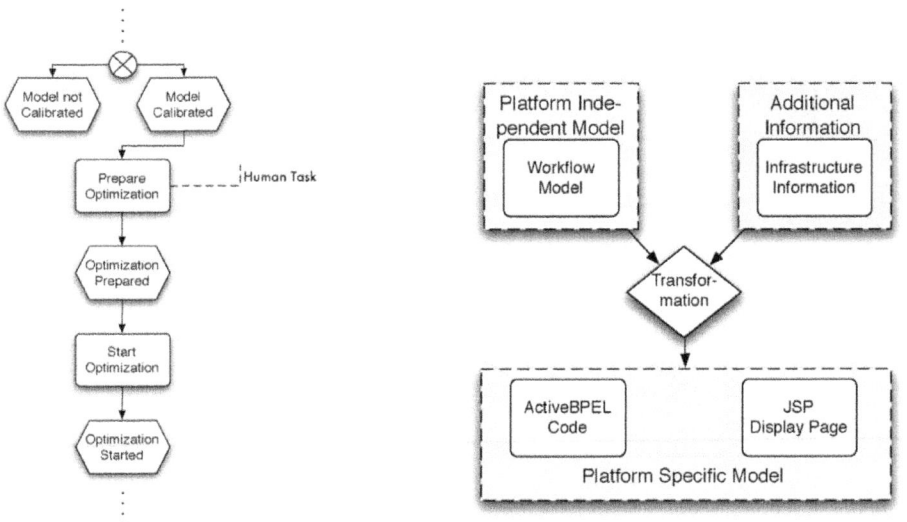

Fig. 9. The left side shows the example process as an event-driven process chain, the right side depicts a schematic view of the transformation for the sample process

Calibrated event triggers a human task Prepare Optimization, where an optimization expert needs to prepare an optimization run (i.e. entering parameters for the algorithm which cannot be determined automatically etc.). When the task is finished, the process will be continued and the optimization can be started. The model has been transferred to the workflow editor and the `Prepare Optimization` function has been annotated as a human task. A GT4 based infrastructure offers the Start Optimization Grid service (in this case: a numerical optimization of a metal casting process), while Prepare Optimization as a human task does not have any specific Grid service representation. Start Optimization expects some parameters to configure an optimization algorithm. When the process is going to be exported, the workflow model is combined with information about the underlying infrastructure (i.e. GT4 and the ActiveBPEL enactment engine) and with the representation technique for human tasks (in this case: the GT4 TLS and the GridSphere portal). The result (shown in fig. 9) is the PSM, consisting of executable BPEL code as well as the auto-generated JSP for displaying the human task. A link between the JSP and the BPEL process is made through the TLS which directly interacts with the workflow on the one hand, and with the GridSphere portlet (the JSP and the implemented portlet class) on the other hand.

In our experiments, the process could be successfully deployed to the ActiveBPEL engine and the JSP was deployed automatically to the GridSphere portal. When the process was executed, a task was created in the TLS by the workflow, and the process stopped and waited for input provided by the specified user. This user could now log on to the portal where the Task List Portlet automatically receives the list of open tasks from the TLS. Processing the task linked the user to the generated JSP, where the appropriate input could be provided and returned to the task list portlet, which immediately informed the TLS about the input provided. The TLS then calls back the waiting process instance (which can be uniquely identified by using the correlation sets), and the process continued and was able to call Start Optimization with the user-provided input.

5.2   Workflow Optimization

The workflow optimization facility was tested using the subprocess mentioned in fig. 5. A depiction of the overall testing process can be seen in fig. 10. The process model was annotated by the workflow designer (1) with the simulation host, the remote desktop host and the user bandwidth as shown in the figure. It was then read by the optimization and transformation facility (2), where the internal process model was modified according to the matched patterns (also see fig. 5). The emitter subsystem of the workflow optimization and transformation facility was configured to produce both output for the Apache ODE engine as well as ActiveBPEL. In terms of MDA, the platform independent model expressing the workflow on a high level is transformed to a platform specific, executable model in this step. The executable process could be deployed on both engines successfully (3) and an end user was able to execute the process on the underlying infrastructure.

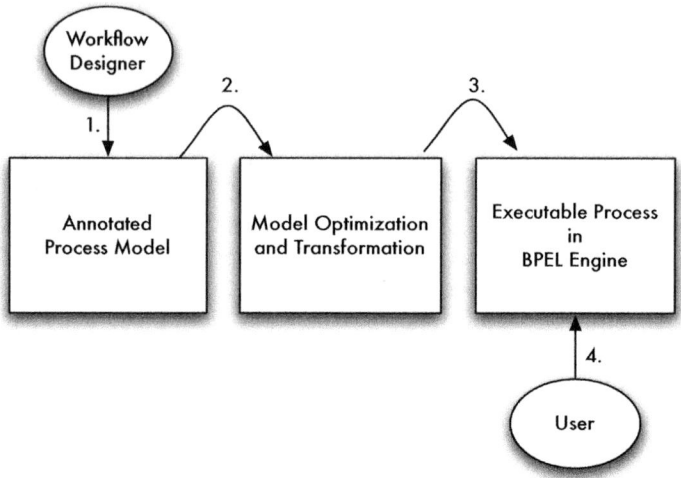

Fig. 10. Schematic of the workflow transformation and optimization process describing the steps from workflow design up to process execution

6   Related Work

In this section, related research in the area of Grid services based workflows is discussed. Since the area of Grid workflow modeling is quite well researched (s. [30] for an overview) and many different approaches and tools exist, we only present some representative approaches.

The P-GRADE Portal [19] is a workflow-oriented Grid portal which integrates both workflow modeling and execution in a collaborative environment. It provides functionality for defining Grid environments, creation and modification of workflows, certificate management as well as controlling and monitoring workflows. However, it does not feature the development of workflows with human interactions nor the creation of user interfaces for human intervention.

Triana [27] is a Grid workflow system that abstracts from underlying technologies by making use of the GAT API. This allows to seamlessly use services which incorporate different technologies, like Condor, Unicore, and WSRF or even low-level services such as SGE or SSH. Like our approach, Triana offers a graphical modeling tool. Quite similar to Triana is the approach taken by Taverna (http://taverna.sourceforge.net/). Both do not offer any support for human tasks in workflows.

The GridFlow [7] workflow management system applies a more complex workflow model. It handles workflows at two levels: a global Grid level and the level of local Grid (typically one or more clusters in the same organization). Workflows for GridFlow are modeled using a graphical editor named GridFlow portal. It provides scheduling capabilities for local Grids and is not designed to support tasks with human interventions.

Wassermann et al. [6] describe their implementation of a BPEL-based environment for visual scientific workflow modeling. It consists of a workflow engine based on ActiveBPEL and a visual editor. To ease the modeling of scientific workflows, the authors introduce several visual abstractions from the BPEL syntax. The visual abstractions are mapped to standard BPEL code so that no modifications to BPEL are necessary. The feasibility of their approach is demonstrated by a real-world example with completely automated workflows from computational chemistry. Nevertheless, the authors do not address human tasks at all.

Mendling et al. [24] have presented an automatic transformation between block-oriented and graph-oriented workflow languages. Furthermore, techniques for automatic transformations to executable processes have been proposed [29], e.g. the transformation from EPC representations to BPEL (see [20,22,23]). The papers mentioned are neither based on MDA techniques nor do they do an automatic optimization of the underlying workflow.

An MDA-approach has been presented by Gardner [14]. Special UML profiles tailored for business process management are used here to generate executable BPEL code. A profile-based transformation from the choreography-language BSS to BPEL has been presented by Hofreiter and Huemer [17]. Again, no automatic optimization is done in these works.

The approach presented by Bauler et al. [5] uses MDA techniques to transform BPMN models to an extended BPMN model due to annotations in the model. The transformation step replaces parts of the BPMN model with already existing sub-workflows which are taken from a repository. A second step then creates excutable BPEL code. The approach represents a static replacement strategy, not allowing to apply dynamic optimization rules, which are necessary for the use cases presented here.

7   Conclusions

In this paper, we have described the problems of workflow designers and integrators when faced with business processes incorporating human tasks and changes in the infrastructure the workflow will run on. The lack of adequate tool support and the complexity of manually trying to create or adjust the workflows while coevally building the user interfaces were discussed. A new approach to solve the problem by utilizing an MDA approach was presented, resulting in visually designing a platform-independent workflow representation and automatically combining it with the underlying platform information and user interface representation techniques. Our approach was validated by applying it to a virtual prototyping process from the metal casting industry.

In the future, the user should get the possibility to change the information presented in the human task user interface, i.e. the layout, by providing a graphical modification system and extending the editor with the functionality. Furthermore, supporting the WS-HumanTask and BPEL4People specifications to gain more standard compliance is desired. This step would also allow workflow designers to combine standard web services and Grid services in a single workflow, and human tasks could be arbitrarily mapped as either a Grid solution or a vendor-specific implementation. Furthermore, the pattern repository for the workflow transformation and optimization facility will be extended to support more rules. Automatic measurement subsystems (e.g. throughput measurement tools) and information Grid services which provide details about a specific Grid node will be implemented to provide even better automatic adjustments to a given infrastructure.

Acknowledgements. The work presented in this paper is partly supported by a grant from the German Ministry of Education and Research (BMBF) (D-Grid initiative, InGrid Project) and by the Ministry of Science and Research of Northrine-Westfalia in the context of the MiGrid-Project. Furthermore, we would like to thank our industry partners ACCESS e.V., Aachen, Germany, Albert Hiby GmbH & Co. KG, Plettenberg, Germany, Fischer & Kaufmann GmbH & Co. KG, Finnentrop, Germany and Co.Com Concurrent Computing, Siegen, Germany for providing the software and parts of the use cases necessary for this work.

References

1. Agrawal, A., Amend, M., Das, M., et al.: WS-BPEL Extension for People (2007)
2. Agrawal, A., Amend, M., Das, M., et al.: Web Services Human Task 1.0 (2007)
3. Allen, R.: Workflow: An Introduction. In: Fischer, L. (ed.) The Workflow Handbook 2001, ch. 1, pp. 15–38. Future Strategies (2000)
4. Apache ODE. The Apache Foundation (2008), http://ode.apache.org (visited)
5. Bauler, P., Feltze, F., Frogneux, E., Renwart, B., Thomase, C.: Usage of Model Driven Engineering in the context of Business Process Management. In: Bichler, M., Hess, T., Krczmar, U., Lechner, R., Matthes, F., Picot, A., Speitkamp, B., Wolf, P. (eds.) Multikonferenz Wirtschaftsinformatik, GITO Verlag (2008)
6. Butchart, B., Cameron, N., Chen, L., Wassermann, B., Emmerich, W., Patel, J.: Sedna: A BPEL-based Environment for Visual Scientific Workflow Modelling, pp. 428–449. Springer, Heidelberg (2007)
7. Cao, J., Jarvis, S., Saini, S., Nudd, G.: GridFlow: Workflow Management for Grid Computing. In: CCGRID, pp. 198–205. IEEE (2003)
8. Culha, B.: Automatic Arrangement of Product Parts, Assemblies and Modules. In: Bouras, A., Gurumoorthy, B., Sudarsan, R. (eds.) Product Lifecycle Management PLM 2005, Inderscience, Geneve (2005)
9. Dörnemann, T., Friese, T., Herdt, S., Juhnke, E., Freisleben, B.: Grid Workflow Modelling Using Grid-Specific BPEL Extensions. In: Proceedings of German e-Science Conference 2007, pp. 1–9 (2007)
10. Dörnemann, T., Smith, M., Freisleben, B.: Composition and Execution of Secure Workflows in WSRF-Grids. In: 8th IEEE International Symposium on Cluster Computing and the Grid (CCGrid 2008). IEEE Press (2008)
11. Foster, I., Kesselman, C. (eds.): The Grid: Blueprint for a New Computing Infrastructure. Morgan Kaufmann Publishers, San Francisco (1999)
12. Foster, I., Kesselman, C. (eds.): The Grid 2: Blueprint for a new Computing Infrastructure. Morgan Kaufmann (2004)

13. Friese, T., Smith, M., Freisleben, B., Reichwald, J., Barth, T., Grauer, M.: Collaborative Grid Process Creation Support in an Engineering Domain. In: Robert, Y., Parashar, M., Badrinath, R., Prasanna, V.K. (eds.) HiPC 2006. LNCS, vol. 4297, pp. 263–276. Springer, Heidelberg (2006)
14. Gardner, T.: UML Modelling of Automated Business Processes with a Mapping to BPEL4WS. In: Proceedings of the First European Workshop on Object Orientation and Web Services (2003)
15. Grauer, M., Reichwald, J., Christian, D., Barth, T.: The Potential of Service-Oriented Computing for Small and Medium Enterprises - Analysis of Value Chains. In: P2P and Grid Track, Multikonferenz Wirtschaftsinformatik, Passau (2006)
16. Grauer, M., Reichwald, J., Barth, T.: A Service-Oriented Grid-Based Infrastructure for Supporting Virtual Prototyping in Manufacturing. In: Oberweis, A., Weinhardt, C., Gimpel, H., Koschmider, A., Pankratius, V., Schnizler, B. (eds.) eOrganisation: Service-, Prozess,- Market-Engineering, vol. 2, pp. 531–548 (2007)
17. Hofreiter, B., Huemer, C.: Transforming UMM Business Collaboration Models to BPEL. In: Meersman, R., Corsaro, A. (eds.) OTM-WS 2004. LNCS, vol. 3292, pp. 507–519. Springer, Heidelberg (2004)
18. Jakumeit, J., Barth, T., Reichwald, J., Grauer, M.: A Grid-Based Parallel Optimization Algorithm Applied to a Problem in Metal Casting Industry. In: 2nd International Conference on Bioinspired Optimization Methods and their Applications (BIOMA), Ljubljana, Slovenia (October 2006)
19. Kacsuk, P., Sipos, G.: Multi-Grid, Multi-UserWorkflows in the P-GRADE Grid Portal. J. Grid Computing 3(3-4), 221–238 (2005)
20. Lübke, D., Lücke, T., Schneider, K., Marx Gomez, J.: Using Event-Driven Process Chains for Model-Driven Development of Business Applications. In: Proc. of the XML4BPM Workshop (2006)
21. Masak, D.: SOA? Serviceorientierung in Business und Software. Springer, Heidelberg (2007)
22. Mendling, J., Ziemann, J.: EPK-Visualisierung von BPEL4WS Prozessdenitionen. In: Proceedings of the 7th Workshop of Software-Reengineering (May 2005)
23. Mendling, J., Ziemann, J.: Transformation of BPEL Processes to EPCs. In: Nüttgens, M., Rump, F.J. (eds.) Proceedings of the 4th GI Workshop on Event-Driven Process Chains, Hamburg, Germany, vol. 167, pp. 41–53 (December 2005)
24. Mendling, J., Lassen, K.B., Zdun, U.: Transformation Strategies between Block-Oriented and Graph-Oriented Process Modelling Languages. In: Lehner, F., Nösekabel, H., Kleinschmidt, P. (eds.) Multikonferenz Wirtschaftsinformatik, vol. 2, pp. 297–312. GITO Verlag, Berlin (2006)
25. Miller, J., Mukerji, J. (eds.): MDA Guide Version 1.0.1. OMG (2003)
26. Singh, M.P., Huhns, M.N.: Service-Oriented Computing - Semantics, Processes, Agents. John Wiley and Sons (2005)
27. Taylor, I., Shields, M., Wang, I., Harrison, A.: Visual GridWorkflow in Triana. Journal of Grid Computing 3(3-4), 153–169 (2005)
28. The Gridsphere Portal Framework (2008), http://www.gridsphere.org (visited)
29. Weber, I., Haller, J., Müller, J.: Automated Derivation of Executable Business Processes from Choreographies in Virtual Organizations. In: Lehner, F., Nösekabel, H., Kleinschmidt, P. (eds.) Multikonferenz Wirtschaftsinformatik, vol. 2, pp. 313–328. GITO Verlag, Berlin (2006)
30. Yu, J., Buyya, R.: A Taxonomy of Workflow Management Systems for Grid Computing. Journal of Grid Computing 3(3-4), 171–200 (2005)

Optimization Approaches in the Strategic and Tactical Planning of Networks for Letter, Parcel and Freight Mail

Hans-Jürgen Sebastian

Deutsche Post Chair of Optimization of Distribution Networks
RWTH Aachen University
Sebastian@or.rwth-aachen.de

Abstract. The increasing market competition and service focus of the customers forces logistics service providers such as e.g. postal organizations and express shipment companies to re-evaluate and to constantly improve their networks for letter, parcel and freight mail. The core service provided by postal companies is parcel and letter mail transportation and delivery. In this market segment there are two key efforts during the last few years: reduction in transportation and delivery time and minimization of costs under service quality constraints. We will analyse the structure of real world distribution networks for letter, parcel or freight mail and describe the respective subnetworks. We will introduce a general approach of heuristic decomposition of such distribution networks using cut-off times and time windows in order to model service quality requirements. Finally we will describe the models, optimization approaches and the implemented Decision Support Systems of three real world cases of subnetworks of distribution networks.

Keywords: postal logistics, distribution networks, letter-, parcel mail, freight, optimization, decision support systems, strategic and tactical planning.

1   Introduction

This article deals with the so-called Postal Logistics area, more precisely, we will focus on distribution networks for letter mail and parcel mail as well. We will introduce the main subnetworks and will describe the logistics processes of transporting, sorting and delivering mail. Distinguishing between the main planning phases of distribution networks - the strategic, the tactical, and the operational planning phase, we will focus on optimization problems and not on multi-criteria or simulation type of problems. After explaining a general heuristic decomposition approach in order to split the overall optimization problem into "smaller," solvable problems for the subnetworks we will identify classes of optimization problems which are characteristic for the respective subnetworks and planning phases as well. This classification is not based on a systematic literature review but on an almost 15 years collaboration between the RWTH Aachen and the Deutsche Post DHL (DPDHL) consisting of numerous research projects and software systems developments. Finally, in order to illustrate our optimization approaches, we will consider 3 cases in detail,

D. Dolk et al. (Eds.): Decision Support Modeling in Service Networks, LNBIP 42, pp. 36–61, 2012.

picking one example from transportation network design (the DPDHL night airmail network), one from the facility location area (the delivery station optimization project) and one from the parcel and freight mail transportation field (DLH's swap body container transportation problem). We start with a short description of a classical distribution network for physical goods in order to show the differences in comparison with the postal logistics distribution networks.

2   Distribution Networks in Postal Logistics

We start with considering a design problem for a (classical) multistage distribution network (Fig. 1).

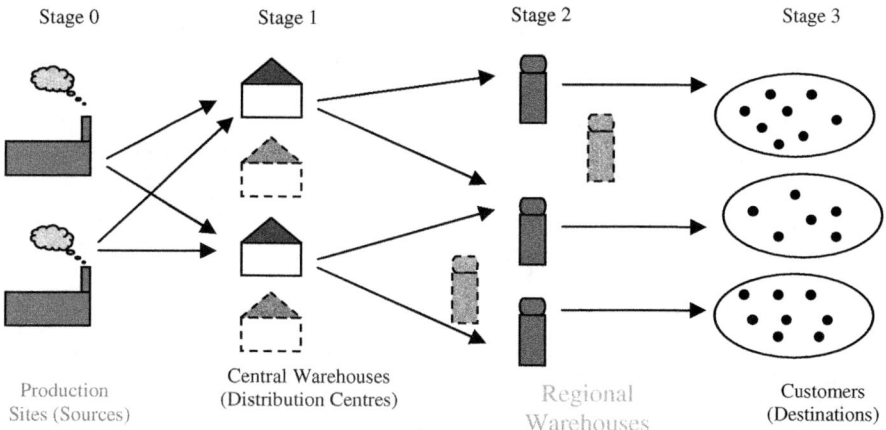

| Stage 0 | Stage 1 | Stage 2 | Stage 3 |

Production Sites (Sources)   Central Warehouses (Distribution Centres)   Regional Warehouses   Customers (Destinations)

Fig. 1. A classical multistage distribution network

There are given production sites (sources) and customers at given locations (destinations). The problem is to select central warehouses (distribution centers) and regional warehouses from predefined sets of potential warehouses and to determine the links for the flow of goods between all four types of objects (production sites, central and regional warehouses, customers). The characteristic properties of such systems are the following:

- Distribution Systems are networks, where nodes representing the objects (described above) of several hierarchical stages are connected by arcs which represent the commodity flow – the flow of goods, articles, products.
- In the nodes and along the arcs processes of commodity transformation in space and time are taking place. (Transformation means e.g. transporting, sorting, storing of the commodities.)
- The general goal of the distribution network is the satisfaction of customer demand in an efficient way.

- In classical distribution networks there are no commodity exchange processes between nodes of the same hierarchical stage of the network
- There is one direction of the flow of goods: from the production sites to the end customers.

These types of distribution networks are extensively discussed in the literature (e.g. see A. Geoffrion, [7])

Our experiences with classical distribution network analysis and design optimization relate to such networks for electrical goods, fashion articles, bath ceramics and glass [1, 33].

A typical distribution network for letter and parcel mail can be described as follows (Fig. 2).

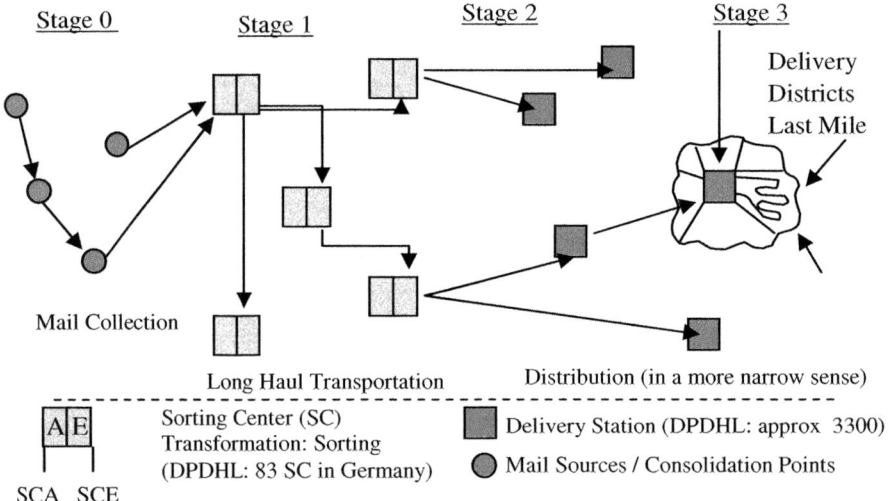

Fig. 2. A distribution network for letter and parcel mail

By using the same stage structure we also used in Fig. 1 we get the stages:

- Stage 0: <u>Mail collection;</u> Collects the mail from different mail sources and uses consolidation points in order to transport the mail to sorting centers.
- Stage 1: <u>Long Haul Transportation;</u> Exchanges the mail between the sorting centers. The idea is to use consolidation and bigger or faster vehicles for the long distances.
- Stage 2: <u>Distribution</u> from sorting centers to mini-hubs (so-called delivery stations) where the final sorting in sequence for the delivery districts takes place
- Stage 3: <u>Delivery (The Last Mile)</u> Postmen visit their delivery districts in order to deliver the mail to the private houses or the business customers.

We will describe the processes at the 4 stages more detailed after a brief comparison of the both network types in figs. 1 and 2.

- There is no "production of goods" at production sites in the Postal Logistics Case. Instead of several 1000's to 10000's of different articles (goods, commodities) which we normally have in a classical distribution network, we are faced with a relatively small number of letter or parcel types in the postal case, which are usually called products.
- But, on the other hand, in the postal case there is a huge number of sources of mail, which are often, at the same time sources and destinations (customers) as well. If we are considering the region of a 5-digit zip-code number, we would (theoretically) have 10^5 sources of mail on an aggregated level, which are also destinations. With other words, in the postal case there is some symmetry between origins and destinations.
- In the postal logistics case there are commodity (mail) exchange processes between the nodes of the same hierarchical stage. For example, the long haul transportation network (Fig. 2) is a network and not just an unstructured stage.
- Finally, the "Last Mile" is much more complex than the stage 3 (Fig. 1) in the classical case is.

Next we go a bit more into the details of the main components of a distribution network for letter and parcel mail introduced before (Fig. 2).

There are subnetworks for collecting mail. Usually each sorting center has its own network for mail collection. The main objects belonging to the <u>mail collection networks</u> are

- mail sources: mailboxes, business customers, filials (consolidation terminals CoP).
- collecting routes to realize the mail transportation to the assigned sorting center.

Two projects at the Deutsche Post Chair of RWTH Aachen dealt with the mail collecting networks. One of them considers mail collection processes for a set of sorting centers at the same time and identifies reassignment possibilities of mail sources to sorting centers [11, 12, 13]. The other project considers the optimization of collection and distribution routes within an area allocated to a sorting center simultaneously and tries, at the same time, to find synergies between letter and parcel mail collecting and distribution [10].

<u>Sorting Centers (SC)</u> for letter or for parcel mail respectively are big automated facilities, which do the sorting-part (the "production") of the networks. Sorting centers for letter mail are divided into two parts SCA and SCE. The SCA sorting center performs sorting of the colleted mail with respect to the destination sorting center. The SCE sorting centers (E means "entrance" from LHT) do sorting processes for the distribution and the delivery (last mile).

Usually the assigned regions to the SCA part and the SCE part of a sorting center are identical. But there is an option to use some of the sorting centers as SCE centers only. Physically the SCA and SCE sorting centers are the same, because of the high degree of flexibility of the automized sorting machines.

There are several types of sorting centers distinguished by their capacity to find good strategies to control the transportation processes within such a sorting center [31, 35, 36].

<u>Long Haul Transportation (LHT)</u> means the global area transportation network between the sorting centers. Consolidation is used in order to transport big quantities

using larger vehicles or using a multi-modal transportation (road-air, road-rail e.g.). In Section 4.1. we will discuss the case of the Night-Airmail Network (NAN) for letter mail in Germany [3, 20] and in Section 4.3. a model which is closely related to the long haul transportation network for parcel mail [9, 32] also within Germany.

Finally, there are the subnetworks for distributing the mail from SCE to the Delivery Stations (DS) and the so-called Last Mile. Delivery stations are mini-hubs, where the final sorting for delivery takes place. The postmen picks up his/her sorted mail and starts the delivery process (last mile) at the DS's. Then he/she moves to the Delivery Districts (DD) he/she has to serve by car, bicycle or by foot in a prescribed sequence. Starting in 1996 one big project of the DPDHL was to find an optimal number and the locations of the delivery stations, provided the sorting centers and the delivery districts are assumed to be given [28, 30]. During this successful project the number of DS's was reduced by about 50%. We will discuss the scientific background of this project in our case-study two in Section 4.2. Currently the problem of optimization of the delivery station locations and the respective allocations are revisited within the project TOPAS [14, 15, 16] resulting in new models, algorithmic approaches and a DSS. In the area of optimization of the last mile, we developed methods and algorithms for postmen problems and arc routing problems [17, 18, 19], which are not in the focus of this article.

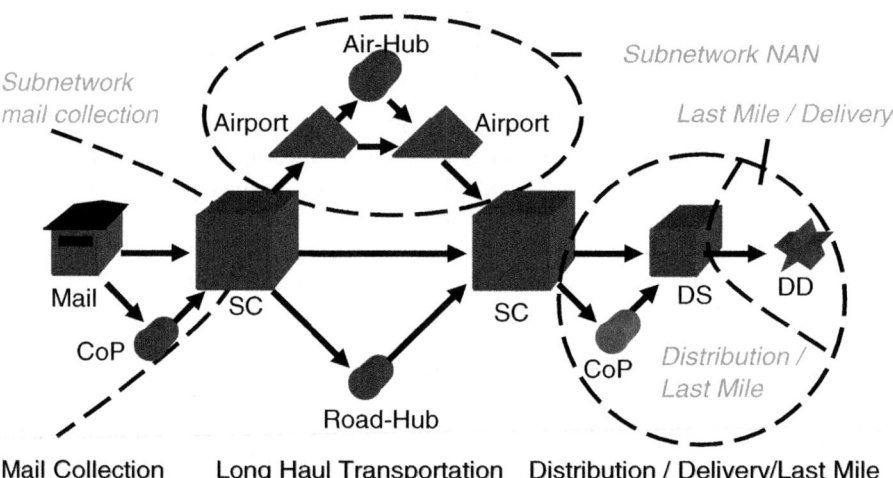

Fig. 3. Schematic view of a distribution network in postal logistics

Fig. 3 shows a more schematic picture of the distribution network for letter and parcel mail. The subnetworks and components are marked using the abbreviations introduced before. If we replace the subnetwork NAN by a respective rail subnetwork and the "mailbox" by "parcel mail sources", we approach the situation of DPDHL's parcel mail network within Germany. In order to illustrate the dimension, the size of an instance of such a distribution network, we will give some characteristic numbers of the DPDHL distribution network for letter mail within Germany:

This network consists of:

40 million final destinations, including 3 million business customers
72 million letters (of different types throughout Germany each working day)
108000 mail boxes
82 sorting centers + the international postal center in Frankfurt
3300 delivery stations (DS) and 12000 sales offices (filials)

The last mile is characterized by:

61000 Delivery districts (DD), where 10500 are visited by foot, 25500 by bicycle and 25000 by car. There are 81000 postmen working for DPDHL within the last mile in Germany.

This huge size of the network does not allow to develop an overall optimization model which has a chance to become solved either exactly or approximately. Therefore, we developed a decomposition-based approach which considers both, subnetworks and different planning phases.

3   The Decomposition Approach into Planning Phases and Subnetworks

3.1   Network Design in Freight Transportation

Letter and parcel mail as well are particular types of freight. Network Design in freight transportation is a field where many attractive work has been published before [4, 5, 8,]. Under network design in freight transportation most of the authors in that field understand: Modeling of the physical transportation network and solution of the task "Shipping goods from origin to destination locations under service-quality requirements". This includes:

− The creation or reengineering of the infrastructure at the locations such as terminals, depots, hubs.
− Selection of the services to be offered.
− Assigning of resources (e.g. vehicles, manpower) to the services.
− Scheduling of these resources.

Because this task is very complex, planning phases have been introduced in order to reduce problem complexity. Usually the following planning phases are considered:

(1) The *Strategic Phase*
This phase deals with long-term type of decisions related to the network infrastructure, e.g. decisions related to
• the quantity and quality of the main resources (locations, facilities, human resources) and the method of acquisition of these resources and
• the selection of services to be offered.

(2) The *Tactical Phase*
Decisions in the tactical phase are mid-term type of decisions related to the design of the service network assuming that the strategic decisions have been made before. These decisions include:

- Service Selection: Definition of the routes on which services will be offered and the characteristics of each service (e.g. frequency or scheduling decisions).
- Traffic distribution: Includes the routes, the services used, the terminals passed through and the operations at these terminals
- Terminal policies: Specification of the consolidation activities at each terminal (e.g. sorting, storing, picking, cross-docking)
- Empty balancing strategies: Repositioning of empties such as vehicles, pallets and containers

(3) The *Operational Phase*

Decisions of the operational phase are short-term decisions made often on-line and in real-time. They are performed by local management, called dispatchers or disponents.

The borderlines between these phases are not crisp. Interdependencies between the phases must be considered. For example, in order to make optimal decisions in the strategic phase, some tactical decisions have to be made simultaneously at least approximately. In case of a location problem it is always necessary to make location and allocation decisions simultaneously. Allocation decisions are related to the transportation network. Many facility location models make a very simple approximation of the related transportation subsystems [22]. Therefore, their acceptance in practice is rather low. A solution would be to consider location and routing decisions (strategic and tactical phase decisions) simultaneously. However, this increases the problem complexity considerably. We will later come back to the respective class of optimization models, the location-routing problems [2, 21, 23-27, 34]. In the project TOPAS C. Hermanns developed an interesting approach to combine strategic and tactical phase decisions [16]. Of course, also the borderline between the tactical and the operational planning phase is as well interesting. It seems that the biggest potential for ensuring a high service quality level and for reduction of cost is in the strategic and tactical phases. However, low quality of managing the operational planning phase can destroy both the service quality and the optimization related cost savings made in the strategic and tactical planning phases. Therefore the operational planning phase is also very important and their regular decisions should be aughmented by a risk management in order to be able to deal with several types of risks which might occur in a freight transportation network.

The considerations discussed above, in particular the planning phases and their overlappings can be applied to the special type of freight transportation we have in the postal area.

All we have to do is to use the specifics of the postal letter or parcel mail system.

As an example we formulate the most important objects for the strategic planning phase of a postal distribution network:

- Origins (sources) for letter or parcel mail; point-like sources as e.g. mail boxes, filials, business customers or area-sources as e.g. 5-digit zip-code areas
- Destinations: private households, business customers or area-destinations depending on the level of aggregation; 5-digit zip-code areas or delivery districts (DD)
- Locations:

- point-like locations useable for mailboxes, sorting centers, delivery stations, airports
- area-locations; zip-code areas, delivery districts, areas allocated to the sorting centers
- facilities; sorting centers (number, size, type, layout configuration), hubs (candidate hubs for long-haul ground transportation are the sorting centers, airports used as hubs), delivery stations (number, size, type, layout configuration)
- Fleets, for example a
- heterogeneous fleet of aircrafts for the LHT-network
- heterogeneous fleet of ground vehicles for the LHT-network, the distribution and the feeding networks

3.2   Services, Time-Windows and Cut-Off-Times

The core of the approach of strategic, tactical and operational type of planning of a distribution network in postal logistics is

- to start with the set of all services such a network could provide,
- to continue with a selection of services and service levels the distribution network should offer and
- to define time windows and cut-off times in such a way that the overall system will become heuristically decomposed into subnetworks (subsystems) which together (as a whole) fulfill the required service-levels and which can be optimized independently on each other (if cut-off times and time windows are not violated) in the sense of cost-minimization.

The list of services could contain e.g. the following services to select:

- LHT-network consisting of ground transportation using trucks only.
- LHT-network consisting of combined rail-road ground transportation.
- LHT-network in a combined transportation mode: air-ground (using trucks only in the ground transportation mode).
- LHT-network using direct service only or using consolidation by introducing hub-locations and -facilities.
- Pick-up routes within the feeding (mail-collection) local networks.
- Delivery routes within the distribution (from SC' to DS's) networks of each sorting center.
- Combined pick-up and delivery routes within the regional transportation networks.
- To-house delivery service by the postmen within the last mile.

The selection of services from such a list (which is much longer in reality) mainly depends on the selected or requested overall service quality level of the whole distribution network. For example, the overall service quality level could be "next-day delivery" or "k-th day delivery ($k \geq 2$)". It may be differ for different types of postal products. For example, within Germany, DPDHL promises next day delivery for each regular letter. More precise, if the letter will be delivered to a mailbox or filial before a cut-off time (last emptying of the mailbox), it will arrive at the destination address next day before 2 p.m.. Of course, such an requirement determines mainly the services which needs to be selected and it determines the cost of running such a network. The next-day delivery service quality requirement for all letter mail simplifies the network design considerably. Sometimes, it is argued, that a network with different service levels for different postal products (and of course different prices for theses letter types) would be more attractive for customers and perhaps even more profitable for the postal organizations. Our research activities show, that it will become much more complicated to optimize and to implement, to use such a network with different service quality levels. In many countries like e.g. the USA, Canada, Russia, China etc. only next-day delivery mail is not realistic because of the geography of the countries. But the analysis of postal systems of those countries show that networks with "k-th day delivery" for different values of k are indeed very complicated.

The usual way to implement the selected service levels is to assign time windows and cut-off times to the predefined subnetworks (see fig. 3) of the overall distribution network.

For example, a service quality level "next-day delivery" may be implemented by the cut-off times and the intervals shown in fig. 4.

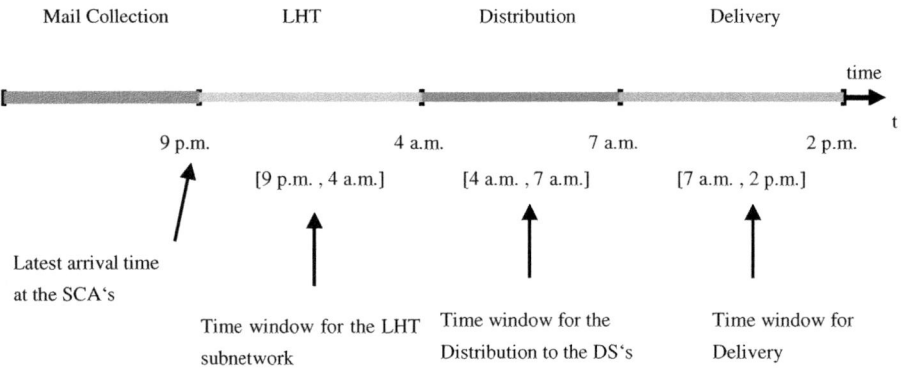

Fig. 4. Example of Cut-Off times and time intervals for subnetworks

The dates in Fig. 4 are very close to the DPDHL German national Letter Mail Network case. In general of course, the time windows and cut-off times must fit the geography of the considered country, the locations, facilities and fleets considered in the strategic planning phase and the services included in the list of available services. For example, without having an air transportation mode for the LHT subnetworks, the time window [9 p.m.; 4 a.m.] for the LHT in Germany would not be realistic. Fig. 4 gives a simplified illustration only. In reality carefully defined time windows are overlapping.

3.3   The Optimization Problems for Distribution Network Design in Postal Logistics

Optimality of a Distribution Network for letter and parcel mail can now (after the preparations above) formulated by a <u>two-phase approach:</u>

Phase 1:
- Decide about the service-quality levels for all considered products
- Project these overall service-quality levels onto a set of time windows and cut-off times for the subnetworks.
- Select feasible services from the list of alternatives (feasible with respect to the time windows and cut-off times).

Phase 2:
- Find a Distribution Network with minimal overall costs under the preconditions defined in phase 1.

That means, service-quality-levels are used as hard constraints, costs are considered to be the objectives of the phase 2 optimization problem. Of course, the phase 2 optimization problem is still too complex. Therefore, in the following, we will split it into the 2-dimensional subsystems structure (see fig. 5) which is determined by the planning-phases and the subsystems as well.

Before doing this, let us remark, that instead of the Phases 1 and 2 introduced above alternative approaches would be possible;

- Trade-off analysis of service quality vs. costs or
- Multi Criteria Decision Analysis (MCDA) approaches.

In our research, the preferences of DPDHL have been clearly expressed into the direction of the 2-phase approach.

Network-Level	Planning Phases		
	Strategic	*Tactical*	*Operational*
Overall Network	Facility Location/Allocation	Transportation Network Design Vehicle Routing	Operations Center
Subnetworks:	Decomposition / Integration of Networks and Services (exact or heuristic)		
- Collection	Location / Allocation	Multi-Depot Vehicle Routing	On-line Optimization for Transporation Subnetworks
- LHT • Hubs • Direct Links • NAN • Airportfeeder	Location / Allocation (Hub Selection) (Airport Selection)	Service Network Design: e.g. Multi-Depot Vehicle Routing and Scheduling	
- Distribution	Location / Allocation (DS) Location Routing	Vehicle Routing and Scheduling	
- Delivery/Last Mile	Capacitated Arc Routing, Postmen Problems		

Fig. 5. Optimization Problems used in different planning phases and subnetworks (Operations Center, see e.g. [29])

In Fig. 5 we show which types of optimization problems are mostly used to solve a problem belonging to a certain planning phase for a particular subnetwork of the overall distribution network in postal logistics and for the overall network as well. We don't go into the details of the operational phase. But in the strategic and tactical planning phases the following classes of optimization models are dominating:

- Facility Location Problems
- Location Routing Problems
- Service Network Design Problems
- Vehicle Routing and Scheduling Problems
- Postmen and Capacitated Arc Routing Problems

Of course, it comes not as a surprise that these classes of optimization problems are most important for postal logistics. In addition, the methodology (optimization methods and algorithms) developed for these problem classes is of course not restricted to the postal application area. However, it is also not focused to that area. Because of the specifics of the postal application and the large scaled problem instances, also new models and solution techniques need to be developed in order to solve real world postal problem instances.

In the following, we will give examples – case studies – which show how to use knowledge from the problem classes mentioned above to solve real world problems in postal logistics. This case studies have been elaborated in cooperation with the DPDHL and with GTS Systems and Consulting.

4   Selected Case Studies

4.1   The Deutsche Post Night-Airmail Network for Letter Mail (NAN)

In the following we will develop the optimization model and describe the solution process. For more detailed description see [3, 20].

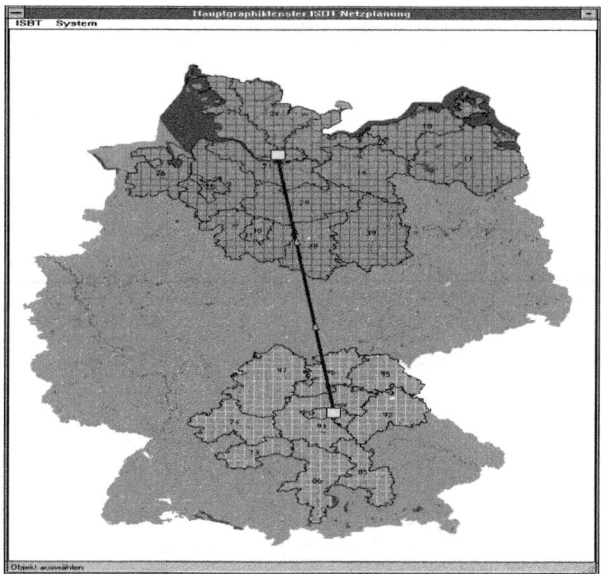

Fig. 6. Why flying is necessary in order to realize next-day delivery?

Because the NAN is one subnetwork of the LHT-network for letter mail it contributes to the mail exchange processes between the 82+1 (International Sorting Center) Sorting Centers for letter mail every night during a time interval of approx. 7 hours (9 p.m. to 4 a.m.). In order to make clear that "flying mail" is necessary within Germany in order to realize the mail exchange process between the sorting centers in the time window of 7 hours one should look to Fig. 6.

There are two airports with assigned sorting center areas. This assignment depends on the departure time of the flight. If the departure time at the airport in southern Germany is early (meaning closely after 9 p.m.) the set of assigned sorting centers areas is rather small, because the mail has to be transported after the cut-off-time (which is 9 p.m.) by car or truck to the airport and the aircraft needs to be loaded. On the other side, early departure means early arrival and that leads to a bigger set of assigned destination sorting center areas, which can be reached by that flight. Finally, within Germany travelling any distance between sorting centers bigger than approx. 300 miles on road within approx. 7 hours seems to be not realistic (even during the night). Therefore, in our approach, we consider all relations (origin SC, destination SC) (83×82=6706 taking into account the symmetry) and assign all relations with a distance greater than 300 miles to the NAN. Later we will see that the model itself can assign also "shorter" relations to the NAN if aircrafts can be better utilized by doing this. Another alternative would be to develop a model which decides this assignment problem under an overall cost objective and not using a simple rule (≥ 300 miles) during a preprocessing.

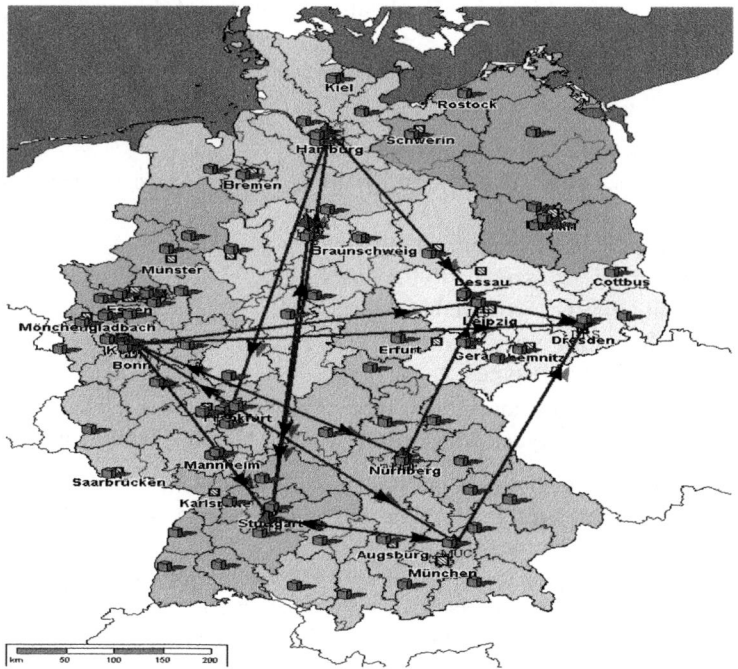

Fig. 7. An example of a direct-flight network

Next we consider the problem of general design alternatives for a NAN. Fig. 7 shows a network consisting of direct (non-stop) flights only, while fig. 8 shows a mixed direct and hub-flight network. It also shows the dimensions from 2005, where Frankfurt airport was used as a hub for hub-flights from and to 6 other airports. The mixed flight network used 10 airports, 13 different aircrafts and 20 flights per night (5 airlines have been involved in that network).]

Fig. 8. The Frankfurt air-hub of the NAN

To explain the main ideas of the modeling process, we introduce the following basic notations:

– A request r is a triple (o(r), d(r), q(r)), where
• o(r), d(r) are the origin, destination locations of the request r (in our case sorting centers)
• q(r) is the quantity to ship from o(r) to d(r)
– **R** – set of all requests assigned to the NAN
– P – set of all airports k involved in the network
– A – set of all aircraft types a, where
  Q_a – capacity of aircraft-type $a \in A$
  n_a – number of available aircrafts of type $a \in A$
  A_k – subset of aircraft types which is allowed for take-off/ landing at airport $k \in P$.

In this model n_a are critical numbers. Sometimes it is not known, which numbers n_a (in particular for smaller aircrafts) can be negotiated. Using – in such case – bigger numbers for n_a might become critical.

Let us now consider the direct flight network design option. In fig. 9 we illustrate the routing of a request r if direct flights are considered only. The request r includes the origin and the destination locations (■ in Fig. 9). Then, one has to select

• a take-off airport and
• a destination airport.

Direct Flight Problem

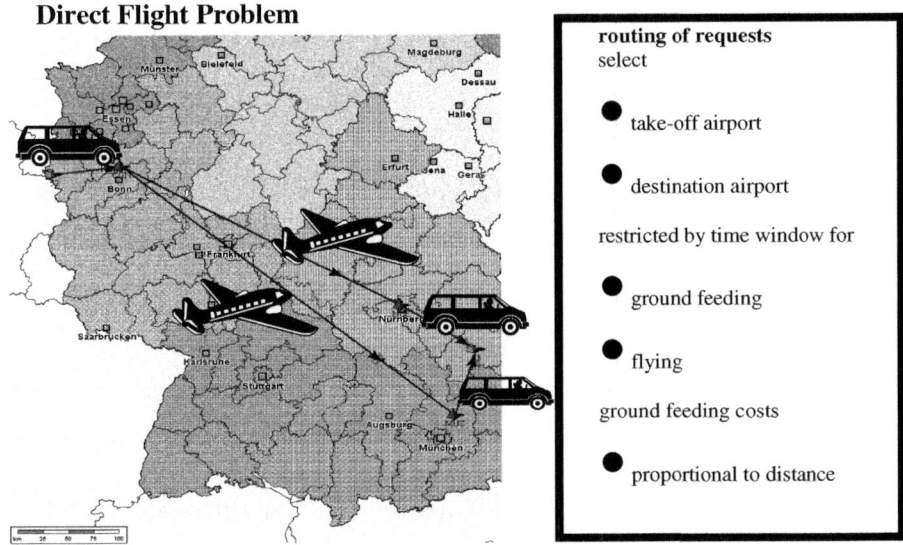

Fig. 9. Routing of a request

These decisions are restricted by time windows for ground feeding and flying. We assume that ground feeding costs are proportional to distance. That means, we use a simple cost model for ground feeding. In the reality ground feeding is realized by routes which might have several stops and use consolidation.

The model we are proposing next belongs mainly to the tactical planning phase, because it finally delivers a schedule for the over-night flights. We define the following main concepts:

– A triple f = (a, k, l) is called a potential flight.
  a stands for an aircraft type; k – for the departure and l for the destination (arrival) airport;
  $a \in A$; $k, l \in P$
  F = {f | f is a potential flight}
  (For Direct Flight Problem (DFP) instances of the NAN for letter mail in Germany we have $500 \leq |F| \leq 1200$.)
– A terminated flight (f, t) is an extension of a potential flight by a take-off time t
  $(f, t) = (a, k, l, t)$, $f \in F$, $t \geq 0$
  If we consider only relevant take-off times t, the cardinality of the set of terminated flights for the DFP-NAN is between 3000 and 20000.
– The central concept is a "loaded flight".
  It is an extension of a terminated flight by a subset R*, $R* \subseteq R$, of requests; (f, t, R*), where (f, t) is a terminated flight.
  Finally, a feasible loaded flight is a loaded flight, where the assignment of requests $r \in R*$ to (f, t) is feasible:
  That means all capacity constraints are fulfilled, and all requests $r \in R*$ are pairwise compatible (can be transported together with the terminated flight (f, t)).

For the DFP-NAN we get from 10^{50} to 10^{60} feasible loaded flights.
With these notations we can model the optimization problem DFP-NAN as follows:

1. Decision Variables

a) Flights (services)
   $y_f \in \{0, 1\}$, = 1, if the potential flight f = (a, k, l) (short: flight) is chosen

b) Feasible assignment of requests to flights
   $x_{rf} \in \{0, 1\}$, = 1, if the request r is assigned to the potential flight f

c) Repositioning
   z_f _ number of repostionings related to f

That means, we use binary (y_f, x_{rf}) and integer (z_f) variables only in order to describe the problem.

2. The objective function

The objective function is to minimize the overall costs of the DFP-NAN:

$$Z = \sum_{f \in F, r \in R(f)} c_{rf}^{feed} \cdot x_{rf} + \sum_{f \in F} c_f^{fix} \cdot y_f + \sum_{f \in F} c_f^{ferry} \cdot z_f \tag{1}$$

The first term computes assignment costs (mainly feeding costs), which appear if a request r is assigned to a potential flight. The second term measures the fix costs related to the use of a potential flight (which are independent on how good or bad that flight is loaded by requests) while the third term evaluates so called ferry costs which might occur if repositioning of aircrafts becomes needed after the transportation process has taken place during night.

3. Constraints

A first group of constraints, the so called coupling constraints determine a master program.

$$\sum_{f \in F} x_{rf} = 1 \quad \text{for all } r \in R$$

(each request needs to be transported)

$$\sum_{f \in F} \delta_f^s \cdot y_f^s \leq n^s \quad \text{for all } s \in CS$$

(number of take-offs, landings, aircrafts of a certain type might be restricted)

$$\sum_{f=(a,k,l) \in F} (y_f + z_f) - \sum_{f=(a,l,k) \in F} (y_f + z_f) = 0$$

(repositioning constraints)

$$K \in P, a \in A, \quad z_f \geq 0 \text{ integer}$$

$$\tag{2}$$

The second group of constraints relates on a single flight, and, therefore, it determines the pricing problem

$$\sum_{r \in R(f)} q_r \cdot x_{rf} \leq Q_a \cdot y_f \quad \text{for all } f = (a, k, l) \in F$$

(capacity constraints for flights)

$x_{rf} + x_{sf} \leq y_f$ for all $f \in F$ where r,s, (with $r \in R(f)$)
are not compatible with respect to f: $r \not\sim_f s$

$y_f \in \{0, 1\}$ for all $f \in F$
$x_{rf} \in \{0, 1\}$ for all $f \in F$, $r \in R(f)$

(3)

This Direct Flight-Problem (1)-(3) has been proven to be NP-hard [3]. Therefore a hybrid Tabu Search – Branch and Bound Heuristic was developed and implemented [3]. The idea behind this heuristic is to enumerate terminated flights and to solve generalized Warehouse Location Problems (WLP). The terminated flights are considered to be the warehouses. This heuristic was used starting in 1999 within the DPDHL software systems (ISBT-Netzplanung [28,6]). However, there have been no tight lower bounds available even for smaller problem instances. Therefore the goal of the PHD-thesis of Stefan Irnich was to compute tight lower bounds and solving small and medium-scale instances to optimality. Irnich considered both, the DFP and the Mixed Hub and Direct Flight Problem (MFP). In that case it is allowed to use one airport as a flight hub where a time window is given for the hub-operations.

On the basis of a Danzig-Wolfe-Decompostion of both the DFP and the MFP models Irnich (S. Irnich 2002 [20]) developed a Branch and Price and Cut solution technique and implemented it.

Using this implementation many real world instances of the DPDHL's NAN problem are solved optimally, for others good bounds are available. These solutions have been used by the DPDHL for negotiation with airlines and also for general insights into the properties of optimal or near optimal solutions of the NAN-problem.

4.2   The Delivery Station Location Optimization Problem

We now go more into the details of the modeling and solving the delivery station location problem, which was already briefly introduced in Section 2.

We assume, that there are given

- a set of potential Delivery Station (DS) locations DS_j , j=1,2,...,m
- a set of Delivery Districts (DD): DD_k , k=1,2,...,n
- a function $ZC_k = f(DD_k)$, which assigns the relevant 5-digit zip-code area to each DD_k.

A zip-code area contains several of the DD's, but not necessarily a DS.

The problem size can be defined by the assigned geographic area of a sorting center, which is partitioned into given zip-code areas, assumed to be given delivery districts, and a finite set of existing delivery stations which could be extended by a set of additional new possible delivery station locations. Then, the problem is to find the optimal number and the optimal locations of delivery stations within this predefined geographic region and, simultaneously, an optimal allocation of the delivery district to the selected delivery stations.

In 1996 the DPDHL used for its national distribution network for letter mail approximately 6400 delivery stations. The goal was to reduce this number considerably within the framework of a general "next day delivery" requirement for all types of letter mail within Germany.

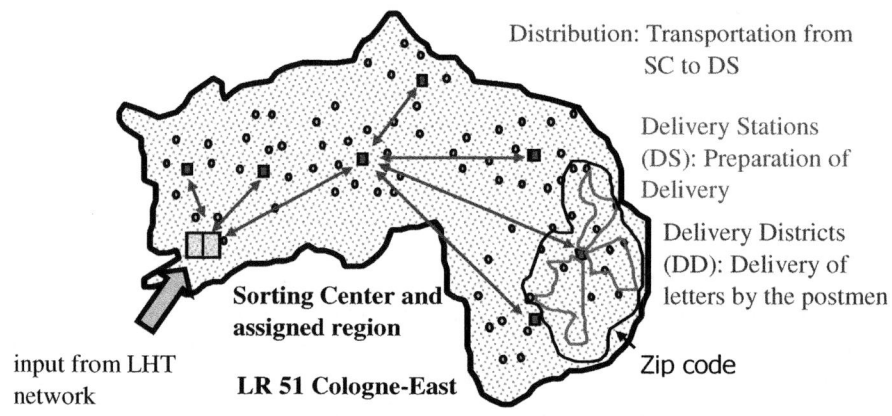

Fig. 10. Sorting Center Region LR 51 Cologne East

Fig. 10 shows as an example the Sorting Center Region LR51 Cologne-East in order to illustrate a subproblem. All together, for each of the 82 sorting centers such a subproblem was required to solve.

We start now to develop the model used to solve that problem by making basic assumptions and introducing the decision variables.

- Selection of the DS's from a given finite set {DS1, ..., DSm} of potential locations (either existing DS's locations or new candidates)
  $y_j = 1$, if DS_j is chosen to become a DS, j=1, ..., m
  (There are capacity constraints of the potential DS-locations; each potential DS_j has a capacity M_j - in terms of number of DD's which might be assigned to that location)
- Allocation variables; assigning delivery districts to delivery stations:
  $z_{kj} = 1$, if delivery district DD_k is assigned to DS_j.

This means, we have introduced m+n·m variables.

- Single Sourcing assumption: Each delivery district is allocated to exactly one delivery station.
- No splitting of a zip-code area is allowed. (Any zip-code area needs to be assigned as a whole to just one delivery station.)
  Under this assumptions, the set of constraints becomes:

$$\sum_{j=1}^{m} z_{kj} = 1 \qquad \text{for each } k=1, \ldots, n \qquad (4)$$

This means single sourcing, because z_{kj} are binary variables.

$$z_{kj} - y_h \leq 0 \text{ for each } k = 1, \ldots, n \quad \text{and} \quad j = 1, \ldots, m \qquad (5)$$

If DS_j is not chosen ($y_j = 0$), no customer (DD) node can be allocated.

$$\sum_{k=1}^{n} z_{kj} \leq M_j \cdot y_j \qquad (6)$$

Capacity constraint: If DS_j is selected, the number of assigned DD's needs to be smaller or equal M_j.

In addition, the compatibility constraints of DD's caused by the "no-splitting assumption of zip-code areas" have to be taken into account.

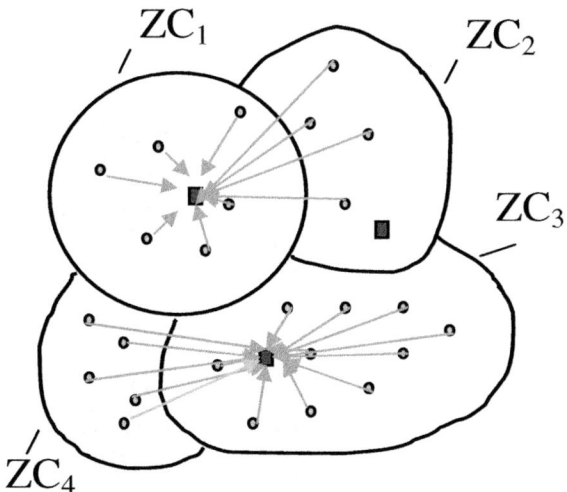

Fig. 11. An example

Fig. 11 shows a selection and allocation in case of m=25 DD's, N=3 potential DS's (two are chosen) and 4 zip-code areas ZC_k.

Finally, the objective function, which represents overall costs, has the following structure:

$$Z = \sum_{k=1}^{n} \sum_{j=1}^{m} c_{kj} \cdot z_{kj} + \sum_{j=1}^{m} \{ f_j \cdot y_j + F_j (\sum_{k=1}^{n} z_{kj}) \} \tag{7}$$

In this overall cost function Z the first term represents the cost for allocation the delivery district DD_k to the delivery station DS_j. The term $f_j \cdot y_j$ denotes costs for "opening" the delivery station DS_j, that means fix-costs of DS_j plus transportation costs from the sorting center SC to DS_j. Finally, $F_j (\sum_{k=1}^{n} z_{kj})$, is a nonlinear function, which represents the immobilia costs of the delivery station DS_j depending on the number of assigned delivery districts.

Summarizing, the objective function (7) is – because of the nonlinear part – not standard in the location theory. However, the modeling of transportation cost in (7) is the same simple approximation, which is normally used in strategic location planning.

The model represented by the explicitly formulated constraints (4), (5) and (6), the additional implicitly given "no-splitting of 5-digit zip-code areas" side constraints and the nonlinear objective function (7) can be classified as a "Capacitated Facility Location Problem with Single Sourcing", additional side constraints and a nonlinear objective function [22]. The single sourcing conditions are causing a NP-hard subproblem, if we relax the side constraints, the nonlinear term in the objective function and if we select feasible values for the location variables y_j. This subproblem is well known as the Generalized Assignment Problem (GAP).

This was the reason for the decision in 1996 to implement a heuristic of the type "Add - and Drop", which is a simple standard type heuristic in the field of facility location.

However the DSS KOBRA [28], which used that heuristic as a solver was extremely successful.

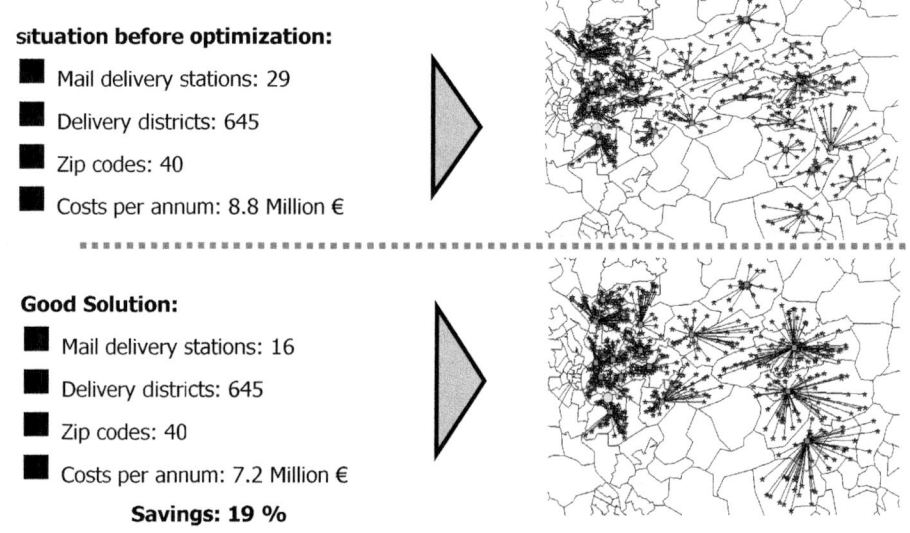

situation before optimization:

- Mail delivery stations: 29
- Delivery districts: 645
- Zip codes: 40
- Costs per annum: 8.8 Million €

Good Solution:

- Mail delivery stations: 16
- Delivery districts: 645
- Zip codes: 40
- Costs per annum: 7.2 Million €

Savings: 19 %

Fig. 12. Savings for the region Cologne East

Fig. 12 illustrates the situation for the region Cologne-East. "Good solution" means a solution generated with the Add - and Drop heuristic based on the model (4)-(7). The number of delivery stations was reduced from 29 to 16, where cost-savings was 19%. Country wide in 1996-1997 using the KOBRA-DSS the number of delivery stations was reduced by more than 3000 (about 50%) with an overall EBITA savings of more than 100 Million Euro per year. Of course, the service quality level – next-day delivery was not touched by this redesign project of the distribution/ delivery part of the network.

Starting in late 2005 the development of new models and a related IT-Tool: TOPAS for delivery station location planning was initiated. The main reasons have been the following:

− Several changes in the distribution network configuration and processes after about 10 years.
− New concepts in letter and parcel mail delivery.
− The progress in the Operations Research area (new optimization models, solution approaches) and much more powerful IT hard- and software.

In the following we will briefly outline the main new concepts and the related changes in modeling. Detailed descriptions of the new models and solver development can be found in [14, 15, 16].

• Integration of the networks for "letter mail" and "parcel mail" in distribution/ delivery.
  (In consequence the sorting centers for parcel mail (33 in Germany) SCP must be considered in addition to the sorting centers for letter mail. Also, delivery stations for parcel mail – called DB (delivery basis) - have to be added.)
• The model (4)-(7) uses approximated transportation costs from or to a DS by direct shipment (Fig. 13).

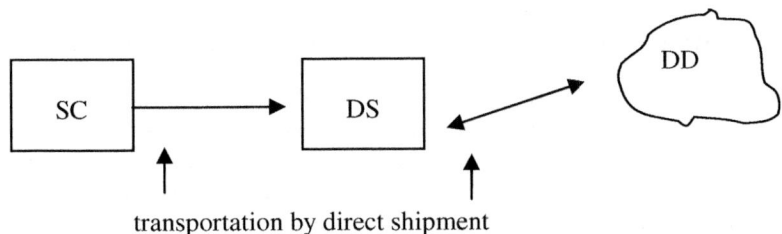

transportation by direct shipment

Fig. 13. Transportation costs approximated by direct shipment

In the reality transportation is organized by tours, either by open tours or by round trips. Therefore, a better approximation of the transportation costs would be an approximation by tours.

The TOPAS project has shown that user acceptance requires new models which approximate transportation costs much better than the "direct shipping" type of models which currently dominate the area of strategic location modeling. Integrating networks is also more challenging than decomposing them. Both aspects together led to new model and solver development and an implemented Tool TOPAS.

Next, we briefly describe the problem of the quality of approximation of transportation costs within strategic Facility Location/ Allocation Models. What, if the distribution process starting at a depot location is not realized by direct shipping but by vehicle routes visiting several customer locations (e.g. delivery stations)? In such a case transportation costs are result of route planning. Route planning, however depends on the depot locations, and, depot locations depend on transportation costs if we use a facility location/ allocation model:

Transportation-costs = f(routes),
Routes = g(depot-location),
Depot-location = h(transportation-costs)

This means, we have cyclic type of dependencies. Therefore, an approach is needed which does simultaneously location- and route-planning. This subarea is called the field of Location-Routing-Problems [2, 24, 23-27, 34].

There are two main approaches to deal with location-routing type of problems in the literature:

1. Approximation methods:
   If the demand allocation is given, there are good approximations of the length of routes and round trips.
2. Heuristics containing a location problem with an explicit routing problem:
   In this area there are sequential, iterative and parallel approaches. Iterative approaches e.g. are Locate First-Route Second heuristics and Route First - Locate Second heuristics [25, 26, 27].

In the TOPAS project a heuristic of the type Route First - Locate Second was developed for the delivery station location optimization problem [16].

4.3   DHL Freight's Transportation Problem of Swap Body Containers

DHL runs daily (more precisely "nightly") a transportation network within Germany, where so called "swap body containers" are carried by trucks or by trains. Each truck can carry exactly two such containers at the same time (therefore the problem is also called the 2-container problem). This network realizes the DHL's long haul transportation network for parcel mail in Germany.

The problem is as follows: Customers order a number of swap bodies. Such an order is called a request, characterized by an origin, a destination, a pickup and a delivery time window. Now, the problem is to assign requests (physically containers) to trucks, to route the trucks and to reposition the empties.

This overall problem was split into subproblems, called modules:

- (1) Modal Split
- (2) Truck Routing: Template Routes
- (3) Truck Routing: Core Routing Process

- (4) Vehicle Scheduling and Assignment
- (5) Repositioning of Empty Containers

The modal split module (1) considers the trade-off between the fixed costs for pre-booked train connections and variable costs for feeding by truck. It also considers the time windows associated with the requests, the train schedules and the necessity to implement a time-staged loading and unloading of the trains. This subproblem can be solved by standard Linear Programming.

Template routes are pre-planned and scheduled regular routes. They are used as a tool for obtaining regularity within the network. The optimization problem in module (2) consists of assigning a set of requests to a set of template routes. It is modelled and solved as an assignment problem.

The core routing process (module (3)) means to combine the remaining requests (those, which are not assigned to template routes) to routes such that the total cost paid to third-party carriers is minimized. There are many constraints one has to consider when performing the core routing process. Here is a selection:

- Time windows of requests and locations
- European drivers' rest break regulations
- Closing of freeways (roads) on Sundays and regional holidays
- Sorting capacities at the parcel mail sorting centers.

An instance of a "core routing problem" contains approximately 3000-5000 requests. We have shown by developing a mathematical model that an exact optimal solution for such large problem instances can not be found in an acceptable solution time. Therefore the truck routing core problem was solved by a parallel insertion heuristic proposed and implemented by T. Grünert [9]. The main idea of this heuristic can be described as follows:

Two requests are called compatible, if they can be transported by the same vehicle. A graph which contains a node for each request and an edge between two nodes, if the nodes represent compatible requests, is called a compatibility graph. Then, the algorithm can be outlined as follows:

1. Compute a compatibility graph on basis of time window and distance information.
2. Find a maximal independent set in the compatibility graph (use the given requests as initial routes).
3. WHILE not all requests have been covered, DO:
    3.1. Compute insertion costs for all requests in all existing routes
    3.2. If any request does not fit into any existing route, then open a new route with this request and assign a vehicle
    3.3. Compute the difference between lowest and 2'nd lowest insertion costs (also called "regret") for all requests
    3.4. Choose the request with the largest regret
    3.5. Insert the chosen request at the best position

Of course, in order to be able to implement this heuristic, the algorithm needs to be formulated more precise and much more detailed.

The objective of the Vehicle Scheduling and Assignment Subsystem (module (4)) is to continuously assign vehicles to routes, which have been generated in modules (2) and (3). This finally means to sell routes to third party carriers. Each such carrier gets a contract guaranteeing a portion of regular routes (template routes), a portion of round trips, a minimum average route length etc. The vehicle scheduling and assignment module bases on a assignment type of model which considers the constraints caused by the contracts with third party carriers. Another possibility is to embed negotiation processes into the analytical model-based approach.

- POP 2 is based on a modular service-oriented architecture.
- It uses an application server approach.
- Communication is via XML/SOAP or text files.

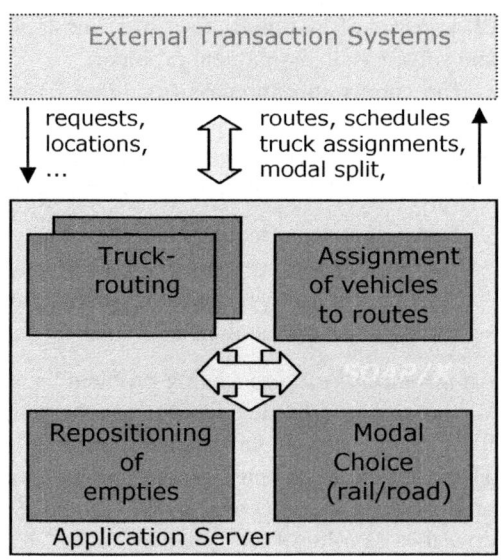

Fig. 14. The architecture of POP2

Finally, in module (5), the problem of cost minimal repositioning empty containers between locations with excess supply and demand is modeled and solved as a specially structured network flow problem. The software system (POP2) which implements the functionality of the above described modules was developed at the RWTH Aachen University as a fist prototype in 2000-2001. Compared to the predecessor system POP1 cost savings between 5% and 10% have been realized using POP2 for real live benchmark problem instances. Therefore a final, extended version of POP2 was developed and implemented by GTS Systems and Consulting GmbH in 2002, which is in daily use since July 2003.

The architecture of POP2 is illustrated in Fig 14.

5   Conclusions

In Section 3 we presented a general heuristic decomposition approach to optimize distribution networks for letter and parcel mail. In Section 4 we described 3 cases which represent the optimization of subnetworks such as e.g. the Night-Airmail

Network (NAN), the delivery station location optimization and the long haul transportation network for parcel mail. There are many more important projects we are dealing with together with DPDHL, e.g. the sorting center location optimization project, optimization of the first and the last mile (postmen problems, capacitated arc routing) and the optimal vehicle routing and scheduling with the subnetworks for collecting and distributing mail.

All these problems (cases) have some common properties:

- Problem instances are "large to very large scale"
- Most of the related optimization problems in that field are NP-hard (and the exceptions are known).
- Special structures are present (patterns of constraints) in particular application scenarios.

From this follows that:

- Exact methods are successful for special models or for small to medium size instances
- Commercial solvers can not deal with the majority of the very large scaled real world applications.

Therefore, we developed and implemented heuristics and methaheuristics (complemented with sharp lower bounds in the case of minimization problems) in order to solve the practical problems in reasonable time and with reasonable accuracy.

We learned some lessons in the fields of project selection, definition and execution as well:

Criteria for a successfully selected project are

- importance for the company
- improvement of customer satisfaction (high service quality)
- considerable cost savings and
- importance for the scientific community.

The key success factor in project execution is joint work of the Operations Research team at the University with the experts in the company. This is in particular necessary for the successful implementation of the project results within the enterprise.

We developed software prototypes of Decision Support Systems (DSS) within most of the joint projects with DPDHL. These IT-Systems are build for expert users (persons, who have a profound knowledge in Operations Research) and for other selected experts of the enterprise.

In some cases our software prototypes have been reimplemented by a software company in order to integrate the IT systems into the IT landscape of DPDDHL.

References

1. Andres, D., Gassen, P., Schiffl, Z.: Standortplanung unter Berücksichtigung von Lagerbeständen, Arbeitsbericht, Deutsche Post Lehrstuhl RWTH Aachen (17) (2005)
2. Bruns, A.D.: Zweistufige Standortplanung unter Berücksichtigung von Tourenplanungsaspekten – Primale Heuristiken und Lokale Suchverfahren, PhD Dissertation, Sankt Gallen University (1998)

3. Büdenbender, K., Grünert, T., Sebastian, H.J.: A Hybrid Tabu Search Branch and Bound Algorithm for the Direct Flight Network Design Problem. Transportation Science 34(4) (2000)
4. Crainic, T., Sebastian, H.J. (eds.): Focused Issue of Transportation Science on Freight Transportation (2004)
5. Crainic, T.: Service network design in freight transportation. In: EJOR, vol. 122(2) (2000)
6. Engelhard, G., Grünert, T., Sebastian, H.J., Thärigen, M., Katz, M., Kuchem, R.: Und ab geht die Post – Transportplanung für den Brieftransport der Deutschen Post AG. OR News (1998)
7. Geoffrion, A.M., Graves, G.M.: Multicommodity distribution system design by Benders decomposition. Management Science 20, 822–844 (1974)
8. Grünert, T., Sebastian, H.J.: Planning Models for Long-Haul Operations of Postal and Express Shipment Companies. European Journal of Operational Research 122(2) (2000)
9. Grünert, T., Irnich, S.: Optimierung im Transport, Band I: Grundlagen. Shaker Verlag, Aachen (2005)
10. Gündüz, H., Luttropp, A., Steffensen, D.: Projekt Regionalverkehre: Analyse von Synergiepotentialen, Arbeitsbericht, Deutsche Post Lehrstuhl RWTH Aachen (40) (2008)
11. Hempsch, C., Irnich, S.: Vehicle Routing Problems with Inter-Tour Resource Constraints. Technical report, Deutsche Post Lehrstuhl RWTH Aachen (2007)
12. Hempsch, C.: BZA-Netzplanung, Arbeitsbericht, Deutsche Post Lehrstuhl RWTH Aachen (20) (2006)
13. Hempsch, C.: Optimierung postalischer Vorlaufnetzwerke, Dissertation, Deutsche Post Lehrstuhl RWTH Aachen (2010)
14. Hermanns, C.: Optimierung der Standortkonfiguration der Zustellstützpunkte im Unternehmensbereich BRIEF der Deutschen Post AG. Arbeitsbericht, Deutsche Post Lehrstuhl RWTH Aachen (2005)
15. Hermanns, C.: Ein Stichfahrten-Modell und ein Tabu-Search-Algorithmus für das zweistufige Standortmodell in TOPAS, Arbeitsbericht, Deutsche Post Lehrstuhl RWTH Aachen (22) (2006)
16. Hermanns, C.: Planung und Optimierung von Auslieferungsstandorten in komplexen Distributionsnetzwerken, Dissertation, Deutsche Post Lehrstuhl RWTH Aachen (2009)
17. Irnich, S.: A Note on Postman Problems with Zigzag Service. INFOR 43(1), 33–39 (2005)
18. Irnich, S., Drexl, M.: Solution of Real-World Postman Problems. European Journal of Operational Research (2007)
19. Irnich, S.: Undirected Postman Problems with Zigzagging Option: A cutting-Plane Approach, Arbeitsbericht, Deutsche Post Lehrstuhl RWTH Aachen (26) (2006)
20. Irnich, S.: Netzwerk-Design für zweistufige Transportsysteme und ein Branch-and-Price-Verfahren für das gemischte Direkt- und Hubflugproblem, Dissertation, RWTH Aachen (2002)
21. Jacobsen, S.K., Madsen, O.B.G.: A comparative study of heuristics for a two-level routing-location problem. European Journal of Operational Research 5, 378–387 (1980)
22. Klose, A.: Standortplanung in distributiven Systemen, Modelle, Methoden, Anwendungen. Physica Verlag, Heidelberg (2001)
23. Laporte, G., Norbert, Y., Taillefer, S.: Solving a family of multi-depot vehicle routing and location-routing problems. Transportation Science 22(3), 161–172 (1988)
24. Lischak, C.: Standortplanung für einen Privaten Paketdienstleister. Dissertation, RWTH Aachen (2001)
25. Nagy, G., Salhi, S.: Location-routing: Issues, models and methods. European Journal of Operational Research 177, 649–672 (2007)

26. Perl, J., Daskin, M.S.: A unified warehouse location-routing methodology. Journal of Business Logistics 5(1), 92–111 (1984)
27. Perl, J., Daskin, M.S.: A warehouse location-routing problem. Transportation Research B 19(5), 381–396 (1985)
28. Pütz, D., Sebastian, H.J., Kuchem, R.: IT Systems of Deutsche Post World Net for Transportation Planning and Control. In: Proceedings of the Workshop IT in Logistics, Berkeley (2003)
29. Sebastian, H.J., Dolk, D., Kuchem, R.: Operations Centers for Logistics – General Concepts and the Deutsche Post Case. In: Proceedings of 34th Hawaiian International Conference on System Sciences (2001)
30. Sebastian, H.J.: Strategic Planning of Distribution Networks in Postal Logistics. In: 3rd US-European Workshop on Logistics and Supply Chain Management, Berkeley (2005)
31. Sebastian, H.J.: Methoden und Potenziale des Operations Research für die Optimierung von Distributionsnetzwerken im Unternehmensbereich Brief der Deutschen Post World Net. Arbeitsbericht, Deutsche Post Lehrstuhl RWTH Aachen (1) (2004)
32. Sebastian, H.J.: Optimization in Postal Logistics (50-minutes presentation). In: INFORMS Practice Conference – Applying Science to the Art of Business, Miami, Florida (2007)
33. Sun, Y.: Europäisches Fashion Netzwerk Design, Diplomarbeit, Deutsche Post Lehrstuhl RWTH Aachen (2006)
34. Wasner, M., Zäpfel, G.: An integrated multi-depot hub-location vehicle routing model for network planning of parcel service. International Journal of Production Economics 90, 403–419 (2004)
35. Winkelkotte, T.: Simulation eines XXL-Briefzentrums, Arbeitsbericht, Deutsche Post Lehrstuhl RWTH Aachen (30) (2007)
36. Winkelkotte, T.: Simulation der Behälterförderanlage eines XXL-Briefzentrums Validierung, Arbeitsbericht, Deutsche Post Lehrstuhl RWTH Aachen (36) (2008)

Adaptation of Optimization Models in Volatile Transport Scenarios

Herbert Kopfer and Jörn Schönberger

Chair of Logistics, University of Bremen, Wilhelm-Herbst-Straße 5,
28359 Bremen, Germany
{kopfer,jsb}@uni-bremen.de
http://www.logistik.uni-bremen.de

Abstract. In online optimization, a sequence of decision model instances is generated and solved consecutively. The definition of a new actualized decision model is triggered by an event that compromises the realization of the so far pursued solution. There is no time to experiment on the right parameters for the new decision model.

In this contribution, concepts for adaptive online optimization of an operational transportation planning problem are presented. Several rules for automatically adjusting the merging decision models of the online optimization problem are introduced and tested. Different approaches with static and adaptive rules for adjusting the objective function or modifying the constraint set are proposed and evaluated. These approaches demonstrate that a flexible balancing between the short-term goals of the single decision problems and the long-term goal of the entire online-problem is possible.

Keywords: online optimization, vehicle routing with subcontraction, model-adaptation, autonomous planning agents, reactive planning, volatile planning situations.

1 Introduction

The fast progress in computer technology and in particular in telematics as well as the enormous cost reduction in information processing enable the nearly synchronous and ubiquitous generation of actual planning data for distributed systems. Especially in the area of operational transportation planning the advanced facilities of telematics provide new chances and challenges for optimization since the occurring processes in this area are naturally distributed and formerly have been rather intransparent for the persons responsible for their scheduling. Research on the optimization of operational transportation problems has a long tradition. However, the investigated optimization models and algorithmic approaches which have been developed for problems of transportation planning during the last decades are only partly appropriate to dynamic problems. They are hardly capable to utilize actualized planning data because they cannot adapt to changing problem situations. That is why much research effort has recently

D. Dolk et al. (Eds.): Decision Support Modeling in Service Networks, LNBIP 42, pp. 62–86, 2012.

been focused *online-optimization* methods, in particular in the area of operational transportation planning. The developed approaches and techniques are able to adjust the solutions to be generated according to new incoming information. Thus, the solution process is getting more flexible and robust which is a pre-requisite to model and solve dynamic optimization problems. This is adequate, if the situation of the solved problems change only slightly caused by relatively small deviations from the target state of planning or by the arrival of few additional input data which has to be integrated in the current solution.

However, if the underlying system which is represented by the online optimization problem changes very drastically and if it changes even with respect to basic planning criteria, it is not enough to resolve the problem each time when actualized data arrives using the same model or solution process. For being able to react to modified basic planning criteria it is necessary to adapt the used solution strategy, too. In order to reach the high degree of flexibility needed in highly volatile planning situations, we present an approach for adapting the actual instances of optimization models used within an online optimization problem. We investigate and present this approach for an application out of the area of operational transportation planning, namely a transportation-scheduling problem with re-planning which is solved in online fashion.

In the considered transportation scenario the solution process must be capable to react to spontaneous and unpredictable events which even alter the so far used planning criteria. We extend the usual and well known concept of online optimization [4] by two additional components. The first component provides a feed-back mechanism which is able to recognize significant changes of the actual planning situation. The second component is responsible for adjusting each single instance of the online planning problem according to the actually recognized planning situation and criteria.

Within this contribution, we present and demonstrate the application of model definition rules which are used to perform the adjustment of the problem instances of an online optimization problem. In Section 2, we regard an online optimization problem as a set of related sub-problems and discuss general aspects of autonomous planning agents solving these sub-problems. Then, in Section 3, we present the dynamic operational transportation planning problem (DOTPP) which is used to demonstrate the application of the proposed extended concept for online optimization. Next, in Section 4, we show how the original online optimization framework can be enhanced by using static model definition rules for a feedback-driven adaptation of problem instances. Furthermore, we define generic strategies for applying such rules to a volatile version of the DOTPP and we combine the approach of model definition rules with a meta-heuristic based on the memetic algorithm search paradigm [18]. Section 5 introduces the application of adaptive model definition rules whose regulative interventions are dependent on the current situation of the online problem. Finally, in Section 6 we report results from comprehensive numerical experiments in which we compare the impacts of static and adaptive modeling rules.

2   Autonomous Adaptation of Interacting Agents

In order to keep a complex system alive and to ensure its profitability, a careful planning of its activities and, most of all, the planning of the activities of all of its components is essential. Therefore, plans are set up which describe in detail how each component of the system has to act. These plans evaluate and coordinate the behavior of each component out of its own local perspective and out of the general global perspective of the entire system.

The components of a hierarchical system are treated as externally controlled units which do not have any authority for taking decisions on their own. On the other hand, in heterarchical systems the components are autonomous units which interact with each other on their own responsibility and are provided with local intelligence and decision authority. In logistics, there is a paradigm shift from hierarchical systems to heterarchical systems, especially concerning the design and control of complex logistic systems. Heterarchical structures grant autonomy to the single system components in order to enable decentralized decision-making. Autonomy of components presupposes that interactive units in non-deterministic systems are able to decide and act on their own authority.

Autonomous units representing components of a complex logistic system can be classified by assigning them to different levels of appearance. At the lowest level, there are autonomous physical logistic units like parcels or containers which are capable and allowed to decide on their handling. At the next level, there are autonomous planning agents like human schedulers or software agents being responsible for the decisions in a delimited problem area and cooperating with agents responsible for adjacent areas. Finally at the upper level, there are autonomous organizational units, e.g. profit centers or partners in a collaborative system constituting a coalition. In our contribution we concentrate on the units of the medium level, i.e. we consider the situation of autonomous planning agents.

Traditionally, most complex logistical planning systems are built in a hierarchical manner. But there is a tendency to redesign such systems in a heterarchical way by constituting a set of interrelated sub-problems for the construction of the system. The objective of increasing the autonomy in logistic systems is a higher degree of robustness and a positive emergence of the total system [29]. Recent research on complex logistic systems aims to explore the limits of autonomy of logistical subsystems and tries to develop techniques for enabling autonomy [8] for typical, formerly hierarchical, logistic systems. Additionally, techniques for determining and installing a suitable or even optimal degree of autonomy for complex logistic systems are investigated. According to this trend the tasks of solving the involved sub-problems are assigned to individual planning agents. These agents are not acting independently, because the sub-problems are coupled in such a way that the relevant impacts between them must be reflected. In homogeneous situations, the coupling refers to a set of related sub-problems with similar structure. Thus, all planning agents apply in principle the same solution process for each sub-problem. However, the solution process of an agent can be adapted to general global requirements and to its internal local requirements.

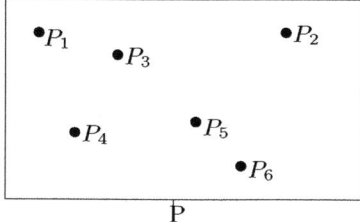

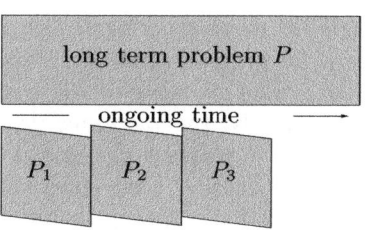

Fig. 1. Spatially related optimization problems (P_i: optimization problem of partner i, P: optimization problem of the entire coalition.)

Fig. 2. Temporal relation of sub-problems P_1, P_2, ...

The aggregation of all sub-problems constitutes a superior decision problem which corresponds to the total problem of the original complex logistical system. The superior problem may have relevant constraints and goals of its own. These superior constraints and goals cannot be judged or even met by a single sub-problem but only by the collaborative behavior of the agents of all sub-problems. The relationship between the single subordinated problems and their relationship to the total superior problem must be respected during the solution process by adaptations performed by the involved agents. By means of a coordinated strategy the autonomous planning agents achieve the simultaneous consideration of subordinated and superior requirements.

There are two typical situations for homogeneous sets of sub-problems forming a superior problem. In the first situation the sub-problems are autonomous nodes which are combined by a spatial relation to a superior problem. In this case, the superior problem is given by a resulting network of cooperating partners. In the second case the sub-problems are combined by a temporal relation. A sequence of short-term problems is considered and their combination to a superior problem yields the corresponding long-term problem. Each temporal sub-problem tries to achieve its own short-term goals and concurrently has to beware the long-term goals which can only be reached by the entirety of the sub-problems. Thus, the coordination process between the sub-problems and their superior problem refers to the adjustment of short-term and long-term planning.

Fig. 1 shows a spatial relation between n partners. Each of the partners respects its individual optimization problem with its own goals and constraints. Each of them acts autonomously and all of them cooperate with each other. The whole coalition has to strive for global goals and to respect global constraints. These goals and constraints are essential for each single partner in order to survive on the long run. Sometimes the global goals of the entire coalition conflict with the individual goals of the partners. Then the goals of the partners must conjointly be adapted to the overall requirements of the entire coalition.

Fig. 2 shows a temporal relation combining several short-term problems to a long-term problem. This is the situation investigated in the context of online-optimization. The online planning process consists in a sequence of problem instances generated by actualizing the problem situation. The optimization of a single instance is performed on the basis of the actual situation resulting from the so far pursued planning process and the newly incoming data. Each instance of the online planning problem pursues its short-term goal using its actual data. Consequently, the planning process of each single instance (short-term problem) generates short-term solutions. Taking the actual solutions of all short-term problems together, they constitute a long range solution for the entire long-term problem. This long range solution is given by the concatenation of all generated short-term solutions. However, the original long-term problem to be solved refers to the entire online-optimization problem for the whole planning period. It has its own long-term goals which are to be achieved by the optimization process. Of course, the concatenation of the short-term solutions does not necessarily comply with the predefined long-term goals. Thus, each instance of the online optimization problem has to be adjusted to both, to the actually incoming new problem data and to the actual state of reaching the pre-defined long-term goals.

The sequence of consecutively solved instances of an online optimization problem resembles a network of problem instances where each single instance represents a node (partner) with its subordinated goal. The short-term objective of a single online problem instance corresponds to the subordinated goal of a single node and the superior goal of the network consists in pursuing the long-term strategy for the entire planning interval. Since the concatenation of the short-term objectives of all single instances sometimes contradicts the superior goal, a model correction might be necessary from time to time. The superior goal is invisible for a single instance and can only be reached by the entirety of all nodes. Using model definition rules it is possible to harmonize the short-term goals of single problem instances with the long-term goal of the collectivity of all problem instances over a longer time period.

The presented approach for extending the usual online optimization concept is useful for harmonizing a homogeneous set of closely related sub-problems taking into account both, the relations between the sub-problems and their relation to the superior problem. The approach is able to handle sub-problems combined by spatial relations as well as temporal relations.

3   Vehicle Routing in a Volatile Environment

We consider an operational transportation planning problem with consecutively arriving customer requests. The planning task consists in solving a dynamic vehicle routing and scheduling problem extended by the possibility of forwarding a part of the incoming requests to external carriers.

3.1   Previous and Related Work

In the scientific literature there exist only few contributions which discuss and explore the vehicle routing problem extended by the possibility of forwarding a part of the requests. Using own vehicles for the execution of requests is called self-fulfillment mode (SF-mode), while entrusting an external carrier with requests is called subcontracting mode (SC-mode). Together with the engagement of an external carrier, the kind of service and the rules of payment for its service (type of subcontracting) are defined. An overview on existing approaches with different types of subcontracting can be found in [13]. The approach for subcontracting presented [26] is applicable for forwarding Less-Than-Truckload (LTL) shipments to external carriers. It is an approach of parameterized subcontracting. Here, the calculation of the freight costs results from isolated price assessments for each request on the basis of a fixed tariff, multiplied with an adjustment parameter which is determined using different criteria such as distance or weight. The adjustment parameter reflects the estimated cost savings which could be realized by the carrier when he integrates the received LTL shipment in a cluster of requests which build a reasonable tour. In order to calculate a reasonable value of the adjustment parameter, an artificial route of a dummy vehicle is constructed in [26].

There are two different strategies coping with incomplete problem data of optimization problems. The a-priori-approach follows the idea of approximating and interpolating missing data by suitable probability distributions. Process decisions are made by optimizing the expected values of the planning goal [22]. The solutions have to be robust in the sense that deviations of estimated data from realized data do not significantly reduce the solution quality with respect to the applied planning goal(s) [12].

Probability distributions are not available for most scenarios of operational transport planning so that the a-priori-approach has received only minor attention so far in this context [11]. Instead, the second strategy consisting in a (repeated) revision of previously made decisions is preferred. A problem in which previously made decisions are allowed (and expected) to be varied one or several times before they are realized is called a dynamic decision problem [3]. The processes must be flexible in the sense that the once made decision can be revised [12].

Zeimpekis et al. [30] give a comprehensive survey of dynamic transport planning problems. Psaraftis [20], [21] provides a detailed differentiation of dynamic vehicle routing and scheduling problems from non-dynamic scenarios and describes the requirements of planning systems managing dynamic transport processes.

Dynamic decision problems are modeled as online decision problems which consist of a sequence of consecutively solved problem instances [15]. Each instance consolidates all data known at its definition time. Whenever significant changes of problem data are detected a new decision model is stated and solved. Static model definition rules predict how to implement additional data into the next instance of the underlying planning model [1]. Dynamic model definition rules [28] work in the same way but it is possible to specify in advance different actions for different time periods. None of these rules is able to reflect and implement unpredictable and ad-hoc variations of the planning criteria into the formalized problem representation. Therefore, adaptive model definition rules are needed, which evaluate the current system state (performance, etc.) and exploit the evaluation results to adapt the model of the appropriate strategy [25]. This *image modification* has been introduced by Bierwirth [2]. Gutenschwager et al. [6] as well as Gutenschwager [7] define a *local objective function* for each instance that differs from the superior planning goal of the whole dynamic decision problem.

A trade-off between solution quality and computational complexity has to be found. Simple one-pass heuristics are mostly used if the controlled system requires an immediate update after a problem variation [1]. This is necessary in real-time process management [17] where the controlled system itself determines the point of time when a process update is required. However, if there is enough time to derive an update of high quality then iterative procedures are deployed [23]. With increased computational power, even the application of meta-heuristic approaches becomes attractive as assessed in [5], [16] and [19]. Ichoua et al. [9] provide a survey on different approaches to solve dynamic transportation planning problems.

3.2   Informal Challenge Description

The presented scenario describes a dynamic decision problem [3]. It is the multi-vehicle version of the traveling repairman problem [10]. The DOTPP generalizes the common vehicle routing problem with time windows [27] in three aspects [14].

Subcontracting. An arriving request can either be fulfilled in the SF-mode using one of the available vehicles of the own fleet or it can be fulfilled in the SC-mode which means that the request is forwarded to a logistic service provider (LSP) who is paid for its execution. The capacity of the own fleet is limited and cannot be increased on the operational planning level. As a consequence, if too many requests are planed to be executed in the SF-mode the request execution will become more and more unreliable since the own vehicles will no more be able to meet the prescribed time windows and some of the requests must even be deferred. If the amount of incoming requests increases even more it will be impossible to fulfill all of the arriving requests by the own fleet. That is why some of them have to be shifted to the SC-mode, anyway. A once subcontracted request cannot be re-integrated into the routes of the own vehicles. The transportation capacity of the external carriers is considered to be unlimited and therefore it is expected that an LSP entrusted with a request will be capable to execute the request on time, i.e. he will meet all prescribed time windows. Consequently, fulfillment in the SC-mode is assumed to be absolutely reliable with respect to time windows, whereas the execution in SF-mode is more or less reliable because its punctuality depends on the degree of utilization of the own fleet. The costs for fulfilling a cluster of requests in the SF-mode arise from the tour that is built for the cluster. These costs depend on the travel distance performed by the vehicle which is executing this tour. For the calculation of the freight to be paid for the SC-mode we use the subcontracting type introduced by Schönberger [26]. The amount of the freight for fulfilling a request in the SC-mode depends on the value of the adjustment parameter. For practical values of the adjustment parameter the execution of a request in the SF-mode is cheaper than in the SC-mode, since the fixed costs of the own fleet are not considered in the optimization process on the operational planning level. The value of the adjustment parameter affects the attractiveness of the SC-mode and thus has influence on the solution process and on the reliability of the optimal fulfillment plan. That is why several different values of the adjustment parameter are used in the experiments for the investigation of the DOTPP in different scenarios.

Uncertain Demand. Only a subset of all requests is known to the planning authority at the time when the fulfillment plan for the DOTPP is generated. The planning authority decides about the fulfillment mode and performs the vehicle routing in the SF-mode for each request as soon as it becomes known. A release of one or more additional requests initiates the revision of the actually valid execution plan. The assignment of a request to the SC-mode is irreversible, whereas the usage of own vehicles is re-planned in the SF-mode. Moreover, requests, so far assigned to the SF-mode, can be excluded from their routes and assigned to the SC-mode. Furthermore, the service of some customers can be postponed (ignoring their time windows) in order to achieve a better clustering for the routes of the own vehicles. Finally, the execution of an already scheduled request can be deferred for the sake of an earlier execution of another request, if this seems to be profitable.

Soft Time Windows. Tardiness at a customer site is allowed in principle, but it causes penalty costs. The penalty costs assure that the optimization process does not merely concentrate on the minimization of the costs but also takes into account the service level provided by the generated solutions. A request is said to be punctual or on time and its fulfillment is said to be reliable, if it is executed during its prescribed time window. The portion of all punctual requests within the entire set of all requests to be fulfilled during a planning interval $[t-t^-;t+t^+]$ is denoted by p_t. Let f_t^e be the number of requests in the entire set of all requests. At time t, the portion p_t contains requests completed punctually within $[t-t^-;t]$ or expected to be completed punctually within $[t;t+t^+]$. Let f_t^{comp} be the number of requests completed punctually within the last t^- time units and let f_t^{expec} be the number of punctually scheduled requests within the next t^+ time units, then $p_t := \frac{f_t^{comp}+f_t^{expec}}{f_t^e}$. The parameter p_t is a performance figure for the actual value of the average punctuality achieved during the given planning interval. During the entire optimization process it is required that a minimum degree of average punctuality p^{target} must be reached. A time interval during which the requirement for the least punctuality ($p_t \geq p^{target}$) is steadily satisfied is called a high quality (HQ) period, and respectively, a low quality (LQ) period denotes a time interval during that the requirement to reach p^{target} is failed.

The overall planning task of the DOTPP consists in finding an optimal fulfillment plan for all incoming requests using the SF-mode as well as the SC-mode and solving this problem dynamically for a given time interval. An admissible fulfillment plan of an instance of the DOTPP has to reflect the usual constraints for route construction, time windows, and maximal vehicle capacity. Additionally, for a sequence of instances the pre-defined minimum value p^{target} for the average punctuality has to be achieved.

Optimality of a plan of a single problem instance is defined with respect to two criteria: cost and reliability. We use a mono-criterion objective function for the definition of the planning goal aspired by an instance of the DOTPP. The objective function is to be minimized. It consists in the sum of all costs: costs for the SF-mode, costs for the SC-mode and penalty costs. The relation of the costs of the SF-mode to those of the SC-mode is given by the adjustment parameter. Reasonable Values for the adjustment parameter ensure that the costs for the different modes are related in the following way: the execution of a cluster of requests combined to a reasonable tour for the SF-mode is cheaper than forwarding the requests of that cluster to an LSP in the SC-mode, but the isolated execution of a single (LTL-)request with an own vehicle in the SF-mode is more expensive than fulfilling it as an LTL-shipment in the SC-mode.

The purpose of the penalty costs is to arrange a desired weighting between cost minimization and service maximization. As the relation between the costs of the SF-mode and the SC-mode is predefined by the type of subcontracting and the value of the adjustment parameter, it is only the amount of the penalty which defines the point of equilibrium between cost reduction and reliability. For a single problem instance of the DOTPP this equilibrium is obtained by the optimal solution of the problem instance i.e. the criteria of costs and punctuality are balanced autonomously for an instance of the online optimization problem. This balancing takes place within each single problem instance and is called local balancing.

The global requirement of average reliability over a period of time is relevant to the superior, long-term problem. It postulates that $p_t \geq p^{target}$ has to be reached during the planning interval $[t - t^-; t + t^+]$, which means that the solutions of the sequence of problem instances of the given time interval must keep the given threshold p^{target}. The reliability of some instances will fall below the aspired limit, because their situation allows the construction of profitable solutions for the SF- and SC-mode with very low execution costs which are used for compensating high penalty costs. This situation is caused by the fact that the equilibrium of those instances is associated with a low reliability. Nevertheless, the threshold for reliability has to be achieved in common and on the long run by all problem instances of that time interval conjointly, while each single instance has to render a cost-minimal service with the required reliability or even has to compensate for a LQ period of earlier instances. The global requirement needs a global balancing between the problem instances. Each instance adapts its behavior by adjusting its optimization model to the global situation depending on the actual value of the average punctuality. Although the global balancing between the different instances relies only on global information, it is performed autonomously. Global balancing assures (a) that the required average value for punctuality is hold, (b) that it can temporarily fall below the threshold if it is attractive, and (c) that it will be rearranged later on by compensating phases of low reliability.

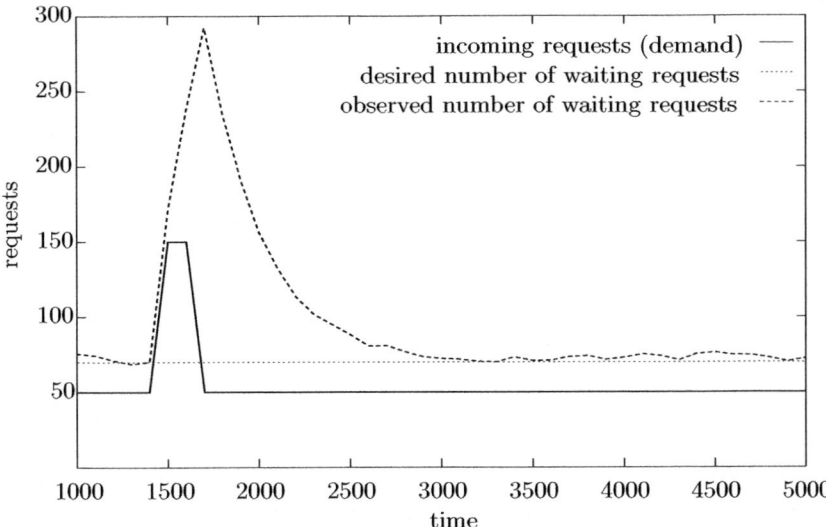

Fig. 3. Demand (continuous line), desired number of waiting requests (dotted line) and observed number of waiting requests (dashed line)

The balance between the long-term goal of average punctuality and the short-term goals of cost minimization can easily be installed for the convenient and stable situation with enough transport resources and a constant stream of incoming new requests. Balancing between the above criteria becomes a difficult and challenging task of adaptation, if the once reached equilibrium is disturbed by exogenous influencing factors which set the system under stress by finding a new equilibrium under consideration of conflicting goals. As an activator for a stressful situation a spontaneous load peak is used (Fig. 3). This load peak causes that a set of waiting requests cannot be fulfilled on time and consequently the average punctuality goes down.

The adjustment of the optimization model of a problem instance can be carried out by modifying the objective function or by altering the set of constraints of the model. In a HQ period the constraints remain unchanged, whereas in LQ periods the solution space is additionally restricted. This restriction requires that all newly arriving requests are to be assigned to the SC-mode until a HQ period has been reached again. Additional restrictions and biasing the objective function for a limited period of time have to be handled very carefully, since they have long-ranging impacts and the process of adapting to their activation and deactivation is very slowly but steady. Thus, it is necessary to find the right moments for activating and deactivating the regulative mechanism in order to prevent an uncontrolled behavior of the online optimization system.

3.3 Decision Model

A sequence of fulfillment plans $FP_0, FP_1, FP_2, \ldots$ must be generated reactively at the ex ante unknown update times $t_0, t_1, t_2, \ldots$ and each single actually active plan is executed until it is updated. A single request r arrives at an update time t_i and attains consecutively different states. Initially, r is known but not yet scheduled (K). Then, r is either assigned to an own vehicle (SF) or subcontracted (SC). If the operation at the corresponding customer site has already been started but not yet finished, the state (S) is assigned to r. The set $R^+(t_i)$ is composed of additional requests arriving at time t_i. Requests completed after the last update time t_{i-1} are stored in the set $R^C(t_{i-1}, t_i)$. The new request stock $R(t_i)$ consists in $R(t_i) := R(t_{i-1}) \cup R^+(t_i) \setminus R^C(t_{i-1}, t_i)$ and the set $R^X(t_i)$ contains all currently available requests belonging to the state $X \in \{K, SF, SC, S\}$ at time t_i.

Let V denote the set of all own vehicles, $P_v(t_i)$ the set of all routes realizable by vehicle v at time t_i and let $P(t_i)$ denote the union of the sets $P_v(t_i)$ $(v \in V)$. If the request r is served in route p then the binary parameter a_{rp} is set to 1, otherwise it is set to 0. A request r, already known at time t_{i-1} and not subcontracted in TP_{i-1} is assigned to vehicle $v(r)$ according to TP_{i-1}. The travel costs associated with route p are denoted as $C^1(p)$. The penalties associated with p are referred by $C^2(p)$. Finally, $C^3(r)$ denotes the subcontracting costs of request r.

In order to formulate a model for a single instance TP_i of the DOTPP at the update times $t_0, t_1, t_2, \ldots$, we define two families of binary decision variables. Let $x_{pv} = 1$ if and only if route $p \in P(t_i)$ is assigned to vehicle $v \in V$ and let $y_r = 1$ if and only if request r is subcontracted.

$$\sum_{p \in P(t_i)} \sum_{v \in V} \left(C^1(p) + C^2(p) \right) x_{pv} + \sum_{r \in R(t_i)} C^3(r) y_r \to \min \quad (1)$$

$$\sum_{p \in P_v(t_i)} x_{pv} = 1 \ \ \forall v \in V \quad (2)$$

$$x_{pv} = 0 \ \ \forall v \in V, p \notin P_v(t_i) \quad (3)$$

$$y_r + \sum_{p \in P(t_i)} \sum_{v \in V} a_{rp} x_{pv} = 1 \ \ \forall r \in R(t_i) \quad (4)$$

$$y_r = 1 \ \ \forall r \in R^{SC}(t_i) \quad (5)$$

$$\sum_{p \in P_{v(r)}} a_{rp} x_{pv(r)} = 1 \ \ \forall r \in R^S(t_i) \quad (6)$$

$$p_t \geq p^{target} \quad (7)$$

The overall costs for TP_i are minimized (1). One route is selected for each vehicle (2) and the selected route p must be realizable by vehicle v (3). Each single request known at time t_i is either fulfilled in the SF- or SC-mode (4) but a once subcontracted request cannot be re-inserted into the routes of the own vehicles (5). An (S)-labeled request cannot be replanned (6) and overall, the percentage p^{target} of all requests must be scheduled on time (7).

3.4   Test cases

The construction of artificial test cases from the Solomon instances [27] is described in [24]. In these scenarios, demand peaks that represent significant changes in the decision situation interrupt constant streams of incoming requests. The costs for the SF-mode are normalized to one monetary unit per travel distance unit. The freight charge in the SC-mode does not depend on the traveled distance of a vehicle but on the distance of transportation of a forwarded request.

For each distance unit of transportation α monetary units have to be paid to an LSP. Each subcontracted request r causes overall costs of $F_r := C^3(r) = \alpha \cdot d(dep, \sigma_r)$ monetary units calculated by multiplying the adjustment parameter α with the distance $d(dep, \sigma_r)$ between the depot dep of the DOTPP and the customer site location σ_r of r. The parameter α is used for adjusting the costs for subcontracting in relation to self-fulfillment costs and is also called tariff level. If the parameter α has the value $\alpha = 2$ then the costs for subcontracting a single request (SC-mode) are equal to the costs in SF-mode for a pendulum-tour fulfilling request r. With respect to the real costs of the fulfillment of a single isolated request (i.e. without bundling) the relation of costs between SC-mode and SF-mode is at least $\alpha = 1$ and at most $\alpha = 2$. That is why values of α with $1 \leq \alpha \leq 2$ are called *comparable freight tariffs*.

4   Online Planning Approach

4.1   Memetic Algorithm Schedule Generation

We use a Memetic Algorithm (MA) realizing a hybrid search strategy consisting of a global genetic search space sampling and a local 2-opt improvement procedure for solving the scheduling model instances $TP_0, TP_1, \ldots$ of the online decision problem introduced in Subsection 3.3.

The genetic search uses a $\mu + \lambda$-population model evolved by the application of the PPSX-crossover-operator [26] and a mutation operator that a) arbitrarily switches fulfillment modes b) shifts requests between selected routes of own vehicles and c) reverses the visiting order of randomly chosen subsequences of arbitrarily selected routes.

The construction of the initial population is generated using the Push Forward Insertion Heuristic [27]. One half of the initial set of solution proposals is generated by deploying the heuristic followed by some random proposal modifications and the other half is completely generated at random without applying any biasing procedure. The evolution process is stopped dynamically if the average fitness of the evolved population does not improve for 10 generations.

4.2   Constraint Handling Techniques

The consideration of constraints during a genetic sampling of a search space requires advanced techniques.

1. *All requests r which are fulfilled unpunctually are collected in the set S_1.*
2. *For each request $r \in S_1$ the savings s_1 are calculated. Here, s_1 is defined as the difference between the travel costs saved by deleting r in its tour and the subcontracting costs F_r.*
3. *If S_1 is empty then goto (5). Otherwise, the requests contained in S_1 are sorted in increasing order.*
4. *Finally, the fulfillment mode of the first request in the sorted list (the one with the highest savings) is switched to subcontraction and the request is deleted from the list. Goto (2)*
5. *The repair has been completed.*

Fig. 4. Procedure REPAIR()

A favorable approach is to design a problem representation, which contains only feasible solutions. As long as the offspring solutions generated by the search operators (crossover and mutation) also comply with the constraints of DOTPP, there will be no infeasibilities corresponding to these constraints. We use the direct problem representation introduced in [26], which ensures that no violations of the constraints (2)-(6) will occur in the maintained population.

Since the punctuality at a customer site depends upon the number and location of the preceding customers in a route it is not possible to code the punctuality constraint (7) into the problem representation.

Repairing Constraint Violations. In order to repair constraint violations of an MA, locally acting heuristics manipulating the genetic material are incorporated into the genetic search. The MA introduced in Subsection 4.1 requires the incorporation of a heuristic which enforces a limitation of its search to the search space restricted by constraint (7). Each recently generated offspring is initially checked for unpunctuality. If the actual average percentage p_t of punctuality is larger than p^{target} then the offspring is accepted and added without further modification to the temporal population. In case that p_t is less than p^{target}, the offspring is repaired using the procedure REPAIR() shown in Fig. 4.

Since the steady application of repairing the genetic material ensures that the global requirement for reliability is met at each time t_i, we refer to this kind of constraint handling for the DOTPP as the "HARD"-technique.

Penalization of Constraint Violations. Generally, if it is not possible to repair the genetic material of an MA completely then those individuals in a population that remain infeasible will be penalized by depreciating their fitness. As a consequence, such penalized individuals become more unattractive and have a smaller chance of being selected during the mating process. It is expected that punished individuals (and their genetic code fragments) will not survive for a larger number of selection iterations so that, at the end, only individuals without any constraint violations form the maintained population.

Besides the "HARD"-technique we use a second constraint handling technique for the DOTPP. The second technique is based on the depreciation of the fitness of individuals and is referred to as the "PEN"-technique. In order to ensure that the requirement of constraint (7) is met by the generated fulfillment plans, we penalize unpunctuality of request fulfillment. For punishment we deploy a piece-wise linear penalty function, which is 0 if no delay is observed and increases proportionally with respect to the delay up to a maximal value of 25 money units for delays longer than 100 time units.

4.3 Basic Re-scheduling Algorithm

As soon as additional requests are released the update of FP_{i-1} to FP_i becomes necessary. The generic decision model TP_i (expressed by (1)-(7)) is used to instantiate $SP(t_i)$. Then, the MA is started to derive a solution FP_i of the current instance $SP(t_i)$ of the DOTPP. This solution is interpreted as the new fulfillment plan FP_i to be executed until further requests are released.

Every time a new decision model instance $SP(t_i)$ is built the MA is re-started to solve the recent instance. Experiments, in which parts of the final population of the previous instance are used to seed the initial population of the next instance, failed because in these experiments the recent population converges rapidly on a bad level even if the crossover and mutation probability are adapted. An analysis of the population development has shown that significantly changing decision situations require a re-initialization of the genetic material in order to enable that the new aspects of the changed situation can be considered explicitly. For this reason, a complete new initial population is formed using the seeding approach described above.

4.4 Experimental Setup

The minimum punctuality to be ensured throughout the complete simulation is set to $p^{target} = 0.8$.

The suitability of the PEN- and the HARD-technique for constraint handling is investigated within several numerical simulations. An experiment $(\alpha, tech)$ is defined by selecting one of the six values for the adjustment parameter $\alpha \in \{1, 1.25, 1.5, 1.75, 2, 3\}$ and combining it with one of the two constraint handling techniques $tech \in \{HARD, PEN\}$. We simulate each scenario $(\alpha, tech, P, \omega)$ in three independent runs $\omega \in \{1, 2, 3\}$ starting with differently seeded initial populations. From the four Solomon instances $P \in \{R103, R104, R107, R108\}$ we derive the request set $R^+(t_i)$ for each instance $SP(t_i)$. Overall, there are $6 \times 2 = 12$ experiments $(\alpha, tech)$ leading to $12 \times 4 \times 3 = 144$ simulated scenarios $(\alpha, tech, P, \omega)$.

The average punctuality realized at time t for the scenario $(\alpha, tech, P, \omega)$ is denoted as $p_t(\alpha, tech, P, \omega)$. For analyzing the impacts of choosing a constraint handling techniques $tech$ with respect to different values of the tariff level α, we observe for each scenario the lowest value of the average punctuality p_t that has been reached. We start the observation after the demand peak has been started at time $t=1500$ and calculate the average quotient

$$\delta(\alpha, tech) := \frac{1}{12} \sum_{\omega=1}^{3} \sum_{P \in \mathcal{P}} \frac{\min_{t \geq 1500}\{p_t(\alpha, tech, P, \omega)\}}{p_{1000}(\alpha, tech, P, \omega)}$$

$p_t(\alpha, PEN)$

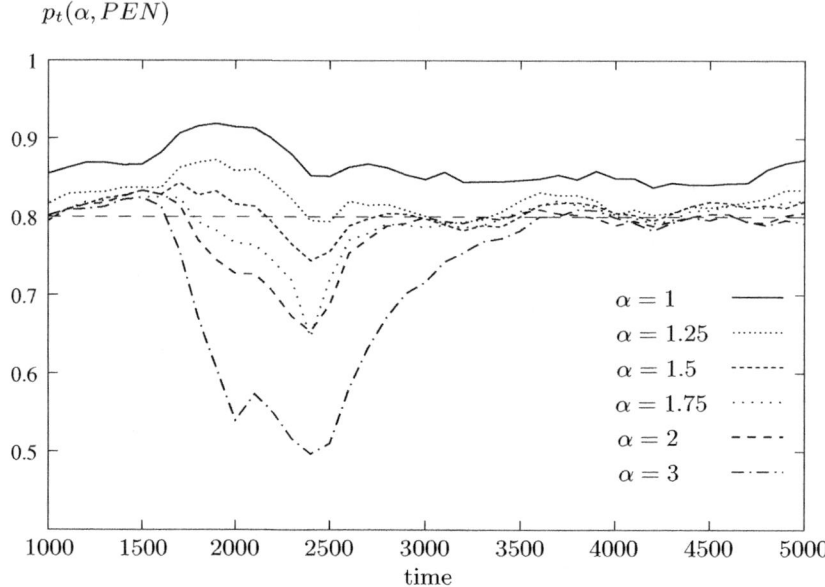

Fig. 5. Development of the punctuality $p_t(\alpha, PEN)$

of the lowest observed value of p_t to its value at time $t=1000$. The quotient $\delta(\alpha, tech)$ is the relative least punctuality of $(\alpha, tech)$, i.e. the average value of the quotients describing the least relative punctuality over all 12 scenarios of an experiment $(\alpha, tech)$. Let

$$p_t(\alpha, tech) := \frac{1}{12} \sum_{\omega=1}^{3} \sum_{P \in \mathcal{P}} p_t(\alpha, tech, P, \omega)$$

denote the punctuality averaged on all scenarios of experiment $(\alpha, tech)$ observed at time t. Then, $T_{\alpha,tech}^{below}$ denotes the first time at which $p_t(\alpha, tech)$ falls below p^{target}. Furthermore, $T_{\alpha,tech}^{heal}$ refers to the time in which an HQ period is finally re-achieved by $p_t(\alpha, tech)$. We define

$$\pi(\alpha, tech) := \frac{T_{\alpha,tech}^{heal} - T_{\alpha,tech}^{below}}{4000}$$

as the percentage of low quality states within the observation interval $[1000, 5000]$.

4.5   Numerical Assessment of PEN and HARD

The PEN-approach can guarantee to keep the threshold of 80% for the average punctuality only for tariff levels α with $\alpha \leq 1.25$ (Fig. 5). The punctuality even increases just after the demand peak is over ($t \geq 1800$) because the routes of the own vehicles are compiled from a larger number of available requests. So, a higher number of matching requests is found. If the tariff level α exceeds 1.5, the SC-mode becomes more and more unattractive. Its actual costs are getting higher than the travel costs plus penalty payments. As a consequence, the SF-mode is preferred although it does not come up with an on-time service. In fact, values of p_t below 50% are observed for $\alpha = 3$. Consequently, the relative punctuality decreases from $\delta(1, PEN) = 98.0\%$ down to $\delta(3, PEN) = 72\%$ as it can be seen in Table 1. Due to the sensitivity of the punctuality $p_t(\alpha, PEN)$ against tariff level increases, the percentage $\pi(\alpha, PEN)$ of low quality states increases from $\pi(0, PEN) = 0$ up to $\pi(3, PEN) = 47.5\%$ (Table 1). A short-time demand peak has therefore a long lasting negative impact on the punctuality of the service.

Table 1. Maximal punctuality decrease $\delta(\alpha, PEN)$

	α					
	1	1.25	1.5	1.75	2	3
$\delta(\alpha, PEN)$	98.0%	97.0%	93.6%	80.7%	81.5%	72.0%
$\pi(\alpha, PEN)$	–	5.0%	15.0%	42.5%	42.5%	47.5%
$\sigma(\alpha, PEN)$	18.8%	13.5%	9.6%	10.9%	5.7%	9.3%

We have recorded throughout the simulation time the percentage of subcontracted requests for each scenario in the parameters $q_t(\alpha, tech, P, \omega)$. The values of these parameters are summarized in

$$q_t(\alpha, tech) := \frac{1}{12} \sum_{\omega=1}^{3} \sum_{p \in \mathcal{P}} q_t(\alpha, tech, P, \omega)$$

for each experiment $(\alpha, tech)$. The maximally observed subcontraction rate

$$\sigma(\alpha, tech)) := \max_{t \geq 1500} q_t(\alpha, tech)$$

indicates the peak of exploitation of the SC-mode.

The main reason for the poor performance of the PEN-technique is caused by the fact that it ignores the usage of the SC-mode if the costs for subcontracting are significantly higher than the sum of travel costs and penalty payments. For $\alpha = 1$ the maximal percentage of subcontracted requests is $\sigma(1, PEN) = 18.8\%$ but for high tariff levels, this portion is significantly reduced ($\sigma(3, PEN) = 9.3\%$, Table 1).

Overall, the PEN-technique is not able to ensure that the minimum average punctuality p^{target} will be reached, if the value for the tariff level increases ($\alpha > 2$). The search for least cost fulfillment plans ignores the SC-mode if the sum of travel costs plus penalty is less than the freight charge to be paid to

Table 2. Maximal punctuality decrease $\delta(\alpha, HARD)$

			α			
	1	1.25	1.5	1.75	2	3
$\delta(\alpha, HARD)$	103.5%	106.5%	104.3%	105.0%	103.2%	101.6%
$\sigma(\alpha, HARD)$	21.6%	15.00%	9.8%	8.1%	7.1%	7.1%

the service provider. We have increased the penalty value in order to overcome this deficiency of the PEN-technique. Improved results could only be achieved exceptionally in singular experiments. The determination of an adequate penalty value requires many tests and is therefore not applicable in an online approach for a problem in which the scarceness of resources varies significantly over time. Volatile data input even requires a continuous re-determination of an appropriate penalty value, but a value for this adaptation can only be found in comprehensive numerical experiments.

The HARD-technique outperforms the PEN-technique. Clearly, by definition, it is $\pi(\alpha, HARD) = 0$ for all investigated tariff levels α. Moreover, the HARD-technique is able to slightly enlarge the punctuality compared to the referential value at time $t = 1000$ (Table 2). It supports the memetic search to evaluate different separations of the request portfolio into SF-mode and SC-mode. Since the constraint (7) ensures that at least 80% of the requests are on time, no penalty costs make the route composition worse.

For comparable freight tariffs ($1 \leq \alpha \leq 2$), a larger percentage of requests is subcontracted (compared to the PEN-technique) as shown in Table 2. It is $\sigma(1, HARD) = 21.6\%$ and this rate falls down to $\sigma(3, HARD) = 7.1\%$ which is smaller than $\sigma(3, PEN) = 9.3\%$.

5   Image Modification Approach

This section describes approaches for a model-based re-scheduling, which explicitly maps the variation of the degree of constraint satisfaction (problem severeness) into the used formal decision model. This mechanism is called *image modification* ([2]) because it affects the representation of the real world problem. Actually, it manipulates the selected formal decision model for the current decision problem instance.

5.1   Static, Dynamic and Adaptive Modeling Rules

To meet the requirement of the minimum average punctuality, both the PEN- and the HARD-technique deploy specific mechanisms that try to enforce the search algorithm to select fulfillment plans in which at least p^{target} percent of all requests are served on time. As soon as the model for updating FP_{i-1} to

FP_i is built, the following mechanisms are applied: adjusting the evaluation of individuals by using penalty values (PEN) or enforcing the compliance with constraint (7) of the DOTPP (HARD). The behavior associated with the PEN- or HARD-technique is determined a priori independently from the current time and from the current system performance or system load. Such a rule for defining components of the optimization model for the next decision instance is called a *static rule*. The PEN as well as the HARD-approach represent realizations of static model definition rules.

Since static rules are defined in advance, it cannot be guaranteed that they remain suitable after a significant change of the decision situation has come up. In our experiments, the PEN-technique works well as long as the system load remains on its original level. In such a situation, the used penalty value is large enough to depreciate solutions with unpunctuality so that detours or even subcontracting are preferred. But if the system load increases during and after the demand peak, the pre-determined penalty value is too low to enforce the subcontraction of unpunctually fulfilled request. The sum of penalty and travel costs has to get more influence for the choice of the fulfillment mode in order to let the SC-mode become the preferred mode for additional requests to be served on time.

A rule that distinguishes several temporal phases and which acts differently in these phases is called a *dynamic model definition rule*, if the corresponding time of each phase as well as the modeling tasks to be carried out are known in advance. Here, we cannot apply any dynamic rule because we do not know the time of load peaks, LQ-periods, and HQ-periods.

Instead of determining modeling rules in advance, it is more promising to decide reactively how to modify a decision model in response to the change of the performance of the represented logistic system. This modification allows the consideration of latest and recent problem variations for the definition of the next model instance. Model definition rules that exploit contextual data are referred to as *adaptive model definition rules*.

The original online decision making framework [15] is neither capable to detect changes in the considered problem situation nor is it equipped with facilities to implement adequate model modifications. In order to overcome these deficiencies, we propose to extend the online decision making framework with adaptive rules.

5.2 Algorithmic Model Adaptation

In order to prepare an automatic recognition of HQ and LQ periods, we first specify the system development which should be aspired starting from the current time t. We select N indicators that map the performance of the considered logistic system at a time t into the N-tuple $(i_1(t), \ldots, i_N(t))$ of real values (the system's state at time t). Let Im_u denote the set of possible values for the indicator $i_u : t \mapsto i_u(t)$. Furthermore, the set $\mathcal{F}(t) \subseteq Im_1 \times \ldots \times Im_N$ is defined to contain exactly all those system states that represent a HQ state. The set $\mathcal{D}(t_i) := [t_i; \infty[\times \mathcal{F}(t_i)$ contains all feasible future system states. It is called the

System Development Corridor at time t_i and serves as a reference that is used to decide whether the current system state is aspired (no model adaptations required) or not (model adaptations required).

The system development corridor for the problem introduced in Section 3 is defined as follows. We use the only indicator p_t mapping the current punctuality into a real value, $Im_1 := [p^{target}; 1]$ and set $\mathcal{F}(t) := [p^{target} + 0.05; 1]$. The corridor $\mathcal{D}(t_i)$ is then given by $\mathcal{D}(t_i) := [t_i; \infty[\times [p^{target} + 0.05; 1]$. Since the system development corridor is already left before p_t has fallen down to p^{target}, there is time to establish countermeasures that lead to a re-increase of p_t.

In order to prepare the right countermeasures, which will lead to re-entering into the system development corridor $\mathcal{D}$, the model of the current decision problem instance is modified. Therefore, at first the intensity of the model adaptation is determined by measuring the displacement of the current system state from the system development corridor. If the displacement is zero (i.e. the system state is in the corridor) then no model modifications are required but if it is large, then a significant re-definition of the so far used model is assumed to be necessary. The function h, which maps the problem severeness (measured by the amount of displacement) to the (real) value expressing the model modification severity, is called the **Intensity Function**.

The proposed Intensity Function h is a function of p_t. It is defined to be 0 as long as $p_t \geq p^{target} + 0.05$ (HQ period), $h(p_t) = 1$ if $p_t \leq p^{target} - 0.05$ (LQ period) and it decreases linearly from 1 down to 0 if p_t increases from 0.75 up to 0.85 (transition state).

The **Implementation Function** H describes the model modifications to be implemented depending on the value of the intensity function h at current time t. We describe the construction of an implementation function H_1 adapting the constraints of the DOTPP in Subsection 5.3. The derivation of an implementation function H_2 modifying the objective function is subject of Subsection 5.4.

5.3   Adaptive Sharpening of the Constraint Set

The severeness of the consecutively solved optimization models changes due to the exogenous modifications of the system load, which finally result in a decrease of the average punctuality p_t. In order to lift up the punctuality again during a LQ-period, we enforce the usage of the SC-mode. In an HQ period, none of the arriving requests is forced into the SC-mode but in an LQ period a large portion of the incoming requests is assigned to this mode. We use the intensity function h to determine the portion to be reassigned. Therefore, a percentage $h(p_t)$ of additionally arriving requests is forced to be assigned to the SC-mode without taking into account the fact that self-fulfillment would be cheaper.

In order to implement a constraint that ensures to intensify the SC-mode, we first call the function $RAND(R^+(t), h(p_t)))$ which selects the percentage $h(p_t)$ of the requests of $R^+(t)$ and collects the selected requests in the set $R^{pre}(t) := RAND(R^+(t), h(p_t)))$. The fulfillment mode of all requests contained in $R^{pre}(t)$

is initially set to subcontraction and it is not allowed to change this assignment later on. The implementation function H_1 is defined to be the set-valued mapping $H_1(t, p_t) := RAND(R^+(t), h(p_t)))$

Now, the next model instance uses the updated constraint (8) instead of the original constraint (5).

$$y_r = 1 \ \forall R^{SC}(t_i) \cup H_1(t, p_t). \tag{8}$$

Since this strategy to adapt the decision model is applied to the constraints, it is referred to as Constraint Set Adaptation (CSAD).

5.4   Situation-Based Adaptation of the Objective Function

The costs of the two fulfillments modes are weighted equally in the original objective function (1) and they are balanced according to the chosen tariff level α. The re-weighting of the costs associated with the two modes is a promising technique for adjusting the balance of modes. In an LQ-period the subcontraction costs are lowered relatively to the self fulfillment costs of a request. As soon as an HQ-period is achieved again, the original weights for the costs of the two fulfillment modes are re-installed.

We define the weight of the subcontraction costs to be 1. The implementation function H_2 controls the weight of the self-fulfillment costs. In an HQ-period, the weight $H_2(t, p_t)$ of the SF-mode is also 1. The tariff level α means, that, one additionally subcontracted request produces costs that are α times larger than the travel costs of an own vehicle from the depot to the location of the customer of the request r. If the weight $H_2(t, p_t)$ of the self-fulfillment costs is larger than α then the subcontracting mode will be selected.

We propose the following procedure to determine the weight H_2. As soon as the punctuality p_t starts falling down towards $p^{target} + 0.05$ or even lower, the weight $H_2(t, p_t)$ is systematically increased until at the end, if p_t is significantly less than p^{target}, $H_2(t, p_t) = 1 + \alpha$. Again, we exploit the piecewise-linear intensity function h introduced in Subsection 5.3 to determine the right intervention degree.

If we define the real-valued function $H_2(t)$ as described in equation (9) then $H_2(t, p_t) = 1$ in HQ-periods, H_2 increases strictly if p_t decreases and if the LQ-period is finally reached, then $H_2(t, p_t) = 1 + \alpha$. We use the function H_2 as implementation function modifying the objective function and replace the original objective function (1) by the adaptive objective function (10).

$$H_2(t_i, p_{t_i}) = \begin{cases} 1, & i = 0 \\ 1 + \alpha \cdot h(p_{t_i}) & i \geq 1 \end{cases} \tag{9}$$

The model $SP(t)$ to be solved at time t is then given by the constraint set (2)-(6) together with the objective function defined by (10).

Table 3. Punctuality decrease $\delta'(\alpha, tech)$

tech	α					
	1	1.25	1.5	1.75	2	3
PEN	-5.3%	-8.9%	-10.3%	-23.1%	-21.0%	-29.2%
CSAD	-10.2%	-9.5%	-10.3%	-10.9%	-9.6%	-10.4%
SDAD	-4.3%	-8.9%	-8.4%	-8.5%	-9.8%	-9.3%

$$\sum_{p \in \mathcal{P}(t_i)} \sum_{v \in \mathcal{V}} H_2(t_i) \cdot (C^1(p) + C^2(p)) x_{pv} + \sum_{r \in \mathcal{R}(t_i)} C^3(r) y_r \rightarrow \min \qquad (10)$$

Since the re-definition of the objective function affects the search trajectory heading of the solving process, we call this approach the Search Direction Adaptation (SDAD) strategy.

6   Computational Experiments

6.1   Layout of the Experimental Field

The average number of vehicles of the own fleet scheduled at time t within the experiment $(\alpha, tech)$ is stored in $v(t, \alpha, tech)$.

Besides the performance figures concerning punctuality described in Section 4, we have recorded the associated costs. Let $C_{\alpha,tech}(t)$ denote the cumulated overall costs realized up to time t in the $(\alpha, tech)$ experiment. The total sum of costs appearing in an experiment is then given by $C_{\alpha,tech}(5000)$.

6.2   Presentation and Interpretation of Numerical Results

In order to analyze the impacts of using different model definition rules, we compare the values of the relative least punctuality $\delta(\alpha, tech)$ achieved by different techniques $tech$ and different tariff levels α. Therefore, we calculate

$$\delta'(\alpha, tech) := \frac{\delta(\alpha, tech)}{\delta(\alpha, HARD)}$$

comparing the relative least punctuality $\delta(\alpha, tech)$ with that of the associated HARD-experiment with the same value of α. These results are compiled in Table 3. Independently from the applied tariff level α, SDAD produces the results with the least deviation from those results observed in the HARD experiment, followed by the results of CSAD and PEN. The last strategy leads to very poor results. In all cases the three strategies PEN, CSAD and SDAD are not able to keep the punctuality on a level as high as HARD is able to do.

Table 4. Percentage of LQ-states $\pi(\alpha, tech)$

				α			
	1	1.25	1.5	1.75	2	3
PEN	–	5.0%	15.0%	42.5%	42.5%	47.5%
CSAD	–	–	5.6%	8.3%	13.9%	19.4%
SDAD	–	–	–	–	5.0%	7.5%

The main conclusion from the analysis of the δ'-values is that both adaptive techniques CSAD as well as SDAD show a similar performance as the static rule represented by the HARD strategy. However, HARD dominates the two adaptive approaches. The usage of a fixed penalty (PEN) does neither lead to satisfying nor convincing results.

The total duration of LQ periods during an experiment increases as soon as the tariff level increases. This can be observed for all modeling rules (Table 4). Using the penalization technique (PEN) a slight growth of the tariff level ($\alpha \geq 1.25$) leads to situations in which the minimum required punctuality p^{target} is not achieved ($\pi(\alpha, tech) > 0$). The rule CSAD cannot prevent LQ periods if $\alpha \geq 1.5$. SDAD is able to prevent LQ periods up to a tariff level of 1.75 and, moreover, in that case the duration of the observed LQ periods is quite short (5%-7.5%).

The application of the static model definition rules HARD as well as PEN lead to a significant sensitivity of the number of subcontracted requests in response to a tariff level lifting (Table 1 and Table 2). In order to allow a comparison of the $\sigma(\alpha, tech)$ values for different model definition rules, we calculate the relative change of the σ-values compared to the values belonging to the HARD experiments:

$$\sigma'(\alpha, tech) := \frac{\sigma(\alpha, tech)}{\sigma(\alpha, HARD)}.$$

The comparison of the results for the different rules, presented in Table 5, shows that the adaptive rules shift a significant larger portion of requests to the SC-mode than the static rules are able to do. This is mainly a consequence of the fact that the adaptive rules implement a deviation from a pure cost optimization strategy.

The analysis of the number $v(t, \alpha, tech)$ of scheduled vehicles of the own fleet shows that the static rules lead to a higher utilization of the own fleet than the application of the adaptive rules. This is indicated by the higher number of averagely deployed vehicles (≈ 10 vehicles) in the experiments with HARD or PEN rule application and an average number of ≈ 8 vehicles for experiments with CSAD or SDAD application. In peak situations, the static rules lead to the deployment of all available own vehicles (25) but if the adaptive model definition rules are used then only 22 of 25 own vehicles are used. After the peak situation

Table 5. Relative increase of the number of subcontracted requests $\sigma'(\alpha, tech)$

tech	α					
	1	1.25	1.5	1.75	2	3
PEN	-12.9%	-10.0%	-1.5%	34.9%	-19.5%	31.4%
CSAD	-1.8%	14.0%	105.1%	150.0%	186.7%	195.2%
SDAD	1.5%	14.0%	64.1%	88.1%	118.9%	133.1%

Table 6. Relative increase $C'(\alpha, tech)$ of the overall costs (comparison to the HARD experiments)

	α					
	1	1.25	1.5	1.75	2	3
NONE	-9.5%	-6.8%	0.5%	4.2%	5.6%	0.4%
CSAD	-7.0%	3.8%	17.8%	28.2%	32.5%	50.4%
SDAD	-5.4%	0.8%	8.0%	11.2%	11.8%	11.4%

is over, the two static rules come along with a longer convalescence time until the average number of 10 deployed own vehicles is finally re-achieved. In comparison, the two adaptive rules show an overreaction and lead to a number of deployed own vehicles that is less than the average number of applied vehicles. Throughout the complete observation period, the number of deployed own vehicles oscillated around its average value at an amplitude that is larger than the amplitude observed for the static rules.

To analyze the cost impacts of a model definition rule replacement, we calculate the relative growth

$$C'(\alpha, tech) := \frac{C_{(\alpha, tech)}(5000)}{C_{(\alpha, HARD)}(5000)}$$

of the overall costs compared to the reference values taken from the HARD-experiments. The $C'(\alpha, tech)$-values compiled in Table 6 show that all strategies lead to additional costs if the tariff level is increased ($\alpha > 1.25$). Since PEN primarily prefers minimal cost fulfillment plans it leads to the least costs. Similarly, the adaptive rule SDAD leads to a small but acceptable amount of additional costs (10%). In contrast, the CSAD rule, which manipulates the constraint set of the model without taking into account any cost criteria, produces unacceptable additional costs of more than 50%.

7   Conclusions

We have extended the online decision making framework by features that allow the detection of an undesired system development as well as the calibration of a formal optimization model. Within comprehensive numerical experiments, we have shown the applicability of this extension as well as its usefulness for managing transport processes in a volatile environment.

Future research efforts will cover the combination of static and adaptive rules as well as investigations about model adaptations if the adaptation costs are limited by a given budget.

Acknowledgment. This research was supported by the German Research Foundation (DFG) as part of the Collaborative Research Centre 637 "Autonomous Cooperating Logistic Processes" (Subproject B7).

References

1. Ausiello, G., Feuerstein, E., Leonardi, S., Stougie, L., Talamo, M.: Algorithms for the online-traveling salesman. Algorithmica 29(4), 540–581 (2001)
2. Bierwirth, C.: Adaptive Search and the Management of Logistics Systems. Kluwer Academic Publishers (2000)
3. Brehmer, B.: Dynamic decision making: Human control of complex systems. Acta Psychologica 81, 211–241 (1992)
4. Fiat, A., Woeginger, G. (eds.): Online Algorithms: The State of the Art. Springer, Heidelberg (1998)
5. Gutenschwager, K., Niklaus, C., Voß, S.: Effiziente Prozesse im kombinierten Verkehr – ein neuer Lösungsansatz zur Disposition von Portalkränen. Logistik Management 5(1), 62–73 (2003)
6. Gutenschwager, K., Böse, F., Voß, S.: Dispatching of an electric monorail system: Applying metaheuristics to an online pickup and delivery problem. Transportation Science 38(4), 434–446 (2004)
7. Gutenschwager, K.: Online-Dispositionsprobleme in der Lagerlogistik. Physica-Verlag, Heidelberg (2002)
8. Hülsmann, M., Windt, K. (eds.): Understanding Autonomous Cooperation and Control in Logistics. Springer, Heidelberg (2007)
9. Ichoua, S., Gendreau, M., Potvin, J.-Y.: Planned route optimization for real-time vehicle routing. In: Zeimpekis, V., Tarantilis, C.D., Giaglis, G.M., Minis, I. (eds.) Dynamic Fleet Management, pp. 1–18. Springer, Heidelberg (2007)
10. Irani, S., Ku, X., Regan, A.: On-line algorithms for the dynamic traveling repairman problem. Journal of Scheduling 7, 243–258 (2004)
11. Jaillet, P.: A priori solution of a travelling salesman problem in which a random subset of customers are visited. Operations Research 36(6), 929–936 (1988)
12. Jensen, M.T.: Robust and flexible scheduling with evolutionary computation. PhD.-Thesis, University of Aarhus (2001)
13. Kopfer, H., Krajewska, M.A.: Approaches for Modelling and Solving the Integrated Transportation and Forwarding Problem. In: Corsten, H., Missbauer, H. (eds.) Produktions- und Logistikmanagement Vahlen, pp. 439–458 (2007)
14. Krumke, S.O., Rambau, J., Torres, L.M.: Real-Time Dispatching of Guided and Unguided Automobile Service Units with Soft Time Windows. In: Möhring, R.H., Raman, R. (eds.) ESA 2002. LNCS, vol. 2461, pp. 637–648. Springer, Heidelberg (2002)

15. Krumke, S.: Online-Optimisation - Competitive Analysis and Beyond. Technical University of Berlin (2001)
16. Lackner, A.: Dynamische Tourenplanung mit ausgewählten Metaheuristiken. Cuvilier-Verlag, Göttingen (2004)
17. Mirchandani, P.: Embedded Algorithms in Real-Time Transportation Systems. In: Rendl, F., Fischer, I., Perdacher, A., Wiegele, A. (eds.) Abstract Booklet of Operations Research 2002, University of Klagenfurt, Austria (2002)
18. Moscato, P.: On evolution, search, optimization, genetic algorithms and martial arts: Towards memetic algorithms. Technical Report 790, CalTech Concurrent Computation Program, California Institute of Technology (1989)
19. Pankratz, G.: Speditionelle Transportdisposition DUV. Wiesbaden (2002)
20. Psaraftis, H.N.: Dynamic vehicle routing: status and prospects. Annals of Operations Research 61, 143–164 (1995)
21. Psaraftis, H.N.: Dynamic vehicle routing problems. In: Golden, B., Assad, A. (eds.) Vehicle Routing: Methods and Studies, pp. 223–248. Elsevier Publishers B.V. (1988)
22. Ruszczynski, A., Shapiro, A.: Stochastic Programming. North-Holland (2003)
23. Sandvoß, E.: Dynamische Tourenplanung auf Basis on Online-Verkehrsinformationen. ProBusiness, Berlin (2004)
24. Schönberger, J., Kopfer, H.: On Decision Model Adaptation in Online Optimization of a Transport System. In: Günther, H.-O., Mattfeld, D.C., Suhl, L. (eds.) Management Logistischer Netzwerke, pp. 361–381. Springer, Heidelberg (2007)
25. Schönberger, J., Kopfer, H.: Autonomous Decision Model Adaptation and the Vehicle Routing Problem with Time Windows and Uncertain Demand. In: Hülsmann, M., Windt, K. (eds.) Understanding Autonomous Cooperation and Control in Logistics, pp. 139–161. Springer, Heidelberg (2007)
26. Schönberger, J.: Operational Freight Carrier Planing. GOR Publications. Springer, Heidelberg (2005)
27. Solomon, M.: Algorithms for the vehicle routing and scheduling problem with time window constraints. Operations Research 35(2), 254–265 (1987)
28. Wasserburger, D.: Dynamische Tourenoptimierung durch verkehrstelematische Daten. In: Schrenk, M. (ed.) Proceedings of CORP, pp. 535–542 (2006)
29. Windt, K., Hülsmann, M.: Changing Paradigms in Logistics – Understanding the Shift from Conventional Control to AUtonomous Cooperation and Control. In: Hülsmann, M., Windt, K. (eds.) Understanding Autonomous Cooperation and Control in Logistics, pp. 1–22. Springer, Heidelberg (2007)
30. Zeimpekis, V., Tarantilis, C.D., Giaglis, G.M., Minis, I. (eds.): Dynamic Fleet Management. Springer, New York (2007)

A Method for Selectively Designing Modeling Languages for Product-Service Systems

Jörg Becker, Daniel Beverungen, and Ralf Knackstedt

WWU Münster, European Research Center for Information Systems
Leonardo-Campus 3, 48149 Muenster, Germany
{becker,daniel.beverungen,ralf.knackstedt}@ercis.uni-muenster.de

Abstract. Confronted with decreasing margins and a rising customer demand for integrated solutions, manufacturing companies broaden their portfolio by offering complementary services. Designing, proposing and providing customer solutions (consisting of physical goods and services) takes place in product-service systems, which may comprise manufacturing companies, service companies and customers. Conceptual modeling is an established approach to support such efforts. In this paper, a method for selectively designing conceptual modeling languages is proposed and demonstrated. Departing from outlining the general properties of value creation in product-service systems, a catalogue of modeling requirements in this area is compiled based on analyzing the perspectives of four sub-disciplines on service research. An evaluation of a set of modeling languages with this catalogue reveals that the languages incompletely address the requirements. Therefore, an approach to selectively design new modeling languages for product-service systems is proposed based on integrating and extending the meta models of other modeling languages.

Keywords: product-service systems, modeling languages, meta modeling.

1 Customer Solutions and Product-Service Systems

1.1 Properties of Customer Solutions

In recent years, service-orientation has increasingly been debated both in research and practice. While some researchers postulate 'service' to be the basic unit of exchange in economies [92, 93], companies struggle to efficiently provide adequate service to their customers. As a subset of this trend, many industries are experiencing a transition from a goods-based to a service-based focus: Traditional manufacturing companies strive to provide physical goods and services as integrated customer solutions [31], which are delivered in relational processes with customers [91].

Generally, offering pure physical goods to customers is seldom done (if not impossible), as can be seen regarding logistics services or promotion services provided along with physical goods in retail. Accordingly, physical goods and services are no longer perceived to be dichotomous [25]. Instead they are rather seen as complementary vehicles to offer value to customers [92, 93]. But regardless of the

D. Dolk et al. (Eds.): Decision Support Modeling in Service Networks, LNBIP 42, pp. 87–117, 2012.
© Springer-Verlag Berlin Heidelberg 2012

ongoing –and sometimes quite philosophical– discourse in academia related to the notions of physical goods, services, or customer solutions, the dominance of the service sector is still increasing [60], shifting companies' focus of attention from providing physical goods to providing customer solutions.

This trend is in particular reflected in the German Mechanical Engineering and Electrical Engineering industries, where many companies strive to professionalize their service business in order to increase their revenues, provide customers with customized solutions, and differentiate themselves from their competitors. Evaluating results from two large-scale empirical studies in both sectors, Stille concludes that turnover related to services has doubled in the Electrical Engineering sector from 9.6% (1997) to 18.5% (2000), while significant gains from 16.8% (1997) to 22.5% (2000) could be identified in the Mechanical Engineering Sector [85]. Mercer Management Consulting recognizes that half of the growth in German Mechanical Engineering in the years 1998–2003 can be allocated to exploiting the potential of the service business. Likewise, the margin realized in the service business (10%) was estimated to be significantly higher than the margin of realized in the physical goods business (2.3%). Furthermore, Mercer states that margins gained from services could be even higher when looking at some leading edge services only, which constantly catch margins of up to 18% [55]. Additional empirical research shows, that companies attribute a high (38.1%) or very high (59.8%) impact on their revenues to their service business [31]. Consistent with these findings, 94.9% of the examined companies planned to expand their business by offering customer solutions in 2007 [86].

The following characteristics have been proposed as being constitutive for customer solutions (see also the discussion in [78] and [9]):

- Customer solutions comprise separately marketable physical goods and services. They are purposefully combined with each other into one coherent value proposition in order to solve a problem for a customer or for a group of customers [31].
- Physical goods components and service components might be substitutable with other components without changing the solution provided. However, this is an optional characteristic [31].
- From the customer's point of view, outcomes of the solution can have tangible and intangible benefits. One motivation for providing customer solutions is to create an outcome for customers and/or providers which is superior to the sum of outcomes of the components [31].
- Customer solutions can be offered as individual value propositions, independent of the physical goods and services they comprise. After a value proposition has been accepted by a customer, customer solutions are delivered in service processes that need to be integrated into the customer's business processes and therefore require customer input (such as information, objects, personnel or other resources) [93].

Services which are often offered as part of customer solutions may correspond to different stages of the traditional product lifecycle, such as a setup, operation or end-of-life stage (Fig. 1). Services in the setup stage may constitute pre-sales services such as requirements engineering, performance analyses, financial services or technical assembly. During the operation stage, service activities as preventive maintenance, corrective maintenance or spare parts logistics are mainly conducted to uphold the operability of the physical good. Referring to the end-of-life stage, any of the physical goods components might be replaced, refurbished and reused, or recycled. Quite often, this might include reallocating machinery to low wage countries for further use.

In practice, the most widely offered services in industrial settings still seem to be 'classic' offerings such as spare part logistics, preventive maintenance/fault repair, consulting, and assembly. It is striking, that most of these services are in fact not new and have a strong physical goods focus. In contrast to this, highly innovative services like cooperative capacity management in value networks, performance contracting business models, or on-demand human resource services are seldom offered.

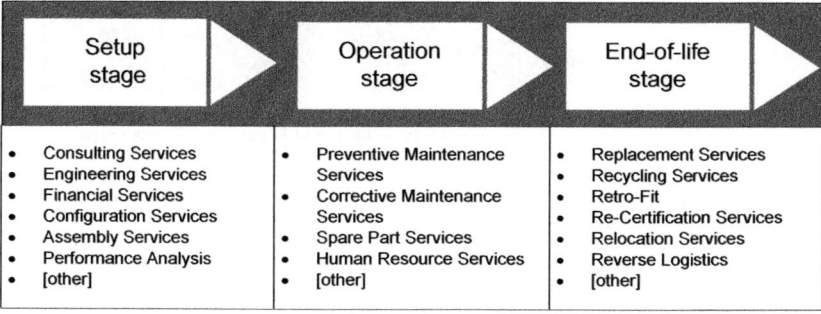

Fig. 1. Exemplary services offered along with physical goods, arranged with respect to a traditional product lifecycle, see also [4, 9]

Some topologies have been proposed to intellectually grasp the characteristics of integrated physical goods and service offerings, an early contribution being the study of Engelhardt, Kleinaltenkamp and Reckenfelderbäumer [25] (Fig. 2). From a service marketing standpoint, they systematize offerings for customers in a two-dimensional framework: On the one hand, the output perceived by the customer may be rather intangible (such as additional knowledge as the result of training to operate a vertical lath) or rather tangible (such as a vertical lath, that has been delivered and assembled). On the other hand, business processes for delivering customer solutions might have to be tightly integrated into the value creation processes of customers (such as providing a vertical lath as-a-service) or can be carried out rather autonomously from customer input (such as spare-parts management offered through a consignment stock). Against the backdrop of this topology, customer solutions can be systematized as being delivered in processes which are to be carried out cooperatively with customers, while they can result in tangible as well as intangible results.

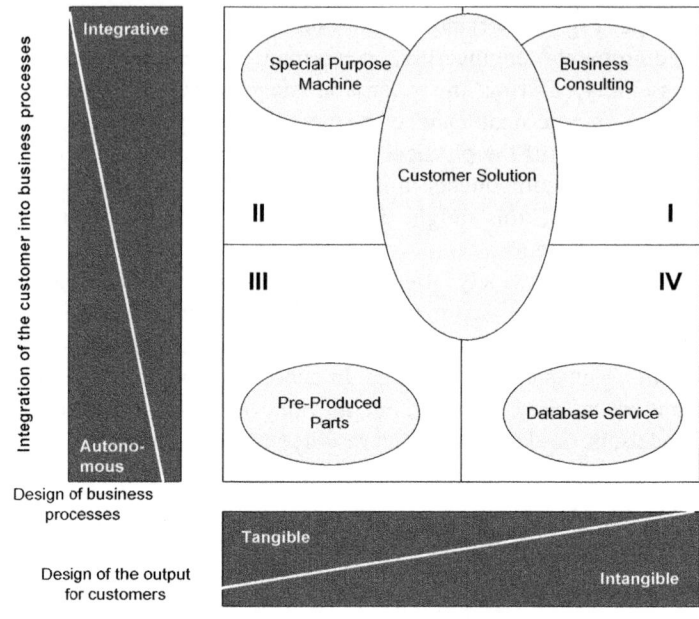

Fig. 2. Customer solutions as sales objects [25], see also [4, 9]

1.2   Value Creation in Product-Service Systems

Several assumptions have been proposed to constitute the creation of value in service systems. It has been argued, that customer solutions can be designed and delivered by the cooperation of manufacturing companies with external service providers [68] or by manufacturing companies themselves. One motivation for networking with other companies is to tap into complementary resource infrastructures and core competencies. On the other hand, the integration of customers into value-creation is a constitutive feature of service processes. Therefore, customers are to be acknowledged as co-creators of value, providing a variety of inputs into the service process [72]. Providers may not offer value but only value proposition, while the creation of value can only take place cooperatively with customers [93]. During this cooperation, value propositions are applied to generate value for customers (i.e. the customer solution). Customers might be consumers (B2C market), other companies (B2B market) or the public sector.

Drawing from an array of previously proposed definitions of Service Systems [51], we conceptualize the term Product-Service System (PSS) [4, 7, 57, 88] to denote a conceptual framework in which the cooperative design and delivery of customer solutions takes place (Fig. 3). In general, two organizational settings are conceivable for providing customer solutions. First, a company might offer physical goods components as well as service components autonomously. This would lead to the need to integrate the offerings in-house in a collaboration of various organizational sub-units (left hand side in Fig. 3). Second, companies might network with other companies in order to provide value propositions that exceed their own resources and capabilities (right hand side in Fig. 3). Either way, both types of settings evoke the need to 'bridge the gap', caused by inconsistent data, different cultures or work practices. Information flows for connecting and coordinating business processes and information systems across organizational borders (represented by arrows in Fig. 3) can be a remedy to bridge this gap. In effect, the organizational units involved in the value creation process contribute offerings that are combined into the actual customer solution. Whereas this solution might be perceived as inseparable from the point of view of the customer, its components have to be traced back to their producers internally for reasons of accountability. Finally, customer solutions can only generate value if integrated into the business processes of a customer (represented by bi-directional arrows in Fig. 3).

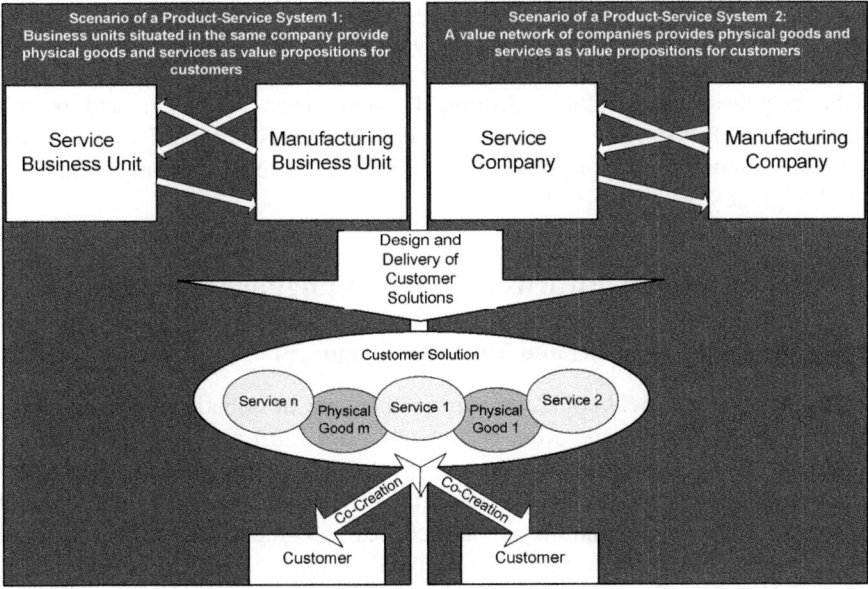

Fig. 3. Cooperative design, proposition and delivery of customer solutions, taking place in Product-Service Systems (PSS), see also [4, 9]

The remainder of the paper is organized as follows:

In the consecutive Section 2, requirements of designing conceptual models with modeling languages in the context of PSS are deduced from four points of view on service science. These perspectives are Engineering, Supply Chain Management, Service Marketing, and Environmental Research. Some key concepts of each discipline are derived, such that an evaluation sheet can be created for modeling languages to be used in the context of PSS. These criteria are different from a similar analysis that we have reported in [4]. Whereas the analysis performed in this paper is focused on criteria from sub-disciplines of service science, the analysis of modeling languages in [4] is guided by a conceptual framework for product-service system engineering. Therefore, both analyses complement each other in identifying the language constructs needed to model phenomena in the PSS domain. In addition, a shortened and updated version of this analysis is offered in [9] with a focus on service description languages.

In Section 3, the method for selectively designing conceptual modeling languages is derived based on proposing a lifecycle model for modeling languages. Consecutively the method is demonstrated to work in the PSS context. Applying the evaluation sheet to a selection of modeling languages from the four disciplines suggests that current modeling languages fall short of addressing issues stemming from other disciplines. In turn, it can be concluded that current modeling languages often lack the expressiveness to thoroughly facilitate the design of conceptual models in the context of PSS. As a strategy to overcome these deficiencies, a meta model integration of the EPC and Service Blueprinting approaches is presented to combine their modeling languages and thus make them more eligible to be applied in a PSS context.

The conclusion and outlook Section 4 summarizes the results and postulates directions for further research on modeling languages. In particular, advancing conceptual modeling languages in PSS can be expected to greatly benefit from multidisciplinary research efforts.

2   Requirements towards Modeling Languages for PSS

2.1   Conceptual Modeling and Modeling Languages

Originating from the fields of Computer Science and Information Systems Research (IS), conceptual models are often used to describe, abstract from, emphasize and explain information concepts. One the one hand conceptual models are designed with respect to unambiguously defined (i.e. specified by means of a meta model) modeling languages. On the other hand they should convey a degree of intuitive understanding for their users. Well designed conceptual models enable members of an interdisciplinary project team to communicate with each other more effectively, regarding concepts such as the structural organization of a company or its business processes [21, 96].

Conceptual modeling has been argued to hold great business potential, for instance to grasp and redesign business processes in the field of business process modeling. Conceptual models used for the development of information systems may explicitly aim at addressing the information needs of key users, senior executives, application designers, and programmers in software development processes. Thus, conceptual models can simultaneously address management issues as well as inform software implementation and business engineering projects on an operational level.

Modeling languages comprise a conceptual aspect and a representational aspect [38]. The conceptual language aspect (ortho-language) defines the meaning of the modeling constructs and relationships among them and constitutes the expressiveness of conceptual models designed with this modeling language. The representational aspect (notation) assigns representation formalisms to the specified constructs to make them easier to grasp and use for stakeholders by reducing the cognitive load imposed on human interpreters. Modeling languages determine the rules according to which conceptual models (or even reference models) have to be designed. Modeling languages can be formally described by meta models, which represent the language concepts and their relationships in a graphical notation. I addition, they can also enable advanced model operations such as specifying a dynamic semantics of models [36].

Using well-established modeling languages to model real-world concepts can accelerate the process of modeling since modelers and users may already be familiar with the modeling language's constructs (think of popular modeling languages such as the Universal Modeling Language, UML). This would lead to more effective communication processes, as well as focus the process of modeling on the crucial aspects of the phenomenon to be modeled.

Therefore, in this paper we report on the adequacy of current modeling languages for generating conceptual models in a PSS context, as well as propose a method for selectively designing new modeling languages based on these premises.

Conceptual models can be used to support designers in dealing with the specific requirements in a PSS context, such as (see also [4] and [9]):

- What are business processes in a PSS context like? How and to what extend might business processes in PSS be improved? What IT support is in place to (semi-)automatically carry out these processes?
- Which organizational units are involved in the process of value creation of customer solutions? What is their role in the process and which components of customer solutions can they provide? How is the integration of providers and customers performed on an operational level?
- How is an entire portfolio of customer solutions structured? Which configurations are allowed to adapt a customer solution to the individual needs of customers without sacrificing its structural integrity?
- How might individual value propositions for customers be derived from the portfolio by combining previously defined physical goods and service modules into customer solutions? Which configuration rules shall be applied in order to derive feasible as well as profitable solutions?
- How much money is a customer willing to pay for a configured solution? What costs are associated with engineering, offering, and delivering a solution for a customer? Which solutions shall providers offer to a customer? Which solutions shall not be offered to a customer, because their creation is undesirable (e.g., non-profitable for the provider)?
- How much negative impact do alternative customer solutions impose on the environment (e.g., ecological footprint)?

2.2   Department-Specific Perspectives of Customer Solutions and PSS

Service Science is a multi-disciplinary research field, involving researchers from various academic disciplines, each of which imposes its own point of view on the subject. We now provide a brief introduction of the perspectives that are usually emphasized by four specific disciplines. From this discussion, we deduce modeling constructs that represent requirements to be addressed by modeling languages in a PSS context. Notably, these disciplines nevertheless also overlap to some extent.

Engineering Disciplines, like Mechanical Engineering or Electrical Engineering, traditionally focus on engineering, constructing, and operating physical investment goods, often with a focus on other manufacturing companies as customers. In the course of an increasing service orientation, many providers have adapted their business models in order to improve the manufacturing processes of their customers themselves, moving to complex value propositions that involve heterogeneous offerings.

Modeling languages for specifying physical goods and production processes have long been established in research and practice. The representation of bills-of-materials is one common and widespread manifestation. A bill-of-materials represents a model of a physical good and breaks down its physical structure into components, parts or even raw materials. Each component or part is manufactured in an identifiable manufacturing process. The activities contained in this process are often described in work plans. In the manufacturing process, each activity is then assigned to a work center in which the activity is carried out.

Consistently, creating physical goods according to formalized specifications has long been the focus of engineering disciplines, which has led to a considerable degree of standardization concerning ways to formally describe manufacturing processes. STEP (STandard for the Exchange of Product model data, ISO 10303-41: Fundaments of Product Description and Support; ISO 10303-42: Geometric and Topological Representation; ISO 10303-46: Visual Presentation) for example has gained particular importance in this respect [2, 66].

Supplementing this perspective, a 'Service Engineering' research movement has emerged in Germany [29] which strives to apply well-proven engineering methods to the design of business services as well (see [15, 16]). This is based on the expectation that services would also benefit from being systematically developed, just like physical goods.

Drawing from the concept of bill-of-materials, the service engineering discipline attempts to decompose services into sub-modules. This would open up opportunities to describe service processes with process models analogous to the work plans used in the manufacturing realm. Fig. 4 depicts a bill-of-materials of a physical product (left hand side) as well as an imaginary bill-of-materials of a service (right hand side). The structural analogy of both models is striking since they both display the structure of sales objects that can be sold to customers based on different hierarchical levels.

It can be inferred that from an engineering point of view representing the structure of physical goods (product engineering) and services (service engineering) and their components (*customer solutions subdivided into components*) is crucial. Based on this specification, work plans comprising activities in production processes can be designed based on which sequence plans and machine capacity schedules can be derived. Work plans are one common feature to be found in current ERP systems.

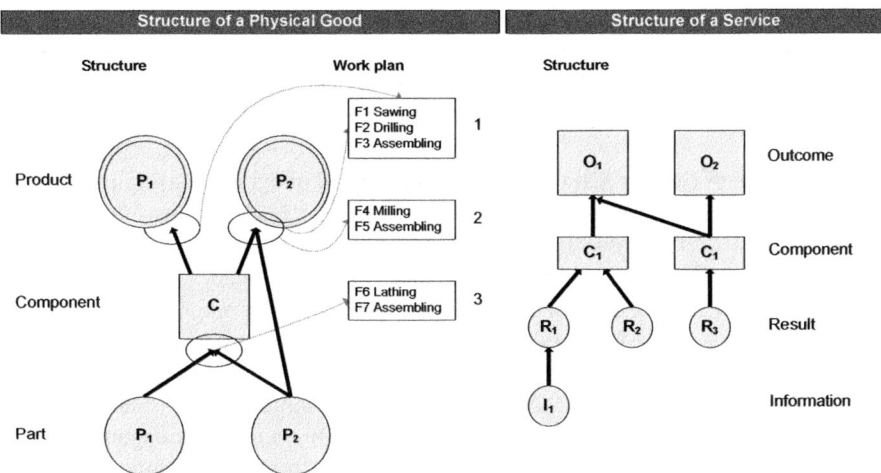

Fig. 4. Comparing a bill-of-materials for a physical good with a bill of materials for a service [48, 75, 9]

Since we will deal with processes and work plans from a Supply Chain Management (SCM) perspective in more detail, we identify three characteristics *control flow, capacity,* and *activities* arising from the engineering perspective. More advanced features of production processes will be dealt with in the consecutive SCM chapter.

A mass-customization business strategy may enable companies to exploit economies of substitution by reusing modules (*reuse of the components as modules*) [30]. Benefits to be gained from modularization include re-using existing knowledge associated with physical good and service modules, reducing performance slippage when incorporating additional modules into the bundle, reducing incorporation costs for suppliers and customers and, perhaps most importantly, making customer solutions modularly upgradeable to cope with changing customer demand (*substitution of modules*) [3, 30]. A prerequisite to assemble customer solutions from modules is to describe them in taxonomies (i.e. is-part-of relationships in a bill-of-materials) of modules as well as establishing non-hierarchical relationships (i.e. configuration rules) between modules. These rules might be inclusive (*configuration rules to specify inclusion (may)*) or exclusive (*configuration rules to specify exclusion (must not)*).

Components might be described by a variety of attributes (*attributes of components*). One particularly important attribute is information about the longevity of a physical good or service module (*longevity*), since often predefined maintenance intervals need to be complied with in order to prolong the warranty period for a machine. To provide information in sufficient detail, product models have to account for a variety of lifecycle phases of the traditional product lifecycle, ranging from setup to end-of-life.

While quality assurance is a mature topic in goods manufacturing, it is especially challenging for service processes, because inspections at the end of the service creation process can only occur after delivery to customers. Therefore, quality standards are important to be followed during any production or service process (*quality standards*). The quality of service as perceived by customers might be explained by a gap-model, as the deviation between expected and perceived service quality [63].

The discipline of **Supply Chain Management** as an integrative discipline drawing from business, engineering, and computer science / IS points-of-view [69], emphasizes the need for streamlining flows and goods and information. In particular, designing sufficient information flows may be necessary to align goods manufacturing and service provision in PSS. Business process management based on information models provides a rich pool of techniques to support such efforts. In addition, setting up efficient processes might be aided by drawing from past successes in Supply Chain Management, Materials Resource Planning (MRP) and Enterprise Resource Planning (ERP) [23]. The discipline of Operations Management (OM) emphasizes the need for multidisciplinary cooperation across several functional areas, such as Human Resources, Marketing or Accounting, to maximize the efficiency in providing customer solutions for customers [7]. In OM, steps from customer analysis to product/service engineering, delivery, and disposal are not viewed in detail, but rather seen as one output of the cooperation [33].

Modeling languages for PSS have to account for these characteristics. Business processes necessary to design and deliver customer solutions include the activities to be carried out in the process of value creation (*activities*), the order in which they have to be carried out (*control flow*), materials to be procured and transported (*flow of materials*), information to be utilized (*flow of information*), and money for physical goods bought or sold to customers (*cash flow*).

It has been stated, that manufacturing processes and service processes differ significantly and managerially [72]. Therefore, a suitable modeling language for PSS must not model service processes in the same way as manufacturing processes, but should take distinctive characteristics of service processes such as customer integration into consideration [76]. Because resources and inputs provided by customers are individual in each service process, modeling languages must be able to represent various customer inputs and various sequences of service processes (*resources to be introduced by customers*). Also production processes for different physical goods or their variants might be different and affect the control flow in manufacturing.

Process cycle times are one important attribute for managing different types of manufacturing and service processes (*process cycle time*). This information can be used for planning resources to be used in the processes, as well as for documenting the processes ex post. For instance, a service incident might be closed and settled with respect to the time that was needed to perform the service process.

Manufacturing as well as service processes might be subject to failure. Consequently, the failure rate should be estimated and considered for planning and scheduling the resource allocation for processes (*failure rate*).

Services processes per se are intangible, but might involve a variety of operant and operand resources during their execution. Operant resources (such as personnel, knowledge, business processes, culture, business relationships) can be seen as the fundamental source of competitive advantage; they are the resources capable of acting on other resources [50, 93]. Operand resources are the resources acted upon when conducting service processes, such as machinery, components, parts, raw materials and other objects (*consumption of operand resources (economic point of view)*).

In the light of services being non-storable, suppliers have to make sure they have sufficient resources at their disposal to carry out the service process when they are requested at the 'moment of truth'. Yet on the other hand, they may want to minimize the time their resources remain idle, waiting for customer input. This optimization problem motivates a resource planning for service processes, as has been applied in manufacturing processes for years. Even so, resource planning for services has been argued to still lag behind resource planning in manufacturing, such as for Supply Chain Management or ERP systems [22]. However, there is an increasingly large body of knowledge on improving the efficiency of service processes, many of which involve queuing theory, since queues are means to 'store' resources until needed in service processes. However, resources for service processes are perishable, such that conceptual models for business services must be able to represent resources and their *capacity*. Resources should be displayed in process models, such that for each function to be carried out the resources to be consumed are depicted and scheduled. During the service process, some *organizational units* and *IT systems and applications* are likely to be involved.

Because PSS might comprise the roles of manufacturers, service providers and customers, it is important to carry out business processes smoothly even across business units and organizations. Integrating information and processes found in the front-end and back-end of service systems has already been identified as a considerable challenge [68, 89]. For example, to offer and deliver a managed truck fleet as a value proposition for customers, a truck manufacturer and a consulting agency have to synchronize their businesses by exchanging documents such as order and bidding documents, schedule dates, or product master data. Therefore, business processes in PSS have to be able to display, which sub-processes must be carried out by manufacturers, service providers, or customers and which activities are to be made visible to others stakeholders.

Due to differing needs of customers and due to different resources and inputs to be introduced into the service process by customers, service processes might be carried out differently each time. Standardizing services can help to provide them in a more consistent quality.

Main points of interest from a **Service Marketing Perspective** on customer solutions (notably represented by Shostack 1982, Vargo and Lusch 2004, as well as a Journal of the Academy of Marketing Science special issue in 2008) comprise offering integrated value propositions for customers [92, 93], determining adequate prices and business models to successfully market these value propositions [87], and integrating the customer into service processes as a co-creator of value [64, 81, 82]. Service settings investigated in this stream of research are often situated in the B2C sector, such as hotel check-in services, health services, or services provided in restaurants.

The emerging research disciplines of Service Science and Service Science, Management and Engineering (SSME) respectively, focus of the design and delivery of services in Service Systems, comprising providers (or even value networks of providers) as well as customers as co-creators of value.

From a service marketing perspective, modeling languages must take distinctive characteristics of services into account. The most distinctive feature of service processes is the integration of customers as co-creators of value into service processes (*resources to be introduced by customers*). Therefore, it is crucial to account for the *line of visibility* and *line of interaction* towards customers [82]. Sampson and Froehle [72] emphasize, that other often cited characteristics of services such as perishability, simultaneity, intangibility, heterogeneity [28] are caused by the integration of the customer into the service process. Additionally, services cannot be produced in advance and thus are non-storable and not easily patentable. In addition to the lines usually postulated by service marketing, *relationships and lines towards stakeholders* can determine the division of labor in PSS, as processes might be outsourced to third party manufacturers or service providers.

Moreover, it is difficult for customers to assess the value of a service in advance of the service process, which makes marketing and pricing services especially challenging. The design of *value propositions* for customers can be supported by modeling constructs to describe, and individually configure and price (*attributes of components*) customer solutions [4]. The value proposition comprises purposefully arranged physical goods and services that jointly fulfill a need for the customer. This integration might necessitate adapting the goods and services components themselves. For instance, a machine layout might be different based on the service processes and the overall business model in which the solution is offered, since remote maintenance solutions need special software components to be running of the machine's hardware. On the other hand, the layout of physical goods greatly influence the service processes to be carried out on this machine.

The *marketing lifecycle* of customer solutions and its components is important to consider, because customers often take services which are in the saturation phase (such as assembly or maintenance services) for granted and might be unwilling to pay for them. In contrast, rather innovative services (such as layout planning or resource optimization services) have only recently been introduced and are more likely to be paid for by customers (*cash flow*). *Service level agreements* (SLAs) might be offered to define the quality level of physical goods and services more consistently and convince customers that the value propositions offered to them will lead to the creation of high-quality solutions that will likely be beneficial for them. Dispatching qualified personnel (*personnel allocation, qualification of personnel*), promising low *failure rates* and short *process cycle times* can be some of the elements dealt with in SLAs.

Apart from these disciplines, customer solutions from an **Environmental Research** standpoint are seen as a means to create customer solutions with less environmental impact [56, 71, 90]. Customer solutions, if offered in performance contracting business models by specialized providers, might allow for resources to be used more efficiently due to exploiting economies of scale. Therefore, value for

Modeling language	Engineering	SCM	Marketing	Environmental
Customer Solutions subdivided into components	X			X
Reuse of the components as modules	X			
Configuration rules to specify inclusion (may)	X			
Configuration rules to specify exclusion (must not)	X			
Substituation of modules or components	X			X
Attributes of components / products	X		X	X
Longevity	X		X	X
Activities	X	X		
Control flow	X	X		
Flow of materials		X		X
Flow of information		X		
Cash flow		X	X	
Process cycle time		X	X	
Failure rate		X	X	
Capacity	X	X		
Consumption of operand resources (economic point of view)		X		
Consumption of operand resources (ecologic point of view)				X
Legal constraints				X
Value proposition for customers			X	
Marketing lifecycle			X	
Line of visibility towards customers		X	X	
Line of interaction towards customers		X	X	
Relationships / lines towards other stakeholders		X	X	
Quality standards	X			
Service level agreements			X	
IT Systems and applications		X		
Data (e.g. master data)		X		
Personnel allocation		X	X	
Qualification of personnel		X	X	
Organisational units		X	X	
Resources to be introduced by customers		X	X	

Fig. 5. Modeling requirements of customer solutions from four different academic points of view, see also [9]

customers can be created in an environmentally 'sustainable' way. Authors arguing from this point-of-view tend to explicitly take environmental aspects into their definitions of customer solutions and PSS [4].

Modeling languages for PSS should address some basic ideas that have significance from an ecological point of view. Most importantly, the **consumption of operand resources (ecological point of view)** during production and service processes should be taken into account, because it may entail some negative environmental impact, for example due to emissions. At the end of its lifecycle (**longevity**), a physical good might be refurbished, relocated or recycled. In these cases, information about the product structure and its components is necessary (**customer solutions subdivided into components**). If modules are to be refurbished, a **substitution of modules** takes place. If modules are recycled, their material might be reused to build other physical goods (**flow of materials**, **attributes of components**).

A division of customer solutions into sub-components and raw materials in connection with adequate attributes can help to quantify this impact, while a modular structure with reusable components can help to spare resources due to exploiting substitution effects and economies of scale. **Legal constraints** (such as WEEE – Waste Electrical and Electronic Equipment (EU 2003) might be important to comply with legal regulations.

Figure 5 summarizes the modeling requirements for customer solutions derived from the four perspectives. The origin of each criterion is displayed, acknowledging that several criteria stem from more than one discipline.

3   A Method for Selectively Designing Modeling Language Support for PSS

The criteria derived from the four research areas can be used to evaluate the support of modeling languages for PSS. However, integrating different modeling languages completely might negatively impact the applicability of the new modeling language due to increased complexity. In contrast to a complete integration, an in-depth analysis provides the opportunity of integrating selected features taken from several modeling languages only. This can be achieved by combining elements taken from the meta models of several modeling languages for creating a meta model for the new language.

Proposing new modeling languages is not necessarily a good strategy in its own right, since the benefit of the new modeling language depends on the current lifecycle stage of modeling support in a specific domain. Therefore, before evaluating and integrating modeling languages for PSS, the current lifecycle stage of a population of modeling languages in the domain of interest needs to be appraised.

3.1   Outline of the Method

When examining modeling languages at a high level of abstraction, it seems conceivable, that they are subject to a lifecycle just like other technologies. Without presenting a validated theory in this paper, we identify several lifecycle stages of modeling languages augmented with examples:

- **Initialization:** When discovering new research areas, no modeling languages will be present. Therefore, one needs to draw ideas from modeling languages existing or proposed in other research areas, which might address some of the new modeling requirements. In the area of Online Analytical Processing Systems (OLAP-Systems), multidimensional modeling was first done using traditional database conceptual modeling approaches such as the Entity Relationship Model (ERM) as modeling languages.

- **Conquest:** Still facing a lack of adequate modeling languages, new modeling languages are developed and proposed to specifically address the modeling needs of the new research area. This might lead to an abundance of new modeling languages. Several strategies for building new modeling languages can be identified: (1) Traditional approaches might be adopted and advanced: Referring to OLAP-Modeling, adapted versions of the ERM (i.e. the ME/RM proposed by Sapia et al. [73]) or UML (i.e. the mUML proposed by Harren and Herden [34]) were proposed. (2) Another approach is to ignore existing approaches and to develop a modeling method from the scratch by defining its conceptual and representational aspects without re-using existing constructs and objects from other modeling languages. Bulos' [17] approach towards OLAP-Modeling can be seen as one striking example. Even for the limited area of OLAP-Modeling, as many as 30 modeling languages can be found, and new modeling languages continue to be proposed [46, 80].

- **Consolidation:** An abundance of modeling languages imposes the need for selection processes in research, teaching, and practical application in companies. Even so, spending this effort might not be justified by a striking uniqueness of the modeling languages. Therefore, conceptual modeling in the domain tends to be subjected to a process of consolidation. In this stage, some languages might emerge as the leading edge methods, which will be gradually advanced without changing the name of the modeling language. Standardization processes accelerate this trend. The field of business process modeling can be seen as a fitting example for this phenomenon: In addition to widely recognized modeling languages such as Petri-Nets or the Event Driven Process Chain (EPC), the Business Process Modeling Notation (BPMN) receives considerable attention. Petri-Nets and EPC are examples of constantly evolving modeling languages, which are not subject to groundbreaking changes. During the consolidation phase, drawing from well-recognized modeling languages is likely to be seen as a desirable way to demonstrate rigor in research papers.

- **Establishment:** The stage of establishment can be seen as final stage of a modeling language's lifecycle. In this stage, few state-of-the-art modeling languages might be identified that can easily be discriminated in terms of the scenarios they support. In the light of their individual strength, there is no stiff competition. As IS can be considered to be a comparatively new research discipline, it can be questioned if any modeling language already has reached this stage, yet the most convincing candidates are ERM or UML Class Diagrams in the area of data modeling.

As stated above, customer solutions are not exactly an entirely new concept (Section 1). Nevertheless, in the light of their increasing recognition, modeling languages for customer solutions have only recently become the focus of attention on a significant scale [42, 61]. Partially, conventional modeling languages are used to display either physical goods or services, but lack the integrative perspective of customer solutions. Even so, some specialized modeling languages have been proposed which their authors claim to be usable in a PSS context. Therefore, we conclude that conceptual modeling in the context of PSS is most likely in the conquest stage at this time.

In the conquest stage, one has to decide whether to build a modeling language from scratch or advance or synthesize existing modeling languages. We propose a four-step method to achieve this. In step 1, conceptual modeling languages are identified in order to explore related work in this area. In step 2, each of the identified modeling languages is evaluated with a set of previously specified criteria. While these criteria need to be derived from the environment in which the modeling language shall be used, the requirements catalog as presented in the preceding chapter can be useful as a reference to inform this process. In the evaluation, it can be ascertained, how well existing modeling languages can be applied to the scenario. In step 3, it has to be decided whether one of the identified modeling languages sufficiently addressed the modeling needs, or if a new modeling language needs to be designed. In the latter case, one needs to determine if the new language can be designed based on selectively integrating the concepts of other modeling languages or if a new modeling language needs to be designed from scratch. In step 4, some selected candidates may be subjected to a more detailed analysis concerning their meta models. Consequently, the meta models of suitable candidates for modification might be integrated with each other or extended by additional language constructs not contained in the original languages (cf. Figure 6).

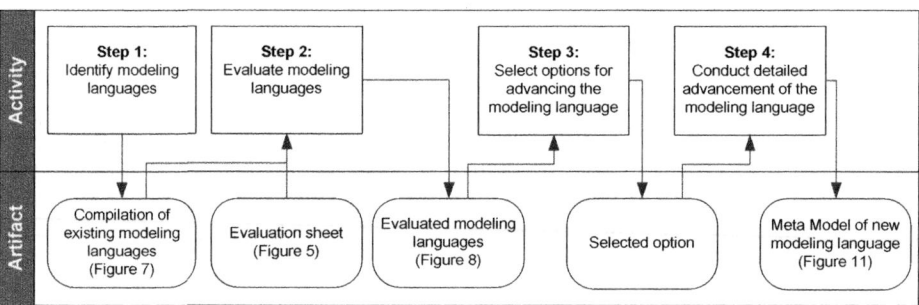

Fig. 6. Proposed method for the selective design of conceptual modeling languages in the conquest stage

3.2   Demonstration of the Method in the Area of PSS

In the following subsections, the proposed method will be demonstrated by designing a new modeling language for a PSS setting, based on integrating the meta models of other modeling languages.

Step 1: Identify Modeling Languages

For advancing modeling languages for customer solutions in the context of PSS, several modeling languages have been identified as suitable starting candidates as enumerated in Fig. 7. From this list, we have selected seven modeling languages for a thorough analysis with the criteria proposed in the requirements catalogue which we have grey shaded in Fig. 7.

Source	Modeling Language
Belz (1997)	Proplan
Bitner, Ostrom, Morgan (2007); Kingman-Brundage (1994); Fließ (2001); Shostack (1981); Shostack (1984); Shostack (2001)	Service Blueprinting
Black et al. (2007)	ITSM-Model
Bley et al. (2003)	Integrated product and process model
Bossmann (2007)	CAD
Botta (2007); Steinbach, Botta, Weber (2005)	PDD-Approach
Congram, Epelmann (1995)	Structured Analysis and Design Technique (SADT)
Corsten, Gössinger (2003)	Framework for integrative Modeling
Dadam et al. (1995)	EPAT
Dietrich, Kirn (2005)	EwoMacs
Emmrich (2005)	Business Integration Model
Gu (1995)	General Product Modeling
Hartel (2004)	Collaborative Blueprinting
Klein (2007)	Model-based Service System Engineering
Klein, Schreiner, Seemann (2003)	K3-Method
Kunau, Loser, Herrmann (2005)	SeeMe
Manavazhi (2000)	Hybrid Modeling Framework
Mason (2002); Pratt (2001); Koonce and Judd (2001); IAI (2008); ISO (1995)	STEP/EXPRESS-G
Maussang, Zwolinski, Brissaud (2005)	Sakao's Service Representation
Rainfurth, Tegtmeyer, Lay (2005)	Industrial Service Blueprinting
Scheer (1994)	Event Driven Process Chain (EPC)
Schmied (2002)	ProMod
Schnieder (2001); Ahrens et al. (2000)	GMA 7.21
Shostack (1977); Shostack (1982); Shostack (1984)	Molecular Model
Winkelmann (2007); Winkelmann and Luczak (2006)	Coloured Petri Nets for Service Simulation

Fig. 7. A compilation and selection of modeling languages, see also [9]

Step 2: Evaluate Modeling Languages

The features of each of the selected modeling languages were matched with the proposed modeling requirements of customer solutions. According to this exploration, the as-is capabilities of the analyzed modeling languages are depicted in Fig. 8. Results can be used to ascertain which features can already be displayed by current modeling languages, while other requirements can be shown to have remained unaddressed. Gaps can be seen as potential areas for extensions with features incorporated from other modeling languages.

Although some modeling languages provide constructs for a variety of requirements, none of the modeling languages is capable of accounting for all the proposed modeling requirements. E.g. interfaces between physical goods and services as well as the configuration and offering of customer solutions are seldom addressed.

In addition to general deficiencies, the investigated modeling languages are unlikely to display features originating from other research areas than the one from which the modeling language emerged. We make the following observations in this regard:

- Modeling languages not originating from an engineering background usually lack a representation of static product data, such as bill-of-materials and lifecycle data (referring to maintenance cycles) on a component level of detail. This seems to suggest that service processes are often conducted without a clear reference to the technical object worked upon in a service process. However, this information would be helpful to inform service technicians, to identify spare parts or to schedule maintenance intervals. In addition, such models could be used to trace all service events that have been performed on a machine. This could, in turn, enable manufacturing companies to make sense of this information in order to offer more sophisticated and reliable performance contracting business models. Moreover, the interdependencies of the physical goods components and service components cannot be modeled in sufficient details, such as to how a bill-of-material of a physical good might change if the underlying business models or service processes are altered. Much work needs to be done here to provide more integrated modeling support.
- Modeling languages not originating from an SCM background tend not to display the IT systems as well as business units involved in service and manufacturing processes. As service processes tend to be labor intensive and require information to be delivered at the correct 'moment of truth', providing these constructs seems to hold significant potential to assign resources and information on time. The ultimate vision is to enable an integrated planning of manufacturing processes and service processes with reference to an integrated pool of resources. This could further increase the overall efficiency of service processes. Just like for product-modeling, various modeling languages exist that can be re-utilized in other languages.
- Modeling languages not stemming from a service marketing point-of-view are unlikely to address the type and intensity of customer integration, e.g. by

displaying the line of interaction and line of visibility towards customers. Acknowledging customers as important members of PSS and as co-creators of value implies accounting for their information and resource input during the service processes. Hence, customers need to be better represented in conceptual models in the PSS domain. This information could be used to improve the overall efficiency of processes of value co-creation between service providers and customers, based on linking up master data and transaction data from either side.

- Environmental aspects remain largely unaddressed by all the evaluated modeling languages. Until now, we failed to identify any formal modeling language specially designed for this purpose. This indicates that new modeling support is needed in this area that cannot be satisfied by integrating the constructs of existing modeling languages. Such modeling support would be desirable in order to model and compare the ecological footprint of customer solution instances in order to select the most sustainable option. In the light of scarce ecological resources and the rise of legal regulations in this area, this issue might constitute a particularly promising vista for future research in PSS modeling.

Step 3: Select Options for Advancing the Modeling Language

The abovementioned deficiencies are not surprising, since the analyzed modeling languages have been designed for particular purposes that are not necessarily in line with all the comprehensive modeling needs found in a PSS context. In addition, no modeling language alone can reasonably include modeling constructs to account for all phenomena found in PSS. Therefore, each designer is likely faced with the need to adapt a modeling language to the particular needs encountered in a scenario.

For business process modeling in a PSS context, this can be done by proposing a new meta model based on integrating other modeling languages. A promising step is to identify the modeling language closest to the desired properties, integrate their meta models [37], and propose additional graphical notations for the new elements. Since meta models of different modeling languages are often specified in different notations also, a first step towards integration is to specify meta models with the same modeling language. Consecutively, a comparison of the meta models can show compatible starting-points for the integration. Eventually, a new meta model is created by integrating subsets from both original meta models. This new meta model can then be used to instantiate conceptual models to represent the desired properties.

Step 4: Conduct Detailed Advancement of the Modeling Language

After the strategy for designing the new modeling language has been set up, the meta model integration has to be performed. In the following, we illustrate this approach by combining features provided by the Event-Driven Process Chain (EPC) and the Service Blueprinting approach.

Modeling language	Molecular Model, Service Blueprinting	SeeMe	SADT	EPC	Coloured Petri Nets for Service Simulation	Business Integration Model	STEP / Express-G	Engineering	SCM	Marketing	Environmental
Customer Solutions subdivided into components	X	(X)	X	-	X	X	X	X			X
Reuse of the components as modules	X	-	X	-	X	X	X	X			
Configuration rules to specify inclusion (may)	-	-	-	-	-	-	X	X			
Configuration rules to specify exclusion (must not)	-	-	-	-	-	-	X	X			
Substituation of modules or components	-	-	-	-	-	-	X	X			X
Attributes of components / products	-	X	-	X	X	X	X	X		X	X
Longevity	-	-	-	-	(X)	X	X	X		X	X
Activities	X	X	X	X	X	X	(X)	X	X		
Control flow	X	X	X	X	X	X	(X)	X	X		
Flow of materials	-	-	-	X	(X)	(X)	-		X		X
Flow of information	-	X	X	X	-	-	-		X		
Cash flow	-	-	-	(X)	-	-	(X)		X	X	
Process cycle time	X	X	-	(X)	-	-	X		X	X	
Failure rate	(X)	-	-	(X)	X	-	X		X	X	
Capacity	-	-	-	(X)	X	-	X	X	X		
Consumption of operand resources (economic point of view)	X	X	X	(X)	X	X	X		X		
Consumption of operand resources (ecologic point of view)	-	-	-	(X)	-	X	-				X
Legal constraints	-	-	X	-	-	-	-				X
Value proposition for customers	-	-	-	-	-	-	-			X	
Marketing lifecycle	-	-	-	-	X	-	-			X	
Line of visibility towards customers	X	-	-	-	-	-	-		X	X	
Line of interaction towards customers	X	-	-	-	-	X	-		X	X	
Relationships / lines towards other stakeholders	(X)	-	(X)	-	-	(X)	-		X	X	
Quality standards	-	-	X	-	X	-	(X)	X			
Service level agreements	-	-	-	-	-	-	-			X	
IT Systems and applications	-	X	X	X	X	(X)	(X)		X		
Data (e.g. master data)	(X)	X	-	X	-	(X)	X		X		
Personnel allocation	(X)	X	X	X	X	(X)	-		X	X	
Qualifikation of personnel	-	(X)	X	-	-	(X)	(X)		X	X	
Organisational units	-	X	X	X	X	-	-		X	X	
Resources to be introduced by customers	X	(X)	(X)	X	X	X	-		X	X	

Fig. 8. As-is capabilities of modeling languages in the light of the modeling requirements of customer solutions, see also [9]

One of the most important goals for service providers is to ensure an appropriate integration with customers in service processes [62]. Recommendations for structuring provider activities that focus on customer interaction have been discussed exhaustively in the (service) marketing literature. Amongst these approaches, Service Blueprinting [10, 27, 81] is characterized by a particularly high degree of differentiation.

The approach differentiates activities at different layers, confined by 'lines'. For example the 'line of interaction' separates customer activities from provider activities, whereas the 'line of visibility' separates customer-perceivable activities of the provider ('onstage activities') from customer-imperceptible activities of the provider ('backstage activities'). A meta model of the service blueprinting approach is depicted in Fig. 9.

As service blueprinting traditionally was rather meant as a diagrammatic illustration of service processes and not intended to be a formal modeling language, we reconstructed the depicted meta model from exemplary models that have been created in the blueprint notation. With its focus on the analysis of customer integration, Service Blueprinting has advantages and drawbacks when compared to the EPC [74].

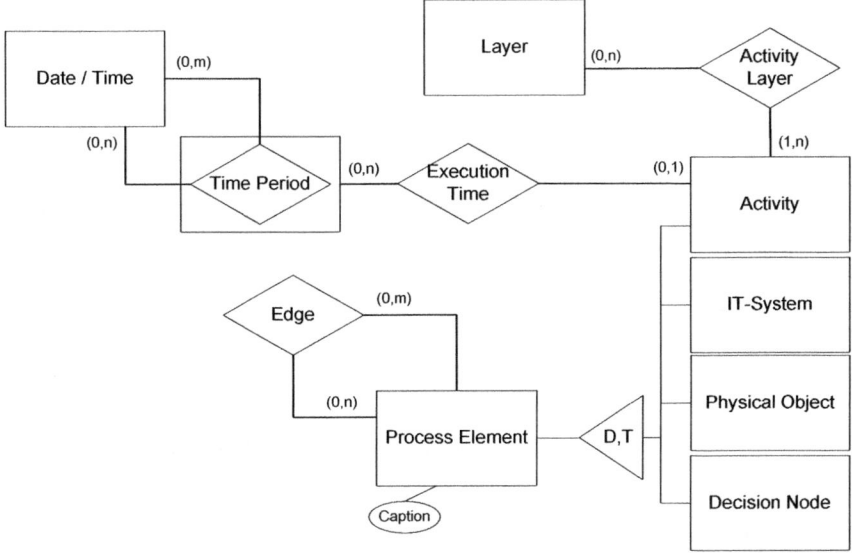

Fig. 9. Reconstructed meta model of the Service Blueprinting approach as proposed by Bitner, Olstrom and Morgan [10]

EPC is one of the central modeling techniques provided in the ARIS framework. EPCs are bipartite, directed graphs which comprise three basic elements (functions, events and logical connectors) indicating the control flow of a business process. The EPC meta model is depicted in Fig. 10. Various extensions of the EPC can be found in specific domains such as knowledge and document management, e-Government, or risk management [58, 59]. From the perspective of PSS, specific extensions with regard to the analysis and specification of customer activities should additionally be made.

The composition of constructs drawn from the languages of Service Blueprinting and EPC can be specified in a new meta model, which comprises elements from both approaches (Fig. 11 depicts an excerpt as an Entity Relationship Model). Areas of

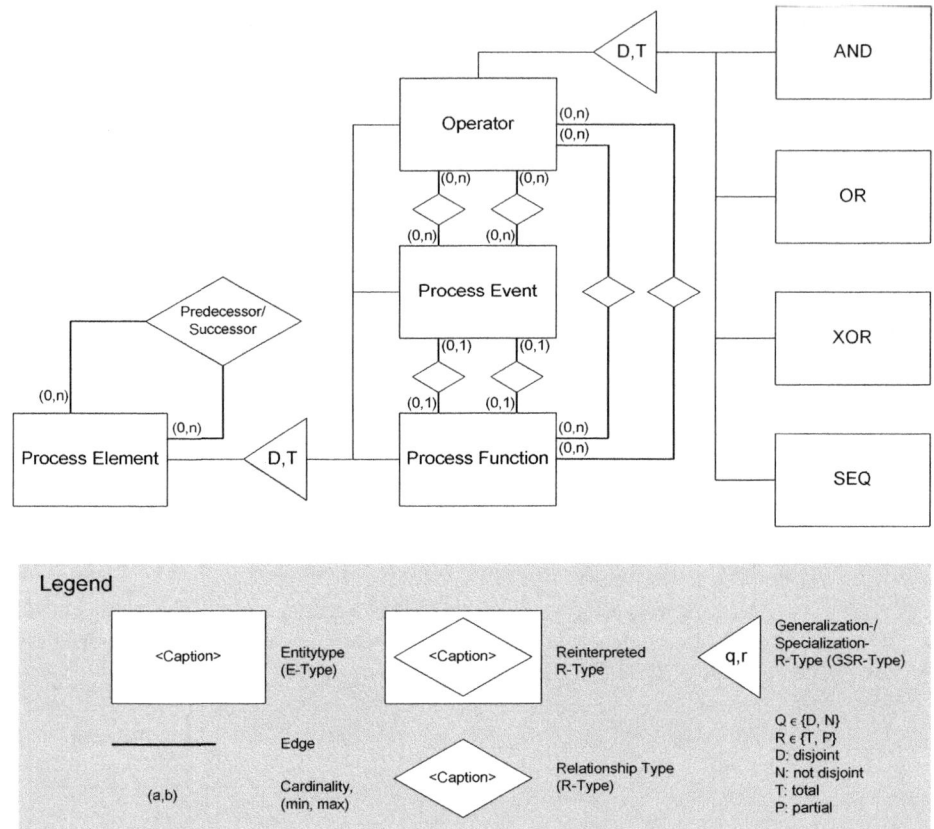

Fig. 10. Excerpt of the meta model of the EPC approach [6]

activity, which are divided by the lines of the Service Blueprinting approach, extend the conceptual aspects of the EPC for a proper analysis of customer activities. Therefore, the new modeling language can display business processes designed with the modeling constructs of the EPC, confined by the lines introduced in the Service Blueprinting approach.

In order to design conceptual models with the new modeling language, graphical notation constructs that correspond to the modeling constructs specified in the new meta model need to be proposed. While some of the notation constructs contained in the integrated modeling languages can be reused, we propose to depict the new 'areas' by means of a swim-lane notation. This leads to a segmentation of the business processes modeled with the EPC notation confined by the lines proposed in the service blueprinting approach. Alternative notations could disregard the swim-lane notation and use a different coloration for the various functions (such as onstage and backstage functions) instead, with each color representing a specific layer.

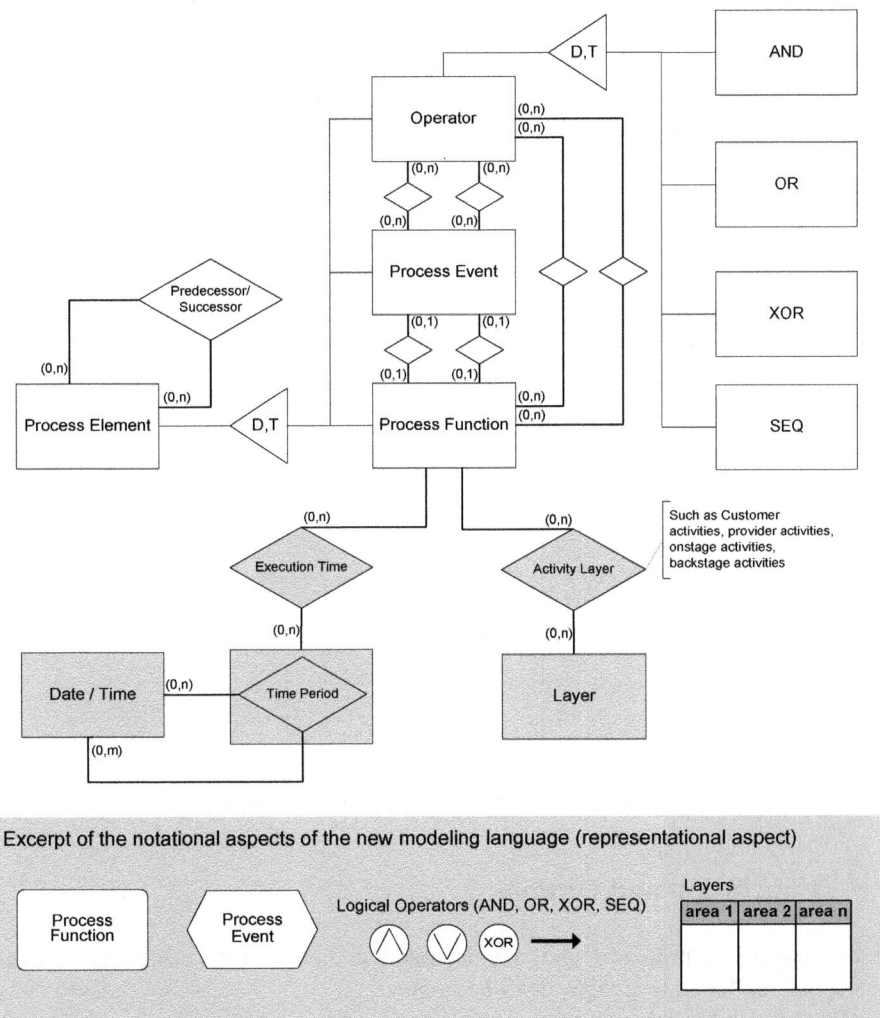

Fig. 11. Conceptual and representational aspects of the new integrated modeling language (elements stemming from the Service Blueprinting approach shaded in grey)

The new modeling language features an increased expressiveness compared to the expressiveness of either of the integrated languages. This is due to new options for designing conceptual models. For instance, due to introducing differing activity areas into the classic EPC notation, the new modeling method is able to support analyses such as 'Where are the interaction points with external stakeholders in our business processes?'. This issue is especially important when designing the integration of the customer into service processes and could not be fully addressed in either of the two original modeling languages alone.

A basic conceptual model created with the proposed integrated modeling language is depicted in Fig. 12 in order to illustrate the proposed swim-lane notation.

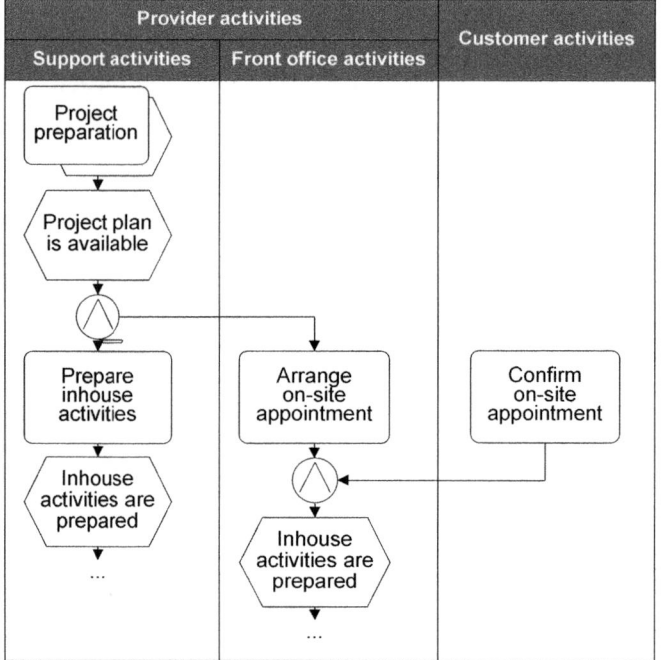

Fig. 12. Basic exemplary model created with the new modeling language

4   Conclusion and Outlook

In this paper we proposed and demonstrated a method for selectively designing conceptual modeling languages in a PSS context.

We started by arguing that the creation and provision of customer solutions is a crucial issue, particularly for traditional manufacturing companies. Designing and delivering customer solutions is however a complex undertaking since it requires the cooperation of various business units, companies and customers in PSS. In particular, an integration of goods manufacturing and service provision requires an exchange of data as well as an integration of business processes among manufacturers, service providers, and customers.

Conceptual models are a well-established means to cope with these challenges. In order to make conceptual modeling usable in a PSS context, the language constructs needed to model objects in this domain have to be specified. Therefore, we derived a catalogue of desired modeling constructs by drawing from four disciplines involved in service research. This complements an analysis that were performed earlier to investigate current modeling languages and reference models in PSS, guided by a conceptual framework for PSS engineering [4]. Moreover, some results were utilized to identify features that need to be incorporated into service description languages [9].

After identifying the modeling constructs desired in PSS settings, conceptual modeling languages can be designed to provide these constructs as well as a suitable graphical notation. As a method to accomplish this, we presented a method to develop, consolidate, extend, and establish modeling language support that was inspired by a general lifecycle model for modeling languages.

To demonstrate the method, we evaluated a selection of modeling languages in the area of PSS, originating from different research areas with the proposed evaluation criteria. We found that adequate support of conceptual modeling by modeling languages for PSS is lacking, as the modeling languages under consideration tended not to adopt an interdisciplinary point of view. Instead, they are restricted to the core phenomena dealt with in the research discipline from which they originate. While this might be satisfactory for the concerns of each discipline alone, the development and operation of sophisticated business models in a real-life PSS context requires data and business processes to be integrated.

To demonstrate the integration of modeling languages for increased expressiveness, we integrated modeling constructs from the EPC and Service Blueprinting meta models. Since no meta model had previously been released for the Service Blueprinting approach, it was reconstructed from analyzing conceptual models designed with this approach. The integrated modeling language incorporates features both modeling languages and therefore is of increased expressiveness.

Notably, the motivation for this paper was not to propose 'yet another' modeling language for PSS, but to propose a method for selectively extending and adapting conceptual modeling languages for this domain. Researchers and practitioners are encouraged to apply the proposed modeling criteria to their own PSS scenarios and design their own modeling languages or data models by selectively building on previous modeling languages.

This paper is, therefore, meant to act as a starting point to develop a more advanced support of conceptual modeling in the area of PSS. With the results we strive to propose directions for extensions to be made to existing modeling languages. This might help to encourage further interdisciplinary research activities carried out in the currently emerging disciplines of Service Science and Service Science Management and Engineering (SSME).

Acknowledgement. This paper was written in the context of the research projects FlexNet and ServPay. Both projects are funded by the German Federal Ministry of Education and Research (BMBF), promotion signs 01FD0629 and 02PG1010. We thank the project management agencies *German Aerospace Center* (PT-DLR) and *Forschungszentrum Karlsruhe* (PTKA) for their support.

References

1. Ahrens, W., Felleisen, M., Schnieder, E., Chouikha, M.: Formale Prozessbeschreibungen - gestern, heute und morgen. Atp – Automatisierungstechnische Praxis 42(9), 24–32
2. Anderl, R., Trippner, D.: STEP: standard for the exchange of product model data, Gabler, Wiesbaden (2000)
3. Baldwin, C.Y., Clark, K.B.: Managing in an Age of Modularity. Harvard Business Review, 84–93 (September-October 1997)
4. Becker, J., Beverungen, D., Knackstedt, R.: The Challenge of Conceptual Modeling for Product-Service Systems – Status-quo and Perspectives for Reference Models and Modeling Languages. Information Systems and e-Business Management 8(1), 12–32 (2010)
5. Becker, J., Beverungen, D., Knackstedt, R., Müller, O.: Model-Based Decision Support for the Customer-Specific Configuration of Value Bundles. Enterprise Modelling and Information Systems Architectures 4, 26–38 (2009)
6. Becker, J., Delfmann, P., Knackstedt, R., Kuropka, D.: Konfigurative Referenzmodellierung. In: Becker, J., Knackstedt, R. (eds.) Wissensmanagement mit Referenzmodellen. Konzepte für die Anwendungssystem- und Organisationsgestaltung. Physica, Heidelberg (2002)
7. Becker, J., Knackstedt, R., Beverungen, D., Glauner, C., Stypmann, M., Rosenkranz, C., Schmitt, R., Hatfield, S., Schmitz, G., Eberhardt, S., Dietz, M., Thomas, O., Walter, P., Lönngren, H.M., Leimeister, J.-M.: Ordnungsrahmen für die hybride Wertschöpfung. In: Proceedings of the GI-Workshop Service Modeling, pp. 95–114. Springer, Heidelberg (2008)
8. Belz, C.: Industrie als Dienstleister. St. Gallen (1997)
9. Beverungen, D., Matzner, M., Müller, O., Becker, J.: Product-Service System Approaches: A Business Perspective on Service Modeling. In: Barros, A., Oberle, D. (eds.) Handbook of Service Description: USDL and its Methods. Springer, New York (in press)
10. Bitner, M.J., Ostrom, A.L., Morgan, F.N.: Service Blueprinting: A Practical Tool for Service Innovation. In: Working Paper / Center for Services Leadership, Arizona State University (2007)
11. Black, J., Draper, C., Lococo, T., Matar, F., Ward, C.: An integration model for organizing IT service management. IBM Systems Journal 46(3), 405–422 (2007)
12. Bley, H., Bernardi, M., Schmitt, B., Zenner, C.: Assembly planning of mini and micro products enhanced by an integrated product and process model. In: Proceedings of the IPAS 2003 (International Precision Assembly Seminar), S. Bad Hofgastein, pp. 31–38 (2003)
13. Bossmann, M.: Feature-basierte Produkt- und Prozessmodelle in der integrierten Produktentstehung. Schriftenreihe Produktionstechnik / Universität des Saarlandes, Band 38 (2007)
14. Botta, C.: Rahmenkonzept zur Entwicklung von Product-Service Systems. Lohmar et al (2007)
15. Bullinger, H.-J.: Service Engineering: Ein Rahmenkonzept für die systematische Entwicklung von Dienstleistungen. In: Bullinger, H.-J., Scheer, A.-W. (eds.) Service Engineering. Entwicklung und Gestaltung innovativer Dienstleitungen, pp. 51–82. Springer, Berlin (2003)
16. Bullinger, H.J., Scheer, A.W. (eds.): Service Engineering – Entwicklung und Gestaltung innovativer Dienstleistungen, 2nd edn. Springer, Berlin (2006)
17. Bulos, D.: OLAP Database Design. A New Dimension. In: Chamoni, P., Gluchowski, P. (eds.) Analytische Informationssysteme. Data Warehouse, On-Line Analytical Processing, Data Mining. Berlin et al., pp. 251–261 (1998)

18. Congram, C., Epelman, M.: How to describe your service – An invitation to the structured analysis and design technique. International Journal of Service Industry Management 6(2), 6–23 (1995)
19. Corsten, H., Gössinger, R.: Rahmenkonzept zur integrativen Modellierung von Dienstleistungen. Schriften zum Produktionsmanagement (58) (2003)
20. Dadam, P., Kuhn, K., Reichert, M., Beuter, T., Nathe, M.: ADEPT: Ein integrierender Ansatz zur Entwicklung flexibler, zuverlässiger kooperierender Assistenzsysteme in klinischen Anwendungsumgebungen. In: Informatik-Berichte / Universität Ulm, vol. (95-07) (1995)
21. Dalal, N.P., Kamath, M., Kolarik, W.J., Sivaraman, E.: Toward an Integrated Framework for Modeling Enterprise Processes. Communications of the ACM 47(3), 83–87 (2004)
22. Dietrich, B.: Ressource Planning for Business Services. Communications of the ACM 49(7), 62–64 (2006)
23. Dietrich, A.J., Kirn, S.: Flexible Wertschöpfungsnetzwerke in der kundenindividuellen Massenfertigung – Ein service-orientiertes Modell für die Schuhindustrie. In: Ferstl, O.K., Sinz, E.J., Eckert, S., Isselhorst, T. (eds.) Wirtschaftsinformatik 2005, Heidelberg, pp. 23–42 (2005)
24. Emmrich, A.: Ein Beitrag zur systematischen Entwicklung produktbegleitender Dienstleistungen. Paderborn (2005)
25. Engelhardt, W.H., Kleinaltenkamp, M., Reckenfelderbäumer, M.: Leistungsbündel als Absatzobjekte. Ein Ansatz zur Überwindung der Dichotomie von Sach- und Dienstleistungen. Zeitschrift für betriebswirtschaftliche Forschung 45(5), 395–426 (2003); EU (2003): Directive 2002/96/EC of the European Parliament and of the Counsil of 27 January 2003 on waste electrical and electronic equipment
26. Fließ, S.: Die Steuerung von Kundenintegrationsprozessen. Deutscher Universitätsverlag, Wiesbaden (2001)
27. Fließ, S., Kleinaltenkamp, M.: Blueprinting the service company: Managing service processes efficiently. Journal of Business Research 57(4), 392–405 (2004)
28. Fitzsimmons, J.A., Fitzsimmons, M.J.: Service Management – Operations, Strategy, and Information Technology, 3rd edn. McGraw-Hill, Inc., Boston and others (2001)
29. Ganz, W.: Germany: Service Engineering. Communications of the ACM 49(7), 79 (2006)
30. Garud, R., Kumaraswamy, A.: Technological and organizational designs for realizing economies of substitution. In: Garud, R., Kumaraswamy, A., Langlois, N. (eds.) Managing in the Modular Age, Architectures, Networks, and Organizations, pp. 45–77. Blackwell Publishing, Malden et al (2003)
31. German Standards Institute (DIN): Publicly Available Specification 1094: Product-Service Systems – Value Creation by Integrating Goods and Services. Beuth Verlag, Berlin (2009) (forthcoming)
32. Gu, P., Chan, K.: Product modelling using STEP. Computer-Aided Design 27(3), 163–179 (1995)
33. Hanna, M.D., Newman, W.R.: Integrated Operations Management: A Supply Chain Perspective, 2nd edn. South-Western, Div of Thomson Learning (2006)
34. Harren, A., Herden, O.: MML und mUML – Sprache und Werkzeug zur Unterstützung des konzeptionellen Data Warehouse Designs. In: Proceedings 2.GI-Workshop Data Mining und Data Warehousing als Grundlage moderner entscheidungsunterstützender Systeme (DMDW 1999), Magdeburg, pp. 57–68 (1999)
35. Hartel, I.: Aufbau und Betrieb eines kooperativen Dienstleistungsmanagements in der Investitionsgüterindustrie. In: Kreibich, R. (ed.) Erfolg mit Dienstleistungen. Stuttgart, pp. 47–54 (2004)

36. Hausmann, J.H., Heckel, R., Sauer, S.: Dynamic Meta Modeling with Time: Specifying the Semantics of Multimedia Sequence Diagrams. Journal of Software and Systems Modeling (SOSYM) 3(3), 181–193 (2004)
37. Höfferer, P.: Achieving business process model interoperability using metamodels and ontologies. In: Proceeding of the 15th European Conference on Information Systems, St. Gallen, Switzerland (2007)
38. Holten, R.: Entwicklung einer Modellierungstechnik für Data-Warehouse-Fachkonzepte. In: Schmidt, H. (ed.) Modellierung Betrieblicher Informationssysteme: Proceedings der MobIS-Fachtagung, Siegen, pp. 3–21 (2000)
39. Hunt, S.D.: On the service-centered dominant logic of marketing. Journal of Marketing 68(1), 21–22 (2004)
40. IAI International Alliance for Interoperability: Data Modeling Using EXPRESS-G for IFC Development,
    `http://www.iai-international.org/Model/documentation/`
    `Data_Modeling_Using_EXPRESS-G_for_IFC_Development.pdf`
    (last accessed: April 11, 2008)
41. International Standards Organization (ISO): Product Data Interchange using STEP (PDES) Part 11 – The EXPRESS Language Reference Manual (1995)
42. Kern, H., Böttcher, M., Kühne, S., Meyer, K.: Ganzheitliche Erstellung und Verarbeitung von Dienstleistungsmodellen. In: Thomas, O., Nüttgens, M. (eds.) Dienstleistungsmodellierung – Methoden, Werkzeuge und Branchenlösungen. Springer, Berlin (2008)
43. Kingman-Brundage, J., George, W.R., Bowen, D.E.: Service logic: achieving service system integration. International Journal of Service Industry Management 6(4), 20–39 (1994)
44. Klein, R.: Modellgestütztes Service System Engineering. Deutscher Universitätsverlag, Wiesbaden (2007)
45. Klein, L., Schreiner, P.: Seemann, C.: Die Dienstleistungen im Griff – Erfolgreich gründen mit System. Stuttgart (2003)
46. Knackstedt, R., Klose, K., Niehaves, B., Becker, J.: Process Reference Model for Data Warehouse Development. A consensus-oriented approach. In: Chen, C.-S., Filipe, J., Seruca, I., Cordeiro, J. (eds.) Proceedings of the Seventh International Conference on Enterprise Information Systems, ICEIS 2005, Miami, USA, vol. III, pp. 499–505 (2005)
47. Koonce, D.A., Judd, R.P.: A visual modeling language for EXPRESS schema. International Journal of Computer Integrated Manufacturing 14(5), 457–472 (2001)
48. Kraemer, W., Zimmermann, V.: Public Service Engineering - Planung und Realisierung innovativer Verwaltungsprodukte. In: Scheer, A.-W. (ed.) Rechnungswesen und EDV: Kundenorientierung in Industrie, Dienstleistung und Verwaltung, vol. 17, p. 574. Saarbrücker Arbeitstagung. Physica, Heidelberg (1996)
49. Kunau, G., Loser, K.-U., Herrmann, T.: Im Spannungsfeld zwischen formalen und informellen Aspekten: Modellierung von Dienstleistungen mit SeeMe. In: Herrmann, T., Kleinbeck, U., Krcmar, H. (eds.) Konzepte für das Service Engineering – Modularisierung, Prozessgestaltung und Produktivitätsmanagement. Springer, Heidelberg (2005)
50. Madhavaram, S., Hunt, S.D.: The service-dominant logic and a hierarchy of operant resources: developing masterful operant resources and implications for marketing strategy. Journal of the Academy of Marketing Science 36(1), 67–82 (2008)
51. Maglio, P.P., Spohrer, J.: Fundamentals of Service Science. Journal of the Academy of Marketing Science 36(1), 18–20 (2008)
52. Manavazhi, M.R.: Hybird modelling framework for synthesizing virtual structures. Construction Management and Economics 18, 415–426 (2000)

53. Mason, H.: ISO 10303 - STEP: A key standard for the global market. In: ISO Bulletin, pp. 9–13 (January 2002)
54. Maussang, N., Zwolinski, P., Brissaud, D.: Design of Product-Service Systems. In: 10th ERSCP (European Roundtable on Sustainable Consumption and Production) (2005)
55. Mercer: Mercer-Analyse, Service im Maschinenbau – Ungenutzte Chancen im Servicegeschäft (2003)
56. Mont, O.: Product-service systems: Panacea or myth? PhD thesis, Lund University (2004)
57. Morelli, N.: Designing Product/Service Systems: A Methodological Exploration. Design Issues 18(3) (Summer 2002)
58. Nüttgens, M., Rump, F.: EPK 2002 – Geschäftsprozessmanagement mit Ereignisgesteuerten Prozessketten. In: Proceedings of the first Workshop der Gesellschaft für Informatik e. V (GI). Trier (2002)
59. Nüttgens, M., Rump, F.: EPK 2003 – Geschäftsprozessmanagement mit Ereignisgesteuerten Prozessketten. In: Proceedings of the 2nd Workshop der Gesellschaft für Informatik e. V. Bamberg (2003)
60. OECD: Enhancing the Performance of the Service Sector, Online Resource (2005), http://www.value-chains.org/dyn/bds/docs/497/Wolf1OECDEnhancingPerformanceServicesSector.pdf (accessed February 20, 2008)
61. O'Sullivan, J.: Towards a Precise Understanding of Service Properties. Dissertation, Queensland University of Technology, Brisbane (2006)
62. Palmer, A., Cole, C.: Services marketing – Principles and practice, Englewood Cliffs, New York (1995)
63. Parasuraman, A., Zeithaml, V.A., Berry, L.L.: SERVQUAL – Multiple-Item Scale for Measuring Customer Perceptions of Service Quality. Journal of Retailing 64(1), 12–40 (1988)
64. Payne, A.F., Storbacka, K., Frow, P.: Managing the co-creation of value. Journal of the Academy of Marketing Science 36(1), 83–96 (2008)
65. Pratt, M.J.: Introduction to ISO 10303 - the STEP Standard for Product Data Exchange. Journal of Computer and Information Science and Engineering 1(1), 102–103 (2001)
66. ProSTEP iViP: Architektur und Aufbau, http://www.prostep.org/de/standards/was/ausbau (accessed December 31, 2007)
67. Quinn, J.B., Doorley, T.L., Paquette, P.C.: Beyond Products: Service-Based Strategy. Harvard Business Review 68(2), 58–67 (1990)
68. Quinn, J.B., Baruch, J.J., Paquette, P.C.: Exploiting the Manufacturing-Services Interface. Sloan Management Review 29(4), 45–56 (1988)
69. Rai, A., Sambamurthy, V.: Editorial Notes-The Growth of Interest in Services Management: Opportunities for Information Systems Scholars. Information Systems Research 17(4), 327–331 (2006)
70. Rainfurth, C., Tegtmeyer, S., Lay, G.: Organisation produktbegleitender Dienstleistungen. In: Lay, G., Nippa, M. (eds.) Management Produktbegleitender Dienstleistungen, pp. 99–119. Springer, Heidelberg (2005)
71. Sakao, T., Shimomura, Y.: Service Engineering: A novel engineering discipline for producers to increase value combining service and product. Journal of Cleaner Production 15, 590–604 (2007)

72. Sampson, S.E., Froehle, C.M.: Foundations and Implications of a Proposed Unified Services Theory. Production & Operations Management 15(2), 329–343 (2006)
73. Sapia, C., Blaschka, M., Höfling, G., Dinter, B.: Extending the E/R Model for the Multidimensional Paradigm. In: Proceedings of the International Workshop on Data Warehouse and Data Mining (DWDM 1998), Singapore, pp. 105–116 (1998)
74. Scheer, A.W.: Business Process Engineering. Reference Models for Industrial Enterprises, 2nd edn. Springer, Berlin (1994)
75. Scheer, A.-W.: ARIS - Vom Geschäftsprozess zum Anwendungssystem, 4th edn. Springer, Berlin (2002)
76. Scheer, A.W., Grieble, O., Klein, R.: Modellbasiertes Dienstleistungsmanagement. In: Bullinger, H.J., Scheer, A.W. (eds.) Service Engineering – Entwicklung und Gestaltung innovativer Dienstleistungen, 2nd edn., pp. 19–52. Springer, Berlin (2006)
77. Schmied, M.: Themenheft Service Engineering 2002, Bonn (2002)
78. Schmitz, G.: Der wahrgenommene Wert hybrider Produkte: Konzeptionelle Grundlagen und Komponenten. In: Proceedings of the Multikonferenz Wirtschaftsinformatik, Munich, pp. 665–683 (2008)
79. Schnieder, E.: Modellkonzepte in der Automatisierungstechnik. In: Engels, G., Oberweis, A., Zündorf, A. (eds.) Modellierung 2001, Bonn, pp. 7–17 (2001)
80. Seidel, S., Knackstedt, R., Janiesch, C.: Procedure Model for the Analysis and Design of Reporting Systems - A Case Study in Conceptual Modelling. In: Proceedings of the 17th Australasian Conference on Information Systems (ACIS 2006), Adelaide, Australia (2006)
81. Shostack, G.L.: Designing services that deliver. Harvard Business Review, 133–139 (January-February 1984)
82. Shostack, G.L.: Breaking free from Product Marketing. Journal of Marketing 41(2), 73–80 (1977)
83. Shostack, G.L.: How to design a service. European Journal of Marketing 16(1), 49–63 (1982)
84. Steinbach, M., Botta, C., Weber, C.: Integrierte Entwicklung von Product-Service Systems. Werkstatttechnik online, Jahrgang 95(H.7/8), 546–553 (2005)
85. Stille, F.: Product-related Services – Still Growing in Importance. DIW Economic Bulletin 40(6), 195–200 (2003)
86. Sturm, F., Bading, A., Schubert, M.: Investitionsgüterhersteller auf dem Weg zum Lösungsanbieter – Eine empirische Studie, Institut für Arbeitswissenschaft und Technologiemanagement, Stuttgart (2007)
87. Sturts, C.S., Griffis, F.H.: Pricing Engineering Services. Journal of Management in Engineering, 56–62 (April 2005)
88. Tan, A., McAloone, T.C., Andreasen, M.M.: What Happens to Integrated Product Development Models with Product/Service-System Approaches. In: Proceedings of the 6th Integrated Product Development Workshop, IPD 2006, October 18–20. Otto-von-Guericke-Universität Magdeburg, Schönebeck/Bad Salzelmen (2006)
89. Teboul, J.: Service is Front Stage: Positioning Services for Value Advantage, Palgrave Macmillan, Basingstone (2006)
90. Tukker, A., Tischner, U.: Product-services as a research field: past, present and future. Reflections from a decade of research. Journal of Cleaner Production 14, 1552–1556 (2006)
91. Tuli, K.R., Kohli, A.K., Bharadwaj, S.G.: Rethinking Customer Solutions: From Product Bundles to Relational Processes. Journal of Marketing 71(3), 1–17 (2007)

92. Vargo, S.L., Lusch, R.F.: The Four Service Marketing Myths. Remnants of a Goods-Based, Manufacturing Model. Journal of Service Research 6(4), 324–335 (2004)
93. Vargo, S., Lusch, R.F.: Service-dominant logic: continuing the evolution. Journal of the Academy of Marketing Science 36(1), 1–10 (2008)
94. Winkelmann, K.: Prospektive Bewertung der kooperativen Erbringung industrieller Dienstleistungen im Maschinenbau durch Simulation mit Petri-Netzen. Shaker Verlag, Aachen (2007)
95. Winkelmann, K., Luczak, H.: Modeling, simulation and prospective analysis of cooperative provision of industrial services using coloured Petri Nets. International Journal of Simulation 7(7), 10–26 (2006)
96. Wolff, F., Frank, U.: A Multiperspective Framework for Evaluating Conceptual Models in Organisatinal Change. In: Proceedings of the 15th European Conference on Information Systems (ECIS), St. Gallen, Switzerland (2005)

SC-CoJava: A Service Composition Language to Unify Simulation and Optimization of Supply Chains

Alexander Brodsky[1,2], Malak Al-Nory[1], and Hadon Nash[3]

[1] George Mason University, Virginia, USA
{brodsky,malnory}@gmu.edu
[2] Adaptive Decisions, Inc., Maryland, USA
[3] Google, California, USA
hadonn@gmail.com

Abstract. The Service Composition (SC) CoJava language extends the programming language Java with (1) a modular service composition framework; (2) an extensible library of supply-chain modeling components such as items, services and business metrics; and (3) decision *choice* constructs for program variables, assertions of constraints and a designation of a program variable to serve as the objective to be minimized or maximized. The SC-CoJava provides not only the procedural "simulation-like" semantics of Java, but also an optimization semantics. The optimization semantics of SC-CoJava amounts to (1) finding an *optimal* instantiation of values into the *choice*-variables, based on automatic construction of a standard optimization model and solving it using a mathematical programming solver, and then (2) executing the Java program procedurally, where all the decision *choice* values are taken from the optimization result.

Keywords: Service composition, Supply chain modeling, Java, Simulation, Optimization.

1 Introduction

1.1 Motivation

Service composition frameworks have emerged not only to support the best selection of services to meet business objectives, but primarily to insure that the resulting overall system is flexible and simple. These frameworks define a service as a particular unit of work that is accessible by independent users and systems through a standardized interface. As a result, the overall system is modeled as a composition of atomic or composite services. A supply chain is a network of services, and thus, can be viewed as a complex service, which is composed of interrelated subservices, such as distribution, transportation, manufacturing, and sourcing. In turn, these subservices may be composed of more basic services, and so on. In this paper we propose the language Service Composition (SC-) CoJava for fast construction of complex supply chain models. The SC-CoJava unified approach supports decisions using both simulation-like models and decision optimization based on Mathematical Programming.

D. Dolk et al. (Eds.): Decision Support Modeling in Service Networks, LNBIP 42, pp. 118–142, 2012.
© Springer-Verlag Berlin Heidelberg 2012

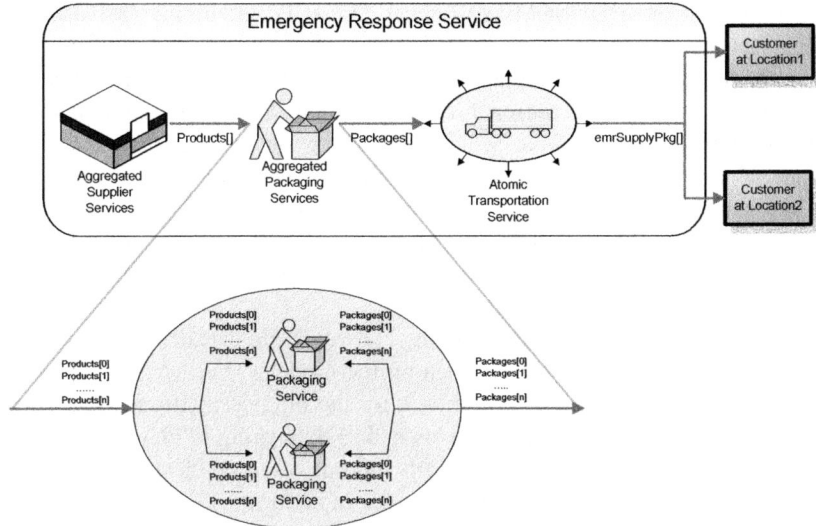

Fig. 1. Emergency Response Service supply chain

Consider an example of Emergency Response (ER) Service, depicted in Fig. 1. This service is responsible for delivering ER packages (with water, food, medicine, blankets,..etc.) to a number of designated ER locations. The service consists of a supply chain that involves (1) transportation services to deliver the packages to ER locations, (2) packaging services, to make the packages from individual products; and (3) supply services, to purchase and deliver individual products to packaging facilities. In turn, transportation services may involve multiple carriers of different kinds (e.g., full-truck-load or less-than-truckload). Similarly, there may be multiple packaging and supply sub-services (see sub-services in Fig. 1 expansion). A typical decision required may be how to deliver the packages to ER locations in the shortest amount of time subject to available resources, or how to minimize total cost within a fixed (short) amount of time. The outcome of such a decision is an actionable recommendation on precisely what packages, in what quantities should be delivered from which packaging facilities and by which transportation carriers, and which products should be purchased, and in what quantities from which suppliers.

1.2   The Challenge: Simulation vs. Optimization

To implement such an optimization problem, a typical Operations Research (OR) approach would be to construct a mathematical model, with decision variables, constraints, and an objective function, possibly using a modeling language such as AMPL [1] or GAMS [2], and then to solve it using an existing mathematical programming solver, e.g., for Mixed Integer Linear Programming (MILP). However, building such models is quite a challenging task, the more so for non-OR professionals, even for those with general computer science and software engineering skills.

As indicated in [3], one reason for that challenge is that the elements of an OR model are abstract constraints, which may have only an indirect connection to elements of a real-world process. For example, one equation may combine elements from several real-world services or devices. In the example of ER service, one equation might involve quantities of each package/product produced by each service (greater than or) equal to the quantities of the same package/product produced by all the other services.

Also, the notions of order and timing of events are usually not explicit in OR models, which puts an additional burden on the modeler. Furthermore, the execution of the optimization is typically a black box for the modeler, with no clear connection to the flow of the real world process. This makes debugging of an optimization model a challenging task. If the optimization fails there is often no clear explanation for the failure. Finally, OR models typically lack the modularity of modern object-oriented (OO) programming languages, so they tend to become difficult to maintain over time (like "spaghetti code").

By contrast, simulations are generally well understood by software developers. The elements of a simulation are state variables and state-transitions, which have a clear one-to-one correspondence with elements of a real-world process. Every quantity from the real-world process is represented by a single state variable, so there is little room for confusion. Real-world time and sequence of events correspond to time and sequence in the running simulation in an obvious way. In the ER Service example, the order in which the services are instantiated is indicated clearly in the simulation process. Also, the "cause and effect" progression of the simulation is easy to follow. If the simulation fails, the exact time and place of the failure is reported. Finally, simulation modelers can practice modern OO software engineering. Complex building blocks can be modeled using simpler building blocks, and so on. In fact, modern OO languages have been derived from early simulation systems. We will show in the next section how complex services in the supply chain, such as the one in the ER example, can be built easily from simple OO components.

While simulation offers numerous advantages in ease of modeling, testing and extensibility, OR modeling has one major advantage. If modeled correctly using a manageable constraint domain such as LP or MILP, an optimization problem can be solved efficiently using existing solvers with sophisticated optimization algorithms. By contrast, no such solvers exist for simulation models. Typically, simulations are optimized by choosing parameters manually. An optimization layer can be added by running a simulation multiple times, with possible heuristics. However, such a search cannot compete with performance of solvers on manageable constraint domains.

The CoJava language [3] proposed a unified model that offers both the advantages of simulation-like process modeling, and the capabilities of true decision optimization. However, in terms of modeling, CoJava only provides a basic Java environment, whereas a higher level of abstraction is desirable for fast modeling of supply chains like the one in the Emergency Response example. SC-CoJava was designed exactly for this purpose as we describe below.

1.3   Contributions

In this paper we propose the language Service Composition (SC) CoJava, describe its syntax and semantics, report on its implementation, and exemplify its use on an emergency response supply chain scenario.

Syntactically, SC-CoJava extends the programming language Java with (1) a modular service composition (SC) framework; (2) an extensible library of supply-chain modeling components such as items, services and business metrics; and (3) decision *choice* constructs for program variables, *assert* statements and a designation of a program variable to serve as the objective to be minimized or maximized.

A modular SC framework is based on the concepts of Items, Business Metrics, Service Information and (atomic or composed) Services, such as Distribution, Manufacturing, Transportation and Sourcing. Conceptually, a Service represents a transformation of incoming Items to outgoing Items and the associated Business Metrics, such as cost, profit or reliability. These SC framework concepts are modeled as Java abstract classes. A hierarchy of supply-chain modeling components that adhere to the SC framework are represented as subclasses of the abstract classes in a Java library. New service classes can be added, whether they are atomic or composed of previously defined service classes (e.g., from the SC library). A simulation semantics of an SC-CoJava program amounts to its execution as a regular Java program, where the variable *choice* statements are interpreted as a random selection of a value from within a given range, while *assert* statements and a designation of a program variable to be minimized or maximized are ignored.

The SC-CoJava provides not only the procedural "simulation-like" semantics of Java, but also an optimization semantics, which amounts to a two-step process. First, SC-CoJava finds an *optimal* instantiation of values into the *choice*-variables, i.e., one that would satisfy all the following *assert* statements, and lead to the minimal or maximal value of a designated program variable. This is done in SC-CoJava by automatic construction of a standard optimization model and solving it using a mathematical programming solver. Second, SC-CoJava executes the program procedurally, as a Java program, where all the decision *choice* values are taken from the optimization result. Note that SC-CoJava does not optimize using multiple simulation runs, but rather using a mathematical programming solver.

To exemplify the SC-CoJava framework, we developed an application to make decisions in emergency response situations. In this application we model the emergency response as a Service that is composed of a number of sub-services, which involve transportation, packaging and sourcing.

This paper is organized as follows. Section 2 discusses the SC framework and SC-CoJava simulation semantics. Section 3 focuses on the optimization semantics of SC-CoJava. Section 4 describes SC-CoJava implementation architecture. Section 5 discusses related work and Section 6 summarizes our results.

2   Service Composition Framework and Its Simulation Semantics

2.1   Conceptual SC Framework

Fig. 2 shows a partially expanded library of supply chain components that adhere to the Service Composition (SC) framework of SC-CoJava. The most important concept is that of a Service, to represent services such as Distribution, Manufacturing, Packaging, Supply, and Transportation. Conceptually, a service represents a transformation of incoming Items to outgoing Items.

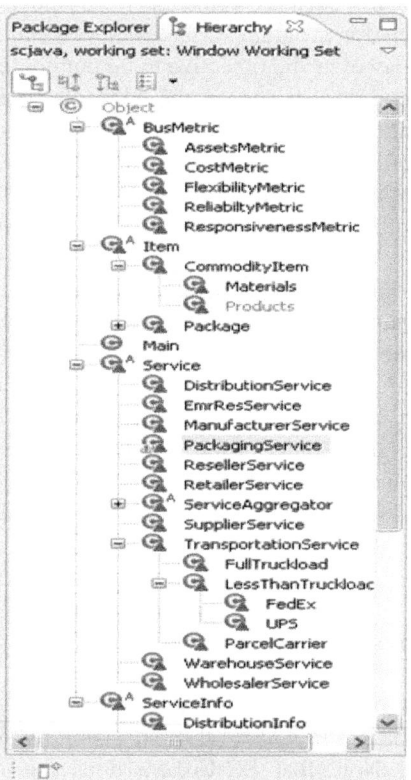

Fig. 2. SC-CoJava library partially expanded

For example, a Manufacturing service transforms Items of type Materials to Items of type Products. A Packaging service transforms items of type Products to items of type Packages. Or a Transportation service transforms Items of type Transportation Package to Items of the same type (with an instance indicating a different location). Some services have only incoming, but no outgoing Items, or the other way around. For example, a Supplier service has only outgoing Items of type Products, whereas a Demand service has only incoming Items.

Incoming and outgoing Items used in Services are characterized by multiple attributes such as quantity and location, which differ across Items of different types. Services are also associated with one or more Business Metrics, such as Reliability, Responsiveness, Flexibility, Assets, and Cost. We designed these metric classes in accordance to the performance measures of the de facto reference in supply chain services, i.e., Supply Chain Operations Reference Model (SCOR) [4]. Also, each Service has an associated Service Information. While Service instance represents a specific dynamic transaction (transformation), its corresponding Service Info instance represents more static parameters. For example, a Supplier Service Info may hold a price list of Items supplied by the Supplier Service, as well as volume discounts and their steps. This data is being used, for example, to compute the Business Metric Cost for a specific set of Items (and their quantities) supplied by a Supplier Service.

Services may be composed of other, more basic services. Fig. 1 shows an example of Emergency Response (ER) Service, described in the Introduction. ER Service has only outgoing Items of type Transportation Package, each characterized by quantity, delivery location, and the description of the more basic Items that compose the package. The ER Service is composed of three sub-services: Aggregated Supplier Services, which supply products to multiple packaging locations; Aggregated Packaging Services, which package products into packages to be shipped to designated ER locations; and a Transportation Service, that delivers incoming Items of type Package from packaging facilities to designated ER locations. In turn, the Aggregated Packaging and Supplier Services are composed of multiple atomic Services.

2.2   Java Representation and Simulation-Like Semantics

For the purpose of this section, we make use of the simulation-like semantics of SC-CoJava, which is the regular procedural semantics of Java. We explain the optimization semantics of SC-CoJava in the next section.

All SC framework components are represented in SC-CoJava as subclasses of the corresponding abstract classes: `Item`, `Service`, `ServiceInfo`, and `BusMetric`. The class Item has a number of concrete subclasses. For example, the class `Products` is a subclass of `CommodityItem`, which is in turn a subclass of `Item`. See Appendix A for all the Java classes that we refer to in this section.

The abstract class `ServiceInfo` has also a number of concrete subclasses. These classes provide specific data relevant to every service. Therefore, for every service type in SC-CoJava library (e.g., `ManufacturerService`, `WarehouseService`, `RetailerService`, etc.) we define a subclass of `ServiceInfo` to instantiate this service (e.g., `ManufacturerInfo`, `WarehouseInfo`, `RetailerInfo`, etc.)

An example of concrete subclasses of type `Service` is the `SupplierService`. The class constructor computes its cost by iterating over its outgoing items, i.e., `outProducts` and looking-up the price of each product at the `supplierInfo`'s price table. The service provides a discount if the cost reaches the specified threshold by the `supplierInfo`. The service then sums the cost (after discounts) and adds its fixed cost to instantiate its `costMetric`.

Similarly, `PackagingService` class constructor computes packaging costs by iterating over the volumes of its outgoing items, i.e., `outPackages` volumes, looking-up the corresponding unit fees in the `packagingInfo` fee table, and multiplying by the packages quantity. `PackagingService` also constructs its incoming items, i.e., `inProducts` by extracting the products objects from its `outPackages`.

`TransportationService` is an atomic service represented as a class that extends `Service`. A constructor of the `TransportationService` class requires providing the transportation information, the outgoing demanded packages, and the possible different locations from which the packages are going to be transported. A private method constructs the incoming items, i.e., `inPackages`, by assigning a non-deterministic value to each package quantity to be transported from each location within the range 0 to the demanded quantity of each package,

$$pkgQty = Nd.choice\ (0, outPackages[p].iQty);$$

In the simulation semantics of SC-CoJava, the default interpretation of the *Nd.choice* methods is the random selection of a real value (of type double) from the interval with boundaries indicated by its actual parameters. In the example above, from the interval [0,outPackages[p].iQty]. (We will explain the optimization semantics of this statement in the next section). The private method also uses an *assert* statement

$$assert\ (totPkgQty == outPackages[p].iQty);$$

which is ignored in the simulation semantics (except for an error message if the assertion is violated). The transportation service computes its cost by iterating over the incoming packages, i.e., `inPackages` and looking-up the location and the destination pair in the fee table of the service, and then multiplying the fee by the package weight and quantity. The service then sums up the costs of all packages, adds the fixed cost of this service, and uses this cost to instantiate the service's `CostMetric`.

Supplier Service Aggregator is an example of the Service Aggregator abstract class and a subclass of the abstract class Service Aggregator. The constructor of the Aggregated Supplier service takes as arguments `SuppliersInfo[]` and the items that should be produced by the service, i.e., `Products[]`. `SupplierSerAgg` does a similar job to the atomic Supplier service, but also constructs the atomic supplier services in the composition. The private method `aggSuppliers()` returns an array of `SupplierService[]`. For each possible supplier service provided by `SuppliersInfo[]`, it constructs a new outgoing items, i.e., `outProducts` with non-deterministic order quantities and use these products to instantiate a new supplier service, such that all the `outProducts` from all atomic supplier services are aligned with the service aggregator `outProducts`.

Note that the *assert* statement specifies that the total quantity of each product in outProducts from all supplier services must be equal to this product quantity in the outProducts of the aggregator, but this statement is ignored in the simulation semantics. A quantity of zero for a specific service would indicate that this service is being omitted from the composition. The aggregator computes suppliers' costs by iterating over each service object and summing up the costMetric objectives.

Other Aggregation Services, such as Transportation and Packaging Aggregators perform similar tasks. They assign non-deterministic values to the quantities from each possible atomic service, while asserting that the items that are consumed and produced by the sub-services are aligned with the items that are consumed and produced by the aggregator.

2.3   Emergency Response Service Example

Once we have a library of atomic and aggregated services, building a new service such as ER service in Fig. 1, can be easily done as follows:

```
class EmrResService extends Service{
    EmrResServiceInfo emrResServiceInfo;
    Package[] outItems;
    CostMetric costMetric;
    EmrResService(EmrResServiceInfo ersInfo,
    Package[] emrSupplyPkg,int[] locations){
            this.emrResServiceInfo = ersInfo;
    this.outItems = emrSupplyPkg;
    TransportationService TS = new
      TransportationService(
      emrResServiceInfo.transportationInfo,
        outItems, locations);
    PackagingSerAgg PSA = new PackagingSerAgg(
                emrResServiceInfo.packagingInfo,
                TS.inPackages);
    SupplierSerAgg SSA = new SupplierSerAgg(
        emrResServiceInfo.suppliersInfo,
        PSA.inProducts);
    this.costMetric = new CostMetric(
        TS.costMetric.objective()+
        PSA.costMetric.objective()+
        SSA.costMetric.objective());
    this.defaultOptObjective = optMetric();
    }
    CostMetric optMetric(){
            return this.costMetric;
    }
}
```

As shown in the code above, the constructor of the class Emergency Response Service (denoted as `EmrResService`) encodes a simulation procedure which uses three of the services in the library; transportation, packaging, and supplier. We instantiate `EmrResService` using three parameters; the service info (i.e., `emrResServiceInfo` that has the info of all the services that are possibly going to be used), the demand (i.e., `emrSupplyPkg`), and the possible locations of the packaging facilities that packages are going to be transported from. The constructor of `EmrResService` does a number of instantiations that simulate the entire supply process. First, it uses all its three parameter arguments to instantiate the transportation service object (TS). Then, it instantiates the packaging service aggregator object (PSA) using for its outgoing items the packages that were constructed by TS as its `inPackages`. Then, it instantiates the supplier service aggregator object (SSA) using the products that were constructed from PSA as `inProducts`. Every instantiated service takes as its own outgoing items, the incoming items which were constructed by the previous service and in turn it constructs its own incoming items. Finally, since `EmrResService` is a service itself, it instantiates a `BusMetric` that is defined here to be a cost metric; simply, it is the summation of all the services `BusMetrics` objectives.

The main program would instantiate `emrResServiceInfo` using one transportation service information, three packaging services information, and two suppliers service information. It would also instantiate the demand, i.e., `emrSupplyPkg`. Having all the input data instantiated, it invokes the constructor of the `EmrResService` class, which simulates the entire process described in the Emergency Response Service example. Lastly, we designate the objective to be the `costMetric` objective, which is the total cost of all the services. Note that in the simulation semantics, this statement is ignored, except for a message indicating the value of the objective in the result of the simulation.

Every time this application is run as a regular Java program, it executes a simulation to the entire Emergency Response Service example. Because a random selection is used by the *Nd.choice* method to select such values as quantities of each package to be shipped from each location to each ER location, and quantities of each product supplied by each supplier, each simulation run would result in a different outcome, including a different total cost of the Emergency Response service. For example, we might run the application three times, and see the following output (produced by the *Nd.checkMinObjective* method in the simulation semantics):

```
objective: 3240404.73
objective: 2812901.62
objective: 2483801.83
```

Note that these numbers do not give the minimum cost for ER service, but merely the costs corresponding to the random selections of values in the simulation runs. The optimization semantics, discussed in the next section automatically makes a selection of values that would minimize the cost of ER service.

3   SC-CoJava Syntax and Optimization Semantics

3.1   SC-CoJava Syntax

By design, the syntax of SC-CoJava is identical to that of the Java programming language, extended with the SC framework and library. Also, it is extended with one special class *Nd*, and a few restrictions on how its methods can interact with the rest of the program. More specifically, SC-CoJava adds the following special class to Java:

```
public class Nd {
  public double choice(double min, double max){..}
  public double checkMinObjective(double objective){..}
  public double checkMaxObjective(double objective){..}
}
```

As mentioned earlier in the examples, the simulation semantics interprets the methods of the class *Nd* as follows. The method `Nd.choice(min,max)` returns a single specific value between min and max, inclusive. Note that the value for min may be negative infinity, and for max positive infinity. The user can use her own implementation of the *choice* method, or use the default SC-CoJava implementation (which is currently a random selection using uniform distribution).

The methods *checkMinObjective* and *checkMaxObjective*, in the simulation semantics, do nothing but output the value of the parameter objective. An SC-CoJava program can also use the Java command

```
assert(booleanCondition)
```

with the standard procedural semantics, namely the program will report an error if the `booleanCondition` is not satisfied.

3.2   Restrictions on the Non-deterministic (Nd) Class Methods

Certain restrictions on how the methods `choice(...)`, `checkObjective(...)`, and the command *assert* interact with the rest of SC-CoJava program are imposed to make the optimization semantics well-defined and computable. To formulate the restrictions, we use the notion of non-deterministic values, or ND-values for short, which we define recursively as follows:

- The output of a *choice* method is an ND-value
- A variable is an ND-value, if it appears on the left-hand side of an assignment with an ND-value on the right-hand side.
- A variable is an ND-value, if it appears on the left-hand side of an assignment that appears in the THEN or ELSE part of a conditional statement, where the Boolean condition is an ND-value.
- The result of an arithmetic or Boolean operation on one or more ND-values is an ND-value.

We also say that a conditional statement is ND if its Boolean condition is ND, a loop statement is ND if its exit Boolean condition is ND, and a method call is ND if it is done from within a ND conditional statement. We also say that a variable, expression, conditional statement etc. are deterministic to mean the negation of being non-deterministic.

The following simple restrictions are imposed in order to make the number of values computed by the program independent of the non-deterministic choices, and associate at most one *checkObjective* method call with each *choice* call and *assert* statement.

- No ND loops
- No ND recursive method calls
- No ND calls for *checkObjective*.

The first restriction controls the number of iterations of each loop. As long as the loop's exit conditions are deterministic, the loop will continue for a deterministic number of iterations. If a loop executed a non-deterministic number of iterations, it would compute a non-deterministic number of values.

The second restriction controls the depth of recursive calls. By prohibiting recursive calls within non-deterministic conditionals, we prevent the depth of recursion from depending on non-deterministic choices.

We do allow arbitrary non-recursive method calls, whether or not they are deterministic, and also recursive method calls as long as they are deterministic. Note that the conditions above are sufficient, but not necessary, to control the number of states in the program. More flexible conditions are the subject for further work.

The third restriction, namely that no *checkObjective* is called from an ND conditional statement, ensures that for any given input to the program, (1) all *checkObjective* method calls have a total ordering, which is deterministic, and (2) every execution path that goes through a specific *choice* or *assert* statement will deterministically "continue" to a unique "nearest" *checkObjective* call (if there is one). In this case, we say that such a *choice* or *assert* statement is in the scope of that nearest *checkObjective* call.

Under the restrictions on the use of non-deterministic values, the reduction to the standard optimization formulation is always guaranteed to work and be correct. However, the resulting formulation may be beyond the constraint domain handled by the available external solver. Thus, similar to OR modeling, a SC-CoJava developer needs to be aware to use only arithmetic expressions that can be handled by the solver employed. For example, if an MILP solver is used, a SC-CoJava program can only use arithmetic expressions that are linear in non-deterministic values (but arbitrarily complex in deterministic values). Or if a non-linear solver such as MINUS or SNOPT is used, a SC-CoJava program can use non-linear arithmetic expressions, but no non-deterministic conditional statements.

3.3   SC-CoJava Optimization Semantics

A sequence of specific selections in non-deterministic *choice* statements corresponds to an execution path. We define a *feasible* execution path as one that satisfies (1) the range conditions in the *choice* statements, and (2) the assert-constraint statements. An *optimal* execution path is a *feasible* path that produces the *optimal* value in a designated program variable, among all *feasible* execution paths.

Case 1: Single checkObjective Call, as Last Program Statement

We assume here that all the restrictions outlined are satisfied. Given a SC-CoJava program *P*, input *I*, and the *checkObjective(v)* statement as the last program statement *S*, we denote by *EP* the set of all *feasible* execution paths e, i.e., execution paths that reach *S*. For a particular *feasible* execution path *e* in *EP*, we denote by $v(e)$ the value of the program variable v at the statement *S*. An *optimal* execution path is a solution to the following optimization problem *OP*:

$$Optimize\ v(e)\quad s.t.\ e\ in\ EP$$

where Optimize stands for Minimize in the case of *checkMinObjective* and Maximize in the case of *checkMaxObjective*. Note that a solution to this problem may not be unique, as more than one *feasible* execution path *e* in *EP* may have the *minimal/maximal* $v(e)$. An *optimal* execution path *e* defines the values for each execution of a *choice* method.

An execution of the program *P* according to the SC-CoJava optimization semantics is a regular procedural execution where the values returned by each *choice* statement are those corresponding to an *optimal* execution path *e*.

Case 2: No checkObjective in the program

In this case, consider a satisfaction problem *SP*: Find *e* in *EP*, where *EP* is the set of all *feasible* execution paths, i.e., those that reach a special NOOP method (which does nothing) at the end of the program.

An execution of the program *P* according to the SC-CoJava optimization semantics is a regular procedural execution where the values returned by each *choice* statement are those corresponding to a *feasible* execution path *e*.

Case 3: One or More checkObjective Calls According to Restrictions

We do not discuss this general case in detail in this paper, nor was it implemented. Here we only provide a general idea. Because of the restrictions, (1) all *checkObjective* method calls have a total ordering, which is deterministic, and (2) every execution path that goes through a specific *choice* or *assert* statement will deterministically "continue" to a unique "nearest" *checkObjective* call (if there is any). In this case, we say that such a *choice* or *assert* statement is in the scope of that nearest *checkObjective* call. The idea here is to consider an execution as split into sections, in the order of *checkObjective* calls, each with the *choice* and *assert* statements in its scope, and apply *Case 1* on all but the last section, and *Case 2* on the last.

3.4   Emergency Response Example as Optimization

We now address the question of what is an *optimal* selection of values in *Nd.choice* statements (instead of a random selection) which (1) satisfies all the requirements of the Emergency Response (i.e., all the *assert* statements), and (2) minimizes the total cost, computed by the simulation. Answering such questions is exactly the purpose of the optimization semantics of SC-CoJava.

The user first defines the simulation model as explained in Section 2. The current implementation of SC-CoJava is integrated in the Eclipse development platform as a stand-alone plug-in. The user can select one or more pre-defined service classes from a library of supply chain modeling components classified by type as shown in Fig. 2. The library includes atomic and composed components, all written in SC-CoJava. Alternatively, the user can extend the library and define his/her own service classes. In that case, the user defines a subclass of the class Service to represent the supply chain, where the method Nd.Choice(double min, double max) is used to indicate any unknown choice constant, i.e., decision variable, and the *assert* construct is used to indicate Boolean conditions that must be satisfied. The user also specifies the input parameters by instantiating Java objects provided in the extensible library.

In the example in Section 2.3, the user defines a class EmrResService as a subclass of the Service class, where the constructor instantiates three services from the library. A transportation service (TransportationService), a packaging service aggregator (PackagingSerAgg), and a supplier service aggregator (SupplierSerAgg). The main program invokes the constructor of EmrResService using the following parameters:

1.   the demand (emrSupplyPkg), which corresponds to two packages, each with different characteristics, such as quantity, delivery location, volume, weight, and type of products included.
2.   the locations of all the packaging facilities, and
3.   the service info (i.e., EmergencyResponseInfo) , which carries the info of all the possible services in the composition).

Table 1 shows the input data used to instantiate the parameters for the EmrResService service class.

Given the input parameters, the constructor of EmrResService instantiates the optimal service object. The SC-CoJava compiler first finds the *optimal* selection of the values of the order quantities represented by the *Nd.choice* statements, satisfying all the *assert* statements, and consequently producing the minimum total cost. This is done by automatically constructing a standard mathematical programming model and sending it to an external solver. For the example above, the solver found the optimal objective of 1772493 after 8 MIP simplex iterations.

Table 1. Input Data for `EmrResService`

Demand Info										
Package	Package 1111					Package 1112				
Quantity	100					200				
Products	includes Product 11 and Product 12					includes Product 13				
Location	2					1				
Volume	20					20				
Weight	200					200				
Supplier Info										
Price for product	Product 11 (Food)		Product 12 (Water)		Product 13 (Medicine)		Discount		After	Fixed cost
Supplier0	50		33		24.7		0.3		50	1200
Supplier1	17.6		20.9		30		0.2		1000	1000
Supplier2	1		2		3		0.1		5	1700
Packaging Info										
Fees by volume	10	20	30	40	50	60	70	80	90	100	Fixed cost
Packaging0	1.5	2.3	7.7	10	11.2	12.5	13	14.5	15	15.9	1278
Packaging1	1	2	7	10	11	12	13	14	15	15	1980
Packaging2	1	2	7	1	1	1	3	4	5	9	20
Transportation Info										
Fees by zone	0		1		2		3		Fixed cost	
0	10		20		30		40		30	
1	20		10		50		60		30	
2	30		50		10		70		30	
3	40		60		70		10		30	

SC-CoJava interprets the optimization results returned by the solver for the user as shown in the excerpt in Fig.3. According to the optimization results, first demanded package (Package 1111) must be delivered from location 1, while the second demanded package (Package 1112) must be delivered from location 0. Both packages should be packaged at Facility 1. Product 13 (medicine) should be ordered from Supplier 2, Product 12 (water) should be ordered from Supplier 1, while Product 11 (food) should be ordered from Supplier 2. The *optimal* objective corresponds to a specific composition of services; as a result, some of the services were instantiated with an order quantity of 0.

After an optimal service object is found, the `EmrResService` constructor operates exactly as a standard Java constructor where each `Nd.choice` is replaced with the optimal choice value. Then the semantics of the `EmrResService` class is identical to that of any Java language class.

In summary, the SC-CoJava compiler (under the optimization semantics) will first determine an *optimal* selection of values in all *Nd.choice* statements (instead of randomly selecting them), resulting in the minimum cost, according to *Case 1* of Optimization Semantics. This is done by an automatic reduction to a standard optimization formulation and solving it on a mathematical programming solver. The SC-CoJava compiler will then run the user program as a regular Java program, where all *Nd.choice* statements select the values from the optimization result.

```
optimize:
    [echo] #### 3. Solving the decision problem...
    [exec] CPLEX 8.0.0: integrality=1e-9
    [exec] CPLEX 8.0.0: optimal integer solution; objective 1772493
    [exec] 8 MIP simplex iterations
    [exec] 0 branch-and-bound nodes
results:
    [echo] #### 4. Interpreting the optimized results...
    [java] Order quantity of product 13 from Supplier0: 0.0
    [java] Order quantity of product 13 from Supplier1: 10000.0
    [java] Order quantity of product 11 from Supplier0: 0.0
    [java] Order quantity of product 11 from Supplier1: 20000.0

    [java] Package1 quantity from loc 0: 0.0
    [java] Package1 quantity from loc 1: 100.0
    [java] Package1 quantity from loc 2: 0.0
    [java] Package2 quantity loc 0: 200.0

    [java] Package1 quantity at Packaging facility0: 0.0
    [java] Package1 quantity at Packaging facility1: 100.0
    [java] Package1 quantity at Packaging facility2: 0.0

solve:
BUILD SUCCESSFUL
```

Fig. 3. Excerpt from the solver results

4   Implementation Notes

SC-CoJava was implemented by extending the language CoJava[3] and with a Service Model and an extensible library of service composition modeling components. Service Model is a Java abstract class that has (1) a number of data members to represent the service information (i.e, `ServiceInfo`, the data part of a service transformation), (2) the default optimization objective, (3) a minimization flag (`minFlag`) which indicates the direction of the optimization, and (4) a data member of type `OptState` (i.e., `state`) which captures the solution status returned by the solver. The status of a solution might be optimal, feasible (might not be the optimal solution), infeasible (the problem proved to be infeasible or unbounded), or no feasible found (i.e., the solver could not process the model far enough to prove anything about the model). `Service` class also has two methods, the first is `optMetric()` which is an abstract method, and thus, its implementation is left to the user to define the business metric to be optimized. The second method is `optObjective()` which is implemented, however, is optional to invoke. An Nd object that is instantiated by the constructor of a class that extends `Service` class represents a SC-CoJava simulation procedure. Then the SC-CoJava (and CoJava) compiler translates a non-deterministic simulation procedure into an equivalent decision problem using a reduction algorithm (see [3]). The resulting decision problem consists of a set of constraints in the modeling language AMPL.

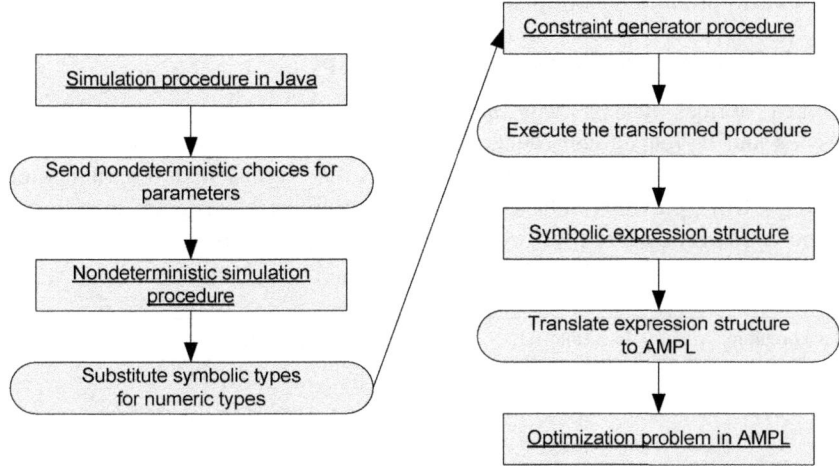

Fig. 4. Implementation Flow

The overall flow of the constraint compiler is shown in Fig. 4. First, a simulation procedure is made non-deterministic by initializing it with values from the non-deterministic *choice* library, and designating its output as an objective value. This requires no change to the procedure itself, only to its parameters and return value. Next, the procedure is transformed to create a constraint generator procedure. This involves uniformly converting all of its numeric data types to symbolic expression data types. Next, the constraint generator is compiled and executed (using a standard Java compiler). The result generated by this procedure is a set of symbolic expression data structures that represent the non-deterministic output of the simulation procedure. Finally, these symbolic expressions are translated into a mathematical programming language AMPL and solved using commercial solver software. In the case of our ER Service example, it required 14 seconds to solve the problem using ILOG CPLEX (MILP) solver on a Dell OPTIPLEX GX260 machine with Intel® Pentium® 4 CPU 2.80GHz and 1 GB of RAM. In the next subsections we give a more detailed description of the translation and the reduction procedure of the constraint compiler.

4.1 Constraint Compiler

SC-CoJava translates a standard Java program into a decision problem that can be solved by various existing optimization engines. The Java program is executed using symbolic expressions in place of the usual numeric data values. Each input to the program is generalized from a simple numeric value to a decision variable representing a range of alternative numeric inputs. Each output of the program is generalized from a particular numeric result to a symbolic expression representing all possible results as a function of the input variables. In effect, SC-CoJava executes the program non-deterministically, following all possible program traces. The result of this non-deterministic execution can be interpreted as a decision problem. The problem objective consists of the symbolic expression for the output we wish to maximize. The problem constraints consist of the constraints implied by the statements that produced the output. The problem solution identifies the program inputs that will produce the optimal program output.

4.2   SC-CoJava Symbolic Expression Data Type

SC-Cojava defines a data type named *NdNumber* that represents a symbolic expression and its related constraints. *NdNumber* is essentially a verbatim record of the operation that produces a new value. Just as the original Java program computes new values from previous values, the "non-deterministic" program composes new symbolic expressions from previous symbolic expressions, as in the following example:

Java program:	Java state:	SC-Cojava state:
int a = 2;	*a --> int(2)*	*a --> NdNumber(2)*
a = a + 1;	*a --> int(2) + int(1)*	*a--> NdNumber(2).add(NdNumber(1))*
	a --> int(3)	*a--> NdOperation("+",*
		NdNumber(2),NdNumber(1))

Each *NdNumber* represents the set of constraints imposed by the program statement that computes a new value. In the previous example, the value of a new *NdNumber* is constrained to be equal to the sum of two previous *NdNumbers*. In the following example, when a new non-deterministic choice is produced, its value is constrained by two inequalities, an upper and lower bound:

Java program:	Java state:	SC-Cojava state:
double a = Nd.choice(- *2.0,2.0);*	*a --> -0.1235*	*a --> NdRange(-2.0, 2.0)*

4.3   SC-CoJava Flow Control

SC-CoJava preserves the semantics of conditional statements by maintaining a set of constraints that correspond to the conjunction of all enclosing conditions. Every assignment that occurs within a conditional statement block is related to the enclosing condition by logical implication, as in the following example:

Java program:	Java state:	SC-CoJava state:
int a = 3;	*a --> int(3)*	*a --> NdNumber(3)*
if (a > 2) a = a + 1;	*a --> int(4)*	*a --> NdSwitch(*
		NdComparison(">", NdNumber(3),
		NdNumber(2)), NdNumber(3) +
		NdNumber(1), NdNumber(1))

Since all state changes in Java are due to assignment statements, guarding assignments in this way is sufficient to accurately reflect the behavior of the conditional statement under all conditions. Java iteration statements are supported similarly to Java conditional statements. All assignments within the body of the iteration are guarded in this way, and the loop is repeated until the loop control cannot possibly be satisfied. The Java *assert* statement has a special significance in SC-CoJava. The *assert* statement makes some set of output values impossible. It has the effect of promoting a Boolean symbolic expression to a global constraint.

4.4   SC-CoJava Constraint Reduction

The *NdNumber* data type implements some simple constraint reduction semantics. These are mostly optimizations to keep the constraints concise. For example, an upper and lower bound is maintained for each *NdNumber*, and if the two are equal, the number reduces to a constant. Booleans values are implemented by constrained integers when the target domain is MILP. When Boolean variables are used in logical implication, they are multiplied by a large constant and used to relax inequality constraints. The following example shows how a Boolean variable is defined and initialized:

Java program:	SC-CoJava state:	AMPL syntax:
boolean a = (3 < 1);	*a-->NdComparison("<", 3, 1)*	*var v integer;*
		v >= 0;
		v <= 1;
		*3 <= 1 + v * 1000000;*
		*1 <= 3 + (1 - v) **
		1000000;

The SC-CoJava symbolic expressions are easily translated to a solver syntax such as AMPL. The tree of *NdNumber* nodes is very similar to the parse tree for a standard decision problem. The AMPL objective function can be produced by an infix traversal of the *NdNumber* tree. The AMPL constraints are produced by requesting constraints for each *NdNumber* node and also including global constraints registered by *assert* statements.

5   Related Work

The majority of the existing supply chain research focuses on the traditional manufacturing aspect rather than the service aspect of the supply chain. The performance of the service supply chain has a different focus of efficiencies based on management of capacity, flexibility of resources, information flows, service performance and cash flow management.   In addition, the variations and the uncertainties in the output are higher in service supply chains [5]. A comparative analysis shows that effective strategies in traditional supply chains might not provide the desired outcome in service supply chains, and therefore dedicated research on service supply chain is required [6]. There has been some research on modeling the service supply chain, such as modeling the software as a service (SaaS) supply chain or the application service supply chain [7]. However, the supply chain is mostly modeled for the traditional objective of cost effectiveness which makes these models very limiting. By contrast, a SC-CoJava Service can be associated with one or more business metrics, such as reliability, responsiveness, and flexibility, thus, SC-CoJava provides a conceptual foundation to modeling the service supply chain for flexible definition of performance efficiencies.

SC-CoJava utilizes constraint modeling and object-oriented simulation paradigms for service compositions in supply chains. Object-oriented simulation has traditionally been approached through procedural object-oriented languages, such as Smalltalk [8] and Java. These languages start with a syntax for variable assignment and add support for modular organization of procedures. There are many specialized object-oriented simulation languages such as Simula [9] and ModSim [10] and there are simulation environments layered on top of existing object-oriented languages such as Silk [11] and Jwarp [12]. There are also productivity tools for supply chain simulation, such as Supply Chain Guru [13] and SDI Industry Pro [14]. These languages and tools allow complex models to be constructed and maintained effectively, but lack support for systematic optimization, based on mathematical programming. Typically, simulation approaches are used when the problem is too complex for existing optimization techniques (e.g., MILP). In contrast, SC-CoJava is designed for cases when existing optimization techniques (and solvers) can be used but allows the problem to be modeled as a simulation-like process. This provides benefits in ease of modeling, testing, and extensibility.

Constraint modeling has traditionally been approached through specialized constraint modeling languages, such as AMPL [15]. These languages start with a syntax for constraints and layer additional support for organizing them. They enable systematic optimization, but they require explicit definition and maintenance of constraint models.

Constraint programming (CP) languages, such as OPL [16], CLP [17], ECLiPSe [18], and ILOG SOLVER [19] allow developers to specify strategies for solving optimization problems, but their modeling component is based on declarative constraints, similar to AMPL. Languages such as Cob [20] and Siri [21] add object-oriented modeling constructs, such as inheritance and encapsulation, to a constraint syntax. Similarly, the COMET language [22] adds object-oriented modeling and control abstractions to constraint-based local graph search using randomization, check-pointing, and meta-heuristics. These languages provide a clean representation for steady-state optimization problems, but they do not model state changes in the direct way that procedural languages do.

The language Modelica [23] might be the most closely related to SC-CoJava in terms of the capability of translating procedural algorithms into declarative constraints. Modelica supports unified models which can define both simulation and optimization problems. The models are translated to equations to be solved by an optimizer or compiled into a sequential procedure. Modelica can translate procedural algorithms into constraint equations within pure functions only (functions without side effects); therefore, it is efficient within a very limited context.

By contrast, SC-CoJava has a thoroughly procedural object-oriented syntax and semantics inherited from Java. SC-CoJava eliminates the boundary between procedures and constraints. SC-CoJava gives developers the flexibility to move model components freely back and forth between procedural algorithms and declarative optimization models. The models developed using SC-CoJava can accommodate any supply chain design with any number of echelons. The SC-CoJava approach provides robust true optimized evaluation of alternative solutions and is more attractive than the complex mathematical programming models.

6   Conclusions and Future Work

To the best of our knowledge, ours is the first work to propose a unified language for both simulation and optimization of service composition in supply chains. Our approach is unique in that it offers the advantages of simulation-like model development, testing and extensibility, while providing true decision optimization based on mathematical programming.

Many questions remain for future research. They include extending SC-CoJava with stochastic and constraint programming capabilities, and utilizing the structure of high-level models to develop optimization heuristics that can work in conjunction with existing MP solvers. Also of interest is a development environment for non software engineers in which a transformation mechanism is used to allow specifying the Java classes from UML models.

References

1. Fourer, R., Gay, D.M., Kernighan, B.W.: AMPL: A Modeling Language For Mathematical Programming. Brooks/Cole-Thomson Learning, Pacific Grove, VA (2003)
2. Boisvert, R.F., Howe, S.E., Kahaner, D.K.: Gams: A Framework for the Management of Scientific Software. ACM Transactions on Mathematical Software (TOMS) 11(4), 313 (1985)
3. Brodsky, A., Nash, H.: CoJava: A Unified Language for Simulation and Optimization. In: van Beek, P. (ed.) CP 2005. LNCS, vol. 3709, p. 877. Springer, Heidelberg (2005)
4. Supply-Chain Operations Reference-Model (SCOR) version 8.0 overview. Supply Chain Council (2007)
5. Ellram, L.M., Tate, W.L., Billington, C.: Understanding and Managing the Services Supply Chain. Journal of Supply Chain Management 40 (2004)
6. Sengupta, K., Heiser, D.R., Cook, L.S.: Manufacturing and Service Supply Chain Performance: A Comparative Analysis. The Journal of Supply Chain Management (2006)
7. Demirkan, H., Cheng, H.K.: The risk and information sharing of application services supply chain. European Jouranl of Operational Research 187, 765 (2008)
8. Goldberg, A., Robson, D.: Smalltalk-80: The Language and its Implementation. Addison-Wesley Longman Publishing Co., Inc., Boston (1983)

9. Dahl, O.J., Nygaard, K.: Simula: An Algol-Based Simulation Language. Communication ACM (9), 671 (1996)
10. Thomasma, T., Madsen, J.: Object Oriented Programming Languages for Developing Simulation-Related Software. In: WSC 1990 in The 22nd Conference in Winter Simulation. IEEE Press, Piscataway (1990)
11. Healy, K.J., Kilgore, R.A.: Introduction to Silk and Java-Based Simulation. In: WSC 1998 in The 30th Conference on Winter Simulation. IEEE Computer Society Press, Los Alamitos (1998)
12. Bizaro, P., Silva, L.M.S.: Jwrap, J.G.: A Java Library for Parallel Discrete-Event Simulation. In: The ACM Workshop on Java for High-Performance Network Computing (1998)
13. Lamasoft, L.: Supply Chain Guru (cited June 14, 2007), http://www.llamasoft.com
14. Phelps, R.A., Parsons, D.J., Siprelle, A.J., The, S.D.I.: Industry Product Suite: Simulation from the Production Line to the Supply Chain. In: The 2000 Winter Simulation Conference (2000)
15. Fourer, R., Gay, D.M., Kernighan, B.W.: A Modeling Language for Mathematical Programming. Management Science (36), 519 (1990)
16. Hentenryck, P.V., et al.: Constraint Programming in OPL. In: Nadathur, G. (ed.) PPDP 1999. LNCS, vol. 1702, pp. 98–116. Springer, Heidelberg (1999)
17. Jaffar, J., Lassez, J.L.: Constraint Logic Programming. In: The 14th ACM SIGACT-SIGPLAN Symposium on Principles of Programming Languages. ACM press, New York (1987)
18. Wallace, M., Novello, S., Schimpf, J.: ECLiPs: A Platform for Constraint Logic Programming. ICL Systems Journal (12), 159 (1997)
19. Puget, J.F., Leconte, M.: Beyond the Glass Box: Constraints as Objects. In: International Logic Programming Symposium, p. 513 (1995)
20. Jarayaman, B., Tambay, P.: Semantics and Applications of Constrained Objects. Technical Report 2001-15 (2001)
21. Horn, B.L.: Siri: A Constrained-Object Language for Reactive Program Implementation. School of Computer Science, Carnegie Mellon University, Pitsburgh, PA (1991)
22. Michel, L., Hentenryck, P.V.: Comet in Context. In: ACM Internation Conference, Proceedings of Paris c.Kanellakis Memorial Workshop on Principles of Computing & Knowledge. ACM, San Diego (2003)
23. Fritzson, P., Engelson, V.: Modelica - a Unified Object-Oriented Language for System Modelling and Simulation. In: Jul, E. (ed.) ECOOP 1998. LNCS, vol. 1445, pp. 67–90. Springer, Heidelberg (1998)

Appendix A

```
class Products extends CommodityItem{
    int locZone;
    double weight;
    Products(int iid, String des, double qty, int loc,
    double wght){
        super (iid, des, qty);
        this.locZone= loc;
        this.weight=wght;
    }
}


class TransportationInfo extends ServiceInfo{
    double[][] fees;
    double fxdCost;
    TransportationInfo(String tsId, double fxCost,
    double[][] fee){
        super(tsId);
        this.fxdCost = fxCost;
        this.fees = fee;
    }
}


class SupplierService extends Service{
    SupplierInfo supplierInfo;
    Products[] outProducts;
    CostMetric costMetric;
    SupplierService(SupplierInfo supplierInfo,
    Products[]outProd){
        this.outProducts = outProd;
        this.supplierInfo = supplierInfo;
        this.costMetric = new
            CostMetric(supplyingCost());
        this.defaultOptObjective = optMetric();
    }
    private double supplyingCost(){
        double cost=0;
        if (this.outProducts.length>0){
    for (int i=0; i<outProducts.length; i=i+1){
      double itemPrice =0;
      for(int p=0;p<supplierInfo.products.length;
```

```
  p=p+1){
            if(outProducts[i].iID ==
            supplierInfo.products[p]){
         itemPrice = supplierInfo.unitCost[p];
       }
     }
     cost=cost+(itemPrice*outProducts[i].iQty);
   }
   if(cost>supplierInfo.thresh){
            cost=supplierInfo.thresh+((1-
            supplierInfo.discount)*(cost-
            supplierInfo.thresh));
     }
  cost=cost+supplierInfo.fxdCost;
         }
         return cost;
   }
   CostMetric optMetric(){
         return this.costMetric;
   }
}


class SupplierSerAgg extends ServiceAggregator{
     SupplierInfo[] suppliersInfo;
     Products[] outProducts;
     SupplierService[] supplierServices;
     CostMetric costMetric;
     SupplierSerAgg(SupplierInfo[] si, Products[]
     oItems){
          this.outProducts = oItems;
          this.suppliersInfo = si;
          this.supplierServices = aggSuppliers();
          this.costMetric = new
          CostMetric(supplyingCost());
          this.defaultOptObjective = optMetric();
     }
     private SupplierService[] aggSuppliers(){
          SupplierService[] ss = new
            SupplierService[suppliersInfo.length];
          Products[] totOutProducts= new
            Products[suppliersInfo.length*
            outProducts.length];
          int i=0;
          for(int p=0;p<outProducts.length;p=p+1){
```

```
        double ordQty = 0;
        double totQty = 0;
        for(int s=0; s<suppliersInfo.length; s=s+1){
          ordQty= Nd.choice(0,outProducts[p].iQty);
          totQty = totQty + ordQty;
          totOutProducts[i]= new Products(
            outProducts[p].iID, outProducts[p].iDes,
            ordQty, outProducts[p].locZone,
            outProducts[p].weight);
          i=i+1;
        }
        assert (totQty == outProducts[p].iQty);
      }
      for(int s=0; s<suppliersInfo.length; s=s+1){
        Products[] newOutProducts= new
               Products[outProducts.length];
        int count = s;
        for(int t=0; t<outProducts.length; t=t+1){
          newOutProducts[t]= new Products(
            totOutProducts[count].iID,
            totOutProducts[count].iDes,
            totOutProducts[count].iQty,
            totOutProducts[count].locZone,
            totOutProducts[count].weight);
          count = count + suppliersInfo.length;
      }
      ss[s]= new SupplierService(
             suppliersInfo[s], newOutProducts);
      }
      return ss;
      }
  double supplyingCost(){
      double cost = 0;
      for (int i=0;i<supplierServices.length;i=i+1){
         cost=cost+
         supplierServices[i].costMetric.objective();
   }
   return cost;
  }
  CostMetric optMetric(){
      return this.costMetric;
  }
}
```

```
abstract class Service{

//0 or more inItems;
//0 or more outItems;
//0 or more BusMetric;
ServiceInfo serviceInfo;
double defaultOptObjective;
int minFlag;
optState state;

abstract double optMetric();
void optObjective(){
    if (state.optimalityFlag==TRUE){
      if (minFlag==
TRUE){Nd.minimize(optMetric());)}
      else Nd.maximize(optMetric());}
    else if (state.optimalityFlag== FAlSE &&
state.infeasiblityFlag==FAlSE
    && state.noFeasibleFound==FALSE){
      if (minFlag==
TRUE){Nd.minimize(optMetric());)}
      else Nd.maximize(optMetric());
      System.out.println(''solution might not be
optimal.'');}
    else if (state.infeasiblityFlag== TRUE){
      System.out.println(''solution is non-
deterministic.'');}
    else if (state.noFeasibleFound== TRUE){
      System.out.println(''solution is non-
deterministic.'');}
   }
}
```

An Ontology-Based Model Management Architecture
for Service Innovation

Omar F. El-Gayar and Amit V. Deokar

College of Business and Information Systems, Dakota State University
820 N. Washington Avenue, Madison, SD 57042 USA
{omar.el-gayar,amit.deokar}@dsu.edu

Abstract. Organizations have indicated renewed interest in service innovation, design and management, given the growth of service sector. Decision support systems (DSS) play an important role in supporting this endeavor, through management of organizational resources such as data and models. Given the global nature of service value chains, there have been ever increasing demands on managing, sharing, and reusing these heterogeneous and distributed resources, both within and across organizational boundaries, through DSS consisting of database management systems (DBMS) and model management systems (MMS). Analogous to DBMS, model management systems focus on the management of decision models, dealing with representation, storage, and retrieval of models as well as a variety of applications such as analysis, reuse, sharing, and composition of models. Recent developments in the areas of semantic web and ontologies have provided a rich tool set for computational reasoning about these resources in an intelligent manner. In this chapter, we leverage these advances and apply service-oriented design principles to propose an ontology-based model management architecture supporting service innovation. The architecture is illustrated with case study scenarios and current state of implementation. The role of potential information technologies in supporting the architecture is also discussed. We then provide a roadmap to make advancements in research in this direction.

Keywords: Services, Services Innovation, Model Management, Ontologies, Service-oriented Architecture.

1   Introduction

The past two decades have witnessed a significant shift in emphasis from traditional manufacturing to service sectors for major economies in the world. Service sector industry verticals such as healthcare, business consulting, and education employ more than 80% of the workforce in the United States [1]. Similar trends have been observed globally with over 20% growth in the service sectors in other countries like Japan, France, Italy, China, and India [2-3]. Traditional manufacturing-based organizations are expanding to become service giants, realizing that beyond reengineering and maintaining efficient processes, service-related capabilities can enhance their business

D. Dolk et al. (Eds.): Decision Support Modeling in Service Networks, LNBIP 42, pp. 143–168, 2012.

models by providing huge service revenues. For instance, IBM's targeted services have undergone expansion from 23% in 1992 to more than 52% in 2006 [4].

Given this pervasiveness of services, much attention is being devoted towards understanding and managing service systems. At a foundational level, service systems are characterized as value-creation networks situated in organizational contexts utilizing people, technology, and informational resources in different magnitudes [2, 5]. However, given that the capabilities in today's emerging services are significantly different from traditional production and service capabilities, the business transformations in developing and managing modern day service systems is a challenging endeavor [3, 6]. Recent industry efforts such as IBM's Service Science, Management, and Engineering (SSME) initiative [5], and initiatives led by consortiums such Service Research and Innovation Initiative (SRII) [7] and Consortium for Service Innovation (CSI) [8] are noteworthy here. Essentially, the focus is on creating service innovations with measurable outcomes.

Service organizations are faced with numerous information management challenges in creating service innovations in today's increasingly complex and dynamic environment. Vast amounts of data and myriads of models of reality are routinely used to predict key outcomes in service systems. Decision support systems (DSS) play a key role in facilitating decision making through management of data and models. The basic thrust of such applications is to enable decision-makers to focus on making decisions rather than being heavily involved in gathering data, and conceiving and selecting analytical decision models. Consequently, decision and management sciences are among the important reference disciplines for managing service systems. Efforts from these disciplines are geared towards providing better decision models to enable effective and efficient decision making. Embedded in such models are measurable metrics and key performance indicators that can lead to improved service innovation and productivity. Sharing and reusing these decision models to support co-creation of value in the service value chain, both at the intra-organizational as well as inter-organizational levels, is one of the key challenges facing service enterprises.

Further, information technology (IT) has opened doors to many new opportunities, including providing new services electronically as well as innovating traditional services through use of IT, leading to increased collaborative efforts in distributed environments. However, in practice, models use a myriad of languages and task specific representations that include textual descriptions of problem statements, modeling languages, and graphical notation. While some model representations offer distinct advantages such as model-data independence, others have data intertwined with the model structure. Also, several representations (and modeling environments) may be used within the same service organization for addressing the same type of model underlying a particular service. To share and reuse models in such environments, individual translators need to be developed for each pair of model representation schemes. This solution is not scalable, particularly in the context of distributed service settings. Thus, in the context of service enterprises, the need for distributed decision support in general, and model management in particular is more today than ever before [9]. Additionally, existing model representations are not directly amenable to architectures supporting distributed environments. Last, but not least, such representation schemes are often paradigm dependent. In effect, without a scalable architecture for managing models in distributed environments that captures the structure and semantics of models as well as preserves model-data, model-solver, and model-paradigm independence, efforts to support "modeling in the large" and to leverage existing investments in models through sharing and reuse are seriously curtailed. In this chapter, we propose an architecture for model management in a heterogeneous and distributed environment. The architecture leverages recent development in service oriented computing, web services, and the semantic web to facilitate model sharing and reuse in such environment and illustrate how such architecture can serve as an enabler for service innovation.

The remainder of the chapter is organized as follows. The following sections presents a brief review of services and service innovation followed by the role of decision models in services innovations and a number of motivating scenarios highlighting the need for a system facilitating the management of models on heterogeneous environments. Next, we provide a detailed description of the proposed model management architecture, and an illustration of the utility of such architecture using a number of representative scenarios for model management. The final section summarizes the main contributions of the proposed architecture and highlights directions for future research.

2   Services and Services Innovation

2.1   The Concept of Services

The services sector truly began to show its presence on the economic front beginning in the 1970s. Given that these initial developments preceded the rise of information technology advances, the services under consideration then were the brick-and-mortar service enterprises (such as restaurants, and traditional banking), what are now termed as "traditional" services, in which the physical environment of service interaction received primary focus.

Definitions of the term "service" abound. Lovelock [10] characterizes services along several dimensions: its nature, the relationship with the client, decisions, economics, and mode of delivery. Fitzsimmons and Fitzsimmons [11] defines service as "a time-perishable, intangible experience performed for a customer acting in a role of co-producer". Gronroos [12] defines services as "processes consisting of a series of activities where a number of different types of resources are used in direct interaction with a customer, so that a solution is found to a customer's problem." Lusch [13] defines service as "the application of specialized competences (knowledge and skills), ... for the benefit of another entity or the entity itself". Implicit in these definitions is the recognition that decision models are key resources utilized throughout the service management lifecycle.

With the advances of information technology (IT), attention is shifting towards "network-based services" also referred to as "emerging services" [3]. Compared to traditional services, these services are differentiated by the fact that they are IT-driven, have low labor requirements, emphasize self-service and high transaction speed, leverage data from multiple heterogeneous sources, are computationally intensive, and focus on mass customization [3]. Online auctioning such as eBay, e-commerce and targeted marketing such as Amazon.com, self-service travel sites such as Travelocity and Expedia are just but few examples of network-based services. Evangelista [14] identify a similar class of services termed as "science and technology based services", where the firms are engaged in innovation activities such as R&D, engineering and technical consultancy including computing and software services. Organizations involved with such services are originators of new technological know-how, which is then diffused to manufacturers and other services. The service activities identified here are located upstream in the innovation and knowledge generation chain, where the goal is to provide appropriate solutions to a variety of information and technical needs and requirements of clients, exploiting available technologies. Harnessing decision support technologies to support these novel breed of services is essential.

With the increasing advances in technology, it can be argued that IT has a critical role to play in supporting the service value chain [5]. Network-based services are essentially dependent on IT for co-creating the value, as well as providing the competitive edge for the provider organization [15] . The role of technology is seen to be twofold. On one hand, technology is dramatically changing the way services are created, designed, and delivered. Research is progressing towards infusing and integrating technology in service encounters such as e-commerce, and self-service systems [16]. On the other hand, technology has a role to play in providing decision support in managing and delivering services and service related artifacts. Artifacts such as decision models underpinning service encounters need to be effectively utilized within organizations and even with partnering organizations across the boundaries. Research in this area is sparse and worthy of more attention [17].

2.2 Service Innovation

Given the ubiquity of services, the area of innovation in services is drawing increasing attention among scholars. The term "innovation" in the context of services has primarily two connotations. Service innovation can imply introduction of a new service offering, analogous to "product innovation", or the development of a new way of managing or delivering a service, analogous to "process innovation". The former can be considered "demand-side" driven innovation with emphasis on growing revenue through market expansion and meeting customer requirements, while the later can be considered "supply-side" driven innovation with emphasis on reengineering and/or improving service management for higher productivity [18]. A strong connection between these two apparently disjoint (strategic vs. operational) views can be noted from an overall service management lifecycle perspective.

Two distinct aspects of service innovation are evident from the literature: organizational innovation and technological innovation [19]. Research along the lines of organizational innovation has focused on developing conceptual tools and models to depict the peculiarities of services such as intangibility, and the highly social nature of interactions [20-21]. On the other hand, research in the area of technological innovation focuses on technological advances and ways in which they can innovate services [22-23]. Thus, it is interesting to recognize multiple and complementary perspectives adopted in studying innovation in services. An example of such emerging perspectives is the notion of "open innovation" or "distributed innovation", which recognizes the interactive nature of modern innovation processes, within and across the service systems [24-25]. It underscores the need to support innovators forming coalitions by sharing their knowledge [26].

Regardless of the definition of services, decision models are an important resource and knowledge objects that underpin any successful service venture and are utilized throughout the service management lifecycle. Recent developments in IT and associated IT-enabled service innovation further emphasizes the increasing role of decision models in providing decision support in managing and delivering services and service related artifacts and in enabling service innovations. The following section elaborates the role of decision models in supporting services and service innovations and highlights the significance of managing these models as an organizational resource.

3   Role of Decision Models in Service Innovation

Krishnan and Chari [27] depict a model (or a model schema) as a formal abstract representation of a decision problem. In other words, models can be conceived as specific formulations of decision situations amenable to certain problem solving techniques, such as simple linear regression, or an LP product mix formulation [28]. Model instances represent specific decision making situations created by instantiating model schemas with appropriate data, and are amenable to computational execution using model solvers to generate model solutions.

Decision models have played a major role in the evolution of manufacturing process and systems towards just-in-time manufacturing and mass customization. Examples of such models were employed in production planning and distribution, facility design, inventory control, and total quality management. With much of the research in operation management (OM) traditionally dominated by manufacturing issues [29], initial efforts focused on adapting and utilizing such models in service design and management. As OM research on services evolved, increased recognition of the distinct characteristics of services and 'breaking free' from the goods-based manufacturing perspective became apparent [29-30]. Along these lines, decision models continued to evolve into models specifically catering to service needs such as yield management and customer selection. Other work emphasized the distinction and similarities between manufacturing and service systems to identify problems (and associated solutions) such as portfolio optimization, workforce optimization, and resource allocation that pertain to both systems [31].

Recent developments in information technology (IT) have been key enablers of service innovations referred to as "emerging services". Examples of such service innovations that are highly dependent on IT include sectors such as financial services and banking, retail, and tourism. Technologies such as Radio Frequency Identification (RFID) and Universal Product Code (UPC) have revolutionized services such as retail and transportation of goods. However, such emerging service innovations enabled by IT have also created challenges with respect to the handling and processing of large amounts of data for decision making (often in real-time), creating what Tien [32] refers to as data rich, information poor (DRIP) problems, i.e., rich in basic transaction data, yet poor in processed data such as derivations, recommendations, and patterns which can form the basis of informed decision making.

Decision models employed within a decision informatics paradigm can provide a feasible solution to the DRIP problem noted above [32]. Decision informatics is comprised of information and decision technologies and is grounded in three disciplines: data analysis, decision modeling, and systems engineering. While data analysis/fusion is concerned with the capture and initial processing of data, decision modeling employs techniques such as optimization and simulation for explicitly supporting decision making, possibly in real time. The research described in this paper builds upon the notion of decision informatics, particularly from a model management standpoint, in supporting the service innovation process.

To better understand the role of decision models in service innovation, we adopt a systems engineering perspective on services [3]. In this perspective, a service system life cycle is composed of the following phases adapted from [33]:

- *Need assessment/Requirements and specification*: The objective is the identification of user requirements and the translation of these requirements into specification for service and supporting processes.
- *Design/Development*: This involves the design of various aspects of the service, e.g., number of servers, delivery and communication mechanisms, etc.
- *Service production and delivery*: In contrast to goods, service production and delivery is co-located in time and space.
- *Service evaluation and optimization*: Following production and delivery, the service is evaluated based on performance measures.
- *Phaseout/Disposal*: A service system may be phased out or replaced by another service based on the results.

Decision models can be used in various phases along the service system life cycle. For example, demand forecasting models can be used in need assessment, while workforce and service portfolio optimization can be used in the design of service innovations. Real-time yield management models may be used in services such as hotels and airlines. Data Envelopment Analysis (DEA) may be used for evaluating service productivity and provide the basis for further innovations as depicted in Table 1.

Table 1. Examples of decision models/application by service system life cycle phase

Service system life cycle phase	*Examples of decision models/applications*
Need analysis	Portfolio optimization (determining the scope, scale and composition of services) and demand forecasting, e.g., [34]
Service design	Queuing models for determining server configurations, e.g., [35]; Workforce scheduling (may also be at the time of delivery, i.e., in real time)
Service production and delivery	Yield (revenue) management, e.g., [36], workforce optimization (workforce level, composition, and assignment), e.g., [37]
Service evaluation and optimization	Data envelop analysis (DEA) [38]

Alternatively, we can view the role of models along Schmenner's Service Process Matrix [39] which distinguishes among various service industries by the degree of labor intensity and the level of interaction and customization involved. Regardless of service type, decision models have been productively employed to address distinct service issues as shown in Table 2.

Models can also be viewed as knowledge objects encapsulating an organization's knowledge about a decision problem in a particular domain. The CSI [8] advocates a knowledge management strategy emphasizing the value of knowledge for enabling organizations to build an organizational learning culture to improve service levels, operational efficiency, and ultimately customer satisfaction. In this strategy, practices and processes focus on the creation, use, and evolution of knowledge. The modeling life-cycle [27] comprised of problem identification, model creation, model implementation, model validation, model solution, model interpretation and model maintenance represent a rich domain for knowledge management practices as advocated by CSI. Central to the life-cycle is the creation and management of models which encapsulates the explicit knowledge captured through the process and codified in the form of models.

Last but not least, recent emphasis on agile business processes and workflows, particularly in the context of service innovation is a major driver for service-oriented computing and architecture. By viewing models as services (as will be described later) within an enterprise service oriented architecture, models can provide the necessary analytics and decision support in real-time to the flexible configuration and re-configuration of business processes and workflows further enabling service innovation.

Table 2. Examples decision models by industry type adapted from Schmenner [39] and Rust [40]

		Interaction and customization	
		Low	High
Labor intensity	Low	*Service factory* Example of industries − Airline − Hotels − Trucking Example of models − Yield management	*Service shop* Example of industries − Hospitals − Repair services Example of models − Layout and queuing analysis
	High	*Mass Service* Example of industries − Retailing − Retail banking Example of models − Data envelop analysis (DEA)	*Professional services* Example of industries − Doctors − Lawyers − Stockbrokers Example of models − Customer selection models

In summary, the following observations are made about the role of models in service innovation:

− Decision models have been developed and used for the design, delivery and management of services. Nevertheless, the ubiquity of IT and the resulting abundance of data further underscore the significance of the development and application of such models in supporting various service life-cycle phases.
− The increased use of software agents as enablers for service innovation [41] coupled with the availability of decision models in machine-readable form (as web services) further expands the support for service innovation.
− Models as knowledge objects encapsulate knowledge involved in the design, delivery, and management of services. The management of these models as a part of an organizational management strategy further supports service innovation as advocated by the CSI [8]
− Decision models as web services support agile business process and service innovation.

In essence, the aforementioned discussion underscores the need for managing models as an organizational resource and a key enabler for service innovation. The following section presents representative scenarios further motivating the need for model management in the context of service innovations followed by a brief review of model management literature highlighting major contributions as well as limitations as enablers of service innovation.

4   Motivating Scenarios

4.1   Scenario 1: Intra-organizational Model Sharing

Consider an organization offering its services in diverse markets, both regionally and internationally. The headquarters uses a marketing simulation model for developing the best marketing mix including the advertising expenditure, product quality index, and product distribution. This model is used in analyzing different what-if scenarios regarding marketing strategies and their effect on the organization's market share and volume. Another branch operating in markets characterized by high variability in demand, different competition conditions, and distribution channels would need to reuse the former model. Reusing such a model will involve customizing the model to take into consideration new parameters and competitive dynamics for this branch's market. Alternatively, various branches may have developed their own models or have adapted existing models to meet their specific requirements. It would be advantageous if each such branch is able to share its models with other branches (including the headquarters) in a seamless manner.

Unfortunately, in practice, such goal is often hampered by lack of awareness of the existence of such models in the first place, heterogeneity of modeling environments resulting in accessibility and compatibility issues, and inadequate (or lack of) documentation that often employs inconsistent semantics complicating the problem of assessing the applicability of a particular model as well as the possibility of customizing such models to the situation at hand. The aforementioned issues are even more prevalent in an inter-organizational setting.

4.2   Scenario 2: Models as Knowledge Objects

Knowledge intensive business services (KIBS) are private organizations that rely heavily on professional knowledge for supplying intermediate products or services that are knowledge based [42]. Examples of KBIS include IT support services, management consultancy, and engineering consultancy. According to Hertog [43], KIBS capture scientific and technological information that is often dispersed across the economy, and tailor such information to meet the needs of its client. KIBS can be considered as catalysts and co-producers of innovation [43]. Interaction between KIBS and their clients involve extensive knowledge flows which take a variety of forms. While tacit knowledge is a significant component of knowledge flow, explicit forms of knowledge such as written reports, project plans, software, and decision models are also prevalent.

In this scenario, consider a management consultancy firm specializing in helping client firms answer questions pertaining to their projected energy demand, cost, and optimal mix of their energy portfolio. The firm relies on a number of decision models for forecasting energy demand and supply, prices for various forms of energy, transportation and distribution costs, etc. A client wishes to use the services of the consultancy firm, specifically the client is interested in integrating the energy price forecasting models developed by the consultancy firm with its own production and distribution models. Given the likelihood that the client may be using different modeling environments and assumptions, such integration may be severely hampered. The situation is further complicated if the client wishes to select and test a variety of such models for their suitability to their particular needs. Such a situation may be encountered with other clients.

4.3   Scenario 3: Model Management Supporting Service Design and Agile Business Processes

The design of a new service frequently involves the use of decision models such as queuing models, resource planning and allocation models, and service portfolio optimization. While such models are often developed in the context of a new service, over time, such models may be applied to other service innovations. For example, consider a parcel delivery company that is experimenting with innovative ways for routing and delivery of packages. In this case, existing routing models may be adapted to reflect various routing configurations. While such a scenario is plausible and feasible using current technology, a number of situations may arise that would constrain such possibilities, namely,

– Decision makers or analysts may not be aware of the existence of such models in the organization in the first place,
– Models may have been developed and implemented using obsolete technologies and no longer accessible,
– Models may lack the documentation necessary for proper utilization.

A model repository in a broader context of a model management system in a heterogeneous environment will help alleviate such situations. The following section highlights contributions and limitations of related work on model management.

5   Related Work on Model Management

Model management (MM) encompasses a variety of functionality including model description, model manipulation, scheduling, execution, and information display. Research in the area of model management emerged since the 1980s in the context of managing models in decision support systems (DSS). Management science and operations research applications provided a fertile environment for this interest. While a comprehensive review of the model management literature can be found elsewhere [28, 44], it is worth noting that much of the motivation behind model management focused around finding ways for developing, storing, manipulating, controlling, and effectively utilizing models in an organization [45]., Some of the important developments are noted below, along with highlighting the need for distributed model management.

In general, models can be seen to conform to a modeling lifecycle, consisting of a complex, iterative process during which several modeling tasks are accomplished.

Some of the modeling tasks are computationally intensive, while others are more subjective and need human judgment and domain expertise. Supporting the modeling life-cycle entails providing a number of functionalities. For example, model creation may involve description, formulation, selection, integration, composition, and reuse of models. The need for providing more expressive power in describing models has driven the research on explicit model representations using meta-modeling techniques such as Structured Modeling (SM) [46]. While model formulation focuses on the knowledge elicitation involved in the development of new models, the remaining steps in model creation aim at leveraging repositories of existing models. Model composition is the problem of generating a sequence of models from a library of available models in response to a particular decision-making situation. Model composition is an important component of model management in the decision support context, where decision models are desired to be composed from individual model units. It is often used interchangeably with the term model integration in the literature. However, we try to distinguish between the two terms based on the approach taken for synthesizing models. Model integration focuses on synthesizing models at the structural or definitional level [47-49]. At this level, different model schemas are integrated in a cohesive manner. Model composition, on the other hand, focuses on assembling models at a functional level [50-52]. Model implementation is concerned with issues related to creating model representations amenable to execution by solvers, with focus on model-data, model-solver, and model-paradigm independence. Post-solution model interpretation deals with issues facilitating the interpretation of results by modelers and decision makers, such as the analysis of the sensitivity of model results to parameter variations, the analysis of the sensitivity of the model to structural changes in the model, and the inspection of model structure.

Most of the MM research since the early 1980s up to the mid-1990s focused on addressing these functionalities and requirements of MM systems. However, over the past decade and a half, additional requirements concerning portability, vendor independence, and compatibility have become critical due to the feasibility of sharing models within and across organizations driven by advances in supporting communication infrastructure. With the exception of Muhanna [9] and few others, very little attention was paid to managing large shared model bases. Accordingly, a major limitation of the aforementioned approaches is their limited support to the requirements for model sharing in a distributed environment. It has thus become critical to meet the increased globalization demands in today's service economy.

Over the past decade, Distributed Model Management Systems (DMMS) have emerged as a new breed of information systems engaged in distributed model management activities such as model creation and delivery, model composition, model execution and model maintenance to fulfill dynamic decision-support and problem solving requests. Bhargava, Krishnan, and Muller [53] propose a web-based architecture for sharing decision models, illustrated using the DecisionNet prototype. The purpose of DecisionNet is to provide decision support technologies accessible electronically to consumers as a service over the World Wide Web instead of being purchased as stand-alone products. In this sense, DecisionNet performs the role of an "agent," mediating transactions between consumers and providers, in essence a "yellow pages" of services. Dolk [54] proposes an integrated modeling environment that utilizes structured modeling for representing models, data warehouses for storing models, and a component-based architecture for plugging in software components based on user needs. Huh, Chung and Kim [55] propose a framework for collaborative model management systems in a distributed environment. The emphasis is on coordinating the changes made to a collection of shared models and propagating the effect of these changes throughout the organization. In the context of optimization models, Ezechukwu and Maros [56] propose an architecture supporting distributed optimization over the Internet.

To facilitate the distribution process of model management, Web services pose as a viable technology to accomplish the mediation task. Web services are based on service-oriented computing principles and provide a standardized way of integrating several application modules using open standards such as XML (Extensible Markup Language), SOAP (Simple Object Access Protocol), WSDL (Web Services Description Language) and UDDI (Universal Description, Discovery, and Integration) over an Internet protocol backbone. In that regard, Iyer, Shankaranarayanan, and Lenard [57] propose a model management architecture emphasizing the use of structured modeling to represent spreadsheet models and an architecture supporting the sharing and reuse of models and data. Also, Madhusudan [58] proposes an architecture in which a "service platform" acts as a mediator by accepting service requests (e.g., from decision support clients), composing applicable models, and orchestrating the execution of the models. Supporting model representation in a web services environment, Kim [59] and El-Gayar and Tandekar [60] propose XML-based representations for analytical models. Both languages are based on the structured modeling paradigm [46] for conceiving, manipulating, and representing models at a higher level of abstraction to facilitate drawing inferences about models.

According to Goul and Corral [61], enterprise modeling refers to the activities, process representations and conceptualizations of an enterprise. The objective is to improve enterprise integration and support analysis of an enterprise. Such models are more likely to exist as a collection of models rather that one monolithic model [62]. As envisioned by Ba et al. [62], a critical element of an enterprise modeling framework is the ability to automate building and executing task-specific models (from existing model fragments) as needed in response to user generated requests. Recent work by Sen, Demirkan, and Goul [63], further extends this notion by proposing an architecture for dynamic and inter-organizational decision support.

In this chapter, we propose an architecture for the management of decision models in a heterogeneous and distributed environment, by building upon previous work on DMMS noted above as well as leveraging recent advances in service-oriented and semantic web technologies. The proposed architecture complements Sen et al.'s [63] architecture at layer 2 "Unified Enterprise Modeling Language (UEML) representation of models" and layer 3 "Decision Support Environment (DSE) middleware" with a focus on models supporting decision making processes in a service enterprise.

6   An Architecture for Distributed Model Management

6.1   Design Considerations

A number of design issues guided the formulation of the proposed architecture. These issues pertain to general DSS requirements for distributed support and to specific requirements for distributed model management. In that regard, we identify the following desirable features and design characteristics of a modeling system [9, 46, 56]:

- a conceptual framework for modeling based on a single model representation format,
- representational independence of model structure and the detailed data,
- representational independence of model structure and the model solution,
- meta-modeling capability to support reasoning about models,
- extensibility for different modeling paradigms, and
- accessibility of decision support resources.

6.2   Models as Services

Conceptually, a model as a loosely coupled component delivering a specific functionality can be conceived as a (computational or web) service. Likewise, a service as an entity abstracting underlying logic can be considered as a model. In reference to the aforementioned principles underlying service orientation [64], and in the context of model management, the following is noted:

- *Reuse*: Much of the work underlying model selection, composition, and integration focuses on finding ways to leverage existing models through reuse.
- *Abstraction*: A model is an abstraction of reality. To facilitate model selection and composition, models commonly expose only the models' description and interface. Note that model integration with its underlying 'white box' assumption is inconsistent with service-oriented principles.
- *Autonomy*: Similar to services, within its boundary (execution environment), models have complete autonomy independent of other models.
- *Loose coupling*: Related to abstraction and autonomy, and in the context of model selection and composition, models are loosely coupled with other models.
- *Statelessness*: Models exhibit statelessness, thereby supporting loose coupling and autonomy characteristics.
- *Composability*: Supporting reusability, models may be composed from other models, and may also participate in the composition of other models.
- *Discoverability*: Models should facilitate their description and discovery for consumption by other models.

In effect, with the exception of model integration and model interpretation, a significant synergy exists between model management, and service-oriented technologies and management. Together, models and model management functionalities wrapped as computational services form the components of the architecture. The proposed architecture highlights opportunities for synergy between these two arenas.

6.3   Distributed Model Management Architecture

The proposed architecture for distributed model management systems builds on earlier work on distributed decision systems, with a particular emphasis on model management, and is illustrated in Figure 1. At the core of the architecture is a service bus, which provides the underlying communication infrastructure for various model management services. The bus supports intra and inter-organization communication among services by implementing web services standards such as SOAP over HTTP. Connected to the bus is a collection of decision support services such as infrastructure management services, user interface services, and model management services. These services provide access to a variety of decision support resources such as models, modeling environments, and solvers. A decision support component acting as a client, can access any of the services connected to the bus irrespective of the physical location of the service. To facilitate intra and inter-organizational communication among services, the architecture adopts XML web services in which all services communicate via Internet protocols (mostly HTTP) and all data messages are sent and received as XML documents.

In this architecture, infrastructure management services may include discovery services for registering (publishing services), and services for configuring, monitoring and operating services. Account management services provide software licenses and access to fee-based services. Adopting XML web services, discovery services are implemented as Universal Description, Discovery, and Integration (UDDI) server managing information about all registered services, i.e., serving as a registry. UDDI uses XML to represent its contents, and contain enough information to direct clients to resources outside it such as web services description language (WSDL) files, which in turn provide information about the functionality of a service and the details necessary to communicate with the service.

Data needed for decision support is available in various formats and is often distributed. Data may reside in containers such as database management systems or data warehouses, or may reside as stand-alone files. Most contemporary database management systems provide support to XML. With the data provider and wrapper services registered with the discovery services, a client component which may be a decision support application or another decision support service would be able to locate and access the desired data. These data management services lie outside the scope of the current architecture; however the architecture is extensible to utilize such data management services.

User interface services are a collection of reusable and sharable components providing functionality for visualizing data and model results, customizing display and access for decision makers, and capturing user input for data and model management services. The presentation layer of a decision support system may use user-interface services as building blocks for developing the interface.

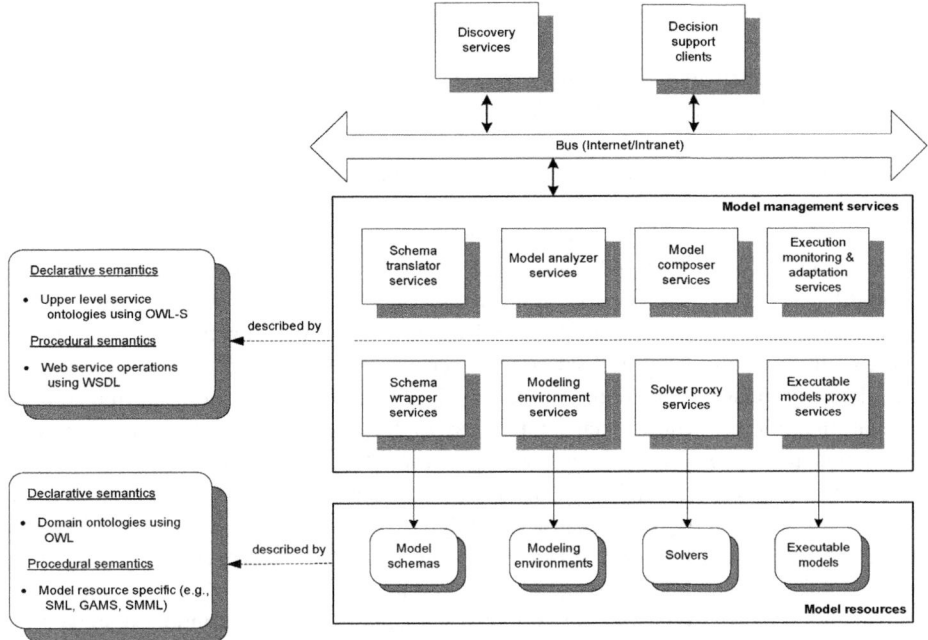

Fig. 1. A semantic web services-based architecture for model management systems

Model management services provide access and management to a variety of modeling resources. These resources include specialized solvers, modeling platforms and languages such as GAMS and AMPL, model schemas represented as text files, e.g., GAMS, and MATLAB models, and models as executable components. Different types of services are needed to utilize the various resources. For executable models and solvers, wrapper services are used to encapsulate the functionality of existing modules as web services. For development environments and platforms such as AMPL or MATLAB, proxy services are used to expose the functionality and to manage the interface with these environments. For model schemas represented as stand-alone non-executable files such as GAMS, AMPL, and XML representations of models, schema wrapper services encapsulate the functionality and purpose of the underlying models and coordinate the interface with other services to successfully execute these models.

Other model management services include services for model translation, model composition, and model analysis. Model translation services represent a repository of services for translating model schemas to/from a variety of popular formats and languages such as GAMS and LINGO to/from SMML. Model composition services in association with the execution monitoring and adaptation services allows for leveraging a collection of models for a specific decision situation by coordinating the execution of such models in a workflow-like manner. Model analyzer services provide functionality for analyzing model results and conducting what-if analysis.

The architecture facilitates service innovation by supporting different phases of the service system life cycle (see Section 3). The needs assessment and specification phase includes knowledge encoding leading to the formulation of specific requests for model retrieval from an existing modeling repository or new model formulations applicable to a specific service context. The service design and development phase includes harnessing discovery services in tandem with model management services depicted in the architecture. The service designer can also utilize other related services such as user interface services, and decision support clients, for facilitating new service design. Model composer services can computationally generate compatible sequences of existing models that can meet the user requirements. These models may be simulated or used in real time, depending upon the life cycle stage. The execution monitoring and adaptation services can guide the service production and delivery phase, while the model analyzer services can help in the service evaluation and optimization phase. Other associated model management services such as schema translator and wrapper services, modeling environment services, solver proxy services, and executable model proxy services can be invoked to conduct the low level model management tasks. Finally, the phase out stage is guided by the results of the model analyzer services to determine the relevance and currency of the model for a particular service application context.

The architecture is distributed in the true sense, in that even the model management functionalities are exposed as web services. This is contrary to many distributed model management approaches discussed in the previous section, where although model resources are distributed, the model management functionalities reside in a centralized manner (e.g., see [58]). This approach has a major advantage in that a decision maker can query, compose, or deploy models using only a thin client, without bearing the burden of model management computations.

Further, two main aspects of the architecture are evident for model sharing and reuse. First, semantic description of models using OWL, provides a mechanism to reason about their properties. Second, the semantics associated with OWL-based ontologies of models is extensible for describing corresponding web services using OWL-S. These semantic web services can then be used either as atomic model units or composed together into composite model units to derive a solution for a particular decision making problem. Since both atomic as well as composite services are described using OWL-S, they can be discovered more effectively through logic-based search techniques, rather than just keyword based search. These two novel aspects of model management are discussed below.

6.4   Semantic Descriptions of Models

Ontologies are explicit conceptualizations (i.e., meta-information) that describe the semantics of information resources. Significant advances have recently been made along the lines of using ontologies for reasoning about resources available on the Web [65] . Model resources such as models, solvers, or executable models that are distributed over the Web can lend themselves to these advances to provide better model management capabilities, particularly in distributed settings. In this section, we discuss some of the relevant advances and standards that are instrumental in realizing the semantic web infrastructure, and their particular application in the context of the proposed model management architecture.

The Resource Description Framework (RDF) is a W3C standard that builds on top of XML to provide a data model for describing resources on the Web in terms of named properties and values, and encoded in a formal, machine-processable format [66]. An RDF description of a resource consists of a set of RDF statements (or triples). Each RDF triple consists of three parts: an object (a resource), an attribute (a property), and a value (another resource or plain literal). RDF Schema (RDF-S) extends RDF by providing a type system for RDF or an ontological vocabulary for describing properties and classes of RDF resources [66]. RDF-S thus provides a way to build an object model with a semantics for generalization-hierarchies of such properties and classes. The Web Ontology Language (OWL) goes a step further by adding more vocabulary for describing properties and classes [66]. Some examples include property type restrictions, equality, property characteristics, class intersection, and restricted cardinality.

Web services are a class of resources that are distributed, similar to models. In the earlier discussion, we built an analogy between models and services. Essentially, web services are self-describing, self-contained software applications that are accessible over the Internet [64]. Web services form a cornerstone of our proposed architecture for model management systems and its relation to semantic web technologies is discussed next.

Currently, models as web services are described procedurally using the Web Services Description Language (WSDL), which lack semantic descriptions of web services [67]. Several research approaches have been proposed to add semantics to web service descriptions [68]. Four submissions to the W3C consortium exemplify these approaches: OWL Web Ontology Language for Services (OWL-S), Web Services Modeling Ontology (WSMO), Semantic Web Services Framework (SWSF), and Web Service Semantics (WSDL-S) [69]. Recently, W3C put forth a modified version of WSDL-S, Semantically Annotated WSDL (SAWSDL) as their recommendation [70]. Analysis of these standards revealed OWL-S to be more amenable to model management, given that it defines its meta-model in the same language that it uses for concrete service descriptions as well as allows for more expressive languages to be incorporated with OWL. OWL-S is hence selected for providing semantics to models, encapsulated as web services in our architecture, and is briefly discussed here. It can also be noted that significant synergy exists between OWL-S and SWASDL, and that research is being conducted on grounding OWL-S in SAWSDL, i.e., relating elements of an OWL-S service description with elements of a WSDL service description [71].

OWL-S is an OWL-based Web Service Ontology language, whose objective is to provide a vocabulary for encoding rich semantic web service descriptions, in a way that builds upon OWL [69]. Service descriptions may be provided using OWL-S that mainly consists of three interrelated sub-ontologies for the top-level concept Service, namely service profile, service model, and service grounding. The service profile is used to express 'what a service does', which may be used for service advertising, constructing service requests, and matchmaking. The service model provides essentially a process model to describe 'how the service works', in the form of inputs, outputs, preconditions, and effects (typically called IOPE), which may be used for service seeking, composing service descriptions, coordinating and monitoring of service executions. However, it can be noted that OWL-S takes the view that a process is not necessary a program to be executed, but a specification of the ways in which a client may interact with the service. There can be three types of processes: atomic, composite, and simple. Atomic processes correspond to the actions a service can perform by engaging it in a single interaction; composite processes correspond to actions that require multi-step protocols and/or multiple server actions; and simple processes provide an abstraction mechanism to provide multiple views of the same process. Finally, the service grounding provides information on 'how the service can be accessed' by mapping the constructs of the process model onto detailed specifications of message formats, protocols, and so forth (typically expressed in WSDL).

Associating semantic metadata to models and other model resources is essential in order to reason about their capabilities. Above mentioned advances in ontologies and semantic web standards facilitate the provision of semantics to model resources through descriptions encoded in the form of their respective *domain ontologies*. Similarly, their corresponding web services as well as other supporting web services, such as model schema translator services, are described in the form of *higher level ontologies*, particularly designed for web services.

Semantic descriptions of models can facilitate multiple uses. They can provide metadata for intelligent searching, browsing, and composing of models by decision makers. Moreover, implicit assumptions, model uses, constraints, and such can be explicitly captured through creation of domain ontologies of models. In fact, certain models may be elaborated in detail to provide, what can be termed as a 'white box' representation of models. Models (or model schemas) described using paradigms such as structured modeling, e.g. using SMML [60], may be semantically expressed to the finest level of detail with domain ontologies. Certain additional elements such as the application domain, model purpose, and so forth, are standardized across every model described with an OWL-based domain ontology. Last, but not the least, these OWL-based domain ontologies can be extended to create higher level ontologies with OWL-S, in order to describe models wrapped as web services. The composer and execution monitoring services can make use of these higher level service ontologies to facilitate model composition functionalities.

Shown below is a snippet of domain ontology for a revenue computation model, described with OWL.

```
. . .
<owl:Class rdf:ID="FinancialModel">
   <rdfs:comment>Used to compute revenues and
                Income
   </rdfs:comment>
   <rdfs:subClassOf rdf:resource="#Model"/>
</owl:Class>
```

```
<owl:DatatypeProperty rdf:ID="hasOutput">
   <rdfs:domain rdf:resource="#Model">
   <rdfs:range
             rdf:resource="&xsd;positiveInteger">
</owl:DatatypeProperty>
...
```

Similarly, shown below is a snippet of the OWL-S service ontology for the revenue computation model.

```
...
<Description rdf:about="#FinancialModel">
    <hasPreCondition>
   <expr:HTN-expression>
       <expr: expressionBody>
     ((computed-price ?product_price)
     (forecasted-demand
                            ?product_demand)
     (production-cost ?pcost)
     (distribution-cost ?dcost))
       </expr: expressionBody>
   </expr:HTN-expression>
    </hasPreCondition>
</Description rdf:about="#FinancialModel">
```

In the following sections, we discuss the implementation of the proposed architecture, followed by illustrative case studies indicating the utility of this architecture in facilitating service innovation.

7   Implementation and Current Status

A research prototype of the proposed architecture has been developed using the J2EE platform. Key model management functionalities include model discovery services, model wrapper and translation services, modeling environment services, solver proxy services, and executable model proxy services. These have been extended based on our prior research effort. The current emphasis is on developing model composer and execution monitoring services. The goal is to utilize the application context encoded in the OWL and OWL-S domain ontologies to semantically extract candidate models that may satisfy the model composition request. The semantic descriptions of models, provided in the form of higher level service ontologies using OWL-S, serve as a building block in how the model composer service may function. The model library is populated with associated ontologies in OWL and OWL-S using the Protégé editor. One of the important developments underway is the ability to provide computational translation of models described using different representation techniques into OWL and OWL-S model ontologies, similar in notion to the work on dynamic decision support by Sen, et al. [63].

8   Case Studies

To demonstrate interaction of the various services comprising the proposed architecture, we have developed a series of Unified Modeling Language (UML) sequence diagrams. Two representative case studies are discussed below.

8.1   Case study 1: Model Sharing in an Inter- or Intra organizational Setting

This case study emphasizes the efficacy of the proposed architecture in addressing some of the issues most frequently encountered in sharing models in an inter- or intra-organizational setting, such as model awareness and the heterogeneity of modeling environments.

In this case study (Figure 2), a decision support client (DSC) wishes to identify a decision model for the problem at hand, e.g., a contract portfolio optimization model or a scheduling model (as described in the motivating scenarios). In the architecture, the DSC may use a discovery service to locate an appropriate model (thereby addressing the awareness issue) and data (if necessary). In this case study, the model happened to be represented in the Structured Modeling Markup Language (SMML), a XML-based representation for mathematical models [60]. This is an abstract representation of model structure that is not suitable for direct execution. Accordingly, when the DSC requests the execution of the model, the SMML portfolio optimization model proxy service uses a translator service to translate the SMML model into a representation such as the General Algebraic Modeling Language (GAMS). To be able to solve the GAMS model, the model proxy server uses the discovery service to locate a proxy service of the respective environment to process the model. The environment proxy service may then use the discovery service to locate an appropriate solver and execute

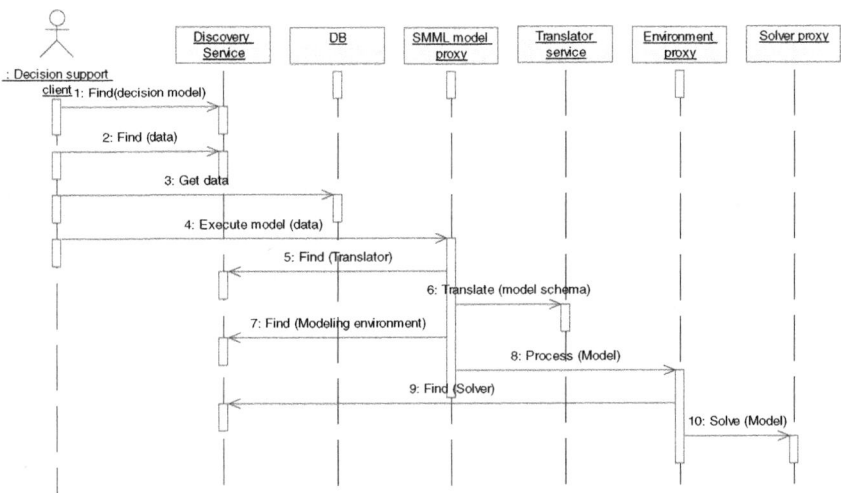

Fig. 2. Case study 1: Model sharing in an inter- or intra-organizational setting

the solver to solve the model. In this case study, a decision maker/analyst would be able to meet his/her decision needs regardless of whether the decision maker (or decision support tool) is familiar to the particular model representation or has access to the modeling environment and solvers necessary to solve the model.

8.2   Case study 2: Model Composition in an Inter-organizational Setting

This case study (Figure 3) demonstrates a typical interaction among model management services for composing a model from existing models and executing them in the appropriate order. An example of such scenario may occur in the interaction between a KIBS firm and its clients as described in the motivating scenarios where a client would wish to integrate its problem specific models with models provided by the KIBS.

In this case study, the decision support client (of the KIBS client) uses the discovery service to first try and locate the desired model. Due to unavailability of such a model, the decision support client then invokes a model composer service with the model request. The model composer service, in turn retrieves the semantic descriptions (OWL-S ontologies) of model resources (bundled as web services). Based on the service profile, and service model descriptions in these ontologies, the composer service extracts the form of inputs, outputs, preconditions, and effects (typically called IOPE, and may be used for service seeking, composing service descriptions, coordinating and monitoring of service executions) for each model resource. In the prototype implementation, Hierarchical Task Network (HTN) planning, which is a class of AI planning algorithms is used to search the state space for potential composition of available model resources to respond favorably to the model composition request. For a detailed example, the readers are referred to [72]. Then, the client uses the execution monitoring services to monitor the execution of the composite service generated. Semantic descriptions of selected model resources are retrieved by the execution monitoring service, since it uses the service model and service grounding descriptions in OWL-S ontologies to coordinate and monitor the ordered deployment of each model resource. In addition to addressing model awareness and heterogeneity issues, this case study demonstrates the use of model semantics to assess the applicability of models to a particular decision situation as well as to compose models (in heterogeneous environments) into new models that address specific needs of the decision maker.

As the ability to support service innovation becomes a major driver of success in service enterprises, facilitating model management for dynamic decision making throughout the service system life cycle becomes imperative. In this chapter, we have discussed the use of decision model management in facilitating service innovation in distributed service environments. The proposed distributed model management architecture is based on the confluence of service-oriented principles and semantic web technology. Design principles supported by SOA emphasize reuse, statelessness, autonomy, abstraction, discoverability, loose coupling, and composability. The proposed architecture for model management systems is novel, primarily in the

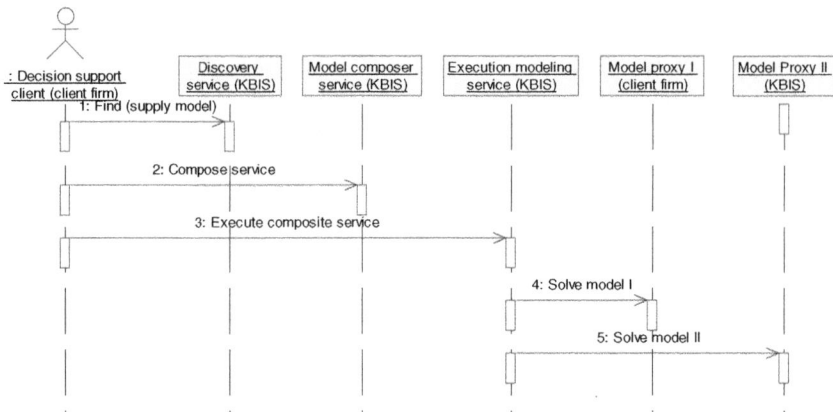

Fig. 3. Case study 2: Model composition in an inter-organizational setting

following two aspects. First, it is completely distributed through the provision for not only distributed model resources, but also distributed model management services. Second, it proposes a semantic layer for model representation that can facilitate automation and reasoning mechanisms, such as model composition. The utility of the architecture in supporting the different service management life cycle phases is highlighted. The motivating scenarios and case studies demonstrate several application areas where such an architecture may be best suited.

Further research is needed in how to reason about models across different service application contexts and industries. Enterprise ontologies have the potential of bringing together the needed semantics for adapting disparate models from different application contexts [61]. Also, model integration is noted to be important component along with model composition, focusing on synthesizing models at the structural (or definitional) level. This capability needs to be further studied in the light of semantic web technologies mentioned in this chapter. The application of model management in supporting agile business processes in service organizations has been noted earlier. However, this perspective needs further attention in terms of integrating workflow technology with model management techniques. Use of process ontologies in this regards seems to be a plausible avenue for further exploration [73]. Such related synergies are likely to create significantly new opportunities for global service organizations competing in an increasingly complex environment and striving for service innovation.

References

1. Hilsenrath, J.E.: The economy: Service sector enjoys growth, but pace slows. Wall Street Journal, New York, NY A.2 (2003)
2. Maglio, P.P., Srinivasan, S., Kreulen, J.T., Spohrer, J.: Service systems, service scientists, SSME, and innovation. Communications of the ACM (Special Issue: Services Science) 49, 81–85 (2006)

3. Tien, J.M., Berg, D.: A case for service systems engineering. International Journal of Systems Engineering 12, 13–39 (2003)
4. IBM: Annual Report (2006)
5. Spohrer, J., Maglio, P.P., Bailey, J., Gruhl, D.: Steps toward a science of service systems. Computer 40, 71–77 (2007)
6. Nambisan, S.: Why service businesses are not product businesses. MIT Sloan Management Review 42, 72–80 (2001)
7. Service Research and Innovation Initiative (2007),
   http://forums.thesrii.org/srii
8. Consortium for Service Innovation (2007),
   http://www.serviceinnovation.org/
9. Muhanna, W.A., Pick, R.A.: Meta-modeling concepts and tools for model management: A systems approach. Manage. Sci. 40, 1093–1123 (1994)
10. Lovelock, C.: Think before your leap in services marketing. In: Berry, L.L., Shostack, G.L., Upah, G. (eds.) Emerging Perspectives in Services Marketing, pp. 115–119. American Marketing Association, Chicago (1983)
11. Fitzsimmons, J.A., Fitzsimmons, M.J.: Services Management: Operations, Strategy, and Information Technology. McGraw-Hill, New York (2004)
12. Gronroos, C.: Service Management and Marketing. Wiley, Chichester (2000)
13. Lusch, R.F., Vargo, S.L. (eds.): The Service-dominant Logic of Marketing: Dialog, Debate, And Directions. M. E. Sharpe (2006)
14. Casati, F., Discenza, A.: Supporting workflow cooperation within and across organizations. In: Proceedings of the 2000 ACM Symposium on Applied Computing, pp. 196–202. ACM Press (2000)
15. Stauss, B., Engelmann, K., Kremer, A., Luhn, A. (eds.): Services Science: Fundamentals, Challenges and Future Developments. Springer, Berlin (2007)
16. Meuter, M.L., Bitner, M.J., Ostrom, A.L., Brown, S.W.: Choosing among alternative service delivery modes: An investigation of customer trial of self-service technologies. Journal of Marketing 69, 61–83 (2005)
17. Rust, R.T.: A call for a wider range of service research. J. Serv. Res. 6, 211 (2004)
18. Mansharamani, V.: Toward a Theory of Service Innovation: An Inductive Case Study Approach to Evaluating Uniqueness of Services. MIT Sloan School of Management, Cambridge, MA (2005)
19. Salter, A., Tether, B.S.: Innovation in Services: Through the Looking Glass of Innovation Studies. In: Research, A.I.o.M. (ed.) Background paper prepared for the Workshop Grand Challenge in Services, Oxford University, UK (2006),
   http://www.sbs.ox.ac.uk/faculty/Sako+Mari/GCS.htm
20. Sundbo, J., Gallouj, F.: Innovation as a loosely coupled system in services. In: Metcalfe, J.S., Miles, I.D. (eds.) Innovation Systems in the Service Economy: Measurement and Case Study Analysis. Kluwer Academic Publishers, Boston (2001)
21. Barras, R.: Towards a theory of innovation in services. Research Policy 15, 161–173 (1986)
22. Quinn, J.B.: Technology in services: Past myths and future challenges. In: Guile, B.R., Quinn, J.B. (eds.) Technology in Services: Policies for Growth, Trade and Employment. National Academy Press, Washington, D. C (1988)
23. Miles, I.: Services in the new industrial economy. Futures 25, 653–672 (1993)
24. Chesbrough, H.: Open Innovation: The New Imperative for Creating and Profiting from Technology. Harvard Business School Press (2003)

25. Coombs, R., Harvey, M., Tether, B.S.: Analysing distributed processes of provision and innovation. Industrial and Corporate Change 12, 1125–1155 (2004)
26. Brown, J.S., Duguid, P.: The Social Life of Information. Harvard Business School Press, Boston (2000)
27. Krishnan, R., Chari, K.: Model management: Survey, future research directions and a bibliography. Interactive Transactions of OR/MS 3 (2000)
28. Chang, A.-M., Holsapple, C.W., Whinston, A.B.: Model management issues and directions. Decision Support Systems 9, 19–37 (1993)
29. Metters, R., Marucheck, A.: Service management - Academic issues and scholarly reflections from operations management researchers. Decis. Sci. 38, 195–214 (2007)
30. Johnson, R.: Service operations management: Return to roots. International Journal of Operations & Production Management 19, 104–124 (1999)
31. Krishnamurthy, A.: From Just in Time Manufacturing to On-Demand Services. In: Hsu, C. (ed.) Service Enterprise Integration: An Enterprise Engineering Perspective, pp. 1–37 (2007)
32. Tien, J.M.: Toward a decision informatics paradigm: a real-time, information-based approach to decision making. IEEE Transactions on Systems, Man And Cybernetics: Part C. Applications And Reviews 33, 102–113 (2003)
33. Sage, A.P., Armstrong Jr., J.E.: An Introduction to Systems Engineering. John Wiley & Sons, New York (2000)
34. Iyer, A.V., Deshpande, V., Wu, Z.: A postponement model for demand management. Management Science 49, 983 (2003)
35. Borst, S., Mandelbaum, A., Reiman, M.I.: Dimensioning Large Call Centers. Operations Research 52, 17 (2004)
36. Paschalidis, I.C., Tsitsiklis, J.N.: Congestion-dependent pricing of network services. IEEE-ACM Transactions on Networking 8, 171–184 (2000)
37. Wright, P.D., Bretthauer, K.M., Cote, M.: Reexamining the nurse scheduling problem: Staffing ratios and nursing shortages. Decision Sciences 37, 39–70 (2006)
38. Charnes, A., Cooper, W., Rhodes, E.: Measuring the efficiency of decision making units. European Journal of Operational Research 2, 428–449 (1978)
39. Schmenner, R.: How can service businesses survive and prosper? Sloan Management Review Spring, 21–32 (1986)
40. Rust, R.T., Metters, R.: Mathematical models of service. European Journal of Operational Research 91, 427–439 (1996)
41. Tien, J.M.: Services Innovation: Decision Attributes, Innovation Enablers, and Innovation Drivers. In: Hsu, C. (ed.) Service Enterprise Integration: An Enterprise Engineering Perspective, pp. 39–76 (2007)
42. Miles, I., Kastrinos, N., Flanagan, K., Bilderbeek, R., den Hertog, P., Huitink, W., Bouman, M.: Knowledge intensive business services: Their role as users, carriers, and sources of innovation. EIMS Publication No. 15, Innovation Programme, DGXIII, Luxembourg (1995)
43. Hertog, P.D.: Co-producers of innovation: On the role of knowledge-intensive business services in innovation. In: Gadrey, J., Gallouj, F. (eds.) Productivity, Innovation and Knowledge in Services: New Economic and Socio-economic Approaches, pp. 223–253. Edward Elgar, Cheltenham (2002)
44. Blanning, R.W.: Model management systems: An overview. Decision Support Systems 9, 9–18 (1993)
45. Muhanna, W.A.: An object-oriented framework for model management and DSS development. Decision Support Systems 9, 217–229 (1993)

46. Geoffrion, A.M.: An introduction to structural modeling. Manage. Sci. 33, 547–588 (1987)
47. Basu, A., Blanning, R.W.: Model integration using metagraphs. Inf. Syst. Res. 5, 195–218 (1994)
48. Dolk, D.R., Kottemann, J.E.: Model integration and a theory of models. Decision Support Systems 9, 51–63 (1993)
49. Liang, T.-P., Konsynski, B.R.: Modeling by analogy: Use of analogical reasoning in model management systems. Decision Support Systems 9, 113–125 (1993)
50. Chari, K.: Model composition using filter spaces. Inf. Syst. Res. 13, 15–35 (2002)
51. Dhar, V., Jarke, M.: On modeling processes. Decision Support Systems 9, 39–49 (1993)
52. Kottemann, J.E., Dolk, D.R.: Model integration and modeling languages: A process perspective. Inf. Syst. Res. 3, 1–16 (1992)
53. Bhargava, H.K., Krishnan, R., Muller, R.: Decision support on demand: Emerging electronic markets for decision technologies. Decision Support Systems 19, 193–214 (1997)
54. Dolk, D.R.: Integrated model management in the data warehouse era. European Journal of Operational Research 122, 199–218 (2000)
55. Huh, S.Y., Chung, Q.B., Kim, H.M.: Collaborative model management in departmental computing. INFOR 38, 373–389 (2000)
56. Ezechukwu, O.C., Maros, I.: OOF: Open Optimization Framework. Department of Computing, Imperial College London (2003)
57. Iyer, B., Shankaranarayanan, G., Lenard, M.L.: Model management decision environment: a Web service prototype for spreadsheet models. Decision Support Systems 40, 283–304 (2005)
58. Madhusudan, T.: A web services framework for distributed model management. Inf. Syst. Front. 9, 9–27 (2007)
59. Kim, H.: An XML-based modeling language for the open interchange of decision models. Decision Support Systems 31, 429–441 (2001)
60. El-Gayar, O.F., Tandekar, K.: An XML-based schema definition for model sharing and reuse in a distributed environment. Decision Support Systems 43, 791–808 (2007)
61. Goul, M., Corral, K.: Enterprise model management and next-generation decision support. Decision Support Systems 43, 915–932 (2007)
62. Ba, S., Lang, K.R., Whinston, A.B.: Enterprise decision support using Intranet technology. Decision Support Systems 20, 99–134 (1997)
63. Sen, S., Demirkan, H., Goul, M.: Dynamic decision support through instantiation of UEML representations. Communications of the ACM 50, 87–93 (2007)
64. Papazoglou, M.P.: Web Services: Principles and Technology. Pearson-Prentice Hall, London (2008)
65. Fensel, D., Hendler, J., Lieberman, H., Wahlster, W. (eds.): Spinning the semantic web: Bringing the world wide web to its full potential. The MIT Press, Cambridge (2003)
66. W3C: W3C Recommendations: (1) Resource Description Framework (RDF): Concepts and Abstract Synatax, (2) RDF Vocabulary Description Language 1.0: RDF Schema, (3) OWL Web Ontology Language Semantics and Abstract Syntax, (4) A Semantic Web Rule Language (SWRL) Combining OWL and RuleML (2004),
http://www.w3.org/2001/sw/
67. W3C: Web Services Description Language (WSDL) 1.1 (W3C Recommendation) (2001),
http://www.w3.org/TR/wsdl
68. Sheth, A., Verma, K., Gomadam, K.: Semantics to energize the full services spectrum. Communications of the ACM (Special Issue: Services Science) 49, 55–61 (2006)

69. W3C: W3C Members Submissions: (1) OWL Web Ontology Language for Services (OWL-S), (2) Web Service Modeling Ontology (WSMO), (3) Semantic Web Services Framework (SWSF), (4) Web Service Semantics: WSDL-S (2005),
http://www.w3.org/2002/ws/swsig/
70. Kopecký, J., Vitvar, T., Bournez, C., Farrell, J.: SAWSDL: Semantic Annotations for WSDL and XML Schema. IEEE Internet Comput. 11, 60–67
71. Paolucci, M., Wagner, M., Martin, D.: Grounding OWL-S in SAWSDL. In: Krämer, B.J., Lin, K.-J., Narasimhan, P. (eds.) ICSOC 2007. LNCS, vol. 4749, pp. 416–421. Springer, Heidelberg (2007)
72. Deokar, A.V., El-Gayar, O.F.: A semantic web services-based architecture for model management. In: Proceedings of the 41st Annual Hawaii International Conference on System Sciences (HICSS-41 2008). IEEE Computer Society, Waikoloa (2008)
73. Therani, M.: Ontology development for designing and managing dynamic business process networks. IEEE Transactions on Industrial Informatics 3, 173–185 (2007)

Virtual Environments for Computational and Analytical Modeling: A Telemedicine Application[*]

Tung Bui[1], Daniel Dolk[2], Alexandre Gachet[1], and Hans-Jürgen Sebastian[3]

[1] University of Hawaii
{Tung.Bui,Gachet}@hawaii.edu
[2] Naval Postgraduate School
drdolk@nps.edu
[3] Deutsche Post Chair of Optimization of Distribution Networks
RWTH Aachen University
Sebastian@or.rwth-aachen.de

Abstract. Virtualization is commonly known in computer science as an abstraction technique of computer resources – physical platforms and resources – so that applications or end-users can seamlessly interact with these resources without the needs to deal with physical requirements. Going beyond the simulation of computer environments and resources, this paper proposes a paradigm for designing complex information systems based upon the concept of virtual modeling. The idea is to allow modelers use a virtual environment that is composed of real modeling platforms to replicate complex real problems, and explore new and virtual problems that might have high potential for real–life applications. Modeling here is not just an effort to find (new) solutions to an existing problem, rather it is also a discovery process seeking to create new (problems). We see this approach as vital in addressing the applications emerging from service science, management and engineering (SSME), which will rely upon computational modeling approaches as much, if not more, than traditional supply-chain based analytical modeling. We illustrate our design methodology with a telemedicine application using Brahms, a multi-agent programming language developed by the NASA.

Keywords: Information Systems Modeling, simulation and decision support, service system, SSME, virtual environments, telemedicine.

1 Introduction

With the advent of high performance computing systems, modeling has become both a process of explanation (e.g., knowledge representation, business process engineering and re-engineering formally coded in executable code) and a process of exploration (e.g., action-driven artificial intelligence software, decision support systems, agent-based simulation). Carley [3] argues that organizational computing has

---

[*] The authors would like to thank Stephen Kimbrough, Wharton School, and Murray Turoff, NJIT, for their inspirational work on virtuality and their suggestions for this paper.

D. Dolk et al. (Eds.): Decision Support Modeling in Service Networks, LNBIP 42, pp. 169–195, 2012.
© Springer-Verlag Berlin Heidelberg 2012

evolved toward an inquiry process related to information, knowledge and computation, and this process has led to a wide range of advanced I.S. applications (e.g., flight simulators, remotely-controlled robots for task-specific applications, and virtual classrooms). Within this expanded scope, modeling can be viewed as a process that not only replicates models of realities but is also capable of creating life-like situations that appear real, yet have no correspondence in reality [29,37]. For example, a computerized business game is modeled after the realities of competition. However, as it becomes a tool for exploring new competitive strategies, the emerging rules of virtual competition might nevertheless lead to real actions. Another classic example is SimCity.

In this paper, we discuss the evolution of both virtuality and modeling in the context of modeling for problem solving with a focus on services science, management and engineering (SSME). We argue that virtuality has evolved to a state in which, only under certain modeling objectives and conditions, should reality be used as a reference. We also contend that modeling under virtual environments requires a new paradigm that views computation as both an experimentation and explanation process. We advocate a paradigm shift in developing a computational model. A negotiated reality – an application environment that situates within the reality-virtuality continuum – requires both the modeler and the users of the model to: (i) use a formal language for describing and explaining the functions and behaviors of a phenomenon and its environment, and (ii) use the power of information technologies to search and experiment with new environments that would best address the problem at hand. Negotiated reality may be a particularly relevant context in which to consider SSME applications since service activities require a much higher degree of cooperation and coordination between provider and consumer than is typically the case with commodity-based economic transactions. We will elaborate this thesis by emphasizing the concepts of computational experimentation and computational explanation.

The paper is organized as follows. Section 2 discusses the evolution of the concept of virtuality. It serves as a foundation to explore in Section 3 how computational modeling and problem solving converge thanks to the joint consideration of reality and virtuality (Fig. 1). In Section 4, we propose a software modeling methodology called Virtual Environment for Computational and Analytical Modeling (VECAM) that applies model management design principles for analytical modeling to generate requirements desiderata for computational modeling environments. Through the discussion of a telemedicine service application, we demonstrate how VECAM can be implemented as a design methodology, one that is particularly relevant to service science, management and engineering (SSME).

2   Evolution of Virtuality

We examine the concept of virtuality in progressive stages, looking first at the role of modeling and simulation in scientific inquiry to see how virtual environments are becoming more integral to that process. We then posit a virtuality spectrum which includes the key concept of *negotiated reality* which we see as one of the distinguishing aspects of services-based applications. We discuss how negotiated reality in concert with virtual environments support SSME concepts and applications.

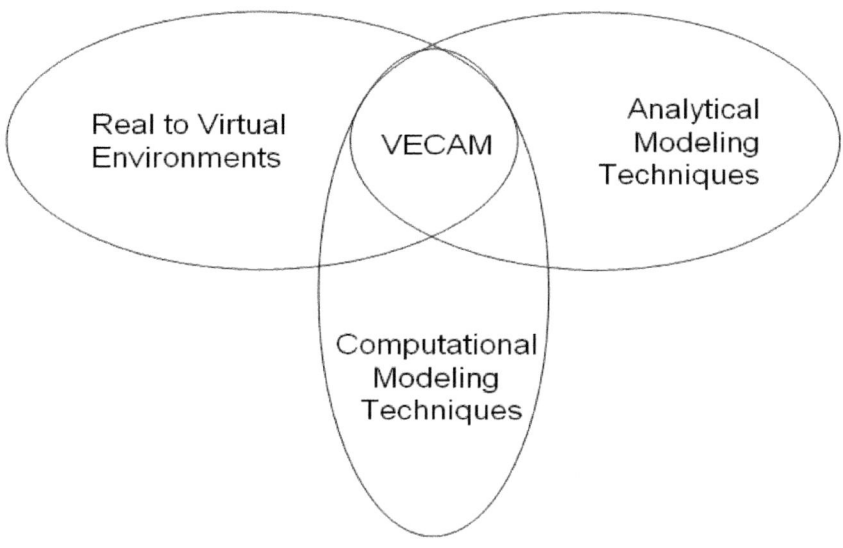

Fig. 1. VECAM framework

2.1   Modeling and Simulation in the Scientific Method

We begin by examining the role of modeling and simulation in the scientific method as characterized by [16]. Fig. 2a shows the traditional interplay between theory and experiment which has earmarked science since the beginning of the Enlightenment until the advent of digital computers. Fig. 2b shows the emergence of modeling and simulation in this process as a result of the use of digital computing. In this scenario, a Model is a formal representation of reality which implements a Theory, and a Simulation elicits the behavior of the Model, usually over time, thus corresponding to an Experiment. Models in this context have largely been what we call analytical models in that they are primarily mathematical in nature, for example systems of partial differential equations, mathematical programming, and the like. We use the term simulation in the larger sense of an experimental design for solving and analyzing a model using various forms of sensitivity analysis and/or goal-seeking, as opposed to the more specific context of various simulation technologies such as discrete or continuous event simulations. Not all models are dynamic, for example, a mathematical programming model for determining the optimal location of a warehouse is spatially, rather than temporally, oriented. Nevertheless, it makes sense to think of an experimental design, or simulation, for testing and analyzing such a model even though it may be time independent.

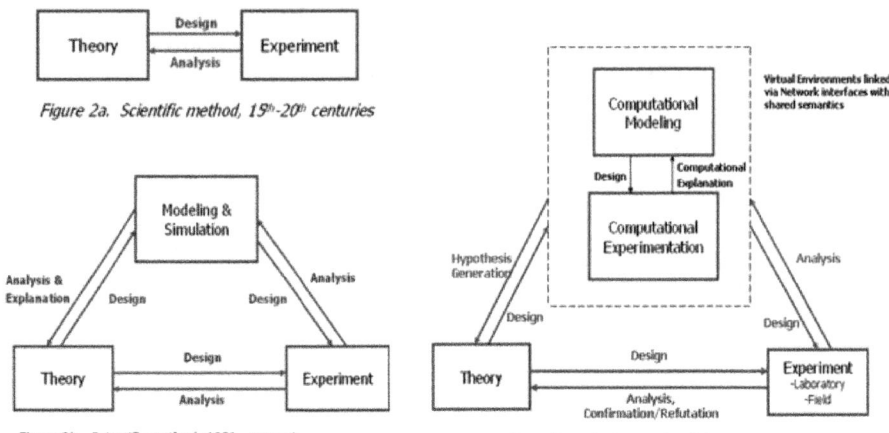

Fig. 2. Role of modeling and simulation in scientific inquiry [16]

Fig. 2c shows the next stage in the scientific method which moves beyond analytical modeling and squarely into the arena of virtual environments. In this scenario, Hamming envisions networks of virtual environments that eventually can be linked via shared semantics. This is model integration in the large, and relies heavily upon computational modeling and the methodology of computational experimentation for the creation and maintenance of virtual environments. We take pains to emphasize that analytical modeling is not rendered obsolete in this context, but rather subsumed and integrated under the umbrella of computational modeling. We will indicate ways in which this can be achieved, specifically through a VECAM architecture.

2.2   The Virtuality – Reality Continuum

According to the Oxford English Dictionary, "virtual reality" is a state or an object that is "not physically existing, but made by software to appear to do so from the point of view of the program or user". This definition depicts a fundamental characteristic of virtuality. According to Turoff, it is a process of *negotiated reality* in which the artifacts of computer systems are adopted by their users as "agreed-upon" reality [37]. In this process, the reality becomes simply more and more artificial [10] while the virtuality becomes more and more real. The virtuality-reality continuum can be explained as a constant search for truth using analytical, experiential, conflictual, synthetic and pragmatic approaches [28].

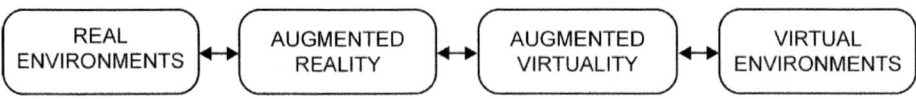

Fig. 3. The evolution of virtuality - from real to virtual environments

Table 1. The Reality-Virtuality continuum with some application examples

REALITY-VIRTUALITY CONTINUUM	APPLICATIONS	CHARACTERISTICS	OBJECTIVES	EXAMPLES
AUGMENTED REALITY	Simulation	Replicate a business behavior	Generate lifelike behavior in either cost-effective or accelerated simulated environment	Queuing applications; flight simulator; technological forecasting; futures research
AUGMENTED VIRTUALITY	e-environments	Create a task in an electronic environment that is different than reality	Use agent-based systems for complex applications on the Internet	e-classroom, Internet-supported distributed teamwork
VIRTUAL ENVIRON-MENTS	Virtual communities (e.g., users' groups)	Social connectedness in cyberspace	Create new communities (e.g., virtual cities with avatars)	MUD (Multi-User Dungeons), MOO (Object-oriented MUDs); Second Life; Facebook groups

Yet, *negotiated reality* implies a number of implicit but fundamental assumptions about modeling that depend on the way the modeler approaches the "reality-virtuality" continuum. As evidenced by several recent systems [22], the reality-virtuality continuum spans from real environments to augmented reality to augmented virtuality and to virtual environments [27] (see Fig. 3 and Table 1). One contrasting dimension of this continuum is the unity of space, time and place in a real environment compared to a dislocation by information and communication technologies and the omnipresence of the WWW in a virtual environment (for example, the traditional classroom versus the distributed e-classroom).

There are two notions that may be relevant here in the discussion of real and virtual environments: *coherence* and *correspondence*. Coherence is a measure of how well a virtual environment holds together internally. Does it exhibit consistent behavior within the boundaries of its environment? Is it believable by the users who interact with it? Does it conform to its internal "laws"? A computer game such as SimCity or a combat simulation would have coherence as a desirable property. Correspondence refers to how well the virtual environment corresponds to a real world counterpart. This is closely related to the concept of "external validation". For example, if we build a synthetic economy, we may want that economy to emulate the real world economy to a specified degree of verisimilitude.

The same is true for many operations research and management science (OR/MS) models, including simulations (e.g., business games). Virtual worlds could also be categorized by the degree of correspondence that is required of them. A recreational computer game such as SimCity may have a low correspondence requirement. Other virtual worlds such as flight simulators may have a partial correspondence requirement that gives the user a sense of the "real world" but not necessarily align completely. An OR model on the other hand may require as complete a correspondence as necessary.

This issue arises in the field of artificial life (AL), for example. AL researchers build elegant virtual environments which mimic the outcomes of evolutionary and biological processes quite impressively. However, they are continually criticized by the scientific establishment for having little, or no, correspondence. The coherence-correspondence relationship has become intertwined and pervasive in the information-based world in which we live (Table 2), and scientists in a number of fields have captured it from a variety of perspectives (Tables 3 and 4).

Kimbrough [21] argues that to deal with complex problem solving, we need a modeling language that is capable of explaining the real world (i.e., extract the basic

Table 2. Characteristics of virtuality

CHARACTERISTICS OF VIRTUALITY	ATTRIBUTES	EXAMPLE
Visual	Unreal, but looking real	Optics: real and virtual picture of an object look the same, but the virtual picture can't be caught on photographic paper
Place	Immaterial, but provided by ICT	Virtual library, virtual database, virtual classrooms
Time	Potentially present	On-line or offline web services or e-communities
Evolution	Existing, but changing	Dynamic reconfiguration of adaptive systems

characteristics of the reality and explain how it works), and of experimenting with it (i.e., use the model that is derived from real-life and experiment with it using conditions that may not (yet) exist in reality). The Delphi method [24] could be interpreted as an example of such a modeling language. Using a structured approach to communications, Delphi could be described as a participatory rituals for reflection and imagination in a highly complex and uncertain scenario [24].

We see the trend towards experimentation as inevitable and it coincides with the growing complexity of the problems to be solved as well as the exponential progress in computer processing capacity. Experimentation in the context of negotiated reality is the iterative search for the virtuality configuration that finds the best interplay between perceptual-motor, cognitive and social aspects of people and computer systems. Thus computational experimentation is both a science of discovery and an engineering design methodology.

Table 3. Computing requirements for virtuality in the Reality-Virtuality continuum

	APPLIC-ATIONS	MODEL	DATA	INTERFACE	INFO-STRUCTURE
REAL ENVIRONMENTS ▼ AUGMENTED REALITY	Simulation	Replicate a close-to-real-life business behavior	Queuing applications; flight simulator	3D GUI; robotics	Stand-alone with advanced real-time sensor or high-performance computing
AUGMENTED VIRTUALITY ▲ VIRTUAL ENVIRONMENTS	e-environ-ments	Achieve a task in an electronic environment that is different than reality	e-classroom, Internet-supported distributed teamwork	Distributed multi-media platform	High bandwidth networks; cloud computing platforms
	Virtual commun-ities	Social connected-ness in cyberspace	MUD, MOO	Instant-Messenger-like technology	Internet; Virtual-ization

Table 4. Definitions of virtuality – An inter-disciplinary perspective

DISCIPLINE	CHARACTERISTICS	SOME REFERENCES
Philosophy	High technology applications of the general principle that humans are self-defining creatures Inquiring systems and reality construction	[24] [36]
Management Science/ Operations Research	Conceptualization and abstraction of real-world via modeling and simulation Inquiring systems (e.g., Delphi)	[28] [29]
Computer Science	Property of a computer system with the potential for enabling a virtual system (in a computer) to become a real system; create model without coding	[23] [37]
Sociology	Departure from everyday reality to construct identity in the culture of simulation, thus eroding boundaries between the real and the virtual; create new forms of identities as they work and play with the new technologies	[34] [36]
Information systems	A new way of representing the world that is proving its value for understanding, monitoring and controlling natural processes; Scenario management	[19]

2.3   Modeling of Service Systems: Negotiated Reality and SSME

The relationship of virtual environments to service science, management and engineering (SSME) is one that has not yet been examined closely, most likely because the field of SSME is relatively new and still searching for guiding principles and concepts.

The formal representation and modeling of service systems is nascent, largely because of the complexity of modeling people, their knowledge, activities, and intentions. Service system complexity is a function of the number and variety of people, technologies, and organizations linked in the value creation networks. The challenge lies not simply in formally modeling the technology or organizational interactions, but in modeling the people and their roles as knowledge workers in the system [25].

Modeling requirements for service systems subsume conventional analytical modeling techniques. Although traditional operations research models, for example, may still play an important role in service system analysis [11], the organic (versus hierarchical) perspective implied above suggests that computational experimentation approaches may be equally, if not more relevant, for capturing the people-based and knowledge-based dimensions of value creation networks.

Consider, as a very simple example, the well known MIT Beer Game simulation which demonstrates how local optimization of activities performed by each node in a beer supply chain (Factory->Distributor->Wholesaler->Retailer) leads to dysfunctional global system behavior such as the bullwhip effect where demand is cyclically over- and underestimated. Kimbrough et al. [20] show how an agent-based representation of the problem leads to a system optimum which is Pareto superior for all nodes in the chain. Although the optimization model can be formulated and solved at the overall system level, it is difficult to envision how it may realistically be implemented. What the Beer Game experiments and the agent-based model suggest is how a negotiated reality environment, one wherein each of the service providers plays the role actually corresponding to his/her "real life" role, may reveal improved service strategies in reality which benefit all players in the supply chain.

One of the salient features of service systems is that participating players must rely more heavily upon cooperation than competition. Inter-network dynamics may be competitive but intra-network processes are largely cooperative. This increased need for cooperation in turn relies heavily upon negotiation (e.g., service level agreements) as a critical element in service-based processes. We therefore return to the negotiated reality aspect of virtual environments as playing a key role in the modeling of SSME.

It appears that computational modeling and virtual environments are in the ascendant as instruments of exploration and analysis of reality, and that this may very likely be the case as well with service-based applications. However, we do not believe that this argues in any way for the obsolescence or decreased importance of the more conventional analytical modeling techniques and environments. As the Beer Game example demonstrates, there is substantive value to both approaches. What we would like to achieve is a synthesis in the form of an architecture for virtual environments which not only supports both analytical and computational modeling, but facilitates their integration in the spirit of Fig. 2c. In the next section, we outline guidelines and design principles for such an architecture.

3 Virtual Environments (VE) for Computational and Analytical Modeling (CAM): An Integrative Approach

This concept paper is an attempt to introduce the reader to the basic notions about virtual environments *for* computational and analytical modeling (VECAM). But what does the "for" really mean? At least two possibilities come to mind: "Virtual environments *in support of* computational and analytical modeling (VE→CAM)" and "Virtual environments *created by* computational and analytical modeling (CAM→VE)". The former in our view emphasizes the *Science of Design* resulting in artifacts such as model management systems, collaborative environments, libraries of meta-heuristic solution procedures and grid arrays for solving systems of large-scale simulation and optimization models. Many other examples could be cited. Broadly speaking, the purpose of these systems is to help modelers solve a wider array of more complex problems than they currently can address feasibly, including the integration of existing models.

The latter is oriented more towards decision-makers, and embodies the traditional view of DSS as "models in support of decision-making". By its very nature, any model comprises a virtual world, by dint of the assumptions it makes about which details of the "real world" to emphasize and which to ignore. Certainly, the agent-based phenomenon plays a central role in this category embracing both the real and virtual worlds. We contend that the essence and potential of virtuality is such that modeling virtuality and using virtuality to model reality present contemporaneously rich opportunities and challenges for the scientific community.

In this section, we adopt the VE→CAM perspective, specifically examining agent-based modeling and simulation (ABMS) platforms for computational modeling in the context of model management research. We observe that ABMS environments are roughly at the same level of software maturity that analytical systems such as optimization modeling were twenty years ago. We apply design principles learned about analytical modeling environments from model management to generate requirements desiderata for computational modeling environments. In this way we hope to achieve a rapprochement that facilitates development of environments which support computational and analytical modeling simultaneously. In the Section 4, we take up the CAM→VE perspective and show how such a system can be used to create a virtual service environment in the telemedicine domain.

3.1   The VECAM Platform

To help bridge the gap between analytical and computational modeling environments, we advocate the definition of a bi-level, integrative framework inspired by the basic principles of analog transmission in the field of telecommunications. In analog transmission, data is transmitted using two components: a carrier wave and a signal. The carrier wave is a waveform that is modulated by the signal that is to be transmitted. This carrier wave is of much higher frequency than the modulating signal (the signal which contains the information). The reason for this is that it is much easier to transmit a signal of higher frequency, and the signal will travel further.

By analogy, the language that we propose consists of two components (Fig. 4). On the bottom level, a formal "carrier" middleware supports the modeling of all the social interactions in the virtual environment and offers the infrastructure needed to explain behaviors and describe environments. On the upper level, an unbounded set of formal languages (by analogy, a set of different signals) support the modeling of cognitive and reasoning operations.

We define this framework as integrative because it unites two families of existing platforms and languages. On the one hand, analytical modeling languages have been around for a long time (for example, mathematical, rule-based, heuristic, analog, and social modeling systems). However, just as an analog signal does not travel far on a conductive medium without a carrier wave, the knowledge created by such languages does not travel far in a virtual environment without carrier middleware. On the other hand, agent-based languages can play the role of the carrier middleware. The next section focuses on the carrier middleware. Section 3.3 focuses on analytical modeling languages.

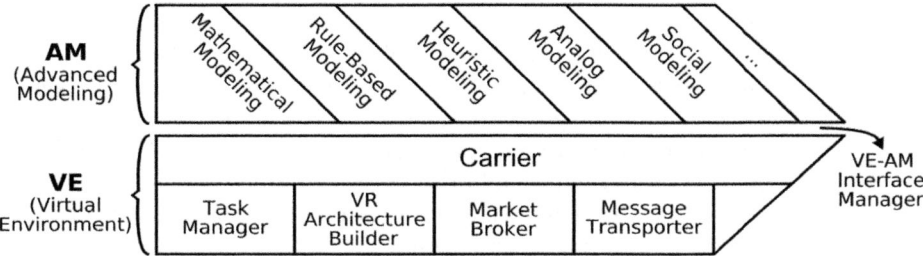

Fig. 4. The VECAM modeling framework

3.2   Carrier Systems to Support Virtual Environments

We use agent-based modeling and simulation (ABMS) platforms as exemplars of computational modeling environments. Recent years have seen a rapid growth in the number of multi-agent platforms, with a current total of at least 150 products[1]. However, modeling software in the ABMS domain is currently at a relatively immature level when viewed from a model management perspective.   For example, [Nguyen 2008] conducted a survey of six popular agent toolkits (SWARM, NetLogo, AnyLogic, Ascape, MASON, REPAST) focusing upon agent structure(s) and the technique(s) for representing agent behavior which each system employs (e.g., state transition graphs, programming language procedures, rules, etc.). Without exception, some level of software coding knowledge is required for the construction and execution of agent-based models using these systems. Further, there are very limited higher level agent representation schemas; of the six systems surveyed, only AnyLogic provides any capability in this realm in the form of state transition graphs for capturing agent behaviors. All systems, however, do provide libraries of reusable executable models which can be retrieved and modified.

This situation is similar in many ways to where modeling software for operations research and management science (OR/MS) applications was two or three decades ago. Linear programming systems, for example, used to employ matrix generators as the standard model representation. This required modelers to view and manipulate models as matrices at a machine level of representation instead of in a more natural mathematical form. Model representation formalisms such as structured modeling [14] and modeling languages such as AMPL were eventually developed to overcome this drawback [12]. As a result, the universe of model builders expanded from the highly focused specialist who had to know Fortran and mathematical programming in

---

[1] UMBC AgentWeb website, *http://agents.umbc.edu*, accessed September 20, 2010.

order to develop models. We would like to replicate the success of software evolution in the domain of OR/MS to the area of agent-based modeling environments, and incorporate some of these design advances into a broad conceptual architecture for a VECAM platform. In this vein, we see the following requirements as desirable, although not exhaustive, features of a computational modeling environment:

1. Generalized representations for agent structure and behaviors. The desideratum here is that model builders be freed from having to be Java programmers in order to build agent-based virtual environments. This, in turn, requires higher level ways of representing agent-based models. Static agent structures are relatively simple, often consisting of little more than attributes one might specify in a normalized relational table. Dynamic behaviors, however, are considerably more complex to represent and may require a portfolio of representation formalisms such as state transition diagrams, workflow diagrams, decision trees, and event diagrams. Higher level languages with corresponding graphical interfaces for specifying agents in these formalisms are necessary.
2. Separation of model representations from data. Agent-based models are typically less data intensive at run time than analytical models. Often the bulk of data processing in ABMS is at the front end of model building in the form of data mining to derive agent behaviors. Nevertheless, any data required for model development and execution should be logically separated from the agent representation.
3. Separation of model representations from solvers. Existing ABMS platforms are best viewed as potential solvers for an agent-based model representation, in the same way that OR algorithms and heuristics are solvers for various mathematical programming representations. Freeing model representations from any particular software platform protocols provides a powerful increase in generalization and flexibility. The cost of this generalization is the need to develop conversion engines for translating model representations transparently into specific solver formats (and vice versa for transmitting results).
4. Reusable model libraries. Models that have been developed, tested and used effectively should be documented and stored for future reuse.
5. Language(s) for experimental design. Specifying agent structure and behavior is only half the battle with agent-based models. As with any simulation technique, it is equally critical to set up experimental designs for analyzing the dynamic behavior of the model.

We re-emphasize that this is not intended to be a complete list of VECAM requirements but rather desirable features culled from decades of model management research into analytical modeling environments [Lindstone and Turoff 2002] which may be transferable to computational modeling systems. However, agent-based models have unique characteristics above and beyond analytical models that facilitate the cultivation of virtuality. We look at three more sophisticated and complex multi-agent ABMS environments: Cougaar, JADE and Brahms (Table 5) in order to extend our requirements list.

Table 5. Examples of platforms to implement the VECAM carrier

	Cougaar	JADE	Brahms
Main supporter	DARPA	Telecom Italia Lab	NASA
Implementatio n language	Java	Java	Java
Availability	Open Source (BSD-like)	Open Source (LGPL)	For research and non-commercial purposes. Licensed to NASA
Real-world use cases	Logistics DSS, military maneuver DSS (US Army); IT management software; Vulnerability analysis (e.g. Electrical grids)	Supply chain management; Holonic manufacturing; Rescue management; Fleet management; Auctions; Tourism	Human-robotic exploration; Modeling work practices onboard the International Space Station (ISS) NASA mission operations, planning, and scheduling
References	Helsinger, Thome et al, 2004 http://www.cougaar.org	Bellifemine, Caire et al, 2003 http://jade.tilab.com /	Sierhuis, J. et al, 2003 http://www.agentiso lutions.com/

Cougaar is "an open-source Java-based agent architecture that provides a survivable base on which to deploy large-scale, robust distributed applications" [17]. Its extreme reliability makes it a very strong carrier middleware in the augmented virtuality area of the reality-virtuality spectrum (see Fig. 2). It offers the features required by any carrier sublanguage. The task manager is based on Cougaar applications. An application includes a set of domains (application data ontologies), a network of agents, and a society configuration (assigning agents to hosts and plugins to agents). The virtual reality architecture builder supports the development of highly resilient distributed architecture. The market broker relies on white and yellow pages repositories. Finally, the message transporter relies on a proprietary agent communication language (high level) and pluggable asynchronous protocols (low level).

With Cougaar, the VECAM interface with the upper layer of our bi-level framework (the modeling languages) is provided through plugins. "A *plugin* is a software component that is added to an agent to contribute a specific piece of application business logic. Each plugin adds domain-specific behavior to the agent" [17]. This definition is perfectly in line with our framework and Cougaar plugins naturally represent the VECAM interface manager shown in Fig. 4.

Table 6. Platform features in the context of the VECAM framework

VE	Cougaar	JADE	Brahms
Task Manager	Based on Cougaar applications	Based on ontologies and complex conversation skeletons	Based on Brahms workframes
VR Architecture Builder (with position on the VR spectrum)	Highly resilient distributed architecture (Augmented virtuality)	Peer-to-peer distributed architecture (Augmented virtuality)	Single VM simulation engine[2] (Augmented reality)
Market Broker	White pages, yellow pages, service discovery	White pages, yellow pages	Single VM namespace
Message Transporter (low level protocols)	Pluggable asynchronous protocols, including RMI, CORBA, HTTP, and UDP, SSL, SMTP	RMI, JICP (JADE proprietary protocol), HTTP, IIOP	Relies on the KAoS middleware; CORBA
Message Transporter (high-level agent communication languages)	Proprietary agent communication languages	FIPA standard compliance Interoperability between J2EE, J2SE, J2ME, and .NET platforms	Proprietary agent communication language Open Agent Architecture (OAA) messages
VECAM Interface Manager	Using plugins	Opacity of the underlying inference engine	Using communication agents and/or Java activities

JADE is "middleware for the development and run-time execution of peer-to-peer applications which are based on the agents paradigm" [4].   JADE shares many similarities with Cougaar. However, it focuses more on mobility than on resilience, and offers better compliance with existing agent standards than Cougaar. The connectivity with the upper layer of our bi-level framework does not use the same plugin architecture. According to [4], "JADE is opaque to the underlying inference

---

[2] Even though Brahms is designed to produce a runtime system from a simulation, the publicly available version of the language is only meant to write simulation models.

engine system, if inferences are needed for a specific application, and it allows programmers to reuse their preferred system. It has been already integrated and tested with JESS and Prolog" (two rule-based languages belonging to the "rule-based modeling" category of Fig. 4). The other elements are described in Table 6.

The third platform, Brahms, is a multi-agent programming language developed by the NASA Ames Research Center [32]. Brahms relates knowledge-based models of cognition (e.g., task models) with discrete simulations and the behavior-based subsumption architecture. Unlike Cougaar and JADE, the publicly available version of Brahms belongs to the augmented reality area of the reality-virtuality spectrum. It is more a simulation engine than a runtime execution engine. The connectivity with the upper layer of our bi-level framework occurs via a specific kind of agent called communication agents. A *communication agent* is "a Java-based agent that interfaces between a Brahms system and other hardware or software components" [9].

Table 6 presents the features of these three platforms in the context of the VECAM framework shown in Fig. 4.

In the context of the VECAM framework, the carrier middleware must support the five requirements displayed in Fig. 4:

1. **A Task Manager**– this manager supports the representation in the virtual environment of tasks associated with the studied phenomenon. For example this representation can take the form of application data ontologies (e.g., for workflow-based planning or logistics), of typical interaction patterns to perform specific tasks (such as negotiations, auctions and task delegations), or to locate behaviors of people and their tools in time and space.
2. **A Virtual Reality Architecture Builder**– this builder supports the development and implementation of the actual virtual reality architecture adapted to the tasks of the studied phenomenon, as represented by the task manager.
3. **A Market Broker**– this broker supports the dynamic matching between entities that need to interact to solve a task or subtask during the study of the phenomenon.
4. **A Message Transporter**– this transporter supports the actual exchange of messages between entities brought together by the market broker. The message transporter manages both the high-level communication languages and the low-level network protocols.
5. **A VECAM Interface Manager**– this manager supports the connectivity between the carrier middleware and the upper layer of the framework, that is to say the Analytical modeling languages.

3.3   Analytical Modeling Languages for VECAM

Connected with the appropriate carrier middleware, modeling languages can be taken out of the often isolated and very domain-specific environments in which they currently reside. Table 7 groups existing modeling languages in five broad categories that could be used together on top of a carrier middleware to solve varied real-life problems. The purpose of this table is to illustrate the broad spectrum of modeling languages that can be integrated in the proposed framework. For example, rule-based languages, such as JESS or CLIPS, can turn underlying agents into experts, injecting in their virtual incarnations knowledge traditionally found in isolated expert systems. Mathematical and heuristics-based languages, such as LPL, GAMS, or AMPL, can turn agents into number-crunching model solvers. Conversely, analog modeling languages can turn passive sensors usually considered as artifacts into reactive agents and group them in sensor networks [ACM 2004]. Finally, social modeling languages, such as ARBAS or ABEL, can lead agents to engage in negotiation and argumentation activities going far beyond the simpler communication patterns usually found in multi-agent platforms.

What we have shown in this section is a conceptual architecture for VECAM which facilitates a fusion of analytical and computational modeling in the service of virtual environments. Borrowing design principles from model management has the potential of liberating agent-based modeling environments from the sole bailiwick of programmers, and simultaneously putting both modeling paradigms on equal footing in terms of computer representation and executability. Meanwhile, the signal-carrier paradigm allows us to differentiate between agent-oriented languages and analytical modeling languages, while still allowing for the fruitful combination of the two in a powerful integrative way. Thus, we have taken a step in extending the notion of virtual environments to accommodate computational models without sacrificing the power and utility of more conventional analytical models.

Table 7. Modeling languages for VECAM

	Mathematical Modeling	Rule-based Modeling	Heuristic Modeling	Analog Modeling	Social Modeling
Methods	Linear and nonlinear programming, differential equations; game theory, queuing theory, linear regression, time series analysis, path analysis, and logistical regression or logic analysis	Forward chaining, backward chaining	Simulated annealing, tabu search, iterated local search, evolutionary algorithms, ant colony optimization, and other meta-heuristics	Sensors-based techniques (thermometer, speedometer, anemometers, barometer, hygrometer, accelerometer, etc.)	Negotiation, argumentation, discussion, articulation

Table 7. (*continued*)

Languages (examples)	AIMMS, AMPL, CPLEX, GAMS, Lindo, LPL, MPL, OPL Studio, Xpress; Prism, SPSS, R, S-Plus	JESS, CLIPS, OPS5, PROLOG	(ad hoc languages)	(ad hoc languages usually embedded with the physical devices)	ARBAS, ABEL
Input	Data	Facts	Data	Stimuli	Positions
Know-ledge base	Models	Rules	Algorithms	Symbols	Social models
Reasoning	Optimization, mining, forecasting	Inference	(Sub)optimization,	Symbolic representation	Inference; optimization
Output	Data	Facts	Data	Data	Propositions
Refer-ences	Huerlimann, 1999; Fourer, Gay et al, 2003; Castillo, 2002	Friedman-Hill, 2003; Giarratano and Riley, 1998; Sterling and Shapiro, 1994	Osman and Kelly, 1996; Voss, 1999	ACM and IEEE, 2004	Wooldridge and Parsons, 2000; Bui, Bodart et al, 1998; Anrig, Haenni et al, 1997

In the next section, we show notionally how to apply a limited version of VECAM architecture to a services-based application. We explore a telemedicine scenario as an example of negotiated reality and show how, using Brahms, we can create an appropriate virtual environment for examining and analyzing this situation. We believe that the computational modeling dimension of VECAM will play an increasingly important role in SSME applications.

4   Modeling Telemedicine Using VECAM

To illustrate the concepts advanced in this paper, we have modeled the virtual environment of a simulated telemedicine scenario [Bui 2000]. Telemedicine is not only a highly services-oriented application but it illustrates well the negotiated reality aspect of SSME environments, and thus the suitability of VECAM for addressing these phenomena. Fig. 5 describes the workflow model of this scenario. Due to the simulation nature of this example, we have chosen the Brahms language as a carrier middleware. We note that Brahms suffers many of the same shortcomings as most ABMS platforms with respect to model management features, but is nevertheless sufficiently powerful to demonstrate conceptually the signal-carrier metaphor central to our VECAM architecture. A real-world implementation, however, would most likely rely upon Cougaar and its resilient architecture. A Brahms model can be used to simulate human-machine systems for what-if experiments, for training, for "user models", or for driving intelligent assistants and robots.

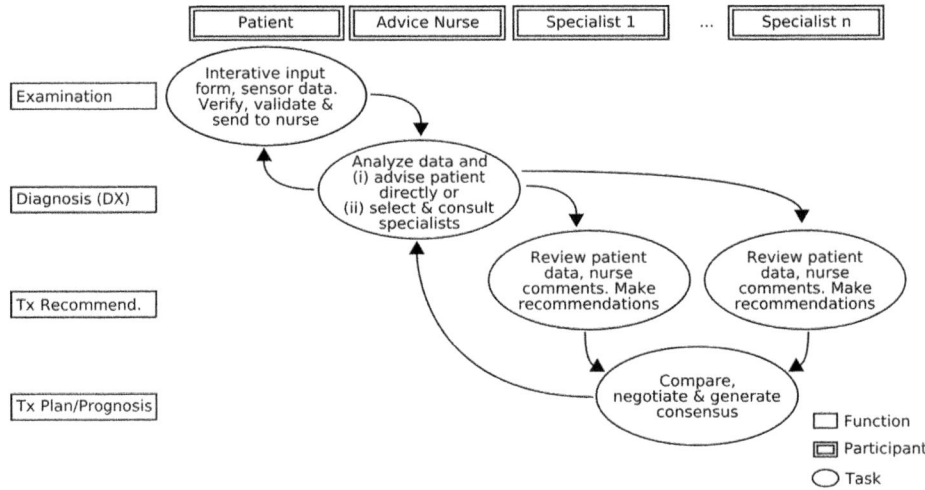

Fig. 5. The telemedicine workflow model

In a negotiated reality, we look for a model that includes aspects of reasoning found in an information-processing model, plus aspects of geography, agent movement, and physical changes to the environment found in a multi-agent simulation. Brahms makes this kind of model possible. Brahms relates knowledge-based models of cognition (e.g., task models) with discrete simulations and the behavior-based subsumption architecture. *Brahms* is centered on the concept of "agents." Agents' behaviors are organized into activities, inherited from groups to which agents belong. *Brahms* differs, however, from other multi-agent systems by incorporating chronological activities of multiple agents, conversations, as well as descriptions of how information is represented, transformed, and reinterpreted in various physical modalities. Activities locate behaviors of people and their tools in time and space, such that resource availability and informal human participation can be taken into account. Fig. 6 can be seen as an instantiation of Fig. 4 for the specific context of this telemedicine scenario.

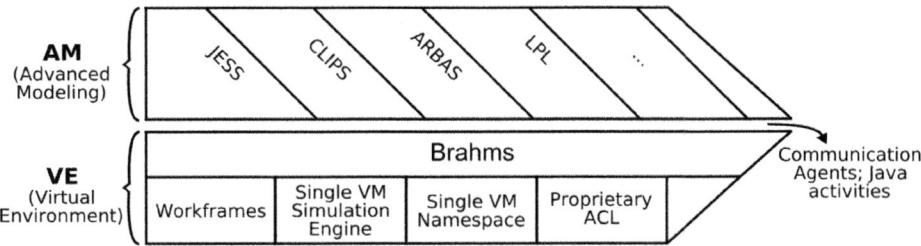

Fig. 6. The bi-level, integrated language adapted to the telemedicine scenario

The Brahms language is built around constructs which can be related to one another according to the structure outlined in Table 8 (Acquisti, Sierhuis et al. 2002). This structure represents the backbone of the simulation engine built by the Brahms virtual reality architecture builder. With this structure, it is possible to accurately model complex man-machine, machine-machine, and man-man social interactions in a virtual environment.

Let's consider the telemedicine example. A specific patient (an agent belonging to the group "Patient") feeling sick (that is to say, having certain **beliefs** about his current health) can engage in a **communication** activity with a device monitoring vital signs (man-machine interaction). Beliefs about the patient's health condition are exchanged during this communication activity. The device in turn connects to the computer of the field nursing station (machine-machine communication), which will alert a nurse on duty (machine-man). In Brahms, the agent group Patient is modeled as in Table 9.

Table 8. An example of VR architecture builder

Groups of groups containing
    Agents who are located and have
        Beliefs that lead them to engage in
            Activities that are specified by
                Workframes that consist of
                    Preconditions of beliefs that lead to
                    Actions, consisting of
                        Communication activities
                        Movement activities
                        Primitive activities
                        Other composite activities
                    Consequences of new beliefs and facts
                Thoughtframes that consist of
                    Preconditions and
                    Consequences

Table 9. An example using Brahms as a carrier platform

```
group Patient {
      attributes:
                 public symbol bloodPressure;
                 public symbol heartbeats;
                 public symbol symptom;
                 public symbol feelings;
                 public boolean newAlert;
      relations:
                 public ExamManager knowsExamManager;
      initial_beliefs:
      activities:
          communicate communicateVitalSigns(ExamManager  examManager)
{
                      max_duration: 300;
                      with: examManager;
                      about: send(current.symptom = s),
                          send(current.feelings = f),
                          send(current.bloodPressure = bp),
                          send(current.heartbeats = hb);
                 }
      workframes:
          workframe wf_recordVitalSigns {
                 variables:
                      forone(ExamManager) examManager;
                 when(
                      knownval(current knowsExamManager examManager)
and
                      knownval(current.symptom != none))
                 do {
                      communicateVitalSigns(examManager);
                 }
```

Message Transporter

Task Manager

The communicateVitalSigns() activity of Table 9 exemplifies the use of the message transporter in the Brahms middleware. The workframe wf_recordVitalSigns is an example of subtask indicating that the communicateVitalSigns() activity must be triggered when the patient feels sickness symptoms (knownval(current.symptom != none)).

The agent group modeling the vital signs device (the ExamManager defined in the relations: section of the Patient group) defines a specific workframe to react to communication activities from the patient (Table 10).

This workframe exemplifies how the market broker of the Brahms middleware matches model elements together. The instruction knownval(current knowsDxTxManager dxTxManager) can be interpreted as "find in the virtual environment the dxTxManager element known to the current element". This dxTxManager is later used by the message transporter during the communicateVitalSigns() activity (last instruction of Table 10).

Table 10. Finding other model elements with the broker

```
workframe wf_sendVitalSigns {
          repeat: false;
          variables:
               forone(Patient) patient;
               forone(DxTxManager) dxTxManager;
          when(
               known(patient.bloodPressure ) and          Market broker
               known(patient.heartbeats ) and
               known(patient.symptom ) and
               known(patient.feelings ) and
               knownval(current knowsDxTxManager dxTxManager))
          do {
               conclude((patient.newAlert = true));
               communicateVitalSigns(patient, dxTxManager);
          }
```

The computer at the field nursing station defines another workframe to react to communication activities from the vital signs device (Table 11).

Table 11. The Brahms middleware interacting with an Analytical modeling language

```
workframe wfr_processIncomingAlert {
     variables:
               forone(TreatmentPlan) treatmentPlan;
               forone(BaseAreaDef) loc;                    VECAM Interface
     when(                                                      Manager
               knownval(current.location = loc))
     do {
               broadcastIncomingAlert(loc, patient);
               createTreatmentPlan(treatmentPlan);
               conclude(
                         (current knowsTreatmentPlan
                          treatmentPlan));
               conclude(
                         (treatmentPlan isDesignedFor patient));
               conclude(
                         (treatmentPlan.shouldBeSentToSpecialist = false));
               broadcastTreatmentPlan(loc, treatmentPlan, patient);
                                   }
                         }
```

In this specific example, the createTreatmentPlan() instruction connects the Brahms middleware to a Java activity calling a rule-based language to establish a preliminary treatment plan.

Fig. 7 illustrates the communication between a (human) patient (John Smith), his exam manager agent in a dedicated device, and the diagnosis agent at the field nursing station (called the DxTxManager in the figure). The figure is a screenshot of the Agent Viewer, the visualization tool of the Brahms language. Each layer shows the active workframe(s) of the agent ("wf") and its corresponding activities ("cw" for communicate activities, "ca" for compound activities, and "pa" for primitive activities). Note that a compound activity (for example, the processIncomingAlert activity of the DxTxManager) is broken down into subworkframes and subactivites. Reasoning activities are represented with light bulbs. In Fig. 7, light bulbs identify simple conclude statements (see Table 11). However, light bulbs in Fig. 8, which represent the negotiation activities between the cardiologist and the psychiatrist, facilitated by a negotiation software agent, represent reasoning activities performed by a dedicated negotiation sublanguage.

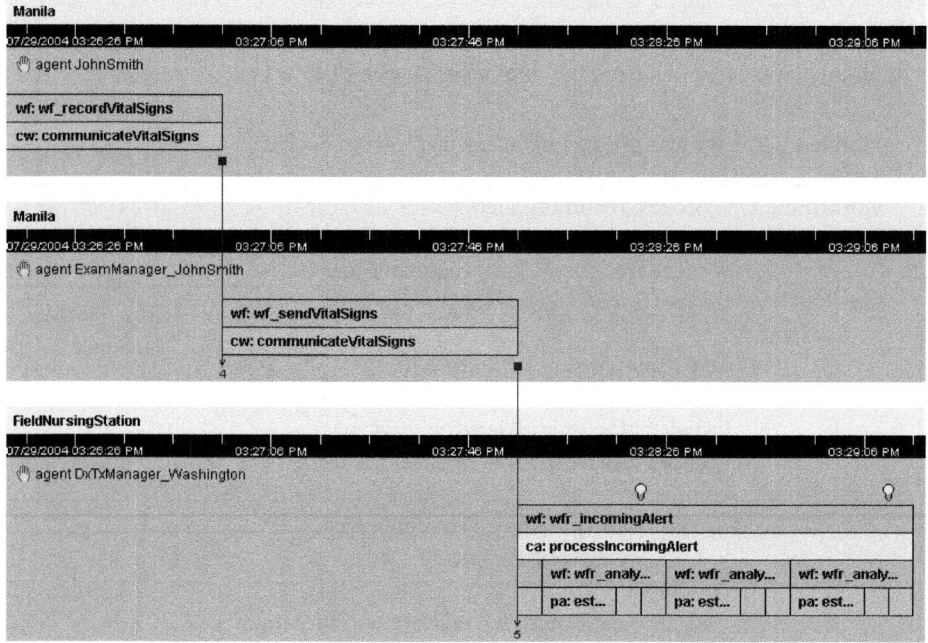

Fig. 7. Interaction between the Patient and the diagnosis agent, via the exam manager agent

Presenting in detail the complete scenario and the *Brahms* syntax goes beyond the scope of this paper. Tables 9 to 11 and Fig. 6 and 7 are only provided for illustrative purposes. However, it is important to understand that a model of activities in *Brahms* does not necessarily describe the intricate details of reasoning or calculation, but instead captures aspects of the social-physical context in which reasoning occurs. For example, the activity createTreatmentPlan() in the workframe of the computer at the field nursing station does not contain any information about the actual operation consisting of establishing a treatment plan based on a preliminary diagnosis. The only information that the Brahms language associates with this activity is its duration and the artifacts (resources) used during the activity (if any).

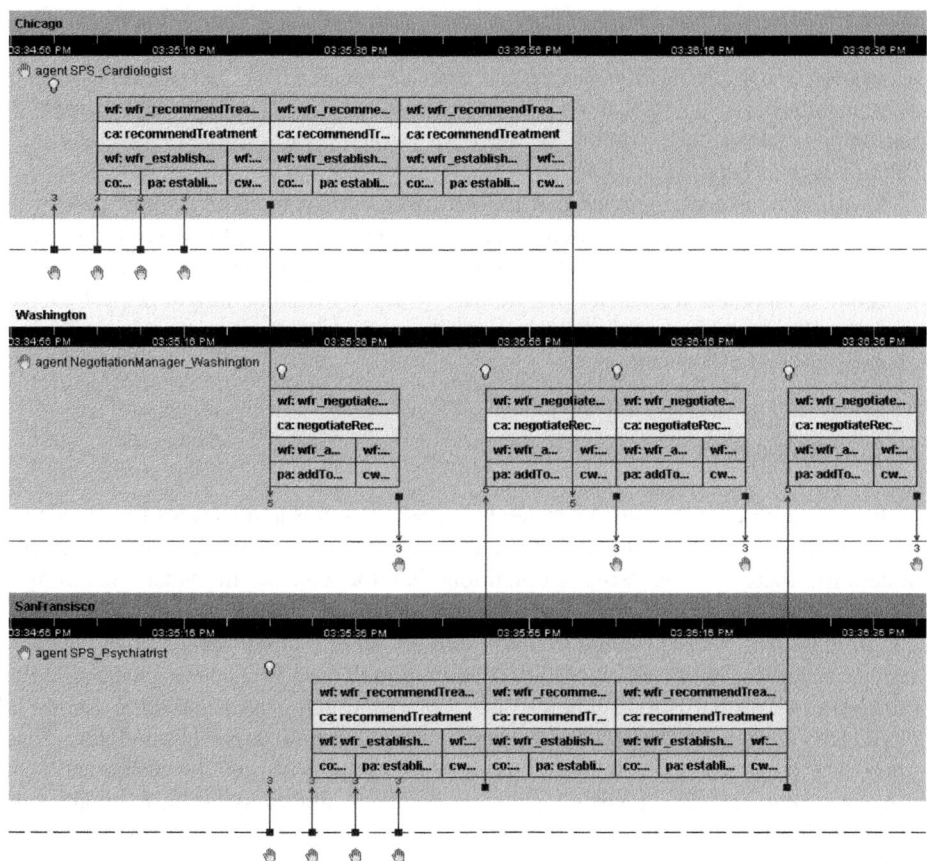

Fig. 8. Negotiation between the cardiologist and the psychiatrist facilitated by a negotiation agent

This is where the second level of our formal language comes into play. The carrier middleware must be "modulated" by other modeling languages or, in other words, the carrier middleware must offer hooks for other formal languages to do some reasoning and processing. For example, we might want to use a formal rule-based sublanguage (such as CLIPS or JESS) to model the actual reasoning happening in the createTreatmentPlan() action (with standard medical diagnosis rules). This language should have access to the belief set of the agent and to the fact set of the virtual environment. It should also be able to conclude new beliefs and facts. In Brahms, such hooks are currently provided in the form of communication agents performing

Java activities. Java activities are primitive activities, but their actual behavior is specified in Java code. Of course, this code could itself call native operations implemented in a different language (for example, the above mentioned rule-based language).

Our telemedicine example also illustrates the possibility to consult one or several specialists if an immediate diagnosis cannot be established by the nurse on duty. However, specialists might recommend conflicting treatment plans for a same patient. As mentioned above when describing Fig. 8, a special negotiation agent could rely on a structured communication language, such as the ARBAS language, to support argumentation and try to reach a consensus between the specialists. Once again, the reasoning operations modeled in ARBAS would be conveyed on the carrier sublanguage as beliefs and facts.

It is important to remember that the set of analytical modeling languages on the second level of our language is unbounded. Computational exploration might require various forms of reasoning and it is mandatory to give modelers and users the freedom to modulate the carrier middleware with the modeling language best adapted to the problem at hand. As such, the modeler would have a tool for computational explanation and experimentation.

5   Summary

With the increased use of virtual systems to make systems applications less dependent on hardware platforms, and the need for a framework to model highly complex situations, there is a growing recognition that the context in which modeling is required needs to be expanded from the traditional formalism of knowledge inquiry and problem solving. This is particularly true for service-based applications which we see as benefiting from advances in computational modeling. We propose a new paradigm – virtual environments for computational and analytical modeling (VECAM) – to help OR/MS/IS researchers explore new ways of modeling based upon negotiated reality. The framework consists of a Virtual Environment – the Carrier – that provides a virtual platform for applications to be built upon, and a Computational and Analytical Modeling module that contains a variety of modeling tools to allow the modeler to model and experiment with a virtuality.

We have successfully developed a virtual telemedicine application derived from a real-life concept of providing distributed, patient-centric emergency care. The migration of this reality to the VECAM platform allows the modeler to experiment with a number of new and virtual environments (virtual medical offices, virtual social network of medical professionals) and new and virtual business practices (medical advising procedures, semi-automated negotiation support). With VECAM as a conceptual basis, we believe we can begin to dramatically enhance, transform, and integrate the nature of modeling processes and environments.

The VECAM framework opens the door to several future research directions. From a model management perspective, an interesting avenue to explore is the model representation of agent-based simulations (ABS). Can higher level representations of

ABS be developed much like modeling languages were for OR/MS applications [Fourer et al 2003], which allow a more abstract and concise specification of models that not only free the modeler and end-user from the chains of learning object-oriented programming but also facilitate the integration of analytical and computational models? From a system design perspective, we might ask whether a different set of design principles is required for building a Carrier, or Virtual, Environment than for a Modeling module. The latter can be constructed from well known system life cycle methodologies, but as [Markus et al 2002] points out in discussing systems for emergent knowledge processes which have much in common with virtual worlds, the landscape may be much less crisp when the set of end users and their respective requirements are not known a priori. Virtual environments are much more likely to exhibit emergent properties which in turn may require a higher degree of dynamic configurability and "fuzzy" design, much like what has been envisioned for the Semantic Web, Adopting a network perspective, there is still much to be learned about combining virtual worlds as suggested in Fig. 2c and the network effects of doing so. As virtual worlds enter and leave such a network, what impact will this have on the process of scientific inquiry and how will this enhance or obfuscate the collaborative decision-making that will be required? How even does one "share" a virtual world in the first place? For example, how can a telemedicine virtual world be integrated with an emergency response counterpart so that medical assistance can be accelerated in times of crises? Also, implicit in the discussion, it seems that technologists understand well the distinction and interaction between virtual reality and reality, this understanding seems to be lost to post-modern sociologists. As an example, when extending the virtuality-reality continuum to the context of crisis management, the interplay between the emergent behaviors in the real worlds (e.g., on-site rescue vs. forum blogs offering resources) [Subba and Bui, 2009] has become an undeniable artefact. These and many more issues arise from thinking about fully idealized virtual environments. We hope that VECAM can be a preliminary step in addressing some of these intriguing questions.

References

1. Acquisti, A., Sierhuis, M., Clancey, W.J., Bradshaw, J.M.: Agent Based Modeling of Collaboration and Work Practices Onboard the International Space Station. In: 11th Conference on Computer-Generated Forces and Behavior Representation, Orlando, FL (2002)
2. Anrig, B., Haenni, R., Kohlas, J., Lehmann, N.: Assumption-based Modeling using ABEL. In: Nonnengart, A., Kruse, R., Ohlbach, H.J., Gabbay, D.M. (eds.) FAPR 1997 and ECSQARU 1997. LNCS, vol. 1244, pp. 171–182. Springer, Heidelberg (1997)
3. Association for Computing Machinery and Institute of Electrical and Electronics Engineers. In: Third International Symposium on Information Processing in Sensor Networks, IPSN 2004, Berkeley, California, USA. New York, N.Y, April 26-27, Association for Computing Machinery (2004)
4. Bellifemine, F., Caire, G., Poggi, A., Rimassa, G.: JADE: A White Paper. Exp. 3(3), 6–19 (2003)

5. Bui, T.: Building agent-based corporate information systems: An application to telemedicine. European Journal of Operational Research 122, 242–257 (2000)
6. Bui, T., Bodart, F., Ma, P.-C.: ARBAS: A Formal Language to Support Argumentation in Network-Based Organizations. Journal of Management Information Systems 14(3), 223–237 (1998)
7. Carley, K.: Computational Organizational Science and Organizational Engineering. Simulation Modeling Practice and Theory 10(5-7), 253–269 (2003)
8. Castillo, E.: Building and solving mathematical programming models in engineering. Wiley, New York (2002)
9. Clancey, W., Sierhuis, M., Kaskiris, C., van Hoof, R.: Advantages of Brahms for Specifying and Implementing a Multi-agent Human-Robotic Exploration System. In: 16th International FLAIRS Conference, St. Augustine, FL (2003)
10. Deleuze, G., Guattari, F.: Anti-Oedipus: capitalism and schizophrenia. Viking Press, New York (1977)
11. Dietrich, B.: Resource planning for business services. Communications of the ACM 49, 7 (2006)
12. Fourer, R., Gay, D.M., Kernighan, B.W.: AMPL: a modeling language for mathematical programming. Thomson/Brooks/Cole, Pacific Grove (2003)
13. Friedman-Hill, E.: Jess in action: rule-based systems in Java, Greenwich, CT, Manning (2003)
14. Geoffrion, A.M.: The Formal Aspects of Structured Modeling. Operations Research 37(1), 30–51 (1989)
15. Giarratano, J.C., Riley, G.: Expert systems: principles and programming. PWS Pub. Co., Boston (1998)
16. Hamming, R.W.: The Art of Doing Science and Engineering: Learning to Learn. Gordon and Breach Science Publishers, Amsterdam B.V. The Netherlands (1997)
17. Helsinger, A., Thome, M., Wright, T.: Cougaar: A Scalable, Distributed Multi-Agent Architecture. In: International Conference on Systems, Man and Cybernetics, The Hague, The Netherlands. IEEE (2004)
18. Huerlimann, T.: Mathematical Modeling and Optimization, An Essay for the Design of Computer-Based Modeling Tools. Kluwer Academic Publishers, Dordrecht (1999)
19. Jarke, M., Bui, T., Carroll, J.: Scenario Management – An Interdisciplinary Perspective. Requirements Engineering Journal 3, 3 (1998)
20. Kimbrough, S., Wu, D., Zhong, F.: Computers play the beer game: Can artificial agents manage supply chains? Decision Support Systems 33, 323–333 (2002)
21. Kimbrough, S.: Computational Modeling: Opportunities for the Information and Management Sciences. In: Eighth INFORMS Computing Society Conferences, Chandler, AZ (2003)
22. Kristensen, B.B., May, D., Jensen, L.K., Gesbo-Moller, C., Nowack, P.: Reality-Virtuality Continuum Systems Empowered with Pervasive and Ubiquitous Computing Technology: Combination and Integration of Real World and Model Systems, University of Southern Denmark (2004)
23. Lendaris, G.: Structural Modeling: A Tutorial Guide. IEEE Transactions onf Systems, Man and Cybernetics 10, 12 (1980)
24. Linstone, H.A., Turoff, M. (eds.): The Delphi Method: Techniques and Applications, NJIT (2002)
25. Maglio, P., Srinivasan, S., Kreulen, J., Spohrer, J.: Service systems, service sciences, SSME and innovation. Communications of the ACM 49, 7 (2006)

26. Markus, M.L., Majchrzak, A., Gasser, L.: A design theory for systems that support emergent knowledge processes. MIS Quarterly 26(3), 179–212 (2002)
27. Milgram, P., Kishino, F.: A Taxonomy of Mixed Reality Visual Displays. IEICE Transactions on Information Systems E77-D(12) (1994)
28. Mitroff, I., Turoff, M.: Philosophical and methodological foundations of Delphi. In: Linstone, H.A., Turoff, M. (eds.) The Delphi method: Techniques and Application, pp. 17–36. Addison Wesley, Reading Massachusetts (2002)
29. Minsky, M.L.: The society of mind. Simon and Schuster, New York (1986)
30. Nguyen, C.: GAME: Generalized agent modeling environment. Naval Postgraduate School M.S. Thesis (2008)
31. Osman, I.H., Kelly, J.P.: Meta-heuristics: theory & applications. Kluwer Academic, Boston (1996)
32. Sierhuis, M., Clancey, W.J., van Hoof Brahms, R.: A multi-agent modeling environment for simulating social phenomena. In: First Conference of the European Social Simulation Association (SIMSOC VI), Groningen, The Netherlands (2003)
33. Sterling, L., Shapiro, E.Y.: The art of Prolog: advanced programming techniques. MIT Press, Cambridge (1994)
34. Stone, A.R.: The war of desire and technology at the close of the mechanical age. MIT Press, Cambridge (1995)
35. Subba, R., Bui, T.: Convergence Behavior in the Blogosphere. In: Proceedings of the Americas Conference on Information Systems (August 2009)
36. Turkle, S.: Life on the Screen: Identity in the Age of the Internet. Simon and Schuster, New York (1995)
37. Turoff, M.: Virtuality. Communications of the ACM 40(9), 38–44 (1997)
38. Voss, S.: Meta-heuristics: advances and trends in local search paradigms for optimization. Kluwer Academic Publishers, Boston (1999)
39. Wooldridge, M., Parsons, S.: Languages for Negotiation. In: Fourteenth European Conference on Artificial Intelligence (2000)

On Deriving Indicators from Texts

Steven O. Kimbrough, Thomas Y. Lee, and Ulku Oktem

University of Pennsylvania, Philadelphia PA 19104, USA
kimbrough@wharton.upenn.edu

Abstract. This paper presents and explores the idea of deriving numerical indicators from texts, that is, converting text data to numerical data that has predictive or diagnostic value. One application of such a general capability is to the provisional identification of networks, or rather, of associations within networks. Conversely, given a network structure among entities that are associated with various texts, the network structure can itself contribute usefully to construction of indicators derived from texts. The focus of the paper is on basic concepts and methods for deriving indicators from texts. Much research remains to be done.

Keywords: text mining, text data mining, data mining, mashing, economic indicators, social indicators.

1 A First Look

It is fun to experiment by counting term frequencies using search engines. One way of doing this is to go to Google's Advanced News Search at http://news.google.com and undertake queries to compare monthly changes in word usage for the news sources indexed by Google. For example, Google reports "about 644 [hits] from Jun 1, 2006 to Jun 30, 2006 for [the search term] recession" and "about 4,440 from Jul 1, 2006 to today [July 30, 2006] for recession." So talk of recession was up, it would seem. We would like to have more than two months of data, of course, but Google presently only supports these queries for the current and previous months. With diligence over time or recourse to other sources, this is a problem that can be overcome.

A more interesting problem is whether counting the appearances of search terms signifies anything important at all. To take the present case, looking back from April 2008, did the uptick in mentions of "recession" and related terms provide evidence that a recession was coming soon? Nouriel Roubini, professor of economics at New York University and economics commentator for Bloomberg News, thought it did (http://www.rgemonitor.com/blog/roubini/137589).

Nouriel Roubini — Jul 24, 2006
It is hard to predict with certainty whether the U.S. and global economy will suffer of serious stagflation or even a recession (my bearish views are fleshed out in my recent blogs here and here). I have been arguing that those risks are large and rising; and I have recently argued that the probability of a US recession in 2007 is, in my view, as high as 50%. In brief, the Three Bears of high oil prices, rising inflation leading to higher policy rates, and a slumping

D. Dolk et al. (Eds.): Decision Support Modeling in Service Networks, LNBIP 42, pp. 196–225, 2012.

housing markets will derail the Goldilocks (of high growth and low inflation) and trigger a sharp U.S. slowdown in 2006, that may turn into a recession in 2007.

One potential barometer of such recession concerns - with all the appropriate caveats - is how many news articles are citing terms such as stagflation, U.S. recession, or recession in general. Here is a brief news-mood summary taken from a brief search on Google News today:

– News Citations of Stagflation: 655
– News Citations of US Recession: 2,870
– News Citations of Recession: 4,850

And it is not just obscure publications that are worrying about stagflation and recession. Recent detailed discussions of such risks were recently front page on the WSJ and on Bloomberg. And the number of private sector folks, experts and academics talking about such risks is rising. The authoritative Mike Mussa, former Chief Economist at the IMF, now puts the odds of a US recession at 25-30% while the Fed's own internal yield curve model now predicts that the probability of a U.S. recession in 2007 is almost 40%. As the proverb says, talk is cheap (if so sweet) but in this case the evidence that many folks and leading media publications are increasingly and systematically talking about recession and stagflation to the tune of 1000s of recent articles and commentaries should be at least a signal, to policy makers and market folks, that these risks may be rising (and the talk is no [sic; so? not?] sweet).

These numbers may not mean much, taken by themselves, since we do not have any base rate information. Perhaps, after all, discussion of stagflation declined over the previous year. Additional queries to Google are listed in table 1.

Table 1. Google search results for various search terms and the corresponding number of search results in two adjoining periods

Search Term	01JUN06 – 30JUN06	01JUL06 – 30JUL06
stagflation	134	438
inflation	7,270	39,200
disaster	6,130	29,800
global warming	2,620	10,500
biofuel	611	2,890
peace	7,250	75,400
prosperity	1,260	7,080
baseball	7,640	92,600

So, it would seem, not only were disasters and recessions upon us, things were getting hotter, too, and there was even much greater interest in peace, prosperity and baseball. One strongly suspects internal bias here. Given that we do not know how Google keeps the records and given that *every* search term increases strongly, one strongly

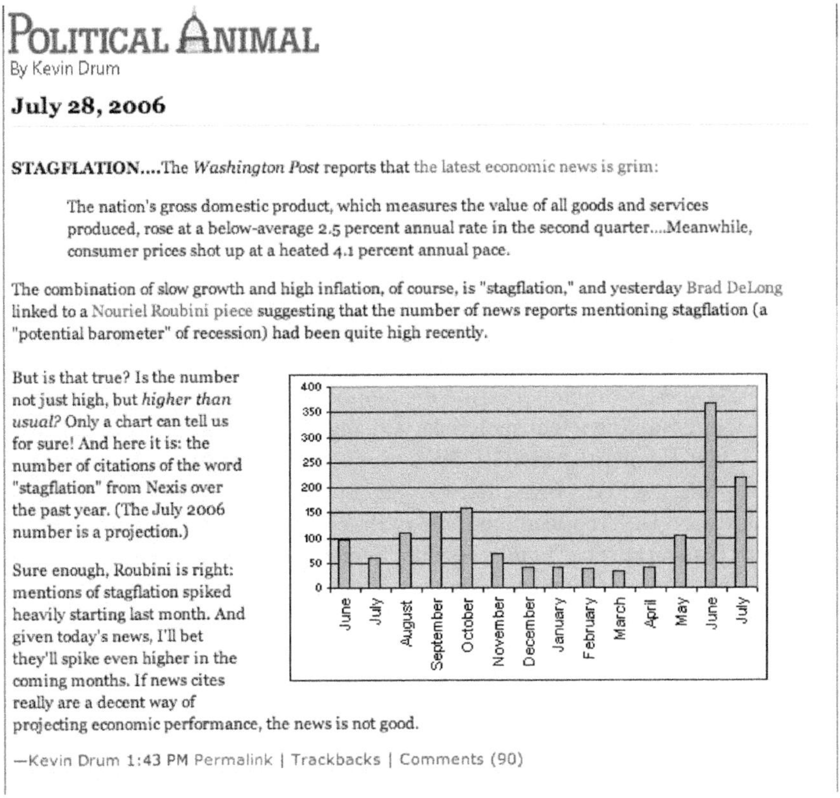

POLITICAL ANIMAL
By Kevin Drum

July 28, 2006

STAGFLATION.... The *Washington Post* reports that the latest economic news is grim:

> The nation's gross domestic product, which measures the value of all goods and services produced, rose at a below-average 2.5 percent annual rate in the second quarter....Meanwhile, consumer prices shot up at a heated 4.1 percent annual pace.

The combination of slow growth and high inflation, of course, is "stagflation," and yesterday Brad DeLong linked to a Nouriel Roubini piece suggesting that the number of news reports mentioning stagflation (a "potential barometer" of recession) had been quite high recently.

But is that true? Is the number not just high, but *higher than usual?* Only a chart can tell us for sure! And here it is: the number of citations of the word "stagflation" from Nexis over the past year. (The July 2006 number is a projection.)

Sure enough, Roubini is right: mentions of stagflation spiked heavily starting last month. And given today's news, I'll bet they'll spike even higher in the coming months. If news cites really are a decent way of projecting economic performance, the news is not good.

—Kevin Drum 1:43 PM Permalink | Trackbacks | Comments (90)

Fig. 1. Kevin Drum on "stagflation"

suspects that Google was aging its document collection. Hits were up recently in all categories because the great majority of documents on hand are comparatively more recent.

Still, if Google is not at least straightforwardly a reliable source, perhaps there are others. The blogger Kevin Drum had a more nuanced take on Professor Roubini's findings.[1]

If, however, we take a somewhat longer view, using Factiva (more or less equivalent to LexisNexis) and querying on "stagflation", we get Table 2. While this is broadly in agreement with Drum's findings on LexisNexis, the longer history of the Factiva data provides no credible support for the hypothesis that in July 2006 there had been a significant uptick in discussion of stagflation. Instead, what we have looks like merely a typical two- or three-month flare-up, of which there was a stronger one in April and May of 2005. Even this is far from established as a pattern. The fact is, these term-count data, these indicators derived from texts, provided no reason whatsoever to believe that stagflation or recession was just around the corner. Which is just as well, since it wasn't.

---

[1] See http://www.washingtonmonthly.com/archives/individual/2006_07/009250.php

Note, however, that in late 2007 and early 2008 the U.S. economy did experience significant slowdown, if not an actual recession. The numbers for this period are in fact much elevated compared to the earlier data.

The term-count data just described are examples of *indicators derived from texts*. In the examples above, the indicators are defined simply by the number of search results over a collection of text documents (Google, Nexis, Factiva). In the past, constructing such an indicator would be anything but simple, requiring manual searching and counting or programming using a customized, source-specific application programming interface (API). Today, the construction of simple indicators based upon aggregating search results over topics and time is facilitated through the use of Web services. Google,[2] LexisNexis,[3] and Factiva[4] all export standardized Web services to facilitate searching and aggregation for such tasks as the construction of indicators. As fully admitted, it is an open question whether these indicators actually provide information on anything besides themselves.

Table 2. "stagflation" document counts on Factiva

Month	Count	Month	Count
January 2005	43	October 2006	73
February 2005	44	November 2006	99
March 2005	51	December 2006	57
April 2005	364	January 2007	47
May 2005	244	February 2007	37
June 2005	72	March 2007	62
July 2005	57	April 2007	187
August 2005	87	May 2007	86
September 2005	145	June 2007	37
October 2005	178	July 2007	52
November 2005	63	August 2007	37
December 2005	53	September 2007	108
January 2006	41	October 2007	77
February 2006	44	November 2007	260
March 2006	55	December 2007	534
April 2006	38	January 2008	530
May 2006	76	February 2008	945
June 2006	247	March 2008	666
July 2006	151	April 2008	327
August 2006	227	May 2008	740
September 2006	140	June 2008	

So our first issue might be parsed as Given an indicator, what does it indicate, with what strength, and how is this known? We'll call this *the validity question* for indicators. Assuming it is possible to get past the first issue, the validity question, the second issue concerns the creation of indicators from texts. Constructing indicators using common term counts from a general and unrefined collection of documents, as on display above, is simple, even naïve. It would be quite surprising if this alone could produce a great deal of information worth attending to. Thus, our second issue is what we will call the

---

[2] http://code.google.com/apis/ajaxsearch/
[3] http://www.lexisnexis.com/webserviceskit/developers/
[4] http://factiva.com/competitiveintelligence-services.html

aptness question for indicators: What are the more apt—more useful—indicators that may be constructed from texts, and how might Web services facilitate their construction? These two issues are not unrelated, but let us discuss them separately.

2   The Validity Question

Indicators derived from texts are a form of quantitative data. As with any data, it is appropriate to ask what, if anything, they are able to predict, either alone or in combination with other data. And, as with any other data, the validation of predictive powers is something for which there are standard, well-established methods, broadly statistical in nature and well known to the empirical sciences. In this regard, data derived from texts has no special status, and indeed is no different than data obtained by any other method. So, while it is inappropriate to notice an uptick in news reports mentioning stagflation and conclude that stagflation is on the way, it is quite appropriate to *test* whether indicator data obtained from news reports can actually be used to make useful predictions.

There is a complication and it applies to all quantitative data. To illustrate, reconsider the stagflation example. You have decisions to make for which the state of the economy in the next few years will have great impact. It matters a great deal to you whether or not stagflation conditions will obtain, and you seek to discern the future. Moreover, the situation is far from clear. The well-tested indicators are not conclusive, yet you must make decisions. Suppose it is true that there has been a recent uptick in news stories about baseball. Are you interested for the sake of your present decisions? Probably not. What about the uptick in stories mentioning stagflation? Probably yes, but not because the uptick leads you to believe that stagflation is on the way. Rather, the uptick creates a *prima facie* reason to attend to it and possibly to make an effort to obtain further information. In the case of an indicator derived from texts, you might consider reading the texts to see what they say.

The larger point is that there is more than one reason why an indicator can be valid, can be worth paying attention to. First, an indicator may be a statistically valid predictor of a condition of import. If so, we may say that the indicator is *statistically valid.* The upshot of our original discussion of word counts of "stagflation" on Google News was that it is a non-starter to consider this indicator to be statistically valid (on the evidence to hand). Second, an indicator may be valuable because it is thought (with justification) to be credibly associated with information that substantially bears on the decision to hand. Such an indicator may be called *investigationally valid.* In brief, while word counts of "stagflation" might not be statistically valid, they well could be (and probably are) investigationally valid in some circumstances. Having an interest in the future state of the economy and noticing a surge of news reports, opinion pieces, blogs, etc. mentioning stagflation, it will often be entirely reasonable to pay attention and to investigate further. And this is where indicator data derived from texts may be different: you can read the documents that produced the data, and you may learn something that will, with warrant, affect your decision.

Indicators and indexes that aggregate indicators (and are themselves indicators) are widely published and used, although it is rare for them to be derived from texts. Familiar, or prominent, examples include:

- Economic indicators. The federal government publishes vast numbers of economic indicators.[5] There are private collectors of indicators.[6] The Conference Board publishes a widely-cited Index of Leading Economic Indicators as well as its Global Business Cycle Indicators.[7]
- Commerce-related indicators
  - Ranking products and services based upon attributes drawn from user-generated online reviews. (See for example [1,19,22,28].)
  - Financial, or investment, analysis using text-based indicators seeks to derive indicators for such commercially interesting events as bankruptcies, risk, and changes in profitability. See [3,5,18,20].
- Environmental indicators. There are sustainability indicators.[8] There are Environmental Treaties and Resources indicators.[9] And others.
- Social indicators. The World Bank publishes social indicators of development.[10] The United Nations publishes various social indicators.[11] as well as its Millennium Development Goals Indicators.[12] Thompson publishing offers its own Essential Science Indicators(TM).[13]

With regard indicators, we may distinguish:

1. What it is a given indicator (or statistic) is (purportedly) about, the event or condition about which the indicator bears information. So, for example, unemployment levels may indicate something about present or future economic growth; similarly the number of building permits issued in the past month may indicate something about levels of housing construction in the near future.
2. How well an indicator indicates. An indicator for X may or may not carry much information about X.
3. How interesting or useful an indicator is. A very weak indicator may be interesting because what it is about is important and no stronger indicators are available.

Generally, indicators are published because they are thought to be useful and important, not because they have been proved to be statistically valid. Validation is typically left

---

[5] http://www.economicindicators.gov/,
http://www.gpoaccess.gov/indicators/index.html
[6] http://www.economic-in-http://dicators.com/,
http://www.rogerseconomics.com/Indicators/index.html
[7] http://www.conference-board.org/,
www.conference-board.org/economics/bci/
[8] http://www.sustainablemeasures.com/
[9] http://sedac.ciesin.columbia.edu/entri/
[10] http://www.ciesin.org/IC/wbank/sid-home.html
[11] http://unstats.un.org/unsd/demographic/products/socind/
[12] http://mdgs.un.org/unsd/mdg/default.aspx
[13] http://scientific.thomson.com/products/esi/

to the user. Indexes, however, are often assembled using statistical modeling techniques and are claimed by their creators to have a degree of statistical validity (e.g., the various economic indexes, which aim to predict performance of particular economies). Typically, these indicators are used both in modeling exercises, in which statistical validity is sought, and less formally as inputs to decision processes, which judge them to be investigationally valid.

As seen in Section 1, one can construct indicators and indexes by composing one or more Web services. In the same way, an indicator or index may itself be exported as a Web service. In particular, we can integrate an indicator directly into a statistical tool for checking validity, as input for constructing another index, or into a decision support tool.

In the remainder of this paper, we focus on investigational validity for indicators derived from texts. This should be seen as a precursor to studies of statistical validity. We suspect that there is ample contribution to decision making to be made on the investigational front, and we wish to explore it a bit here. Where applicable, we will point out how indicators can be constructed from and exported as Web services. For now, we will consider the second issue before us.

3   The Aptness Question

Investigationally valid indicators command our attention for decision making. Mere occurrence counts of "stagflation" and "recession" on Google or Factiva may or may not. The aptness question may be stated as follows: Under what conditions and in what sorts of ways can indicators—indicators derived from texts—be obtained that warrant attending to during decision making? This is a large question, certainly too large to be treated definitively in any single paper, let alone in a paper that introduces the question. Our present aim is more modest. By presenting examples of plausibly apt indicators derived from texts, we demonstrate that the aptness question has favorable answers. There are ways, as we shall show, of deriving indicators from texts, which indicators merit consideration during decision making. Here, then, are a few examples.

Forecasting economic events, with real money on the line, is as difficult a prediction task as there is. Any simple way of predicting economic trends or other events that would affect stock prices can be expected to be arbitraged away quickly. Predicting other kinds of events and conditions will often be easier. The aptness of deriving indicators from texts may well be favorable for more promising tasks. For example, searching Factiva on "global warming" yields the results shown in Table 3.

It is evident that the number of recorded mentions of "global warming" has increased substantially since 1990 and that an important transition was made between 1996 and 1997. We do not know how much of the increase in the counts of articles mentioning global warning is attributable to Factiva's collection policies. Perhaps the periodicals indexed have changed greatly since 1990. Other possibilities are conceivable but implausible: Perhaps the average periodical has gotten longer. *Prima facie*, taking the data at face value, however, simple document occurrence counts on "global warming" seem to have increased about 20-fold between 1990 and 2008, and there seems to have been a significant uptick during the 1996-7 period. If you are concerned with the amount of "play" that global warming is getting in the popular press—perhaps because you engaged in strategic planning or public relations for a petroleum company—then it is not unlikely that you would find the data in Table 3 investigationally interesting.

A legitimate worry about the data in Table 3, just noted, is the possibility that the underlying document base varies so as to produce misleading results. One way to address this worry is to select a fixed number of periodicals that existed and were indexed throughout the time period in question. Table 4 Left reports the number of articles containing "global warming" and appearing in either *The Wall Street Journal* or *The Washington Post*.

Table 3. All sources ("global warming") on Factiva. (*Document counts for 2008 are for 1 January – 19 June).

Year	Count
1990	6262
1991	4493
1992	8074
1993	3724
1994	3541
1995	4057
1996	4687
1997	16827
1998	13777
1999	11422
2000	17582
2001	17514
2002	13271
2003	10753
2004	21817
2005	33880
2006	58591
2007	129958
2008*	45770

Comparing the results in Tables 3 and 4 Left we see that they are broadly in agreement: during 1990–2 a baseline is established, during 1993–6 a new, lower baseline obtains, a strong uptick occurs in 1997, followed by a general increase until the present. In short, there is remarkable agreement.

The term "sustainability" has become focal for many interested in environmental issues, broadly construed. In ordinary language and in its recent environmental context, "sustainable" as applied to a system or process connotes maintainability over a long period of time because a renewable balance has been achieved. The fact of global warming, together with the fact that it is caused in large part by such "greenhouse" gases as carbon dioxide and methane, strongly suggests that unconstrained burning of fossil fuels (petroleum and especially coal) is not sustainable. Heating of the earth will halt it, working either by human foresight and planning or by shutting down civilization, if not our species. The principal policy goals of what may be called the sustainability movement are described in this representative passage (http://www.anavogroup.com/sustainability.html, accessed 31 July 2006):

> The 'sustainability' movement strives to bring technologies and processes to the marketplace that support both basic human needs, and often socially accepted comforts, while being environmentally benign and economically viable.

The same site asserts that "Sustainability is Gaining Traction":

> Today, sustainability perspectives and innovations are becoming mainstream at a dizzying pace.

Table 4. *The Wall Street Journal* or *The Washington Post* on Factiva Left: ("global warming"). Right: ("sustainability") *Document counts for 2008 are for 1 January – 19 June.

Table 5. Left: All sources ("sustainability") on Factiva. Right: All sources ("sustainable development") on Factiva. (*Document counts for 2008 are for 1 Jan. – 19 Jun.)

Year	Count
1990	294
1991	189
1992	238
1993	102
1994	81
1995	78
1996	82
1997	268
1998	224
1999	169
2000	242
2001	337
2002	221
2003	169
2004	318
2005	467
2006	803
2007	1386
2008*	583

Year	Count
1990	16
1991	16
1992	14
1993	12
1994	15
1995	12
1996	11
1997	34
1998	18
1999	29
2000	32
2001	41
2002	69
2003	95
2004	101
2005	88
2006	117
2007	155
2008*	83

Year	Count
1990	376
1991	527
1992	891
1993	1195
1994	1833
1995	2188
1996	3291
1997	5688
1998	7226
1999	9405
2000	11329
2001	13013
2002	22118
2003	27154
2004	34102
2005	40259
2006	51298
2007	76410
2008*	43296

Year	Count
1990	649
1991	781
1992	2316
1993	2069
1994	3580
1995	3298
1996	4292
1997	6155
1998	6839
1999	8797
2000	9693
2001	11195
2002	26659
2003	17626
2004	20180
2005	23852
2006	25380
2007	33758
2008*	16052

From the data, it would indeed appear that global warming is "gaining traction." What does a similar investigation say of sustainability? Tables 4 and 5 supply supporting evidence. Table 4 reports on the counts of articles in *The Wall Street Journal* or *The Washington Post* that mention "sustainability." The pattern broadly resembles that for "global warming": there is an appreciable uptick in 1997 and continued growth from there. Table 5, left, repeats the query, now with all the news sources that Factiva indexes, with quite similar results. Finally, Table 5, right, queries all news sources on Factiva for "sustainable development," a phrase closely associated with the sustainability movement. The usual pattern roughly reasserts itself.

It is apt to count occurrences of "global warming," "sustainability," and so on if your aim is to discover whether associated topics are "gaining traction." For some purposes and for some decisions, the evidence presented here would constitute sufficient warrant to judge that both global warming and sustainability are increasingly topics of general concern. For other purposes and decisions, the evidence would not suffice, but would be interesting nonetheless because it presents a *prima facie* case, whose significance would trigger further investigation. Such investigation might take many forms, including deriving other indicators from texts, and actually reading indicated documents, as well as more traditional forms such as undertaking public surveys.

4   Further Methods

The previous section, §3 on aptness, constitutes a basic demonstration of the aptness, at least in some circumstances, of deriving indicators from texts. The methods we employed—essentially calculating hit counts of news articles (counts of documents returned by the searches) and categorizing the hits by year—were quite elementary. Our purpose in this section is to indicate some additional methods that may be used for effectively—aptly, to coin a neologism—deriving indicators from texts.

The aptness of deriving indicators from texts may, as we have just argued, be enhanced by judicious choice of topic. It may also be enhanced by careful selection of source documents. Factiva is just one of very many potential sources of documents and its focus, broadly news articles, is narrow. Other sources of interest include:

1. Other commercial document indexing and retrieval services, such as LexisNexis and ABI-Inform.
2. Organizational archives and repositories, including technical reports and working papers.
3. General Web queries with search engines such as Google and Yahoo!
4. Specialized Web queries, e.g., using Google Scholar.
5. Directed Web queries, e.g., using `wget` given a list of URLs.
6. Regulatory files, e.g., SEC filings (10-K, 10-Q, etc.), EPA and OSHA filings, and their analogs outside the United States.
7. Patents and patent applications (both US and non-US).

Systematic exploration of all methods and sources is well beyond the scope of this, or any single paper. We content ourselves here with examples to illustrate our basic points. However, even a few examples are sufficient to illustrate how Web services may also support additional approaches for deriving indicators from text. Next, we discuss some useful methods, using a document base of 800,000+ US patents, published between 1999 and 2004.

4.1   Categorization of Indicators

A very useful way of generalizing, or abstracting, the aptness examples in §3 is to see the reports, presented in the various tables, as examples of arrays of triples, each consisting of the *value* of an *indicator* in a *category*. For example, in the first row of Table 4 (page 204) we find: 1990 and 16. The indicator is the count of articles containing "sustainability". The category is a complex one (double in this case): appearing in 1990 and in either *The Wall Street Journal* or *The Washington Post*. And the value is 16. Notice that there is a many-to-many relationship between indicators and categories. In Table 4 one indicator's values are shown for several categories (the year changes). Conversely, we might fix the year and the periodicals (constituting the category) and vary the indicators, using, for example, "biofuels", "water resistant" and so on.

Table 6 illustrates the generalization. Here the indicator is the count of documents containing the term biodegradable. The categories are US patents published in the period 1999-2004 × USPTO classification class. We see that classes 424 and 514 of the USPTO classification scheme have apparently identical class descriptions (they in fact do, weirdly, as do 606 and 604).

Notice that the table displays a *pattern* of information: values of the indicator are displayed across multiple categories. This *pattern-oriented* query—showing a non-random distribution of values for multiple categories—is in distinction to the *record-oriented* queries familiar to users of Internet search engines. Record-oriented queries return lists of documents; pattern-oriented queries return scores (data values) for categories of documents. See [7] for discussion of the distinction between record-oriented and pattern-oriented queries.

Patterns of indicators can be constructed by composing multiple Web services together. In this case, we can combine data from news sources and the USPTO classification scheme into a denormalized relational structure using a service like Yahoo's YQL (http://developer.yahoo.com/yql/) Multi-dimensional queries can then produce some classes of pattern-oriented results [7].

Table 6. Counts of US patents, 1999-2004, mentioning "biodegradable" by USPTO classification scheme classes, in descending order

Class Num.	Count	Class Description
424	1638	Drug, bio-affecting and body treating compositions
514	1624	Drug, bio-affecting and body treating compositions
435	1063	Chemistry: molecular biology and microbiology
510	563	Cleaning compositions for solid surfaces, auxiliar
623	415	Prosthesis (i.e., artificial body members), parts
606	358	Surgery
604	280	Surgery
428	275	Stock material or miscellaneous articles
536	233	Organic compounds – part of the class 532-570 ser
530	221	Chemistry: natural resins or derivatives; peptides
210	211	Liquid purification or separation
528	187	Synthetic resins or natural rubbers – part of the
430	159	Radiation imagery chemistry: process, composition,
600	137	Surgery
525	117	Synthetic resins or natural rubbers – part of the
524	111	Synthetic resins or natural rubbers – part of the
264	106	Plastic and nonmetallic article shaping or treatin
47	91	Plant husbandry
523	79	Synthetic resins or natural rubbers – part of the
134	79	Cleaning and liquid contact with solids
427	78	Coating processes
508	74	Solid anti-friction devices, materials therefor,
8	74	Bleaching and dyeing; fluid treatment and chemical
252	69	Compositions
800	68	Multicellular living organisms and unmodified part
162	68	Paper making and fiber liberation
106	63	Compositions: coating or plastic

4.2   Calculating More Nuanced Indicators

So far, the indicators we have discussed have been functionally trivial: they are simple summations of term counts. While there is much to be said in favor of simplicity, there is no reason not to use complex functions and multiple parameter inputs if that proves useful. To illustrate, the following is a small step in that direction.

Figure 2 is an example outcome which indicates the number of "energy efficiency" related patents that have been granted to the indicated companies between 1999 and 2003 and their relevancy to the topic. The relevancy score is obtained as follows:

Relevancy= ((Total number of times "energy efficiency" is mentioned in patents where there is at least one mention of "energy efficiency")/(Total number of patents where "energy efficiency" is mentioned at least once)) × 10 (scaling factor).

The Figure 2 graph indicates that although Air Products has the most patents related to "energy efficiency" among the top chemical companies interested in this concept, Kimberly Clark's patents are more strongly connected to "energy efficiency." Similarly, the most popular energy efficiency topics covered in these patents are found very quickly but not included in this document.

In this particular example, nuanced indicators come not only from document searches but also through text processing of each document in the search result. A number of Web services supporting text mining (see http://u?compare.org/ and http://www.alchemyapi.com/) enable the analysis of individual text documents and larger text collections. The process for constructing more nuanced indicators composes a text processing Web service with a document search Web service.

4.3   Ontologies

An ontology, in the currently popular sense of term as deployed in the information sciences, is "a specification of a conceptualization" (accessed 2006-08-20: http://www.ksl.stanford.edu/kst/what-is-an-ontology.html). To elaborate:

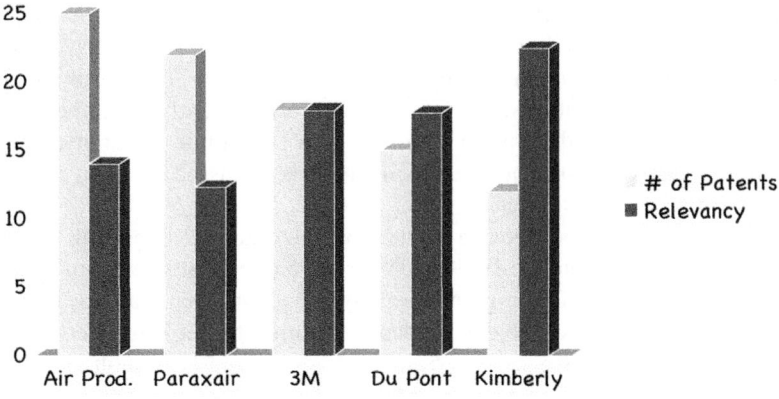

Fig. 2. Two measures of "energy efficiency" in patents

A body of formally represented knowledge is based on a conceptualization: the objects, concepts, and other entities that are assumed to exist in some area of interest and the relationships that hold among them ....A conceptualization is an abstract, simplified view of the world that we wish to represent for some purpose. Every knowledge base, knowledge-based system, or knowledge-level agent is committed to some conceptualization, explicitly or implicitly.

An ontology is an explicit specification of a conceptualization. The term is borrowed from philosophy, where an Ontology is a systematic account of Existence. For AI systems, what "exists" is that which can be represented. When the knowledge of a domain is represented in a declarative formalism, the set of objects that can be represented is called the universe of discourse. This set of objects, and the describable relationships among them, are reflected in the representational vocabulary with which a knowledge-based program represents knowledge. Thus, in the context of AI, we can describe the ontology of a program by defining a set of representational terms. In such an ontology, definitions associate the names of entities in the universe of discourse (e.g., classes, relations, functions, or other objects) with human-readable text describing what the names mean, and formal axioms that constrain the interpretation and well-formed use of these terms. Formally, an ontology is the statement of a logical theory.

The author adds in a footnote that

Ontologies are often equated with taxonomic hierarchies of classes, but [sic; with?] class definitions, and the subsumption relation, but ontologies need not be limited to these forms. Ontologies are also not limited to conservative definitions, that is, definitions in the traditional logic sense that only introduce terminology and do not add any knowledge about the world ....

Thus, a taxonomic classification system may constitute a form, perhaps a minimal form, of ontology. The work we describe in this paper pertaining to ontologies is in the main focused on use of taxonomic classification systems. There is, however, no fundamental reason to so limit the employment of ontologies for deriving indicators from texts. It is merely a matter of convenience for present purposes. Drawing on expertise from a number of sources (including one of the authors of this paper), we have constructed a rudimentary ontology (*qua* taxonomic classification system) on the subject of biofuels in the context of sustainability. Our biofuels ontology currently encompasses about 600 n-grams (words or word phrases) as leaves in a taxonomic hierarchy. The ontology continues to evolve; in consequence specific reports discussed here may not fully reflect its current, more complete, state.

Table 7 presents representative n-grams from our ontology along with their frequency counts in US patents from the 1999-2004 period. Notice that 'methanol' appears much more than any other biofuel n-gram, strongly suggesting that many of its occurrences are unrelated to biofuels. Table 8 probes this notion by looking at co-occurences of biofuels n-grams. Here we see that 5,367 patents contain 'vegetable oil' and of these 1,996 contain 'methanol', suggesting a fairly strong association between vegetable oil and methanol in the context of biofuels. The nature of that association must, of course, be discovered by other means, such as reading in the patent documents themselves.

Table 7. N-grams from the biofuels ontology and their frequencies in US patents, 1999-2004

ngram	count(ngram)
methanol	52653
biodegradable	10222
ethanol	3355
viscosity	3015
recyclable	2909
energy efficient	2240
solar energy	1978
air pollution	1947
fuel efficiency	1822
emulsions	1182
methane	894
increase productivity	739
water pollution	483
water usage	393
energy reduction	214
emulsification	207
greenhouse gases	197
wind energy	194
transesterification	158
fuel pump	124
higher energy efficiency	102
waste reduction	95
viscosity reduction	33
water efficiency	18
reduction in usage	9
environmentally sustainable	5
lower water usage	4
organic certification	4

Table 8. Counts in n-grams in US patents, 1999–2004, among the 5,367 documents containing 'vegetable oil'

ngram	doc. count
methanol	1996
biodegradable	520
ethanol	101
emulsions	65
viscosity	63
recyclable	31
water pollution	26
air pollution	21
methane	17
emulsification	10
solar energy	10
transesterification	9
energy efficient	8
used vegetable oil	6
increase productivity	6
fuel efficiency	5
water usage	3
wind energy	3
waste vegetable oil	2
greenhouse gases	1

One of the services an ontology provides is to draw our attention to topics of import, and how they are commonly described, in the subject to hand (here, biofuels). This is one way in which the expertise embodied in the ontology is leveraged. We note that this motivation is also present in the concept of *exemplary documents* developed by Blair and Kimbrough [4]. Their notion might be summarized as a concept for building ontologies by identifying key or important—their word is *exemplary*—documents in an area and then to using information retrieval methods—particularly *seed searching*—to exploit the ontologies. This is a promising idea which remains to be investigated rigorously.

A number of general purpose ontologies are publicly exported via Web services for use in constructing indicators and indices. Among them, a Wikipedia API (unofficially at http://www.programmableweb.com/api/wikipedia and an official API coming soon via http://wikipedialab.org/en/index.php/Wikipedia_API) and the forthcoming DMOZ API for Open Directory (http://blog.dmoz.org/bloggers/bob-keating).

4.4   Information Mashing

Information mashing is a new term of art, referring to the aggregation of information from multiple sources to serve a common purpose. The earliest very clear articulation that we have found of the term and the idea is by Ellen Miller of the Sunlight Foundation (`www.sunlightfoundation.com`) in her blog on April 28, 2006 (`http://www.sunlightfoundation.com/node/465`). She writes:

> Information Mashing. Don't you just love that term? It's one of the major goals of Sunlight and while we've been working on it for the past couple of months we have a ways to go before it happens in any substantial way. Our goal is simple: integrate in a user-friendly way individual data sets (like campaign contributions, lobbyists and government contracts) that makes the whole larger than the sum of its parts.
>
> We'd like to create something we've dubbed an "Accountability Matrix." A website where, with one click you can look up a major donor and see not just their campaign contributions, but also their lobbying expenditures, the names of members who've flown on their private jet, the names of former congressional staffers they've hired, and so on.
>
> In a nutshell, we want to make information more liquid and more accessible to the public.

She has politics and public policy specifically in mind. Generalizing this is the notion of a vaim, a value-added information mash. (See `http://opim.wharton.upenn.edu/~sok/asadai/vaim-faqs.pdf` and `http://opim.wharton.upenn.edu/~sok/asadai/vaim-design-faqs.pdf`.) The vaim concept generalizes to any subject area of interest (e.g., sustainability) and explicitly adds the notion of adding value through leading edge software technology. The key point, however, is the generalization of what she calls the "Accountability Matrix." This is essentially a way of associating information items in a useful way. Her example is a good one. There are documents (including Federal Election Reports) about campaign contributions and there are documents (e.g., press releases, newspaper stories) about hiring of former congressional staffers. What Miller is asking for is a system that would facilitate the explicit association of (certain types of) information items.

The general principle is that fact *A and B*, that *A is associated with B*, may well be much more significant than either the fact *A* or the fact *B* in isolation. We call this the *pattern principle* or the *connecting the dots principle*. For further discussion, see [7]. A vaim is a system that works to implement the pattern principle, using documents from multiple sources to make explicit associations among information items.

Here, to illustrate, is a simple example of information mashing. We have built a second ontology, this one for firms active in the biofuels space. By extracting assignee information from the patents and using string-matching queries, we can use the company ontology to obtain patenting information regarding the biofuels companies. Which companies hold patents? In what years? What are the n-grams present? In addition, we downloaded all of the publicly-available Web pages at each company's site and indexed them with the original biofuels n-grams. In consequence we have two document collections—patents and company Web pages—each indexed with the same two ontologies—biofuels n-grams and biofuels companies. This effects a 'mashup' and affords comparison of patent topics and word patterns with Web page topics and word patterns. Table 9 presents a small example.

As befitting a Web-based phenomenon like mashups, there are a number of Web services supporting the construction of mashups. Among them, Yahoo Pipes (`http://pipes.yahoo.com/pipes/`) and Google's Mashup Editor, which has been superseded by the App Engine (`http://code.google.com/appengine/`), are well known. Commercial tools such as those supported by IBM's Mashup Center 2.0 are also available (`http://www-01.ibm.com/software/info/mashup-center/`).

Table 9. Example n-gram patterns by firm

Organization	N-gram	count(ngram)
Biodiesel Industries	biodegradable	9
Biodiesel Industries	greenhouse gases	3
Biodiesel Industries	air pollution	2
Biodiesel Industries	water pollution	1
Biodiesel Industries	recyclable	1
BioDiesel International	biodegradable	5
BioDiesel International	recyclable	1
BioDiesel International	greenhouse gases	1
Biodiesel Technologies Inc.	greenhouse gases	2
Biodiesel Technologies Inc.	air pollution	1
Biodiesel Technologies Inc.	biodegradable	1
Biofuels Corporation plc	biodegradable	5
Biofuels Corporation plc	greenhouse gases	3
Biofuels Corporation plc	air pollution	1
Cargill	biodegradable	15
Cargill	waste reduction	4
Cargill	increase productivity	3
Cargill	organic certification	3
Cargill	environmentally sustainable	1
Cargill	greenhouse gases	1
Cargill	water usage	1
Detroit Diesel Corporation	fuel efficiency	57
Detroit Diesel Corporation	recyclable	1
Filter Speciality Inc.	air pollution	2
Filter Speciality Inc.	biodegradable	1
Filter Speciality Inc.	recyclable	1
Greenline Industries	biodegradable	1
Greenline Industries	recyclable	1
Neste Oil	biodegradable	3
Neste Oil	recyclable	1
Neste Oil	air pollution	1
Patriot Biofuels	biodegradable	2
Patriot Biofuels	fuel efficiency	1

4.5   Information Extraction

Information extraction is a term of art in the information sciences:

> Information extraction (IE) is a type of information retrieval whose goal is to automatically extract structured or semistructured information from unstructured machine-readable documents. It is a sub-discipline of language engineering, a branch of computer science.

(http://en.wikipedia.org/wiki/Information_extraction, accessed 2006-8-20; see [13] for a summary of the state-of-the-art.) What has gone by the name of information extraction does not include the derivation of indicators from texts that we describe here. Instead, IE has focused on extracting particular facts from texts; it has been, as we say, record-oriented rather than pattern-oriented. See, e.g., [6] for an example of using information extraction techniques to find uses for products from patent documents. [11] is an example of deriving hazardous events data from news sources, but the extraction was done manually and would not be classified today as *information extraction*. This said, deriving indicators from texts is surely a form of information extraction in a broad, ordinary language sense.

Further, it is certainly the case that information extraction and deriving indicators from texts are complementary. We used basic forms of information extraction on the patent documents to obtain such data as dates, assignees, and classifications, which we used to obtain many of the results described above. Our view is that any and all methods that prove useful are welcome for converting texts into data and deriving indicators. We merely observe that these methods are not presently well collected. Some are standard in the the IE community, some in the broader information retrieval community, some are new (including some of our techniques) and originate outside either community. Together, we believe, these techniques can be very effectively deployed for deriving indicators from texts.

4.6   Association Distributions

The derived indicators we have discussed so far have all been scalar quantities, mainly document counts, or some richer function, organized by category. Vector indicators consisting of multiple scalar indicators have been investigated and found effective for information discovery (in Dworman's Ph.D. thesis, [8]; see [7] for an overview). In particular, Dworman investigated categorized patterns of term co-occurrences. We can illustrate this in our present context, with patent documents and ontologies for biofuels and biofuel firms.

The biofuels firm Cargill was found to have 136 patents in our patent document base. Table 10 shows the distribution of biofuels n-grams for Cargill patents. Detroit Diesel, another biofuels firm, has 102 patents, but a very different n-gram profile, as Table 11 shows. Finally, we can compare these firms with patenting from MIT. During the 1999-2004 period MIT scored 657 patents, resulting in the biofuels n-gram distribution shown in Table 12.

Finally, two points about association patterns. First, the vectors introduce an additional aspect of pattern-oriented retrieval. Now we compare and assess different distributions (vectors) consisting of multiple scalar values. Second, Tables 10–12 *illustrate* the method. They hardly exhaust its variations. Our indicator-category-value framework remains apt, but now our indicators are vector (or distribution) patterns. This forecloses no option regarding creation of more complex categories. For example, we might compare n-gram distributions among (assignees × patents containing the n-gram 'vegetable oil'). This is the level of complexity investigated by Dworman, although in entirely different subject domains. We have illustrated above use of a simpler category; obviously much more complex ones are available should they prove useful.

5   Categorized Document Bases with Normalized Hits

In a CDB (categorized document base [15]) the documents in the collection are tagged with taxa from classification systems. The documents tagged with a common taxon may be said to form a subcollection. If we query a CDB we can return counts of documents (numbers of 'hits') by category or subcollection that match our query. These hit numbers may be of considerable interest.

Assume, for example, that we have a document collection pertaining to biofuels in which each of the documents is mapped to one or more firms from the S&P 500. Querying the collection results in matches between the query and a number of documents in the collection. It is then possible to count the number of matching documents (i.e., the 'hits') by subcollection or taxon, that is by firm from the S&P 500.

The utility of having such hit information for a query is substantial in principle. If our collection of documents is interesting and relevant to a given topic and the query is of interest for a given purpose, then the hit counts may have investigational (or stronger) validity for comparing distinct taxa. The hit counts are not, however, comparable with each other unless they are normalized in an appropriate way across the various subcollections, each constituted by the documents associated with a given taxon.

This normalization can be done in any of a number of ways. Perhaps the most obvious is to obtain a 'raw' hit count score and modify it by a factor representing the relative size (in any of a number of senses, including number of documents, number of words, and so on) of the subcollection to hand. A second approach, which would appear to be equally valid, is to construct the subcollections in such a way that they are sized more or less equally. Then with equal-sized normalization we can compare the raw hit counts directly. It is impossible to know a priori which normalization will be most useful in a given situation. Only future experience will be dispositive on this matter.

To illustrate, we used Yahoo! to identify and download a collection of about 1000 biofuels-related documents (973 were actually obtained). We then mapped each firm in the S&P 500 to the 30 most relevant documents from the collection (for that firm). Interestingly, this mapping resulted in the use of 946 (of the 973) documents. No document was associated with more than 40 firms and only 3 documents were associated with more than 30 firms.

The result was *not* equal-sized subcollections. Only 326 of the S&P 500 firms hit at all. Of these, 203 firms/taxa had fully 30 associated documents in their subcollections.

Another 24 had between 20 and 29 associated documents. Reducing the cutoff point further, 248 firms had more than 10 associated documents.

Even though not every firm/taxa was represented in the subcollections and the subcollections were of differing sizes, the matching can be considered a soft normalization. All but 80 of the S&P 500 firms were either well represented (more than 10 associated documents) or were absent entirely from the matching. Thus, approximately and we think good enough for many investigatory purposes, the represented firms were represented equally. Corresponding subcollections are roughly comparable for purposes of noticing unusual numbers of hits.

Querying the collection on 'glycerol' (an important by-product of making biodiesel) and ordering the hit categories in descending order of hit intensity produces the information in Table 13. Querying on 'transesterification' (an important process in the making of biodiesel) produces the information displayed in Table 14.

Results are easily proliferated with the existing system (biofuels documents stored in a database, indexed for full text retrieval and indexed by S&P 500). Beyond 'glycerol' and 'transesterification' any reasonable query can be issued, and the resulting data obtained, along with the underlying documents. Beyond this, the approach applies to any collection of documents to which a classification scheme is matched in the manner described. We submit that with such a system, the bar for investigational validity of these indicator data is readily surpassed.

Figures 3–5 illustrate the concept of CDBs with Normalized Hits in a deployed prototype system, called Sizatola Categorization Engine. In these figures we see demonstrated the mashing (matching) of a classification system and a document collection, and some of the resulting possibilities thereby created. Here the classification is the UNSPSC (Standard Products and Services Classification, www.unspsc.org) system, which consists of some 22,000 taxa and aims to classify all of the world's products and services. We obtained 10 documents for each of the UNSPSC taxa, thereby creating a CDB suitable for equal-sized normalization.

UNSPSC is a four-level classification system. The figures illustrate a query sequence that navigates the hierarchy. In Figure 3 the user queries the top level of the hierarchy (consisting of separate *segments*, in the argot of UNSPSC) for high viscosity. As we see, only one segment is implicated, *Chemicals including Bio Chemicals and Gas Materials*. There are 629 hits. Figure 4 shows that in the segment for *Chemicals including Bio Chemicals and Gas Materials*, only one family, *Additives* is implicated. Selecting a specific family expands that family to the class level. Figure 4 also depicts the class level for *Additives*. A user can further drill down from the class level to the commodity level of UNSPSC taxonomy. In Figure 5, the user has expanded the list of commodities for the class *Mud removal mixtures* revealing two alternatives. As also seen in Figure 5, expanding a specific commodity reveals the documents that match the particular leaf level of the hierarchy. The user may view the hits as stored or may go to the original URL and explore further.

With just a few quick clicks the user is able to exploit the hierarchical classification system, as mapped to the document collection, and the pattern of hits created by the query in order to focus attention on very specific, and often quite surprising, topics.

Table 10. Biofuels n-gram patterns for Cargill. 136 patents in all. Note: "pesticides?" matches to "pesticide" and "pesticide" and similarly for other "s?" constructions. See also Tables 11 and 12.

ngram	count(ngram)
viscosity	63
methanol	44
biodegradable	41
vegetable oil	36
transesterification	27
ethanol	21
landfill	16
emulsions?	13
waste water	9
methane	8
waste disposal	6
water treatment	5
collectors?	3
energy efficient	2
waste water treatment	2
sustainable	2
emulsification	2
emulsions	1
waste management	1
water supply	1
fresh water	1
greenhouse gas	1
pesticides?	1

Table 11. Biofuels n-gram patterns for Detroit Diesel. 102 patents in all.

ngram	count(ngram)
fuel pumps?	9
fuel efficiency	9
viscosity	3
methanol	2
heating systems?	2
emulsions?	1

Table 12. Biofuels n-gram patterns for MIT. 657 patents in all.

ngram	count(ngram)
ethanol	89
methanol	75
viscosity	63
emulsions?	58
biodegradable	47
collectors?	15
methane	12
energy storage	10
sustainable	7
fuel efficiency	6
solar energy	6
emulsification	5
heating systems?	3
fuel pumps?	2
pesticides?	2
drinking water	2
water supply	2
energy efficient	2
space heating	1
waste disposal	1
energy ratios?	1
pollution prevention	1
waste minimization	1
waste water	1
landfill	1
municipal waste	1
waste production	1
water treatment	1
energy balance	1
transesterification	1
vegetable oil	1

Table 13. Top match scores on 'glycerol' for 'biofuels' documents, by S&P 500 company

Score	Company
4	Jack Henry & Associates
4	Ultra Petroleum
4	United States Steel
3	Ameron International
3	PAETEC Holding
3	Manhattan Associates
3	SI International
3	SRA International
3	Cleveland-Cliffs
3	Hewitt Associates
3	Brinker International
3	Burlington Northern Santa Fe
3	American Tower
3	International Speedway
3	Wendy's International
3	Crown Castle Intl
3	Lennox International
3	CAI International
3	Bucyrus International
3	NII Holding
2	Endo Pharmaceuticals
2	Dollar Thrifty Automotive Group
2	Arch Coal
2	Spirit Aerosystems Holdings
2	Coeur d'Alene Mines
2	Automatic Data Processing
2	Adobe Systems
2	Computer Sciences
2	Valeant Pharmaceuticals
2	Armor Holdings
2	Trinity Industries
2	Leisure time
2	Watson Pharmaceuticals
2	Armstrong World Industries
2	Hovnanian Enterprises
2	Cavco Industries
2	Mohawk Industries
2	Reliance Steel & Aluminum

Table 14. Top match scores on 'transesterification' for 'biofuels' documents, by S&P 500 company

Score	Company
8	Alexander & Baldwin
6	Pioneer Natural Resources
6	United States Steel
5	PAETEC Holding
5	Ultra Petroleum
5	Palm
5	American Tower
5	NII Holding
4	Penn Virginia
4	Burlington Northern Santa Fe
4	King Pharmaceuticals
4	Manhattan Associates
4	Jack Henry & Associates
4	Watson Pharmaceuticals
4	Hewitt Associates
4	Cleveland-Cliffs
4	Sigma Designs
4	Chevron
3	Global Payments
3	ConocoPhillips
3	Panera Bread
3	Barr Pharmaceuticals
3	Endo Pharmaceuticals
3	Arch Coal
3	Stage Stores
3	Valeant Pharmaceuticals
3	Hovnanian Enterprises
3	Crown Castle Intl
3	Adams Respiratory Therapeutics
3	Sykes Enterprises
3	Werner Enterprises
3	Reliance Steel & Aluminum
3	Forest Laboratories
3	Automatic Data Processing
3	Silicon Laboratories
3	Foundation Coal Holdings
3	Steel Dynamics
3	Hewlett-Packard

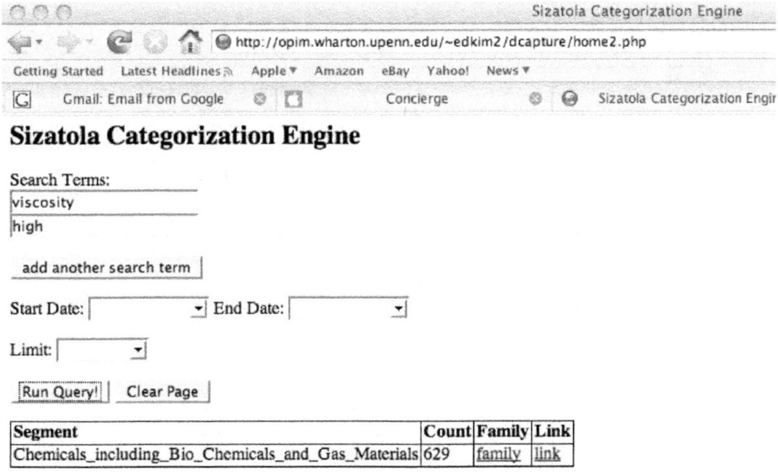

Fig. 3. SCE: Simple AND Query (viscosity and high) with UNSPC Taxonomy and 10 Documents per Taxon, Using the Drill Down Interface at the Top Level (Segment) of the UNSPC Taxonomy

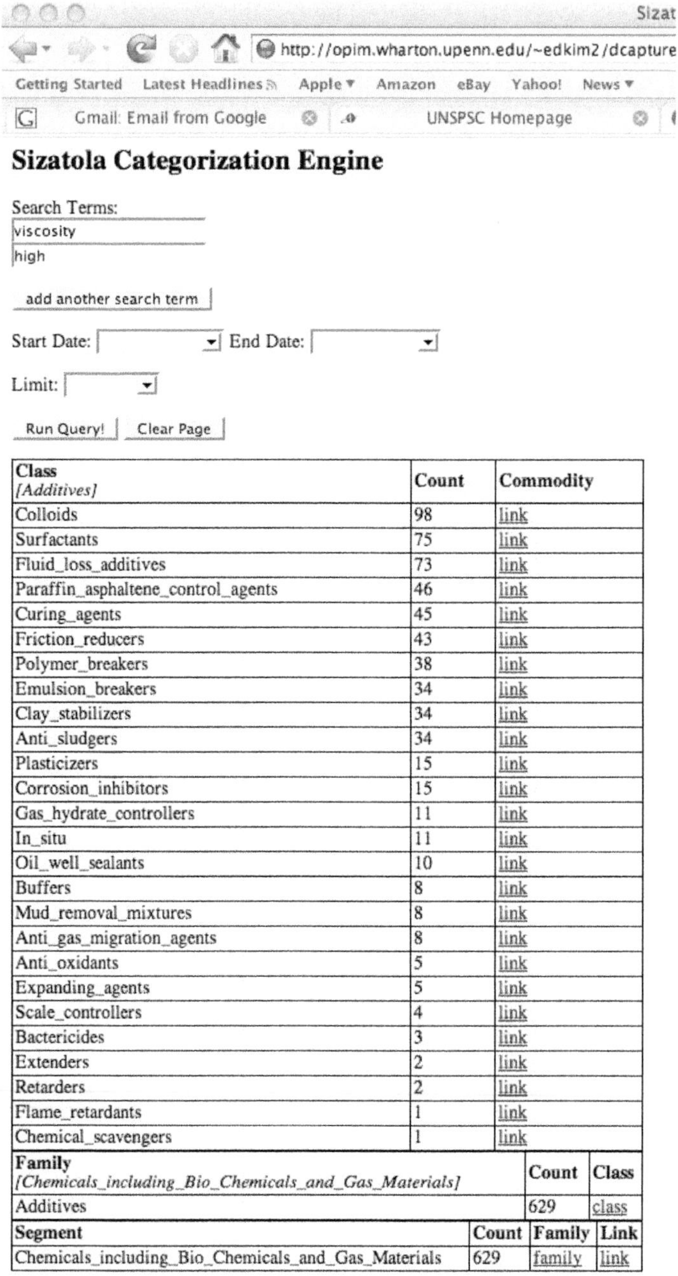

Sizatola Categorization Engine

Search Terms:
viscosity
high

add another search term

Start Date: ▼ End Date: ▼

Limit: ▼

Run Query!   Clear Page

Class [Additives]	Count	Commodity
Colloids	98	link
Surfactants	75	link
Fluid_loss_additives	73	link
Paraffin_asphaltene_control_agents	46	link
Curing_agents	45	link
Friction_reducers	43	link
Polymer_breakers	38	link
Emulsion_breakers	34	link
Clay_stabilizers	34	link
Anti_sludgers	34	link
Plasticizers	15	link
Corrosion_inhibitors	15	link
Gas_hydrate_controllers	11	link
In_situ	11	link
Oil_well_sealants	10	link
Buffers	8	link
Mud_removal_mixtures	8	link
Anti_gas_migration_agents	8	link
Anti_oxidants	5	link
Expanding_agents	5	link
Scale_controllers	4	link
Bactericides	3	link
Extenders	2	link
Retarders	2	link
Flame_retardants	1	link
Chemical_scavengers	1	link

Family [Chemicals_including_Bio_Chemicals_and_Gas_Materials]	Count	Class
Additives	629	class

Segment	Count	Family	Link
Chemicals_including_Bio_Chemicals_and_Gas_Materials	629	family	link

Fig. 4. SCE: Simple AND Query (viscosity and high) with UNSPC Taxonomy and 10 Documents per Taxon, Using the Drill Down Interface at the Third Level (Class) of the UNSPC Taxonomy, under the Segment Chemicals_including_Bio_Chemicals_and_Gas_Materials and under the Family Additives

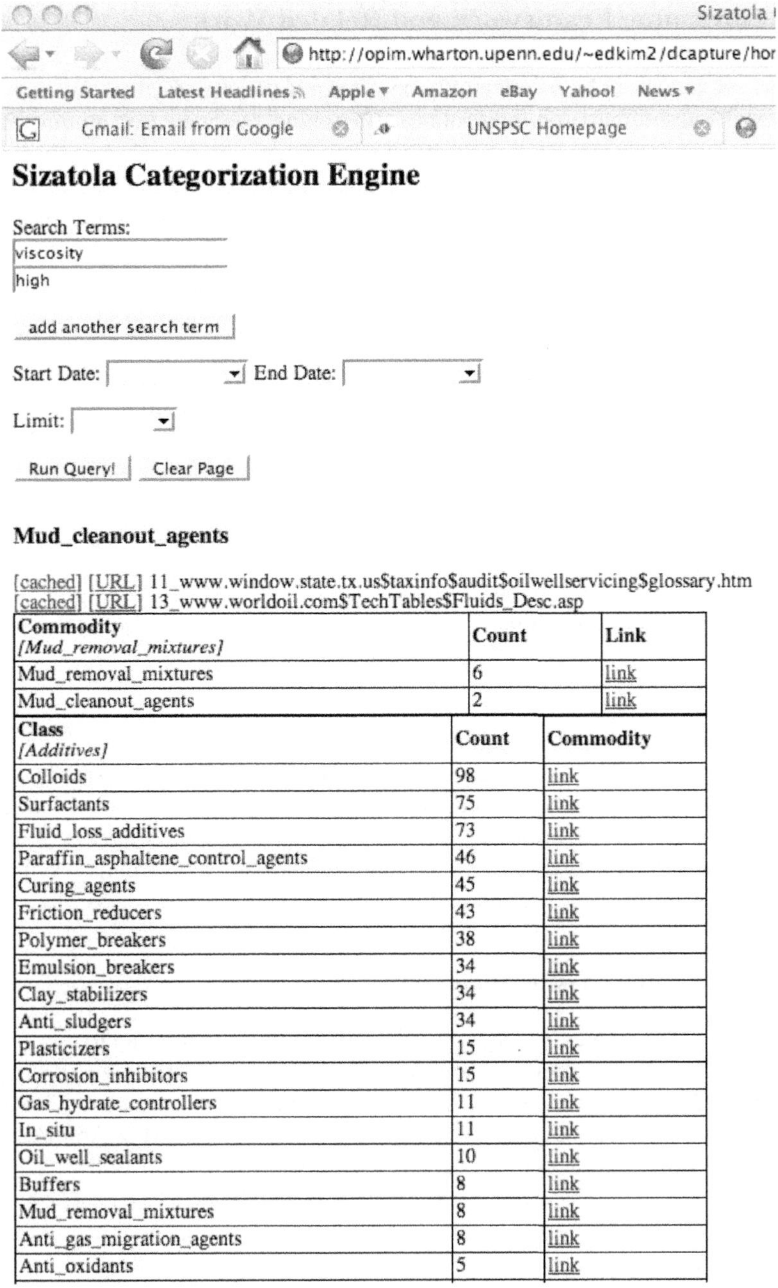

Sizatola Categorization Engine

Search Terms:

viscosity

high

add another search term

Start Date: [▼] End Date: [▼]

Limit: [▼]

Run Query!   Clear Page

Mud_cleanout_agents

[cached] [URL] 11_www.window.state.tx.us$taxinfo$audit$oilwellservicing$glossary.htm
[cached] [URL] 13_www.worldoil.com$TechTables$Fluids_Desc.asp

Commodity [Mud_removal_mixtures]	Count	Link
Mud_removal_mixtures	6	link
Mud_cleanout_agents	2	link

Class [Additives]	Count	Commodity
Colloids	98	link
Surfactants	75	link
Fluid_loss_additives	73	link
Paraffin_asphaltene_control_agents	46	link
Curing_agents	45	link
Friction_reducers	43	link
Polymer_breakers	38	link
Emulsion_breakers	34	link
Clay_stabilizers	34	link
Anti_sludgers	34	link
Plasticizers	15	link
Corrosion_inhibitors	15	link
Gas_hydrate_controllers	11	link
In_situ	11	link
Oil_well_sealants	10	link
Buffers	8	link
Mud_removal_mixtures	8	link
Anti_gas_migration_agents	8	link
Anti_oxidants	5	link

Fig. 5. SCE: Simple AND Query (viscosity and high) with UNSPC Taxonomy and 10 Documents per Taxon, Using the Drill Down Interface at the Fourth Level (Commodity) of the UNSPC Taxonomy, under the Segment Chemicals_including_Bio_Chemicals_and_Gas_Materials and under the Family Additives and under the Class Mud_removal_mixtures and under the Commodity Mud_cleanout_agents

6   A Governing Framework and Related Work

Categorized document bases are hardly new, even if the term CDB is. What is particularly new is our emphasis on their role in text mining. We view text mining, or knowledge discovery in text (KDT), as an effort to discover new knowledge. In distinction, information retrieval is about finding relevant documents. Heretofore, categorization of text has mainly been used to support retrieval, rather than—as emphasized here—discovery.

Retrieval succeeds if the documents identified in response to a query are in fact (comparatively) highly relevant to the query, or to the intended goal of the user who has formulated the query. (For present purposes we ignore this important distinction.) Discovery succeeds if we find patterns of information that are surprising and warrant follow on investigation. In short, patterns that are investigationally valid.

A general framework will help articulate this idea and serve to point to related work. We call this the C-M-A framework for knowledge. How in general may knowledge—interesting, investigationally valid patterns of information—be obtained from collections of text (as well as other information items)? In the C-M-A framework there are three salient steps

1. Categorization/classification
2. Measurement
3. Association

which we discuss individually beginning in the next section.

In the context of the C-M-A framework (or process), our philosophical view is that interesting, investigationally valid patterns of information *constitute* knowledge. To discover interesting, investigationally valid patterns of associations among categorized measurements simply *is* to discover knowledge. We allow that there may be many ways of discovering knowledge, but this is surely among them.

6.1   Categorization/Classification

A CDB is created by categorizing (classifying, applying a taxonomy to, etc.) the documents in a collection. A number of ways are available, discussed below, for categorizing documents. Also, more than one classification scheme may be applied to a body of documents. Indeed, faceted indexing systems, such as the Getty's Art & Architecture Thesaurus, consist of multiple classification systems, each called a facet (`http://www.` `(getty.edu/research/conducting_research/vocabularies/aat/;` see also `http://www.getty.edu/research/conducting_research/` `vocabularies/`).

Documents are routinely classified both by manual methods and by automated methods. Among the automated methods, *text categorization*, *document clustering* and *automated indexing* name the principal families of approach.

Document classification by supervised learning methods, referred to as *text categorization*, has been extensively researched in the context of information retrieval and, to a lesser extent, text mining. Good overviews are available in [9,13,16].

Document classification by unsupervised methods, also known as *document clustering*, has likewise been extensively researched in the context of information retrieval and, to a lesser extent, text mining. Good overviews are available in [9,13,16].

Automatic indexing (also *automatic classification* and *automatic document classification*) names a body of method and research arising from the information and library science communities [24,29] that has aimed in large part at algorithmic creation of document indexes. This literature has focused almost exclusively on information retrieval. Exploring its relevance for KDT presents an exciting prospect.

We note that *sentiment analysis* and *information extraction* [9,13,16] name two important and very active areas of research and development in information retrieval and in text mining. *Sentiment analysis* is "A technique to detect favorable and unfavorable opinions toward specific subjects (such as organizations and their products) within large numbers of documents [it] offers enormous opportunities for various applications. It would provide powerful functionality for competitive analysis, marketing analysis, and detection of unfavorable rumors for risk management." (Accessed 24 August 2006: `http://www.trl.ibm.com/projects/textmining/takmi/sentiment _analysis_e.htm`.) See [12,17,19,25,31,26]. They are, or have been, less central to document classification. In the future, however, it is entirely possible that these techniques could make important contributions here as well.

Manual methods for document classification predated by far all of the automated methods and have been studied in depth in the information science literature. In a typical regime, a *controlled vocabulary* (aka: classification system, taxonomy, etc.) is created and indexers are trained to read documents and apply the vocabulary terms as appropriate. This has been found to be an expensive and not terribly reliable process.

Interestingly, manual classification has come back in force with the fielding of *tagging* systems seen at such sites as del.icio.us (`http://del.icio.us/`), Flickr (`http://www.flickr.com/`), and Google's email system (`http://mail.google.com/`). These and other applications have spawned the *folksonomy* concept, a folksonomy being a taxonomy created from the bottom up, by the folk.

> Folksonomy (also known as collaborative tagging, social classification, social indexing, and social tagging) is the practice and method of collaboratively creating and managing tags to annotate and categorize content. In contrast to traditional subject indexing, metadata is generated not only by experts but also by creators and consumers of the content. Usually, freely chosen keywords are used instead of a controlled vocabulary [30]. Folksonomy is a portmanteau of the words folk and taxonomy, hence a folksonomy is a user generated taxonomy. (`http://en.wikipedia.org/wiki/Folksonomy`, accessed 2008-6-22)

Invention of the term is credited to Thomas Vander Wal, who maintains a related blog and Web site (`http://www.vanderwal.net/folksonomy.html`, accessed 2008-6-22). A popular article in *Salon* in 2005 stimulated much interest in folksonomies [23]. "Folksonomies – Cooperative Classification and Communication Through Shared

Metadata" by Adam Mathes has been highly regarded in this community.[14] And there is the inevitable entry from *Wired*, "Order out of chaos" by Bruce Sterling (`http://www.wired.com/wired/archive/13.04/view.html?pg=4`, published April 2005, accessed 2008-6-22).

The considerable hoopla about folksonomies has generated inevitable questioning of their usefulness (*D-Lib Magazine* is a good source, recently `http://www.dlib.org/dlib/november06/peterson/11peterson.html`). Even so, a major folksonomy software project is underway in the museums and archives world, called Steve (`http://www.steve.museum/`). For those interested in KDT, developments in folksonomies bear monitoring.

All of these approaches are potentially useful for deriving indicators from text. Whether, or how well, they work can only be determined by experience and careful empirical investigation. The illustrations presented above use mainly other methods. For example, patent documents are published in categorized form. Today they typically use XML and a raft of special tags for mark up and categorization. To create a CDB one does what we did: process the documents to capture the categorization information (date, patent number, inventors, etc.), store the categorization information in a relational database, and index the body of the documents with a convenient full text system, preserving the associations between the document's text and its categories.

The illustrations in §5 used two different methods. First, we obtained a collection of documents on a particular subject (here: biofuels) and then we mapped classification systems to the collection by taking the n most relevant documents for each taxon in the classification scheme. This method draws upon and is described in [14]. Second, we used the taxa of a classification system to retrieve relevant documents (in this case from the Web). The resulting collection was categorized by the taxa simply because each document in the collection was causally obtained by some taxon or other. This method draws upon and is described in [15].

6.2 Measurement

In information retrieval we apply an algorithm to a query and a *collection* of documents in order to produce a relevance score for each *document*. The score may be binary 1-0 (relevant or not) for matching retrieval (by document) or graded by relevance on a finer scale, in the case of relevance ranking retrieval (by document).

In KDT we apply an algorithm to a query and a *CDB* in order to in order to produce a relevance score for each *category* (or combination of categories). Again, the score may be binary 1-0 (relevant or not) for matching retrieval *by category* or, much more likely, graded by relevance on a finer scale, in the case of relevance ranking retrieval *by category*.

In short, what fundamentally distinguishes information retrieval from text mining are the objects of retrieval. In the case of information retrieval the objects are individual documents, for which we seek relevance scores. In the case of text mining the objects are categories of documents (categorized sub-collections of documents), for which we seek relevance scores.

---

[14] `http://www.adammathes.com/academic/computer-mediated-communication/folksonomies.html`, accessed 2008-6-22.

We are not aware of much research on measuring *category* relevance to a query. In the examples we presented above we largely relied on counts of matches to a query produced by a pattern-oriented retrieval engine (typically a boolean search engine). In some cases we reported the counts directly, in others we reported functional transformations.

It is easy to imagine other forms of measurement for category relevance. One might, for instance, use the average or the maximum of the relevance rank scores for the documents in a category. Or one might treat all of the documents in a category as one large document and use standard IR methods on the resulting document set. Various forms of query expansion might be applied, either to the query or to the process of identifying the documents to be in a given category. This is an important area for future investigation.

6.3 Association

By *quantity* let us mean the value of a particular measurement on a category. Thus, for example, if the category is plasticizers and 15 is the measurement value on this category for the query *high AND viscosity* (see Figure 5), then we say that 15 is the quantity (of the query *high AND viscosity* on plasticizers). Note that quantities are inherently numeric. This is without loss of generality. Even nominal data (e.g., country of residence, state, gender, marital status) may be coded numerically. Specific quantities may be defined on nominal, ordinal, interval or ratio scales. The quantities in our examples in this paper are all ratio scaled.

For the sake of discovering knowledge we compare different quantities in order to determine whether or not there is an association between (or among) them. Does one co-vary in a non-random fashion with another? If so, then the two quantities have a non-random association or, to be brief, simply an association. And if there is an association, then one quantity indicates the other (to some degree or other). (The point generalizes to groups of quantities.)

In sum, given quanties—categories and numerical measurements for them—produced by applying a scoring engine to a query on the CDB, we have demonstrated the deriving data (or indicators) from text. We have reduced the text mining problem to the more familiar realm of data exploration and analysis. In the examples above we used simple tabular and graphical means to display data (derived from text) in one and two dimensional forms. More complex forms are described in [15] and merit further investigation. Related ideas are presented in [21].

The fundamental point here is that the concepts and methods we have described for converting documents to data are fully general and open up to text mining the richly endowed world of statistics and data mining. As a general fact, knowledge is discovered by discovering non-random associations among quantities. Our point is that categorization and measurement operations on collections of text provide suitable and productive quantities, comparison of which will often lead to knowledge discovery.

7 Discussion

Broadly speaking, we would like to make two points. First, we have observed that data may be—indeed very often are—valuable indicators for decision making even in the absence of established statistical validity. If data are known to be statistically reliable indicators, that is certainy welcome and to be sought after. The press of events, however, will often preclude decision making in the presence of this kind of statistical certainty. This is well accepted. Investigational aptness is often available even if statistical validity is not. What is done is to employ subjective judgment (e.g., "A rising divorce rate would seem to indicate that families are under increasing stress and traditional norms are weakening") and a preponderance of indicators (divorce rate, suicide rate, labor participation rate, . . .) to weave together a plausible story to support action. Social science, public policy, and works by "public intellectuals" largely fit this form. Robert Putnam's *Bowling Alone* [27], Francis Fukuyams's *Trust* [10], and Eric Beinhocker's *The Origin of Wealth* [2] are just three of many excellent examples.

Our second point, to which most of the paper is devoted, is to demonstrate that useful data—data that can serve as indicators for decision making—can be derived from bodies of texts in a variety of ways. The examples we have presented include well-known and established techniques, new techniques, and combinations thereof. Moreover, these techniques are supported by any number of existing or emerging Web services that both standardize and simplify the construction of indicators and indexes. We have assumed on the basis of face validity that there is a *prima facie* case in favor of the value of deriving indicators from texts and we have concentrated on demonstrating something of the rich variety of ways in which this may be done. This hardly exhausts the topic. Our aim instead has been to open it for further investigation.

References

1. Archak, N., Ghose, A., Ipeirotis, P.: Show me the money! Deriving the pricing power of product features by mining customer reviews. In: ACM SIGKDD International Conference on Knowledge Discovery and Data Mining (KDD 2007), San Jose, CA. ACM (August 2007)
2. Beinhocker, E.D.: The origin of wealth: Evolution, complexity, and the radical remaking of economics. Harvard Business School Press, Boston (2006)
3. Balakrishnan, K., Ghose, A., Ipeirotis, P.: The impact of information disclosure on stock market returns: The Sarlanes-Oxley Act and the role of media as an information intermediary. In: Workshop on Economics and Information Security (WEIS 2008) (Dartmouth College), File (2008), http://weis2008.econinfosec.org/papers/Ghose.pdf
4. Blair, D.C., Kimbrough, S.O.: Exemplary documents: a foundation for information retrieval design. Information Processing and Management 38(3), 363–379 (2002)
5. Cecchini, M.: Quantifying the risk of financial events using kernel methods and information retrieval, Ph.D.thesis, University of Florida, Gainesville, FL (2005)
6. Chen, G.T., Kimbrough, S., Lee, T.: A note on automated support for product application discovery. In: Dutta, A., Goes, P. (eds.) Proceedings of the Fourteenth Annual Workshop on Information Technologies and Systems (WITS 2004), Washington, D.C, pp. 128–133 (2004)
7. Dworman, G.O., Kimbrough, S.O., Patch, C.: On pattern-directed search of archives and collections. Journal of the American Society for Information Science 51(1), 14–23 (2000)
8. Dworman, G.O.: Pattern-oriented access to document collections, Ph.D. thesis, University of Pennsylvania, Philadelphia, PA, Available as a working paper, Department of Operations and Information Management (1999)
9. Feldman, R., Sanger, J.: The text mining handbook: Advanced approaches in analyzing unstructured data. Cambridge University Press, Cambridge (2007)
10. Fukuyama, F.: Trust. The Free Press, New York (1995)

11. Glickman, T.S., Terry, K.S.: Using the news to develop a worldwide database of hazardous events: A report of the results of a 75-day experiment, with recommendations for further action, National Science Foundation research grant no. SBR-9309369 report, Center for Risk Management, Resources for the Future, Washington, DC (1994)
12. Hu, M., Liu, B.: Mining and summarizing customer reviews. In: Proceedings of Knowledge Discovery in Databases, KDD 2004 (2004)
13. Jackson, P., Moulinier, I.: Natural language processing for online applications: Text retrieval. John Benjamins Publishing Company, Amsterdam (2002)
14. Kimbrough, S.O., MacMillan, I., Ranieri, J.: Process and system for matching products and markets. United States Patent 7,257,568 (August 14, 2007), www.uspto.gov
15. Kimbrough, S.O., MacMillan, I., Ranieri, J., Thompson, J.D.: Categorized document bases. United States Patent Application 20070106662 (May 10, 2007), http://www.uspto.gov
16. Konchady, M.: Text mining application programming. Charles River Media, Boston (2006)
17. Lee, T.Y.: Use-centric mining of customer reviews. In: Proceedings of the 2004 Workshop on Information Technology and Systems, WITS (2004)
18. Lee, T.: Learning industry-specific voluntary disclosures from SEC 10-K regulatory filings, Winter Information Systems Conference (University of Utah, UT) (March 2008)
19. Liu, B., Hu, M., Cheng, J.: Opinion observer: Analyzing and comparing opinions on the web. In: Proceedings of WWW 2005 (2005)
20. Li, F.: Do stock market investors understand the risk sentiment of corporate annual reports? In: Working paper SSRN 898181, University of Michigan, Ann Arbor, MI (2006)
21. Lauw, H.W., Lim, E.-P., Pang, H.: TUBE (Text-cUBE) for discovering documentary evidence of associations among entities. In: Proceedings of the 22nd Annual ACM Symposium on Applied Computing, SAC 2007, Seoul, Korea, March 11-15, pp. 824–828. ACM (2007), http://www.acm.org/conferences/sac/sac2007/; Indicators from Texts 29 (2009)
22. Lee, T., Li, S., Wei, R.: Needs-centric searching and ranking based on customer reviews. In: IEEE Conference on Electronic Commerce, Washington, D.C. IEEE (July 2008)
23. Mieszkowski, K.: Steal this bookmark!, Salon, www.salon.com (February 2005), http://dir.salon.com/story/tech/feature/2005/02/08/tagging/index.html
24. Moens, M.-F.: Automatic indexing and abstracting of document texts. The Information Retrieval Series, vol. 6. Springer, Germany (2000) ISBN: 978-0-7923-7793-1
25. Nasukawa, T., Yi, J.: Sentiment analysis: Capturing favorability using natural language processing. In: Proceedings of the Second International Conference on Knowledge Capture (K-CAP 2003) (October 2003)
26. Popescu, A.-M., Etzioni, O.: Extracting product features and opinions from reviews. In: Proceedings of HLTEMNLP (2005)
27. Putnam, R.D.: Bowling alone: The collapse and revival of American community. Simon & Schuster, New York (2000)
28. Scaffidi, C., Bierhoff, K., Chang, E., Felker, M., Ng, H., Chun, J.: Red Opal: Product-feature scoring from reviews. In: ACM Conference on Electronic Commerce, San Diego, CA. ACM (June 2007)
29. Salton, G., Wong, A., Yang, C.S.: A vector space model for automatic indexing. Communications of the ACM 18(11), 613–620 (1975)
30. Voss, J.: Tagging, folksonomy & co - renaissance of manual indexing? In: Proceedings of the International Symposium of Information Science, pp. 234–254 (2007)
31. Yi, J., Nasukawa, T., Bunescu, R., Niblack, W.: Sentiment analyzer: Extracting of sentiments towards a given topic using NLP techniques. In: The Third IEEE International Conference on Data Mining, ICDM 2003 (November 2003)

An Ontological Framework
for Model-Based Problem-Solving

Huub Scholten and Adrie J.M. Beulens

Logistics, Decision and Information Sciences, Department of Social Sciences,
Wageningen University
{Huub.Scholten,Adrie.Beulens}@wur.nl

Abstract. Multidisciplinary projects to solve real world problems of increasing complexity are more and more plagued by obstacles such as miscommunication between modellers with different disciplinary backgrounds and bad modelling practices. To tackle these difficulties, a body of knowledge on problems, on modelling and on models to solve problems, has been made explicit and organised in ontological knowledge bases, which are structured in layers, ranging from generic to detailed and specific. This approach facilitates the solution of the 'language' and communication problem between team members from different disciplines, between the project team and its commissioner and other stakeholders and also makes parts of the knowledge reusable. Finally, we developed tools, available as Web-based services, that enable to fill the knowledge bases and support modelling projects (guidance from the knowledge base, logbook and project management). The modelling approach, the ontologies and the tools together constitute a more complete and better modelling framework.

Keywords: model-based problem-solving, problem ontology, modelling ontologies, model ontology, (web based) services, mathematical models.

1   Introduction

Managers and policy makers are currently confronted with decision making problems of great and increasing complexity. This complexity results amongst others from:

- Increasing scope of the problem situation and the variety of properties and relationships of that problem situation to be considered.
- Moreover, an ever increasing variety of stakeholders have their own views and requirements related to the problem situation and opportunities at hand. Stakeholders may encompass, governmental organizations, NGOs, interested members of societal groups, companies, banks, etc. Each stakeholder may have his own influence and stake in a problem situation and view on how it changes due to implemented decisions. As a consequence each stakeholder – in his own way – will try to affect and is being affected by decision making processes and the implementation of decisions [44].

D. Dolk et al. (Eds.): Decision Support Modeling in Service Networks, LNBIP 42, pp. 226–256, 2012.
© Springer-Verlag Berlin Heidelberg 2012

- These stakeholders also have their own view on requirements with respect to the management, organization and constituent parts of the process in which decisions and their evaluations are developed. In brief, in the business and political context, stakeholders require solutions to these problems swiftly, cost effectively and transparently while taking into account the diversity of requirements mentioned.

Mastering this complexity in both an effective and efficient manner often requires a project approach where a multidisciplinary team (including the commissioner):

1. Obtains and shares a vision of the nature and extent of the problem situation at hand.
2. Obtains and shares a vision on how to tackle the problem. Such visions entail consideration of the scope of the study, the solution approach, expected results, duration, costs and resources used. For complex societal, business and technological problems, this often calls for an approach where knowledge and models are used to obtain insight into the problem situation and to generate and evaluate decision alternatives. That vision is then to be translated into an explicit specification of the project.
3. Identifies and uses available (certified) resources (data, models and solvers) of stakeholders in a cost effective manner.
4. Executes a commissioned project in compliance with the explicit project specifications obtained when developing the shared problem and solution approach, and within the scope of identified (distributed) resources.
5. Executes the project in compliance with Quality Assurance (QA) requirements, including transparency [35,36].

This chapter focuses on how knowledge can be used to support model management in the most general sense, i.e. the organization, execution and management of modelling projects in which multidisciplinary teams use models to solve highly complex problems for water management and water stress mitigation. This chapter outlines what kinds of knowledge are needed to support model management. Parts of this body of knowledge have been made explicit in tools that are available as services on the Internet and we indicate how we will implement and use the other dimensions of knowledge in future activities.

The next section will outline modelling problems. Section 3 will summarize our overall approach and how we use knowledge, formalized in ontological knowledge bases, to support modelling. Section 4 will introduce the knowledge bases and section 5 the tools to work effectively with the knowledge bases in the framework. Section 6 will be dedicated to the use and reuse of the framework. This chapter ends in section 7 with a discussion of the conclusions.

2   Modelling Problems

Our extensive experience with model management projects has helped us to identify critical factors that influence functional and performance requirements for developing complex modelling projects.

Increased Quality Assurance awareness and requirements for modelling projects have been fuelled by a multitude of problems and bad experiences with model-based studies in the past. Refsgaard *et al.* [24] and Scholten *et al.* [36] enumerate several reasons for these problems:

- Ambiguous terminology and a lack of mutual and shared understanding between key-players (modelers, clients, auditors, stakeholders and concerned members of the public);
- Miscommunication between the modeler and end-user on the possibilities and limitations of the modelling project resulting in the overselling of model capabilities;
- Miscommunication between modelers with different disciplinary backgrounds;
- Malpractice in the form of careless handling of input data, inadequate model set-up, insufficient calibration and validation and model use outside of its scope;
- Lack of data or poor quality of available data;
- Insufficient knowledge about processes;
- Confusion on how to use model results in decision making;
- Lack of documentation and transparency of the modelling process, leading to projects which can be audited or reconstructed with great difficulty, if at all;
- Insufficient consideration of economic, institutional and political issues and a lack of integrated modelling.

We will use the term *language problem* for the first three reasons (i.e. ambiguous terminology and miscommunications) for modelling problems summarized above.

An additional complicating factor is associated with the increased need for supporting multidisciplinary problem solving. Over the last decades we have observed changes in the character of model-based problem solving projects from single discipline, single person, academic-oriented research model studies to multidisciplinary, decision support-oriented projects, in which teams of members with different backgrounds and roles must collaborate. Such projects typically integrate several subprojects belonging to various application domains and are executed by internationally distributed teams. During recent years, the complexity of model-based decision support has been extended even further to include rigorous socio-economic impact assessments as well.

Moreover, there are often legal prerequisites to decision making that require public participation in the decision making process, e.g. the European Union Water Framework Directive and similar legislation. Participatory processes with public and stakeholder participation in complex decision making can have three levels of involvement: (1) being informed, (2) being consulted and (3) active involvement, i.e. discussions, influence on the policy agenda, participatory design of solutions, involvement in decision making and participating in implementation [20,21,22,25].

In response to these changing requirements we introduced the concept of *New Modelling* to support decision making by multidisciplinary modelling teams, working across multi-application domains, using methodology from a variety of modelling paradigms[1] and adopting participatory involvement. This expanded approach to

---

[1] *Modelling paradigm* can be defined as: Model type and associated format, solver and methodology.

modelling enables the exploration of more complex questions and addresses quality assurance requirements, but also makes modelling more difficult. Team members with different scientific backgrounds encounter more communication problems, which, in turn, makes managing multidisciplinary projects such as model-based water management a cumbersome affair [35].

Refsgaard and Henriksen [23] and Refsgaard *et al.*[24] review responses of the research community to these problems. Most recommendations focus on providing scientific and technical guidance on how to decide what to model and how to carry out various steps in the modelling work to achieve the best and most reliable results. Existing modelling guidelines, mostly nationally based, focus on a single domain in contrast to integrated models [24]. Furthermore, these guidelines vary worldwide. Resulting model outcomes and decisions based on them are often non-transparent, irreproducible, non-auditable and not fully comparable among different countries.

Beulens and Scholten [2] add two other problems to the above list:

- In the acquisition phase the problem owner has to select the modeler, i.e. a consultant or other organization that has the right expertise for the problem to be solved. In this tendering procedure the problem owner may make a completely wrong choice for a problem solver. This can cause various problems, including inadequate expertise to solve the problem.
- In the project start-up phase, major decisions such as which problem related process to include and which type of model to use can start the problem-solving process on a completely wrong track if improperly implemented.

Most of these problems deal with the *process dimension* of multidisciplinary modelling projects, but a consistent, well-structured view is also needed on the problem to be solved and on the models, which are instrumental in model-based problem solving. To support the effective and efficient solution of the above outlined modelling problems, we have developed a *New Modelling Framework* consisting of ontological knowledge bases that contain definitions for the *process dimension* of multidisciplinary modelling, structured knowledge about the *problem dimension* (including an object system with relevant aspects of the problem situation) and knowledge about the *model dimension* (what are available models for analysis and design complete with their properties, requirements and available solvers). The framework with the three ontological knowledge bases is augmented by a *meta-ontology* with basic terminology and a tool box to set up and edit the ontological knowledge bases and to support organization, execution and management of modelling projects.

3   Approach

3.1   Framework Outline

A major challenge in multidisciplinary collaborative projects is to support solving *language problems* that may occur in such projects. This paper discusses an ontological framework to support multidisciplinary teams in model-based problem-solving, focused on, but not restricted to, (continuous) simulation for environmental and ecological applications in water management. The overall objective is broader in scope, however, and intended to be generalizable to other application domains and modelling paradigms.

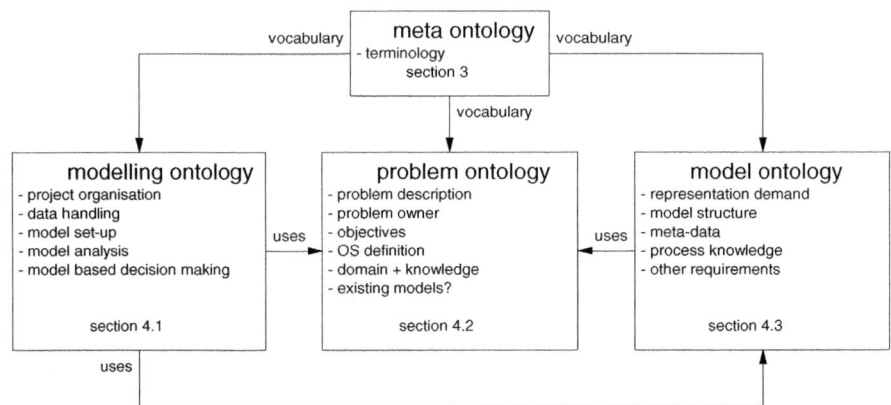

Fig. 1. A structured ontology for multidisciplinary problem-solving, consisting of 4 interrelated ontologies. At a highly abstract level, the ontologies are concepts (presented as rectangles) and the relationships between the ontologies depicted as arrows.

The framework consists of knowledge bases (KBs) and tools. The KBs have an ontological structure with *concepts* and *relations* between these concepts. *Instances* of the ontological concepts contain the content of a KB (see section 3.4.1). The knowledge containing part of the framework consists of four (associated) ontologies: on *modelling*, on *problems* (and the associated object system), on *models* and the *meta-ontology* with basic terminology, needed to describe the other three ontologies. Instances of the first three ontologies are filled with actual knowledge (on modelling, on problems and on models) and embody so three knowledge bases. The overall structure of the four knowledge bases is presented in Fig. 1. The ontologies described with their relationships and the meta-ontology, when properly filled, provide for a common language over disciplines and cultural backgrounds and thus facilitate overcoming the *language problem* identified in section 2.

The overall concept of the framework presented in this paper, has been discussed in more detailed in Scholten [34]. The modelling knowledge base (further referred to as *modelling-KB*) and associated modelling support tools were developed within the HarmoniQuA[2] project [36].

---

[2] HarmoniQuA is an acronym for *Harmonizing Quality Assurance in model-based catchment and river basin management*. From 1 January 2002 to 31 December 2005. HarmoniQuA was supported by EC's FP5 within Key Action "Sustainable Management and Quality of Water" of the Energy, Environment and Sustainable Development Programme. Contract Number: EVK1-CT-2001-00097.

3.2   Use Cases

In order to provide some insight into the needed functionality and content of the framework ontologies we now identify three types of users of the support system using associated high level Use Cases.

The first type of user consists of the members of the modelling team that run the modelling project (see *Use Case 1* in section 3.2.1). The second type of users consists of domain experts who are the source of the knowledge in the knowledge bases. In the case of the modelling-KB this group was composed of modelling experts in model-based water management and knowledge engineers with some modelling experience (see *Use Case 2* in section 3.2.2. The third type of users consists of researchers and system engineers who aim to extend the application domains of the framework (see *Use Case 3* in section 3.2.3).

3.2.1   *Use Case 1*: Running a Modelling Project

When an organization has a complex problem to be solved and mathematical models can be instrumental in solving it, an employee of the problem owning organization (further referred to as problem owner) will select and arrange a modelling team. The team selection process is governed by subjective selection criteria such as the problem owner's view of the problem, the problem owner's expertise in relevant modelling paradigms and the application domain, and the problem owner's personal qualities. This modelling team selection typically results from dialogue between the problem owner and a small number of modelling organizations the problem owner is familiar with.

After the selection of the team, the team members fine tune the modelling project preparations and start to collaborate within the team to consider one or more models for solving the problem at hand. Nowadays, such collaboration is often complex, given the multidisciplinary team and the often mandatory involvement of various stakeholders and the public. The team members will collaborate in different roles (problem owner or client, modeler, auditor, stakeholder and public) and are often geographically dispersed, ranging from different rooms in one building to different countries or even continents. To better facilitate collaboration, they need a shared vision on what to do and how to do it.

This is provided by guidance from the modelling-KB, the content of which is a shared and accepted vision of subject matter experts within the professional modelling community. This guidance is based on a definition of the modelling process by decomposing the modelling process into steps, the steps into tasks and the tasks into activities. To perform tasks and activities, teams or team members can use methods and tools. Steps, tasks, activities, methods and tools are explicitly described in the modelling-KB and will be passed on to all team members, filtered for the team member's role and the type of application domain relevant for that team member.

Furthermore, team members have to communicate what they have done in the project. Providing guidance and recording what team members do in a modelling journal is enabled by the M̲odelling S̲upport T̲ool, MoST. Each team member uses this tool in his own workspace both to receive dedicated guidance and to track progress and results. MoST also exchanges and synchronizes these personal model journals of team members with a server-based Internet or LAN application. The server application synchronizes each team member's model journal and broadcasts the complete updated model journal to each team member. The result is that team members share a single modelling journal. This integrated journal has the additional benefits that it enables project managers to plan and manage the project, helps to produce reporting to the client, and leaves an audit trail for internal and external project assessment.

3.2.2   *Use Case 2*: Editing the Modelling-KB

In the HarmoniQuA project, MoST and the modelling-KB have been developed. During and after the project the knowledge base had to be maintained as required by a substantial part of its users. The knowledge base was developed using the Protégé platform, which supports developing ontologies. In addition to Protégé a web-based knowledge base editor (KB-editor) has been developed to facilitate editing the modelling-KB by domain experts without knowledge engineering skills.

In a typical editing session the modelling-KB can be populated, maintained or corrected. In such sessions domain experts (e.g. an expert in groundwater modelling, an expert in socio-economic modelling) are responsible for the content of the modelling-KB, related to their fields of expertise. With the KB-editor all others can comment on the modelling-KB content. The responsible domain expert subsequently proposes changes to a wider group of modelling experts and changes the modelling-KB according to a shared and agreed vision.

3.2.3   *Use Case 3*: Creating New Knowledge Bases

Setting up a new knowledge base is the work of specialists in knowledge engineering. They discuss with domain experts what kinds of knowledge are available that must be organized and structured. The ontological structure of the knowledge base should reflect this. For the modelling-KB, a draft version has been created by a small group consisting of three experts in model-based water management in cooperation with two experts in ontological knowledge engineering. They started to decompose the modelling process and used this decomposition structure as an ontology for modelling (and other collaborative processes). The results have been presented to and discussed with a larger group of 25 experienced modelers. These discussions resulted in an updated modelling-KB, however the initial structure remains largely unchanged, except for some minor improvements.

3.3   Functional Architecture of the Framework

Based on the *uses-cases* of section 3.2, an outline of the functional architecture is presented in Fig. 2. The top part reflects typical usage for model-based problem solving by a multidisciplinary team. The lower part depicts how the content of knowledge bases is edited by domain experts and how the structures are created by knowledge engineers.

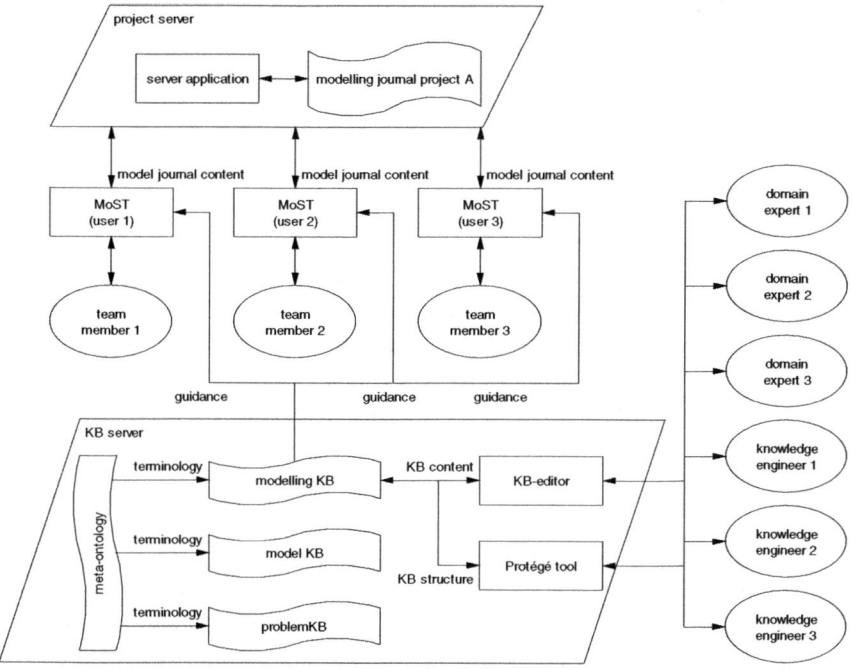

Fig. 2. Outline of the functional architecture of the framework for model-based problem-solving. The model knowledge base and the problem knowledge base are not included. *Rectangles* represent tools, *ovals* represent users, *parallelograms* represent servers and *waves* represent ontologies / knowledge bases.

3.4   Layered Ontological Knowledge Bases

3.4.1   What, Why and How Ontologies

The most widely used definition of ontology is by Gruber [10,11]: an ontology is an explicit specification of a conceptualization. Gruber [11] states further, that a conceptualization is an abstract, simplified view of the world that we wish to represent for some purpose. In an AI-context a conceptualization refers to what can be represented in terms of concepts and the relationships among them, reflected in the representational vocabulary [10]. Borst [5] adds to this definition that there should be consensus about the meaning of the concepts and the relations between them, resulting in the following definition: an ontology is a formal specification of a shared conceptualization. Scholten [34] extends this definition to: *an ontology is a precise, formal specification of knowledge, shared by a group of persons and providing sufficient vocabulary so that it can be formalized for its purpose, is understandable for its human users and manageable for its machine users (computers).*[3]

---

[3] Compared to the other definitions, two new terms are introduced in this definition: *users* and *purpose*, but these terms are also used by the authors of other definitions (e.g. [7,10]) in a similar way, but they did not include them as such in their definitions.

Gruber [11] links ontologies with their *purpose*, which should not be confused with their field of application. Here we follow the scheme of intended purposes for ontologies proposed by Uschold *et al.* [43], who distinguishes three groups of uses of ontologies: communication (between people, between machines and between machines and people), interoperability (between machines, e.g. web agents) and systems engineering (explicit specification for knowledge or software related systems and checking the match between requirements and design).

Many studies on ontologies focus on knowledge engineering aspects of ontologies and on developing domain factual knowledge ontologies (e.g., [5,6,7,10,11]). For our purpose an ontological approach is not a goal unto itself, but is instrumental only in the development of knowledge bases that can be (re)used in multidisciplinary projects, i.e. a *meta-ontology*, a *problem-KB*, a *model-KB* and a *modelling-KB* with special emphasis on modelling for water management within the HarmoniQuA project. The steps described in [34] were followed in the development of the modelling-KB:

1. *Design of an ontological structure*: First, the essential process concepts (step, task, activity, etc.) and the relationships between them have been defined, together representing the ontological structure;

2. *Development of a knowledge acquisition tool*: a knowledge acquisition tool has been developed to populate the modelling-KB; it is called the KB-editor (see section 3.5);

3. *Implementation of the KB as instances of the ontological structure*: a small group of modelling experts and knowledge engineering experts implemented the modelling-KB in instances of the concepts in the ontological structure, which was then reviewed by a larger group of water management modelling experts;

4. *Development of a tool to use the KB for a specified purpose*: a tool to use the modelling ontology has been developed, Modelling Support Tool (MoST), which will be discussed in section 5.

The meta-ontology has been developed incrementally. When a concept was missing from the other ontological knowledge bases, it was added to the meta-ontology. The problem-KB and the model-KB have been developed in a series of modelling studies discussed in sections 4.4 and 4.5.

3.4.2   Layered Ontological Structure

The four ontologies that we developed consist of a *structural part* with concepts and relations between the concepts and of *instances*, in which the concepts contain their content. The structure of the ontological framework resembles a tree with the meta-ontology as root and three branches for the *modelling-KB*, the *problem-KB* and the *model-KB* (Fig. 3).

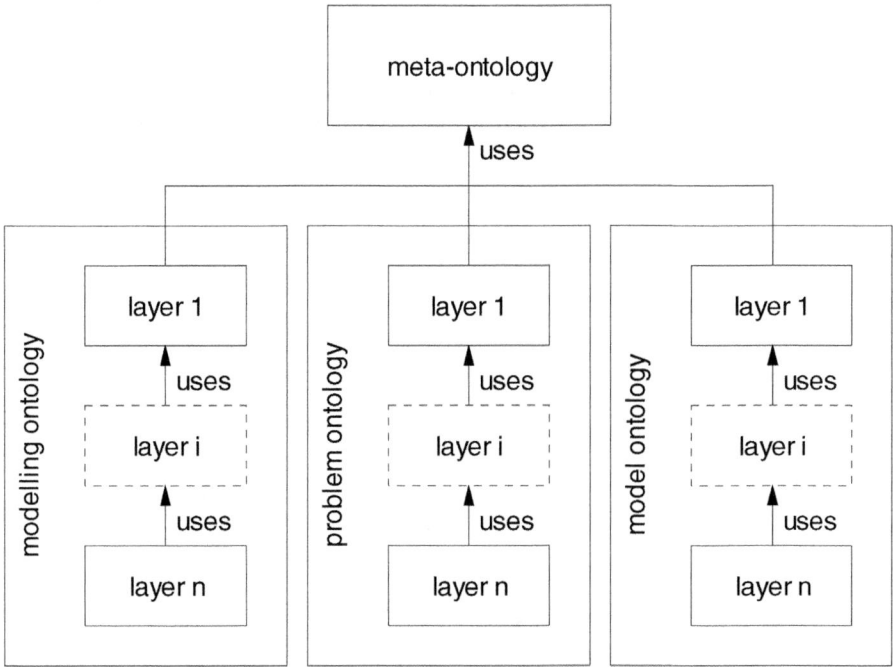

Fig. 3. The ontological modelling framework consisting of four ontologies. The meta-ontology contains basic terminology and the three others (modelling, problem and model-KB), have so called ontological layers of increasing specialization. Here, three layers are depicted, i.e. *layer 1*, *layer i* and *layer n*). Rectangles are *concepts* and arrows are *relations*.

In most cases ontologies are developed and used with two *ontological layers*: the *structure layer* and the *instance layer*. But more ontological layers may give more expressive power to support the assembly of ontologies. *Ontological layer i* should provide all knowledge necessary to define, discuss and use the knowledge structured in *ontological layer i+1*. In this way, a structured framework of ontologies allows ontology developers (domain experts) to add coherent detailed content, separated from other details and not mixed up with more generic knowledge that is located in a higher ontological layer. This is not a new idea, because ontologies have always been assumed to be combined into more powerful ones, whether by combining ontologies 'in the same ontological layer' or in hierarchical structures as in the 'Standard Upper Ontology'[4] or similar initiatives (Cyc[5], core-ontology[6]). In our approach, each tree

---

[4] An up-to-date overview can be found at http://suo.ieee.org

[5] *OpenCyc* is the open source version of the Cyc technology, the world's largest and most complete knowledge base and reasoning engine, developed by Cycorp. An overview can be found at http://opensyc.org

[6] A *core* ontology is a very basic, minimal, bootstrapping ontology, consisting of the minimal concepts required to develop other ontologies. The meta-ontology discussed here is a core-ontology for multidisciplinary problem-solving.

branch is layered with the top layer (close to the meta-ontology) containing more generic concepts and the lower layers more specialized, detailed concepts and instances.

The layered structure in the proposed framework is one of its innovative qualities. This structure provides an appropriate level for specialists to describe all their disciplinary details, but it also facilitates communication on the included knowledge

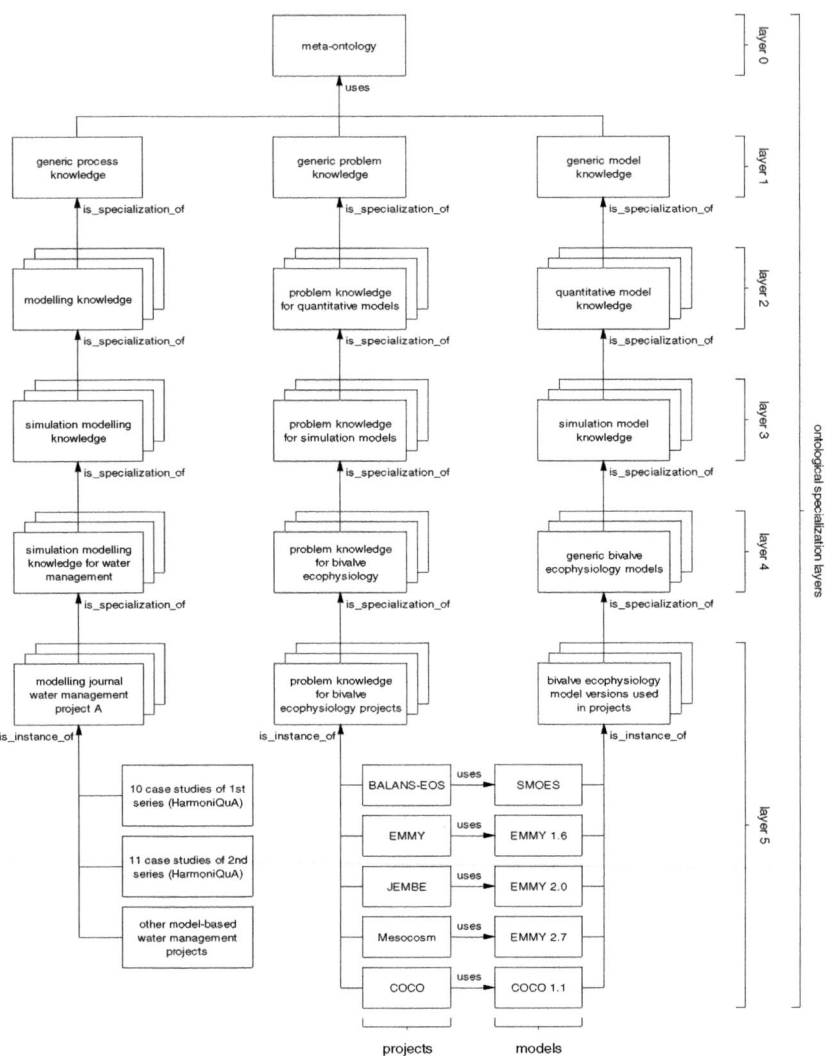

Fig. 4. Overview of the knowledge structure used in the ontological framework, showing what is realized and used in research projects. The structure is layered with stepwise specialization from the generic top (meta-ontology) to the detailed concepts at the bottom. A set of three concepts indicates a bifurcation in the tree. The side branches at the bifurcations are left out in the next (more specialized) ontological layer.

between less specialized team members at a less detailed, shared generic level, when they must collaborate in projects and be able to understand each other to some degree. That is the chosen method to support solving the *language problem*: communicate on the level of shared concepts and extend these to more specialist concepts on a lower level.

Fig. 4 depicts the outline structure of Fig. 3, but augmented with real, implemented situations in terms of modelling projects, problems and models. The mainstream branches shown in Fig. 4 are complete and detailed (section 4.1). The top meta-ontology provides basic terminology (section 4.2). The left main branch (*process ontology*) is focused upon modelling using (mainly) continuous simulation models and resulting in a knowledge base with modelling guidelines for water management (section 4.3). The central branch (*problem-KB*) and the right branch (*model-KB*) are populated with detailed knowledge on bivalve ecophysiology and associated simulation models (section 4.4 and 4.5).

3.5   Toolbox to Support Model-Based Problem-Solving

In addition to the ontological knowledge segment of the framework, a set of tools has been developed to support knowledge base set-up, population and maintenance, and the set-up and execution of modelling projects.

The free, open source ontology editor and knowledge base framework, Protégé, has been used to establish the structured ontologies with increasing levels of specialization and the KB with modelling guidelines (Stanford Center for Biomedical Informatics Research [42]). Protégé has been extended by building a plug-in for XML-export, according to a predefined XML-format, interpretable for the modelling support tool that has to co-operate with the KB.

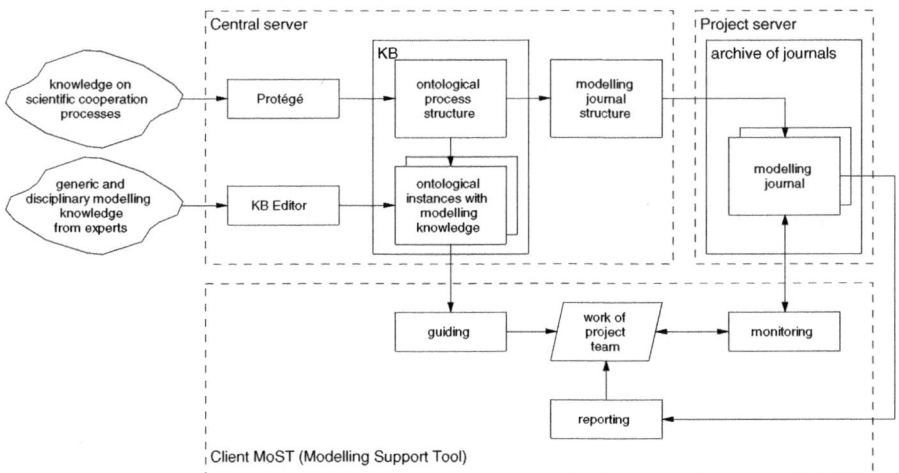

Fig. 5. Sketch of the client-server architecture with the Modelling Support Tool, MoST, the ontological *modelling-KB*, outlining MoST's major functions: guiding (from the *modelling-KB*), monitoring and reporting. Modelling journals are located on a project server (from [35])

To populate the KB, a web-based KB-editor has been developed, which acts as a front-end between domain experts, who are unskilled in knowledge engineering, and the knowledge base implemented in Protégé. The KB-editor also handles authorization issues and ensures that users can work concurrently in the system by locking knowledge elements under revision to overcome authors entering conflicting updates [14]. This KB-editor has been extended to support better other types of collaborative research processes and other types of ontological knowledge bases. Furthermore, the KB-editor enables development of glossaries related to the content of a knowledge base. These glossaries can be used to connect terms in the guidance text, provided by MoST to its users, by hyperlinks to their explanations in a glossary.

The Modelling Support Tool (MoST) supports the work of modelling teams in their daily practice by presenting modelling guidance from the modelling-KB, monitoring what is done by each team member and facilitating project management by providing detailed data on what is done by whom in the project as well as on resources used or spent [36].

4   Knowledge Bases

4.1   Problem, Model and Modelling Knowledge Base

The modelling-KB, the problem-KB and the model-KB are developed for different purposes, in different contexts, filled with content from different application domains and are in different stages of implementation. This will be explained here briefly. The remaining part of this section will present and discuss in more detail the meta-ontology (section 4.2), the modelling-KB (section 4.3), the problem-KB (section 4.4) and the model-KB (section 4.5).

The modelling knowledge base has been developed for the HarmoniQuA project. The main objective of the modelling-KB is to provide guidance and straightforward use of the modelling knowledge contained in the Modelling Support Tool, MoST. The main requirements for the modelling-KB are:

- Explicit representation of modelling knowledge;
- Flexible structure;
- Sharing of knowledge by many experts;
- Ease of update and maintenance;
- Appropriate security;
- Platform independence.

The requirements dictated the design of the KB towards the use of ontologies. The structure and content of the modelling-KB will be discussed in section 4.3.

The resulting implementation of the modelling-KB for model-based water management and Modelling Support Tool, MoST, was initially reviewed internally, and subsequently shared with the larger modelling community in water management through meetings and publications [24,36]. Results so far, i.e. from using the KB in an educational context, in 21 professional test cases and some other projects, have shown that our design decision was a sound one. Most requirements have been met and for those which have not, substantial efforts will be spent to handle gaps and inconsistencies in the content of the KB and to make it a generally accepted methodology for modelling in water management.

The problem-KB and the model-KB are less mature and have been developed on a more ad hoc basis [34]. The current content of the problem-KB and the model-KB can best be seen as a side-product of the series of papers on bivalve ecophysiology models [26,29,30,41,]. These ontologies were based on the models used in these papers. In contrast to the process ontology on modelling, which has been developed and populated by a group varying between 5 and 25 persons, the knowledge of the problem-KB and of the model-KB have been derived from the expertise of only a few researchers during a long series of discussions on developing and subsequently structuring simulation models representing the physiological response of 'blue mussels', *Mytilus edulis* L. on varying ecological inputs, including food supply. The structure of these ontologies, specified in the more detailed and specialized ontological layers, has been largely evoked from building this series of models. During model development natural ontological layers became visible in the body of knowledge at hand. The structure and content of the problem-KB and the model-KB will be discussed in sections 4.4 and 4.5. So, the framework contains all three knowledge bases, where the contents of the problem-KB and model-KB are restricted to rather specialized biological knowledge on bivalve ecophysiology issues.

4.2   Meta-ontology

To begin developing the ontological framework for model-based problem-solving, we followed a bootstrap approach [3,34] very similar to the one advocated by Uschold *et al.* [43]. This approach has similarities with approaches used in semantic data modelling [8] and in Ontolingua's *Glossary of Ontology Terminology*[7].

We use a simple and well-defined language (limited set of terms) required for generic processes in general and modelling project processes specifically as a starting vocabulary for a meta-ontology. Uschold *et al.* [43] uses the following basic terms for deriving the business ontology: *entity, relationship, role, subclass of, attribute, axiom* and *instance*. Date [8] uses similar concepts such as: *entity, property, entity type, relationship, subtype, domain* and *instance*. Ontolingua uses *ontology, class, relation, slot, subclass, function* and *axiom*. For a comparison of these bootstrap terminologies, we refer to [34].

We created a new, more extensive and richer vocabulary, which in concert with the bootstrapping terminology, comprises our meta-ontology. The meta-ontology includes, but is not restricted to:

- Bootstrapping concepts: *ontology, concept, relation* (hierarchical, preference), *attribute, property, instance, function, axiom*;
- Bootstrapping relations: *is_a, has, specialization_of, instance_of, property_of, performed_by, uses*;

---

[7] See: http://www-ksl-svc.stanford.edu:5915/doc/frame-editor/glossary-of-terms.html

- Basic meta-ontology: *action, actor* (human, machine), *team, process, project*;
- Multidisciplinary meta-ontology: *science, discipline, paradigm,* (application) *domain, theories and hypotheses, practices, methodology, model, problem, object system, role*;
- Additional terminology: *inheritance, specialization, generalization, abstraction, aggregation, ontological layer.*

We discuss the main branch ontologies and associated knowledge bases in the sections 4.3 – 4.5. A full discussion of all the concepts and relations of the meta-ontology is presented in [34].

4.3   Modelling-KB

Here we will discuss the layered structure and the content of the process-KB, instantiated for the modelling process. A major aim of the HarmoniQuA project was to establish a multidisciplinary modelling methodology for water management. This objective has been met by realizing a detailed knowledge base with modelling expertise for multidisciplinary modelling for water management, providing users in different roles guidance on what they have to do, within all supported domains and for different job complexities.

The part of the methodology on how to model for water management is not new. The content of the modelling-KB is based on existing knowledge and existing guidelines for model-based water management [1,4,19,28,33,39,40,45]. However, the existing modelling guidance is substantially extended. The modelling-KB is available as a service and publicly accessible. The modelling-KB can best be used in combination with the Modelling Support Tool that supports actual modelling by multidisciplinary teams, in which team members play different roles. In water management projects we distinguish roles such as modeler, water manager, auditor, stakeholder and concerned members of the public (see section 5). In addition MoST monitors all modelling activities, and provides a variety of methods to use and help produce reports for various audiences and audits. MoST and its modelling guidelines thus support model management in general and project management for this level of complex, multidisciplinary modelling efforts.

The *process ontology* (of which *modelling* is a specialization) is built on top of the *meta-ontology*, in a layered structure of increasing specialization, described in section 3.4.2. Here we summarize the content per ontological layer, indicate some main concepts and leave out all other concepts and properties associated with each concept:

- Layer 1 (generic process knowledge) with concepts like *guideline, step, task, method, activity, role*, etc.
- Layer 2 (modelling knowledge) with concepts like *modeler, client / manager, expert, auditor, modelling paradigm, modelling practices*, etc.
- Layer 3 (simulation modelling knowledge) with concepts like *describe problem and context, identify data availability, summarize conceptual model and assumptions, construct problem specific model, select calibration parameters, perform calibration, validate model, determine scope of applicability of model, simulate scenarios*, etc.

- Layer 4 (simulation modelling knowledge for water management) with concepts like simulation modelling for the following sub-domains of water management *hydrodynamics, groundwater, precipitation-runoff, flood forecasting, surface water quality, biota / ecology, socio-economics*. Next to these set of (instantiated) sub-domains of application, many concepts of ontological layer 3 have a special meaning in this more specialized layer 4, e.g. 'conceptual model' in the task *summarize conceptual model and assumptions* has completely different meanings in the sub-domains *groundwater modelling* and *precipitation-runoff*.
- Layer 5 (modelling journal for water management) will not be discussed here, but briefly in section 5.4.

A comprehensive overview of ontological layers in the process branch of the framework is given in [34].

4.4   Problem-KB

The *problem-KB* is less mature than the *modelling-KB*, as it lacks a proper implementation in Protégé and there are no tools to use its content directly. Nevertheless it can be useful as a skeleton with consistent terminology to describe knowledge on problems and associated aspects of object systems, especially as this knowledge has to be represented within a simulation model.

The *problem-KB* has subsequently been tested in the set of models on bivalve ecophysiology [26,29,30,41], which indicates that organizing knowledge on problems in a problem-KB is useful to develop simulation models and facilitates reuse. Its usefulness would substantially increase with he availability of a tool which can structure such a body of domain factual knowledge on problems and make it available within model development software.

The *problem-KB* (mainly instantiated for bivalve ecophysiology) uses also the terminology of the *meta-ontology*. It is structured with ontological layers of increasing specialization, described in section 3.4.2. Here we summarize the content per ontological layer, and indicate selected main concepts, omitting all other concepts and properties associated with each concept:

- Layer 1 (generic problem knowledge) with concepts like *object system entity, object system relation, object system aggregation, object system structure, problem description, problem topic, problem context, wanted solution, problem solving methodology, problem domain, functional knowledge, structural knowledge, process knowledge*, etc.
- Layer 2 (problem knowledge for quantitative models) with concepts like *static object system entity, variable object system entity, observable object system entity, non-observable object system entity, physical knowledge, physics process, biological process, chemical process*, etc.
- Layer 3 (problem knowledge for simulation models) with structural related concepts, problem subject related specializations, like *pollution, disturbed ecosystem, nature conservation, climate change* and process related concepts (often specializations of concepts from *layer 2*) like:

o   *biological process* (layer 2): e.g. *ecological process, physiological process, biochemical process*;

o   *biochemical process* (layer 2): e.g. *endothermic process, exothermic process*;

o   *transport process* (layer 2): e.g. *water quantity transport, dissolved mater transport, particulate matter transport*;

- Layer 4 (problem knowledge for application domains, i.e. instantiated with *problem knowledge for bivalve ecophysiology*) with concepts like

    o   Food related processes: *clearance, filtration, pre-ingestive selection, ingestion, absorption, faeces production*;

    o   Respiration and excretion related processes: *rest respiration, active respiration, excretion*;

    o   Reproduction related processes: *gametogenesis, spawning*;

    o   Allocation and growth related processes: *growth reproductive compartment, growth storage compartment, growth somatic compartment, growth (organic part of) shell*;

- Layer 5 (problem knowledge for a project) will not be discussed here, but we refer to [34], which provides a comprehensive overview of ontological layers in the problem branch of the framework.

4.5   Model-KB

The *model-KB* is also not very mature, as it lacks a proper implementation and tools to use it. Nevertheless it appears useful in the limited number of models that were based on it. To improve the *model-KB*, it should be integrated in model development tools, using the *problem-KB* content to translate the knowledge from the problem-KB directly or with help of a modeler into a model.

The *model-KB* is based on the expertise and (simulation) traditions of our research group[8], which has 30 years of experience in modelling & simulation (M&S) methodology and M&S software (e.g., [9,15,16,17,32,38]). The *model-KB* has been further molded by requirements established in the development of implemented and published models.

The *model-KB* (mainly instantiated for bivalve ecophysiological models) also uses the terminology of the *meta-ontology*. It is structured with ontological layers of increasing specialization, described in section 3.4.2. Again, we summarize the content per ontological layer and indicate selected main concepts :

- Layer 1 (generic model knowledge) with concepts like *model, representation power (structural, behavioral), model objective, model scope, base model, model paradigm, model assumption, model component*, etc.

- Layer 2 (quantitative model knowledge) with concepts like *optimization, simulation (continuous, discrete), agent based modelling, model mode (conceptual, mathematical, computer), model application, numerical model*

---

[8] Information Technology Group at Wageningen University, Netherlands, http://www.inf.wur.nl/UK/

solver, objective function, model quantity (model variable type, model parameter type, model function type), model expression, model input, model output, etc.

- Layer 3 (simulation model knowledge) with structural related concepts, like *observable variable, not-observable variable, model equations (differential, algebraic), model experiments, model scenario, experimental frame* and *model quantity* related concepts (often specializations of concepts from *layer 2*) like:
  - ○ *model variable type* (layer 2): e.g. *state variable, auxiliary variable*;
  - ○ *model parameter type* (layer 2): e.g. *constant parameter, observed parameter, decision parameter, calculated parameter, free parameter*;
  - ○ *model function type* (layer 2): e.g. *spatio-temporal series, spatial series, time series, tabular function, basic function, other function*;
- Layer 4 (generic simulation models for application domains, i.e. instantiated with *simulation model knowledge for bivalve ecophysiology*) all concepts are instantiation of the above outlined concepts of ontological layer 3;
- Layer 5 (specific simulation models in a project) will not be discussed here, but we refer to [34], who provides a comprehensive overview of ontological layers in the problem branch of the framework.

4.6   Connections between the Knowledge Bases

In the previous sections we have elaborated on the concepts incorporated in the different layers of the ontologies of the knowledge bases. If we look at them in more detail, it can easily be discerned that the concepts contained within the first three layers provide for the common part of the shared language to be employed by all team members in a project. The concepts in lower layers are more specialized. If the concepts in these lower layers are always attached to the concepts in the upper layers, we may assume that we are able to contribute to solving the *language problem* in projects between all modelling team members involved. The ontological structure of the framework will assure that this condition is met.

5   Modelling Support Tool (MoST)

5.1   Introduction to MoST

In the previous sections we briefly described functional requirements to be met by a support tool. In line with these requirements the Modelling Support Tool can work in different modes with components to set up and edit projects (section 5.2), obtain guidance (section 5.3), monitor what teams actually do in a project (section 5.4) and report what has to be done (section 5.5). Detailed descriptions of the tool and its usefulness for model-based water management are given by Scholten *et al.* [36].

The relation between the Modelling Support Tool and the other components of the system are depicted in Fig. 5 with emphasis on how the components interact with each other and the role of team members and domain experts in this system. MoST can be used either in *local projects* (a single user, typically a modeler) or for *online projects*, in which members of a multidisciplinary team collaborate in a model-based problem-solving project.

5.2   Setting-Up Modelling Projects

Projects have to be defined in the project initialization phase by a project initiator (further referred to as administrator). First the administrator defines one or more subprojects (each related to one or more application domains). Subsequently each subproject has to be fine-tuned in terms of relevant tasks from a comprehensive template. Next team members (called users) have to be added, each getting a role (administrator, manager, modeler, auditor, stakeholder, public) with appropriate authorizations at the task level, i.e. permissions to *read*, *write* or *decision making* (i.e. deciding whether to continue with the next task or to redo some previous ones).

In order to evaluate modelling projects and help auditors, a *scoreboard* template is provided, which can be modified for the project at hand by project administrators and the problem owner (i.e. clients of the project). During project execution, auditors must fill scoreboards as part of their evaluation activities.

5.3   Guiding Modelling Projects

The guideline component provides different views on the KB: the *tree view*, the *flowchart view* and the *task view*. These views are the major panels on the screen in the guideline component (Fig. 6). The guideline component can also be used outside the context of running a modelling project.

The **tree view** resembles standard MS-Windows trees[9] and enables browsing project steps and tasks much like MS-Windows Explorer allows browsing directories and files. Symbols indicate the nature of the concepts: red ovals for *steps*, yellow rectangles for *(ordinary) tasks*, blue diamonds for *decision tasks*, and green hexagons for *review tasks*.

The **flowchart view** provides another type of browsing through the network of *steps* and *tasks*, but also features a structured view with the order of *tasks* and of *redo-loops*. Arrows indicate the order and have tool-tips to see their origin *task* or destination *task*.

The task view presents a textual description of the chosen concept (*guideline, step* or *task*). It shows the content of a task, organized with tabs for *task description* (definition and explanation of the task), *activities information* (list of activities and description of each activity), *methods information* (list of available methods and their brief descriptions); *pitfalls and sensitivities* (an overview of the risky elements in the task) and *other information* (relations to other tasks, software aspects, references, inputs and outputs). The descriptions of tasks in this view contain discipline related terminology, which is further explained in the glossary and accessible through hyperlinks in the task view.

---

[9] A *tree view* is a graphical diagram used to display the hierarchal structure of items, such as directories and files on a disk.

One of the major objectives of the overall system is customizing the guidelines for each team member with respect to their roles, the domains / disciplines involved, and the specific project characteristics. This is achieved by filtering the guidance for these properties according to what is relevant for that specific user. Filtering automatically updates the *tree view*, the *flowchart view* and the *task view*.

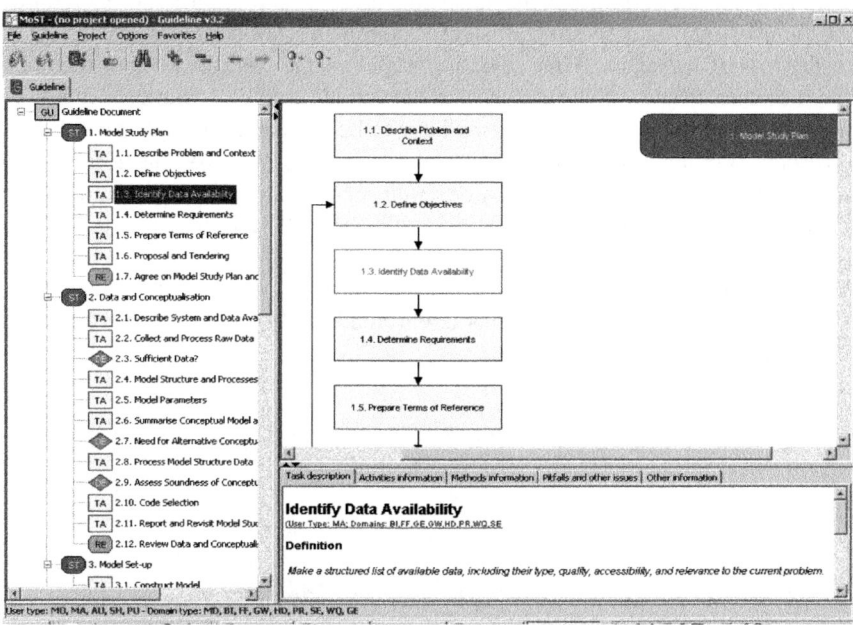

Fig. 6. Screen dump of guideline component of MoST in the case where no project has yet been opened, showing menu bar, tool bar and guideline component tab at the top and the tree view, the flowchart view and the task view in the central part of the screen. In the tree view Task 1.3 has been chosen and the guideline component synchronizes the other views by setting the pointer to the same activity in these views.

5.4   Monitoring Modelling Projects

Keeping records in the form of creating a modelling or project journal, is essential in the project execution phase, as it enables audits and the reconstruction of projects. This monitoring component of MoST is complex in its user interface and its functionality.

The project execution component provides three views of which two involve the KB: the *tree view* and the *task view*. The third view, the *activity view*, presents what actually is done in the task at a very detailed level (*activity level*) . These views are the major panels on the screen in the project execution component (Fig. 7).

The **tree view** (left section in Fig. 7) displays all the tasks in the project and the status of these tasks. This view can be used to browse through the tasks and also to inspect the status of each task in the subproject. Different icons are used to show this status. A transparent rectangle indicates a task not yet started. A yellow rectangle indicates a task that has already started, but not yet finished. If it is finished, a green checkmark is displayed. Skipped task are shown with a red cross.

The **task view** (lower right in Fig. 7) is similar to the task view in the guideline component of MoST (section 5.3). It provides guidance on the task that is selected in the tree view, with tabs to select the sections on the guidance for that task.

The **activity view** (upper right panel in Fig. 7) is the main panel to record what team members do, and to store this information in a modelling journal for sharing with the rest of the team. After selecting a *task* in the *tree view*, team members can provide *details, actions and outcomes* and attach all kind of documents in any format to the modelling journal. *Methods used* have to be indicated. *Activities* can be skipped and *resources* edited. In less complex projects one can also work at *task level*, which requires fewer details. If a task is a *decision task* or a *review task*, authorized team members can decide whether to continue with the next task or redo some part of the modelling process.

Browsing through the *tasks* should be done in the *tree view*, but – depending on if the prescribed order in the guidelines is enforced, *tasks* have to be performed in the designated order.

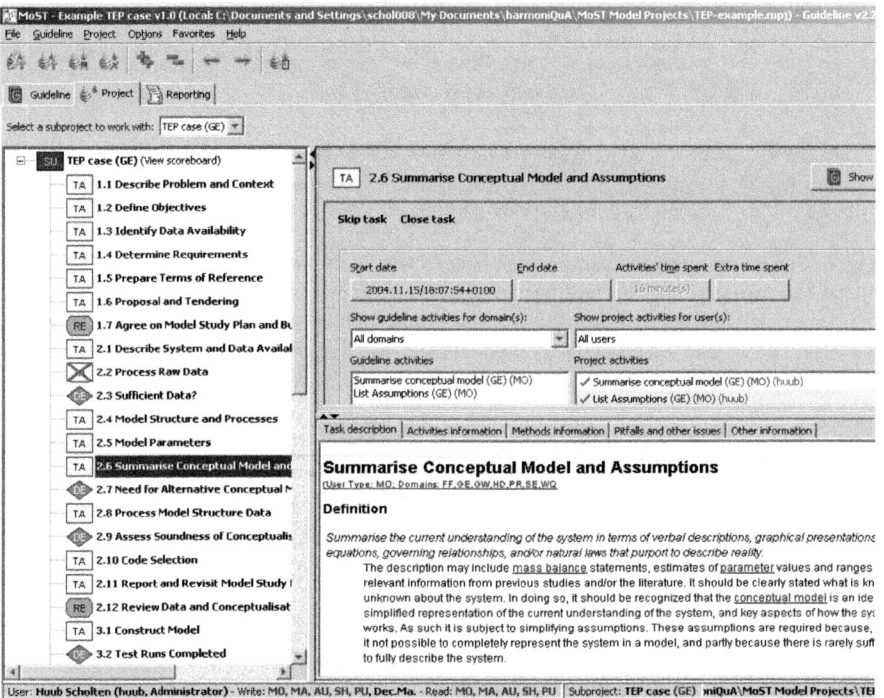

Fig. 7. Screen dump of MoST in the case where a project (TEP case (GE)) has been opened showing the menu bar, tool bar, component tabs and subproject dropdown box in the top and the tree view, task view and activity view in the central part of the screen

5.5   Reporting on Modelling Projects

During a modelling project and after its completion, there is a strong need for various types of reports about the execution of the project. All reports will be generated from the content of a modelling journal. Two aspects of reports are of interest here: its *intended use* and its *audience*. The use may vary from informing other team members, management checks on progress, to the final report for the client of the modelling study. Audiences are also diversified, including scientists, managers, professional engineers, (lay) stakeholders and interested members of the general public. Therefore MoST includes powerful means to generate reports for specific purposes and audiences.

5.6   Training Material and Help

MoST is a complex tool and novice users need some training before they can benefit from all its features to support modelling teams in their daily routine. Therefore, comprehensive training material has been developed for students and professional modelers in water management[10]. This training material consists of written material, presentations, exercises that encourage using MoST in a test case project and many screen-recording movies on MoST, its KB, a case study and some background information. The screen recording movies have a typical length of one to two minutes and are accompanied by an instructor's voice. The movies allow trainees to work individually, at their own pace. Using the movies also allows the instructor both to explain in words and to show by demonstration. The movies are the core part of the training material and serve as a sort of animated help facility to help users work with MoST. In addition to the training material a *help function* has been implemented with the summarized information of the training material.

5.7   Testing

The experiences with MoST so far are promising. MoST has been evaluated within the HarmoniQuA project in 21 test case studies, 15 professional workshops, a professional survey, and a stakeholder survey. Furthermore, it has been used successfully in 6 university courses. Finally it has been appraised with a web based user questionnaire. Several modelling projects use it now. An evaluation of MoST can be found in [31] and more comprehensively in [34]. Based on these test results it may be concluded that MoST is a new and innovative way of supporting multidisciplinary modelling for water management [36], as it combines modelling guidance with tool support during the whole life-cycle of model-based problem-solving projects.

6   Reuse and Extension of the Framework

The ontologies of the framework have been used in different ways and with different intensities. The *meta-ontology* has been used in more modelling projects and was extended as soon as terminology to develop the other ontologies was discovered to be

---

[10] The training material is accessible from www.HarmoniQuA.org/training

missing. The *problem-KB* and *model-KB* can be used to describe problems and associated object systems in case a (simulation) model has to be used to solve a problem at hand. All instances of these two ontologies are related to bivalve ecophysiology problems and models.

The *modelling ontology* is a specialization of the more generic *process ontology* and has been used extensively in combination with MoST. Here we focus on the knowledge in the process branch of the ontological framework and began discussing ways to extend the use of the framework for the modelling branch in combination with MoST [28].

Implementation of ontological layers in the KB (see Fig. 3 and Fig. 4) facilitates the use and reuse of knowledge and tools. We define (in the process branch) ontological layers 0 (meta-ontology), layer 1 (generic process knowledge), layer 2 (simulation modelling knowledge) and layer 3 (generic simulation modelling knowledge for application domain) of the modelling ontology in combination with MoST, as the *simulation modelling support technology*. In HarmoniQuA we combined this modelling technology with ontological layer 4 (generic simulation modelling knowledge for model-based water management), referring to this as MoST and its *modelling-KB*. In addition to layer 3 (generic simulation modelling knowledge for application domain), water management (sub)domains are detailed in layer 4, i.e. (at present) *hydrodynamics*, *groundwater*, *precipitation-runoff*, *flood forecasting*, *surface water quality*, *biota* and *socio-economics*. There are plans to extend this set of domains with *activated sludge modelling*. For this purpose ontological layer 4 has to be extended with knowledge about this extra domain (Scholten and Kassahun, 2006). In a similar way the *simulation modelling support technology* can be used for modelling in other application domains. So far interest has been shown from experts in other application domains, such as modelling for ecological and environmental restoration of river basins, crop growth modelling and science and policy integration for coastal assessment. Using the framework for these other application domains will require a new content of ontological layers 4 and 5, containing specialized modelling knowledge for that domain and related projects [28].

If we want to support other processes than modelling, the *modelling support technology* has to be tailored to a *process support technology*. This will require adaptations in all parts of the framework, i.e. the process branch (until now referred to as the modelling branch), the problem branch, the model branch, ProST and the KB-editor.

An example of using the *process support technology* for other processes can be found in the AquaStress project[11]. This project addresses water stress mitigation by providing various water stress mitigation options (technical, management, institutional and others), scientific evaluation of options (multi-criteria analysis, simulation, case based reasoning, etc.) for case studies at specific sites and by supporting participatory processes, in which stakeholders and public participate in selecting and evaluating water stress solutions (Scholten and Kassahun, 2006). Other examples of reusing the *process support technology*, which are not implemented so

---

[11] See www.aquastress.net

far, include the implementation process of WFD (Water Framework Directive), supply chain management and the drug development process for SME's in biotechnology and the pharmaceutical industry.

The required adaptations to the framework to support other processes in addition to modelling, will be discussed here briefly using an example project on water stress mitigation (AquaStress project), in which modelling is instrumental only for some detailed solutions.

In the *process branch* of the framework the *meta-ontology* (with generic terminology) and *ontological layer 1* (generic process knowledge) can be reused providing concepts like *process, step, task, activity, method*, and *tool*; which are generic enough to be reused. We define new processes on water stress mitigation for test cases at the test sites Velt and Vecht (Netherlands) and Iskar (Bulgaria) by filling in instances of more detailed ontological layers 2, 3 and 4 (see process-KB[12] for overview and details).

The *problem branch* of the framework is adapted in a similar way and problem knowledge related to AquaStress is defined for one or more case studies of all test sites (see site-KB[13] for overview and details).

The *model branch* of the framework needs to be modified most rigorously, as models are not a problem-solver type for the water stress mitigation approach in AquaStress. Instead of models, *options* are the more appropriate instruments, preferably in combination with *indicators*. The AquaStress glossary[14] defines *option* as 'measure to combat water stress and interventions for water stress mitigation, including policy mechanisms, economic tools, administrative initiatives, participatory processes & education and cost-effective broadly supported decisions for sustainable water management'. *Indicator* is defined as 'variable that summarizes large amounts of data into a single value, which can then be compared over time or between countries and regions to reveal changes and differences. They also provide a means of communicating information about progress towards a goal (such as sustainable resource management) in a significant and simplified manner.' So *options* are instruments to mitigate water stress and *indicators* are instruments to quantify water stress in many dimensions and before and after applying an option. Although *option* and *indicator* are not models, they share some characteristics with models. Models and *options* are both problem-solving instruments and models and *indicators* are both quantitative instruments. For details on *options,* see the option-KB[15], and for details on *indicators* consult the indicator-KB[16].

Applying the New Modelling framework to the AquaStress situation also requires significant adaptations to the tools. Although MoST is a powerful tool to support modelling, it has a number of limitations due to its focus on (simulation) modelling, especially for water management. To support other collaborative multidisciplinary projects, such as water stress mitigation in AquaStress, MoST had to be extended to

---

[12] http://harmoniqua.wau.nl/aquastress/edit?&type=Process

[13] http://harmoniqua.wau.nl/aquastress/edit?type=Site&PageSize=20

[14] http://harmoniqua.wau.nl/aquastress/edit?&type=GlossaryTerm

[15] http://harmoniqua.wau.nl/aquastress/edit?&type=Option

[16] http://harmoniqua.wau.nl/aquastress/edit?&type=Indicator

match AquaStress' functional requirements. The new version of MoST which supports a wider spectrum of collaborative processes is now called P̲rocess S̲upport T̲ool (ProST). New features in ProST include a more flexible structure of the process knowledge base (e.g. user defined roles), multilingual user interface, multilingual knowledge bases and a more extensive support for project planning and management with deadlines and resource allocation.

To extend the usability of the framework for other collaborative processes than modelling, the KB-editor (section 3.5) must also be redesigned. The present version facilitates development of knowledge bases in Protégé for various processes, problems, instruments (models, options, indicators) and glossaries.

7   Discussion

7.1   Introduction

Model-based problem-solving is a mature and powerful instrument for comprehensive analysis and decision support. Problem-solving projects have shifted from monodisciplinary to multidisciplinary while simultaneously problem-solving modelling has generated more model types and associated modelling paradigms, leading to the potential for more complete analysis [18]. These changes in turn have created many new problems that hinder appropriate modelling. To overcome some of these problems, we have proposed to structure relevant knowledge explicitly in the form of knowledge bases. In our approach knowledge has been organized into four ontological knowledge bases (KBs): a *meta-ontology* (with basic terminology), a *modelling-KB*, a *model-KB* and a *problem-KB*. Each of these KBs has layers of increasing specialization, ranging from very generic to very specialized. These ontological layers facilitate reuse of KB content, especially the more generic ontological layers, and greatly help solve the *language problems* identified in section 2. A series of software tools and services has been developed, including the KB-editor to facilitate developing KBs (on processes, problems and problem-solving instruments like models) and glossaries in Protégé, and the Modelling Support Tool to support multidisciplinary modelling project teams by providing guidance, monitoring, and reporting and management capabilities.

ProST (Process Support Tool), the more generic successor of MoST, supports a wider range of projects, in which teams of researchers and professionals collaborate in multidisciplinary problem-solving processes. Finally, training material and a help function flatten the learning curve.

7.2   Scientific Innovation

Regarding the ontology for processes, instantiated for model-based problem solving in water management, and the other ontologies (*meta-ontology*, *problem-KB* and *model-KB*), the most innovative aspects are the structural framework of four ontologies with layers of increasing specialization (Fig. 3 and Fig. 4). The layered structure is innovative and facilitates content-specific conversations between human users of the ontology and computer programs. The latter is realized in the following way: an ontological *layer x* provides the language and terminology to discuss concepts and relations at the more specialized (and thus less generic) *layer x+1*. Furthermore, the layered ontology structure enables the reuse of at least the more generic (less specialized) layers for other purposes. This reuse has only been implemented and tested for the process ontology and not yet for the other ontologies.

7.3   QA for Modelling

Compared to state-of-the-art quality assurance guidelines for model-based water management such as the Dutch GMP Handbook [45], the Bay-Delta modelling protocol [1] and the Australian groundwater modelling guidelines [19], the modelling guidelines discussed by Scholten *et al.* [36] are more complete and flexible. This is reflected in its knowledge base (KB) by including several water management modelling sub-domains, targeted at different types of users and job complexities. Furthermore, and most importantly, the ideas and implementation of the supporting tool MoST is novel, as no other guidelines have attempted to prepare such a tool [36].

The available quality standard, ISO 9000 and those built on top of the ISO 9000 family[17] are not focused on modelling and simulation. They are not sufficient for modelling and simulation because they are not specific enough (ISO 9000) or else are focused on different fields of application. The approach followed for model-based water management in the HarmoniQuA project (modelling-KB and MoST) matches the basic ideas of ISO 9000, i.e. describing what to do (process definition), monitoring and recording what is done, comparing what is done with what should have be done, and testing for satisfactory (intermediate) products and results (assessing the soundness of the conceptual model, calibrated model, validation and uncertainty analysis of scenario runs, etc.). These are all, to some extent, part of the modelling process and simultaneously focused on finding flaws in resulting products of the modelling process. The HarmoniQuA approach combines testing products, e.g. model validation, with a process approach.

It is clear that (simulation) modelling has profited from the modelling-KB and MoST. The other parts of the ontological framework, i.e. the problem-KB and the model-KB, have a less direct effect on quality assurance of model-based problem-solving for water management or other application domains, but nevertheless help to develop, analyze and apply models in a more transparent and auditable way.

7.4   Multidisciplinary Collaboration

Many real world problems that can be analyzed with model-based problem-solving have a distinctly multidisciplinary character. The difficulties due to the multidisciplinary character of real world problems are not completely solved by our approach, but model-based problem-solving teams are supported to deal with these hurdles, mainly by facilitating mutual understanding via a complete and consistent terminology covering all disciplines and application domains at hand and tool based support for multidisciplinary teams in projects.

---

[17] See for an introduction: http://www.iso.org/iso/iso_catalogue/management_standards.htm

7.5   Public Participation

MoST (and its successor ProST) facilitates public participation at the first two basic levels: informing and consulting stakeholders and the public. If members of these groups are added to the problem solving team in MoST or ProST, they can read or write parts of the project journal within the limits of their authorization. The third level of participation is more active as it consists of discussions, influence on the policy agenda, participatory design of solutions, involvement in decision making and participating in implementation [20,21,22,25]. To facilitate the latter, most intensive, type of participatory involvement, the guidelines in the process-KB have to be adapted.

7.6   Present Status and Future Plans

The New Modelling Framework is rather comprehensive, as it consists of tools and a set of linked knowledge bases. Tools that are implemented and used are the KB-editor, developed to populate the knowledge bases (see section 3.5), and MoST (and its successor ProST), developed to use the knowledge bases and support modelling (see section 5). The knowledge bases are designed to represent knowledge of various levels of detail and specialization and they can be extended as discussed in this chapter.

In summary, at present all KBs are structured and populated with knowledge on water management modelling, water stress mitigation and bivalve ecophysiology, as described in section 4. It is in use for practical modelling studies (e.g. [12]) and in educational courses at MSc level[18].

We also plan to use the problem-KB and the model-KB in the context of a new framework that aims to chain environmental Web services (e.g. data, models and modelling tools) automatically [13,37]. Here it will facilitate semantic interoperability between user requirements and the elements of the Web service chain and to assure a sound coupling of the Web services.

7.7   Modelling Problems Solved

The problems in model-based water management discussed in section 2 are partly solved with the development of MoST and its modelling-KB. The glossary is an answer to *ambiguous terminology used in modelling,* while the explicit guidelines in the KB help to promote *mutual understanding in multidisciplinary modelling teams. Malpractice* cannot completely be banned in modelling projects, but the guidelines direct professionals to model according to 'Good Modelling Practices' and to avoid some of the unprofessional practices, including *careless handling of input data, inadequate model set-up, insufficient calibration and validation* and *model use outside of its scope.* The widespread problem of *too few data* or *the poor quality of available data* will obviously not solved by the methodology and tools presented here; this is also the case for *insufficient knowledge on processes. Miscommunication of the modeler to the end-user on the possibilities and limitations of the modelling project* and *overselling of model capabilities* are still possible, but modelers are guided to avoid these pitfalls. Furthermore, the model journals enable end-users to do

---

[18] E.g. see http://www.inf.wur.nl/UK/education/INF-31806MFNC/

proper audits and to check the translation of model results into end-user advice. This will also help to avoid *confusion on how to use model results in decision-making*. Furthermore, the model journals are a direct answer to the problem of *lack of documentation and transparency of the modelling process, leading to projects which cannot be feasibly audited or reconstructed*. Finally, MoST and its KB distinguish socio-economics as a separate and essential domain of water management, which helps to avoid *insufficient consideration of economic, institutional and political issues and a lack of integrated modelling*.

We have shown that modelling problems in water management can be effectively solved with MoST and its *modelling-KB*. We also proposed a more explicit approach to describe the combination of a problem, a suitable model for its solution, and a computer executable object system for the problem. The goal of the *problem-KB* is to contain all relevant knowledge to be coupled to or included in a model. Moreover, we perceived a need for a more formal, ontology based, approach to describe models, directly linked to the *model-KB*. Finally, a *meta-ontology* is proposed for the basic terminology. The total proposed framework is more than just MoST and the modelling-KB, however the latter products are more extensively realized. The other elements of this framework are not less important, but their usefulness remains to be proven [34] until all its elements are implemented and supported by a toolbox supporting its use. This will require substantial additional effort. Despite the limited realization of the framework, it is reasonable to claim that the most used part (MoST and its modelling-KB) improves the quality of model-based problem-solving, especially for water management, by providing guidance and rendering the modelling process more transparent.

7.8   Concluding Remarks

The proposed ontological framework describes and structures relevant knowledge about processes, (e.g. modelling), models and problems. Its relevance is determined by its purpose. We do not intend to describe the entire *world*, but only aspects that are relevant for a specified purpose. These aspects are views on relevant concepts of *what is*, filtered by science, scientific observation technology and some purposeful reason. Therefore, there can be no single, *perfect* ontology, but many useful ones depending on some specified purpose. We have created an ontological framework that is useful for its overall purpose, i.e. better modelling practices. If one invests substantial resources for such a construct, it is desirable to make it as general as possible, i.e. reusable for other problems, models and modelling paradigms. The degree to which the proposed framework can be reused will demonstrate its genuine value.

Acknowledgement. The present work was carried out within the projects *HarmoniQuA* (partly funded by the EC in FP5 under Contract EVK1-CT2001-00097, www.harmoniqua.org) and *AquaStress* (partly funded by the EC in FP6 under Contract 511231, www.aquastress.net). The authors want to thank all researchers involved in these two projects, especially Ayalew Kassahun and Peter Gijsbers, involved in both projects, Theodore Kargas and Jens Christian Refsgaard, involved in HarmoniQuA and Michiel Blind, involved in AquaStress. The authors are also grateful to Pasky Pascual (EPA, Washington, USA), Nils Ferrand (Cemagref, Montpellier, France) and Hugh Middlemis (Aquaterra, Kent Town, Australia), who acted as external reviewers of MoST and its modelling knowledge base. The constructive comments of three anonymous reviewers are acknowledged.

References

1. BDMF, Protocols for Water and Environmental Modelling. Bay-Delta Modelling Forum (2000), http://cwemf.org/Pubs/Protocols2000-01.pdf
2. Beulens, A.J.M., Scholten, H.: An ontological framework for structuring process knowledge specified for the process of model-based problem solving. In: Makowski, M. (ed.) 18th Workshop on Methodologies and Tools for Complex System Modelling and Integrated Policy Assessment, IIASA, Laxenburg, Austria, September 6-8, pp. 4–8 (2004)
3. Beulens, A.J.M., Scholten, H.: Towards a process ontology for a model based support system for problem solving: the ontology bootstrap problem. International Journal of Knowledge and Systems Sciences 2, 30–34 (2005)
4. Blind, M.W., Scholten, H., van Waveren, R.H.: Model for success. Water 21 October (2000)
5. Borst, W.N.: Construction of engineering ontologies for knowledge sharing and reuse. University of Twente, The Netherlands, Enschede (1997)
6. Chandrasekaran, B., Josephson, J., Benjamins, V.: Ontology of tasks and methods. In: Eleventh Workshop on Knowledge Acquisition, Modelling and Management, Banff, Alberta, Canada (1998)
7. Chandrasekaran, B., Josephson, J., Benjamins, V.: What are ontologies and why do we need them? IEEE Intelligent Systems 14, 20–26 (1999)
8. Date, C.J.: An introduction to database systems, 8th edn. Addison-Wesley Publishing Company, Reading (2004)
9. Elzas, M.S.: Desktop modelling and simulation environments. In: Huntsinger, R.C., Karplus, W.J., Kerckhoffs, E.J., Vansteenkiste, G.C. (eds.) Simulation Environments: Symbol and Number Processing on Multi and Array Processors, pp. 389–393. Society for Computer Simulation, Zeist (1988) ISBN
10. Gruber, T.R.: A translation approach to portable ontology specifications. Knowledge Acquisition 5(2), 199–220 (1993)
11. Gruber, T.R.: Towards principles for the design of ontologies used for knowledge sharing. International Journal of Human-Computer Studies 43, 907–928 (1995)
12. Højberg, A.L., Refsgaard, J.C.: Quality assurance in water resources modelling: NOVANAQuA. Geological Survey of Denmark and Greenland, Copenhagen, p. 75 (2009), http://www.vandmodel.dk/xpdf/novanaqua.pdf
13. Kassahun, A., Kramer, M.R., Scholten, H., Beulens, A.J.M.: CHESS Integrated Framework – Mapping problem solving tasks to web services. In: The 22nd International Workshop on Complex Systems Modelling (CSM), pp. 23–27 (2009)
14. Kassahun, A., Scholten, H.: A knowledge base system for multidisciplinary model-based water management, Summit on Environmental Modelling and Software. In: 3rd Biennial Meeting of the International Environmental Modelling and Software Society, Burlington, Vermont, USA, July 9-12 (2006)
15. Kettenis, D.L.: Issues of parallelization in implementation of the combined simulation language Cosmos, University of Technology, p. 260. Delft (1994)
16. Klepper, O., Van der Tol, M.W.M., Scholten, H., Herman, P.M.J.: SMOES: a Simulation Model for the Oosterschelde EcoSystem. Part I: Description and Uncertainty Analysis. Hydrobiologia 282/283, 437–451 (1994)

17. Kramer, M.R., Scholten, H.: The Smart approach to modelling and simulation. In: Heemink, A.W., Dekker, L., Arons, H.d.S., Smit, I., van Stijn, T.L. (eds.) Proceedings OF EUROSIM 2001, Shaping Future with Simulation, The 4th International EUROSIM Congress, in which is Incorporated the 2nd Conference on Modelling and Simulation in Biology, Medicine and Biomedical Engineering, Delft, The Netherlands, TU Delft, 6 pages on CD-ROM, June 26-29 (2001) ISBN: 90-806441-1-0

18. Makowski, M.: A Structured Modelling Technology. European Journal of Operational Research 166, 615–648 (2005)

19. Middlemis, H.: Murray-Darling Basin Commission. Groundwater flow modelling guideline. Aquaterra Consulting Pty Ltd., South Perth (2000)

20. Pahl-Wostl, C., Hare, M.: Processes of social learning in integrated resources management. Journal of Community & Applied Social Psychology 14, 193–206 (2004)

21. Pahl-Wostl, C.: Towards sustainability in the water sector - the importance of human actors and processes of social learning. Aquatic Sciences 64, 394–411 (2002)

22. Pahl-Wostl, C.: Actor based analysis and modelling approaches. The Integrated Assessment Journal 5, 97–118 (2005), http://journals.sfu.ca/int_assess/index.php/iaj/article/view/167/110

23. Refsgaard, J.C., Henriksen, H.J.: Modelling guidelines - terminology and guiding principles. Advances in Water Resources 27, 71–82 (2004)

24. Refsgaard, J.C., Henriksen, H.J., Harrar, B., Scholten, H., Kassahun, A.: Quality assurance in model based water management - review of existing practice and outline of new approaches. Environmental Modelling & Software 20, 1201–1215 (2005)

25. Ridder, D., Mostert, E., Wolters, H.A. (eds.): Learning together to manage together: improving participation in water management, University of Osnabrück, Osnabrück, p. 115 (2005), http://www.harmonicop.info/handbook.php; ISBN 3-00-016970-9

26. Rueda, J.L., Smaal, A.C., Scholten, H.: A growth model of the cockle (Cerastoderma edule L.) tested in the Oosterschelde estuary (The Netherlands). Journal of Sea Research 54, 276–298 (2005)

27. Scholten, H.: An ontological approach in quality assessment of modelling and simulation. In: Heemink, A.W., Dekker, L., Arons, H.d.S., Smit, I., van Stijn, T.L. (eds.) Proceedings of EUROSIM 2001, Shaping Future with Simulation, The 4th International EUROSIM Congress, in Which is Incorporated the 2nd Conference on Modelling and Simulation in Biology, Medicine and Biomedical Engineering. TU Delft, Delft, The Netherlands 6 pages on CD-ROM (2001) ISBN: 90-806441-1-0

28. Scholten, H., Kassahun, A.: Supporting multidisciplinary model-based water management projects: a user perspective, Summit on Environmental Modelling and Software. In: 3rd Biennial Meeting of the International Environmental Modelling and Software Society. Burlington, Vermont, USA, July 9-12 (2006)

29. Scholten, H., Smaal, A.C.: Responses of Mytilus edulis L. to varying food concentrations - testing EMMY, an ecophysiological model. J. Exp. Mar. Biol. Ecol. 219, 217–239 (1998)

30. Scholten, H., Smaal, A.C.: The ecophysiological response of mussels in mesocosms with reduced inorganic nutrient loads: simulations with the model EMMY. Aquatic Ecology 33, 83–100 (1999)

31. Scholten, H., Beulens, A.J.M.: Testing ontological support for multidisciplinary model-based problem-solving for water management. In: Makowski, M. (ed.) Knowledge Creation and Integration for Solving Complex Problems. The 19th International Workshop on Complex Systems Modelling (CSM) jointly with the 6th International Symposium on Knowledge and Systems Sciences (KSS), IIASA, Laxenburg, Austria, August 29-31, pp. 51–55 (2005) ISBN

32. Scholten, H., Van der Tol, M.W.M.: SMOES: a Simulation Model for the Oosterschelde EcoSystem. Part II: calibration and validation. Hydrobiologia 282/283, 453–474 (1994)
33. Scholten, H.: Good Modelling Practice. In: Makowski, M. (ed.) Abstracts of the 13th JISR-IIASA Workshop on Methodologies and Tools for Complex System Modelling and Integrated Policy Assessment, IIASA, Laxenburg, pp. 57–59 (1999)
34. Scholten, H.: Better modelling practice: an ontological perspective on multidisciplinary model-based problem-solving, Social Science, Information Technology Group. Wageningen University, Wageningen (2008), http://library.wur.nl/wda/dissertations/dis4562.pdf ISBN 978-90-8585-304
35. Scholten, H., Kassahun, A., Refsgaard, J.C.: Managing multidisciplinary model based water management projects. In: Gourbesville, P., Cunge, J., Guinot, V., Liong, S.-Y. (eds.) 7th International Conference on HydroInformatics, Nice, France, September 4-8, vol. 3, pp. 2231–2238. Research Publishing (2006)
36. Scholten, H., Kassahun, A., Refsgaard, J.C., Kargas, T., Gavardinas, C., Beulens, A.J.M.: A methodology to support multidisciplinary model-based water management. Environmental Modelling & Software 22, 743–759 (2007)
37. Scholten, H., Kassahun, A., Beulens, A.J.M.: Chaining environmental Web services: composing a Web service chain. In: The 22nd International Workshop on Complex Systems Modelling (CSM), pp. 46–50 (2009)
38. Scholten, H., De Hoop, B.J., Herman, P.M.J.: SENECA 1.2: a Simulation Environment for ECological Application (Manual), DIHO, Yerseke, p. 150 (1990) ISBN 90-74638-01-5
39. Scholten, H., Van Waveren, R.H., Groot, S., Van Geer, F., Wösten, H., Koeze, R., Noort, J.J.: Good Modelling Practice in water management. In: Proceedings HydroInformatics 2000, International Association for Hydraulic Research, Cedar Rapids, Iowa, USA (2000)
40. Scholten, H., Van Waveren, R.H., Groot, S., Van Geer, F., Wösten, H., Koeze, R., Noort, J.J.: Improving the quality of model-based decision support: Good Modelling Practice in water management. In: Schumann, A., Xia, J., Marino, M., Rosbjerg, D. (eds.) Regional Management of Water Resources. Proceedings of Symposium S2 of the 6th Scientific Assembly of the International Association of Hydrological Sciences, Maastricht, The Netherlands, July 18-27, pp. 223–230. IAHS, Maastricht (2001)
41. Smaal, A.C., Scholten, H.: EMMY: an ecophysiological model of Mytilus edulis L. In: Smaal, A.C. (ed.) Food Supply and Demand of Bivalve Suspension Feeders in a Tidal System. Rijksuniversiteit Groningen, pp. 147–190, Groningen (1997)
42. Stanford Center for Biomedical Informatics Research Welcome to Protégé, http://protege.stanford.edu/ (accessed August 21, 2009)
43. Uschold, M., King, M., Moralee, S., Zorgios, Y.: The Enterprise Ontology. In: Uschold, M., Tate, A. (eds.) The Knowledge Engineering Review. Special Issue on Putting Ontologies to Use, vol. 13 (1998)
44. Weide, A., van der, Beulens, A.J.M., Van Dijk, S.: Project Planning and Management, Lemma (2003) ISBN 90 5931 1523
45. van Waveren, R.H., Groot, S., Scholten, H., Van Geer, F., Wösten, H., Koeze, R., Noort, J.: Good Modelling Practice Handbook, STOWA, Utrecht, RWS-RIZA, Lelystad, The Netherlands (in Dutch, English version) (1999), http://informatics.wur.nl/researchprojects/pub-pdf/gmp.pdf

Knowledge Pentagram System
and Applications

Yoshiteru Nakamori[1] and Andrzej P. Wierzbicki[2]

[1] School of Knowledge Science, Japan Advanced Institute of Science and Technology (JAIST),
Asahidai 1-1, Nomi, Ishikawa 923-1292, Japan
nakamori@jaist.ac.jp
[2] National Institute of Telecommunications, Szachowa 1, 04-894 Warsaw, Poland
A.Wierzbicki@itl.waw.pl

Abstract. The chapter reviews recent advances in describing processes of knowledge and technology creation using models of such processes that stress and utilize the a-rational abilities of human mind such as tacit knowledge, emotion, instincts, intuition. To such models belong Shinayakana Systems Approach, SECI Spiral, Knowledge Pentagram or i-System, Creative Space and diverse knowledge creation spirals that can be distinguished in this space. The chapter discusses the relations between such models in detail and indicates diverse applications such as knowledge archive systems, an evaluation system for research activities and environments in academia, technology roadmaps; this chapter illustrates another application, that of fresh food management system. The main thesis of this chapter is that such models can be used as prototypes of network services supporting knowledge management and generally creativity.

Keywords: tacit knowledge, intuition, emotion and instincts, rational use of irrational mind capabilities, organizational and academic knowledge creation.

1 Introduction

Many approaches to describe processes of knowledge and technology creation have appeared in recent 20 years. Their specific feature is that they try to represent the role of and utilize the irrational or a-rational creative abilities of the human mind, such as tacit knowledge, emotions and instincts, and intuition [35]. In management science a novel approach was developed by Nonaka in 1992, with an international publication: *Knowledge Creating Company* [26]. This is the now-renowned *SECI Spiral*, with its process- and algorithmic-like principle of organizational knowledge creation. This principle is revolutionary because it stresses steps leading to knowledge increase surely, based on the collaboration of a group in knowledge creation and on the rational use of irrational mind capabilities, namely tacit knowledge, which consists of emotions and intuition.

Historically, the first of such approaches is *Shinayakana Systems Approach* by Sawaragi, with a publication in Sawaragi and Nakamori [32], in the field of decision and systems science. Being systemic and influenced by the soft and critical systems

D. Dolk et al. (Eds.): Decision Support Modeling in Service Networks, LNBIP 42, pp. 257–278, 2012.

tradition, it did not specify a process-like, algorithmic recipe for knowledge and technology creation, only a set of principles for systemic problem-solving. To these principles belong: using intuition, keeping an open mind, trying diverse approaches and perspectives, being adaptive and ready to learn from mistakes, and being elastic like a willow but sharp as a sword in short, *Shinayakana*, implying a synthesis between soft and hard systemic approaches.

Further development of the *Shinayakana Systems Approach* was given in Nakamori [22] in a systemic and process-like approach to knowledge creation called *Knowledge Pentagram System* or *i-System*. The five ontological elements (or subsystems) of this system are *Intervention* (and the will to solve problems), *Intelligence* (and existing scientific knowledge), *Involvement* (and social motivation), *Imagination* (and other aspects of creativity), and *Integration* (using systemic knowledge). True to the *Shinayakana* tradition, there is no algorithmic recipe for how to move between these ontological nodes: all transitions are equally advisable, according to individual needs. Thus, *i-System* stresses the need to move freely between diverse dimensions of creative space.

From a viewpoint of social science, Zhu explored the *i-System* as a (re-)structurationist model for knowledge management [24]. Viewed through *i-System*, knowledge is (re-)constructed by actors, who are constrained and enabled by structures that consist of a scientific-actual, a cognitive-mental and a social-relational front, mobilize and realize the agency of themselves and of others that can be differentiated as intelligence, imagination and involvement clusters, engage in rational-inertial, postrational-projective and arational-evaluative actions in pursuing sectional interests.

The *i-System* has several applications such as a guideline to develop a knowledge archive system, technology roadmaps, an evaluation system of research activities and environments in academia, and a fresh food management system; the last will be shortly illustrated in this chapter.

2   Knowledge Pentagram System

This section presents the Knowledge Pentagram System or the *i*-System for knowledge integration and creation and its relation to the new concept of the Creative Space [35]. The five ontological elements of Pentagram System are *Intelligence*, *Involvement*, *Imagination*, *Intervention*, and *Integration* correspond to five diverse dimensions of the Creative Space. We discuss the meanings and functions of these dimensions in knowledge integration and creation. We also discuss the relation of the *i*-System to Far East philosophy and to "*Shinayakana Systems Approach*".

2.1   Creative Space

We have shown in [35] how we can fruitfully generalize the SECI Spiral from [26] by adding more nodes in the basic dimensions of the spiral, thus obtaining the concept of Creative Space; this is illustrated in Fig.1 and Fig.2. Essentially, the epistemological dimension of SECI Spiral is enriched by splitting *tacit knowledge* into its two specific parts: *emotive knowledge* and *intuitive knowledge,* and the other dimension (called ontological in [26] and more precisely social in [35]) is enriched by adding the third level of *humanity heritage* to the levels of *individual* and *group.* This way, a three-by-three matrix is distinguished, indicating nine nodes of Creative Space shown in Fig.2; there are also diverse transitions between these nodes (called in [26] knowledge conversions). While, for example, the nodes of individual emotions and individual intuition just show more specifically which parts constitute individual tacit knowledge, the consideration of the three nodes of humanity emotive, intuitive, and rational heritage is a very important addition to SECI Spiral: every process of knowledge creation is in fact based on humanity intellectual heritage, called the third world by Popper [29], but including its rational, intuitive and emotive parts (the latter two not considered directly by Popper).

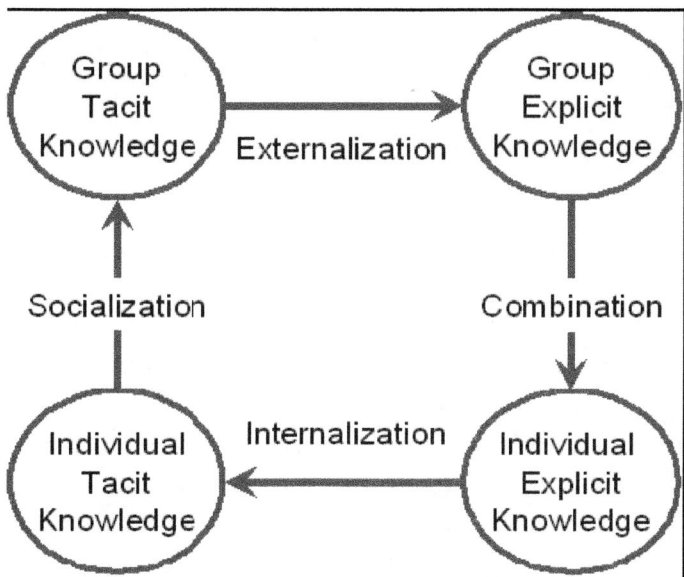

Fig. 1. The SECI Spiral (Nonaka and Takeuchi [26])

In this way, new descriptions of creative processes can be obtained. For example, while the four nodes in the lower right-hand corner of Fig.2 represent the known SECI Spiral, the four nodes in the upper left-hand corner of Fig.2 represent another theory of knowledge creation, the Theory of Regress of Motycka [18], describing the processes of basic knowledge creation in time of a scientific revolution, such as during the creation of quantum theory; this theory can be also represented as a spiral which consists of transitions Abstraction - Regress - Mythologization - Empathisation, hence ARME Spiral; for more detailed description and analysis, see [34] and [35].

However, the Creative Space has certainly more dimensions than just the epistemological and social dimensions used in Fig.1 and Fig.2. This is stressed, for example, by Nakamori's *i*-System - see [23]; its five ontological elements are *Intelligence, Involvement, Imagination, Intervention,* and *Integration* and they might correspond actually to five diverse dimensions of Creative Space; thus, they stress the need to move freely between more dimensions of this space. These five ontological elements were originally interpreted as nodes, as illustrated in Fig.3.

Because the *i*-System is intended as a synthesis of systemic approaches, *Integration* is, in a sense, its final dimension (in Fig.3 all arrows converge to *Integration* interpreted as a node; links without arrows denote the possibility of impact in both directions). The beginning node is *Intervention*, where problems or issues perceived by the individual or the group motivate their further analysis and the entire creative process.

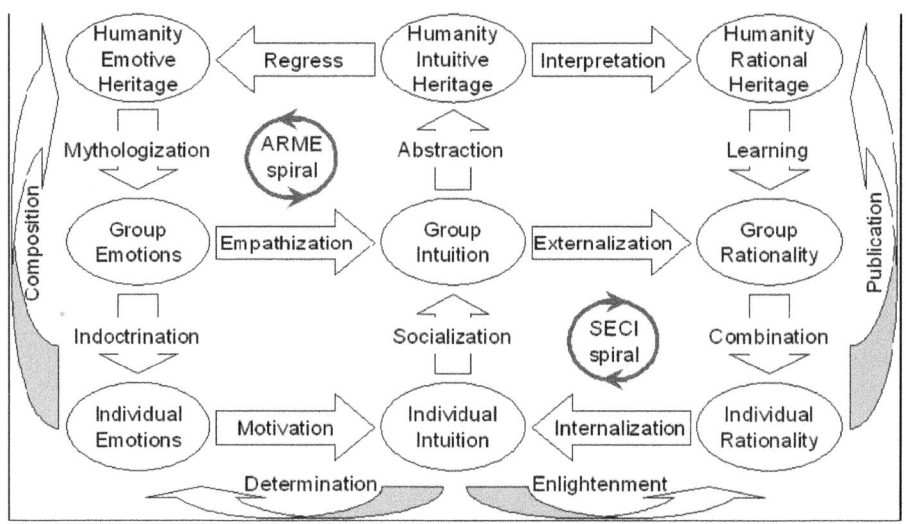

Fig. 2. The basic dimensions of Creative Space [35]

The node *Intelligence* corresponds to various types of knowledge, the node *Involvement* represents social aspects. The creative aspects are represented mostly in the node *Imagination*. Observe, however, that the node *Intelligence* - together with all existing scientific knowledge - corresponds roughly to the basic epistemological dimension (*Emotive – Intuitive – Rational* Knowledge) of Creative Space. The node *Involvement* stresses the social motivation and corresponds roughly to the basic social dimension (Individual - Group - Humanity Heritage) of the Creative Space. When analyzing these dimensions we have found that binary logic is inadequate and even rough, three-valued logic barely sufficient for a detailed analysis. For example, it is not only necessary to distinguish between the knowledge on the level of individual,

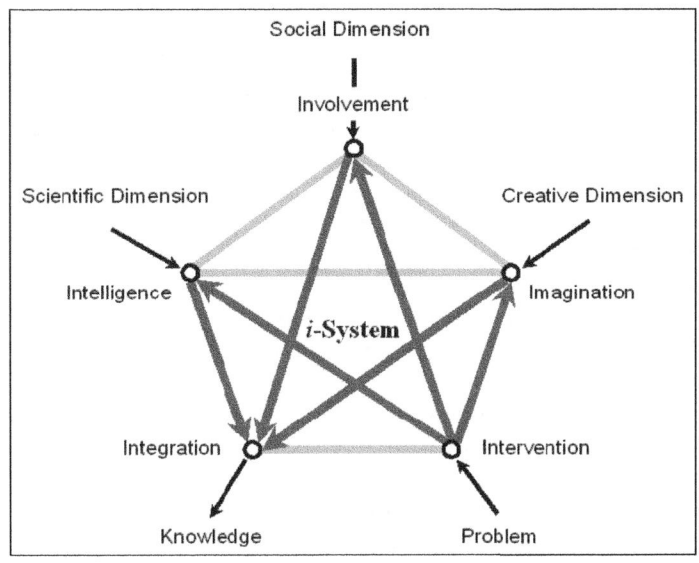

Fig. 3. Knowledge Pentagram System or *i*-System

group and humanity heritage; it is also important to distinguish motivation related to the interests of the individual, the group and humanity. While an organization operating in the commercial market rightly stresses the interests of the group of people employed by it (or of its shareholders), educational research activity at universities might be best promoted when stressing the individual interests of students and young researchers; on the other hand, the interests of humanity must be protected when facing the prospect of privatization of basic knowledge.

However, other nodes presented in Fig. 3 indicate the need to consider other dimensions of Creative Space, and additional dimensions result in additional complexity. The dimension *Imagination* seems to be an essential element of only individual intuition. All creative processes can be related, on the other hand, to three levels of *Imagination*: *Routine - Diversity - Fantasy*; we shall discuss the importance of this distinction in the following text.

2.1.1   Dimension of Imagination

We start with the dimension *Imagination*. We utilize imagination in diverse degrees depending on the character of a creative process. The lowest level is *Routine* – that involves imagination, but in a standard, well-trained fashion. We are able to use imagination more strongly, to involve an element of *Diversity* - but we must be motivated to do this by professional pride, pure curiosity, monetary rewards etc. Finally, we have also the highest level of imagination, which might be called *Fantasy*. The 20th Century tradition of not speaking about metaphysics (started by Wittgenstein [36]) relegated fantasy to the arts and the emotions. However, fantasy is an essential element of any highly creative process, including the construction of technological devices and systems.

Here we encounter a difficulty in the graphic representation of Creative Space: to represent its three or more dimensions on paper, on a two-dimensional plane, might be difficult. As we well know, it is possible to represent three-dimensional objects, while for the representation of four-dimensional objects there are only some inadequate tricks. Consider the possibility of three-dimensional representation of Creative Space, in which, say, the additional dimension *Imagination* would be indicated by three layers of nodes of the space. Already this representation is would be too complex and such an idea serves only to illustrate an obvious conclusion: Knowledge and technology creation are essentially very complex processes; all models of creative processes are just simplifications, necessary for a better understanding but far from fully representing reality.

2.1.2   Dimension of Intervention

The dimension *Intervention* is difficult to consider separately in Oriental philosophy and culture, with their concepts of unity of mind and body and unity of man and nature: the will to do something is not considered as a separate phenomenon, it is simply a part of being, and being should be such as not to destroy the unity of man and nature. In a culture seeking consensus and harmony, such an explanation and such principles are sufficient. Occidental or Western culture pays more attention to the problems related to human intervention and will. Western culture has a long history of philosophic debate of the issues of will and freedom of intervention. The seminal points of this debate start just after the Enlightenment era, in German pre-romanticism, first with the concept of self-realization, then in the *Kritik der praktischen Vernunft* (Kant [13]) with its radical concept of freedom: a man is free in a radical, transcendental sense, self-determining not as a natural being, but as pure moral will.

> This unity of self-determination, moral life, autonomy and freedom, expressed best by Kant's statement *the starlight sky over me and the moral law in me*, was exhilarating for his contemporaries and still remains a powerful motivation for the representatives of Western culture.

The concept of will, of freedom to act and intervene, has been for many centuries and still remains one of the central ideas of Western or Occidental culture. Concerning any creative activity, it is clear that the role of motivation, of the will to create new ideas, objects of art, technological devices, etc. is a central condition of success. Without *Drive, Determination, Dedication* no creative process will be completed.

By *Drive* we understand here the basic fact that creativity is one of the most fundamental components of self-realization of man. *Determination* is the concentrated Nietzschean will to overcome obstacles in realizing the creative process. *Dedication* is a conviction that completing a creative process is right in terms of Kantian transcendental moral law.

2.1.3   Dimension of Integration

The dimension of *Integration* in the original *i*-System (see Fig.3) is a node intended to represent the final stage, the systemic synthesis of the creative process. Thus, in this stage we should use all systemic knowledge; applying systemic concepts to newly created knowledge is certainly the only explicit, rational knowledge tool that can be used in order to achieve integration. Thus, any teaching of creative abilities must include a strong component of systems science.

The apparently simplest is *Specialized Integration*, when the task consists of integrating several elements of knowledge in some specialized field. But even this task can be very difficult as, for example, the task of integrating knowledge about the diverse functions of contemporary computer networks. It becomes more complex when its character is *Interdisciplinary*, as in the case of the analysis of environmental policy models. However, the contemporary trends of globalization result today in new, even more complex challenges related to *Intercultural Integration*, as in the case of integration of diverse theories of knowledge and technology creation. In fact, the *Intercultural Integration* of knowledge might be considered a defining feature of a new interpretation of systems science.

3   Pentagram System, Shinayakana Systems Approach and Critical Systems Thinking

In summary, the knowledge creation system called the Knowledge Pentagram System or the *i*-System is comprised of five elements - dimensions, nodes or subsystems:

1. *Intervention*: Taking action on a problem situation which has not been dealt with before. First we ask: what kind of knowledge is necessary to solve the new problem? Then the following three subsystems are called on to collect that knowledge.
2. *Intelligence:* Raises our capability to understand and learn things. The necessary data and information are collected, scientifically analyzed, and then a model is built to achieve simulation and optimization.
3. *Imagination*: Creating our own ideas on new or existing things. Complex phenomena are simulated based on partial information, by exploiting information technology.
4. *Involvement*: Raising the interest and passion of ourselves and other people. Sponsoring conferences and gathering people's opinions using techniques like interview surveys.
5. *Integration*: Integrating heterogeneous types of knowledge so they are tightly related. Validating the reliability and correctness of the output from the above three subsystems.

We can interpret these elements variously - either as nodes, or dimensions of Creative Space, or subsystems. In the last interpretation, while the 1st and the 5th subsystems are, in a sense, autonomous, the 2nd, 3rd and 4th subsystems are dependent on others; it is generally difficult for them to complete their missions themselves, and thus we can interpret them as a lower level system with similar structure to the overall system.

Even if the *i*-System stresses that the creative process begins in the *Intervention* dimension or subsystem and ends in the *Integration* dimension or subsystem, it gives no prescription how to move in between. There is no algorithmic recipe how to move between these ontological nodes or dimensions: all transitions are equally advisable, according to individual needs. This is true to the *Shinayakana Systems Approach* tradition that is in a sense further developed by the *i*-System. Thus, for a better understanding of the *i*-System it is useful to comment also on the *Shinayakana Systems Approach*.

The *Shinayakana Systems Approach* is a systemic approach developed by Sawaragi and Nakamori for several years prior to its publication [20]. The approach proposes a synthesis, an integration of hard and soft systemic methods, integration from the perspective of Japanese philosophy and culture. In the the *Shinayakana Systems Approach*, Sawaragi and Nakamori tried to resolve the controversy between hard and soft systems traditions by using Far East philosophy: both hard and soft sides are necessary, we must use them in harmony and seeking consensus. Most important is the principle of openness to diverse soft systems approaches while preserving the strength and variety of hard systems approaches, the principle of being hard and soft at the same time.

In fact, *Shinayakana* means both soft and hard - elastic like a willow and sharp as a sword. Because of their synthesis of soft systems thinking with Oriental philosophy, the authors of *Shinayakana Systems Approach* did not formulate any spirals, any algorithmic processes, only a general description of principles – although both authors are also specialists in hard systems practice and could propose algorithmic processes. The *i*-System is in fact a continuation of *Shinayakana Systems Approach* with slightly more algorithmic tendency - although, as we already observed, *i*-System gives no precise prescription how to move between ontological nodes or dimensions, true to the *Shinayakana* tradition.

On the other hand, the *Shinayakana Systems Approach* and the *i*-System give a different way to the synthesis of soft and hard systemic approaches than Critical Systems Methodology (CSM) or Critical Systems Thinking, see, e.g., [11]. CSM tries to broaden the approach of Soft Systems Methodology (SSM) [6], but preserves the assumption of the superiority of soft systemic approaches made by SSM. The *Shinayakana Systems Approach* and the *i*-System treat both hard and soft systemic approaches as equally important, following Far Eastern philosophical principles of harmony, integration and methodological simplicity.

4   Road-Mapping

The *i*-System can be called a knowledge creating system. The system integrates statistical data and individual persons' fragmentary knowledge, and then creates new knowledge nobody had before. Such knowledge must be tacit in origin, otherwise it would not be new. Therefore, the system should have a process to convert tacit knowledge into explicit knowledge. This means that the members of the project or relevant people constitute a part of the system. For this characteristics, the *i*-System can be used for constructing technological roadmaps.

4.1   Intervention

Intervention can be understood as a motivational dimension, a drive, or determination, or even dedication to solving a problem. Starting a road-mapping process can be thus thought as an intervention for issues motivating strategic plans. In this dimension, first, initiators of the road-mapping process should have a deep understanding what is the motivation for making the particular roadmap. Second, they should also know what roadmaps and road-mapping are, what advantages road-mapping has, and how to do road-mapping. Third, initiators or coordinators must also consider who should participate in the road-mapping team and motivate them to join, customize a road-mapping process and schedule, and let all participants know the purpose and schedule and their roles in road-mapping.

4.2   Intelligence

Intelligence has two aspects: rational, explicit and intuitive, tacit. It is a duty of the coordinator and of all participants of a road-mapping process to search for relevant explicit information. In this task, the following methods of support could be helpful:

- *Scientific databases*: The access either to disciplinary or to general scientific databases such as Scopus, ScienceDirect, etc., can be very helpful for researchers to understand what has been done, what is being done, and what should be done.
- *Text mining tools*: The amount of scientific literature increases very fast, thus help in finding relevant explicit information is necessary.
- *Workshops*: in which many experts are involved. Here some selected groupware, such as Pathmaker, could be applied to structure and manage discussions among experts.

In fact, the third method involves already some elements of intuitive or tacit knowledge of experts. But an important aspect of good intelligence is individual reflection on and interpretation of the explicit information previously obtained.

4.3   Involvement

Involvement is a social dimension, related to two aspects: societal motivation and consensus building in the group of participants. Road-mapping in a group is a consensus building process. This process might include many researchers, experts, and other stakeholders. There are following important aspects in this dimension.

- *Participation of administrative authorities and coordinators*: If administrative authorities are involved in the coordination of the road-mapping process, then this helps it to proceed smoothly.
- *Customized solutions*: Preparing a template of a solution for the road-mapping process also helps it to proceed smoothly. There are many existing solutions that might serve as templates, such as T-plan [28], disruptive technology roadmaps [16], interactive planning solutions for personal research roadmaps [17], etc.
- *Internet-based groupware*: The use of internet-based groupware can contribute to *Involvement*.

4.4   Imagination

Imagination is needed during entire road-mapping process; it should help to create vision. Participants are encouraged to imagine the purposeful future where should we go and the means how to get there.

- *Graphical presentation tools*: Graphical presentation tools can help people to express and refine their imagination.
- *Simulations*: Simulations can enhance and stimulate imagination, especially concerning complex dynamic processes.
- *Critical debate*: This is probably the most fundamental way of promoting imagination.
- *Brainstorming*: Brainstorming is, in a sense, a counterpart of critical debate; it encourages people to generate and express diverse, even fantastic ideas, and is directly related to imagination.
- *Idealized design*: Idealized design is a unique and essential feature of Interactive Planning approach [1],[2],[3] which is regarded as a basic method for solving creative problems.

4.5   Integration

Integration must be applied several times during road-mapping, at least when making a first-cut, refined, and the final version of roadmap. Integration includes all knowledge of the other four dimensions, thus is interdisciplinary and systemic. Diverse rational systemic approaches, such as *Analytical Hierarchy Process* (AHP) [30] and *Meta-Synthesis Approach*, see Gu and Tang [9], might be helpful. However, in order to be creative and visionary, integration cannot rely only on rational, explicit knowledge, must rely on preverbal, intuitive and emotional knowledge. Therefore, software with a heuristic interface and graphical representation tools are essential for help in this dimension. For example, the number of nodes and links in a roadmap might be large, difficult to master by an unaided human brain. A properly chosen perspective of graphical representation of the roadmap might be thus essential. In order to choose such perspective, a heuristic interface can be applied to infer the preferred features of graphical roadmaps.

5   Sociological Interpretation

This section explores the *i*-System as a (re-)structurationist model for knowledge management. Viewed through the *i*-System, knowledge is (re-)constructed by actors, who are constrained and enabled by structures that consist of a *scientific-actual*, a *cognitive-mental* and a *social-relational* front, mobilise and realise the agency of themselves and of others that can be differentiated as *intelligence*, *imagination* and *involvement* clusters, engage in *rational-inertial*, *postrational-projective* and *arational-evaluative* actions in pursuing sectional interests. The exploration presented here intends particularly to unpack the structure, agency and action "black boxes", investigate the complexity, ambiguity and emergent properties internal to each of them, as well as those implicated in the relationships between. While structure complexity provides possibilities for innovation, agency complexity allows actors exploit those possibilities in differing ways. Knowing (in-forming) and practice (intervening) are seen as constituting each other, from which knowledge is emerging and embodied, over time, "back" into structures and agency. The exploration draws mainly upon institutionalism, structuration theory, critical realism, actor-network theory as well as Confucianism, Taoism and Zen Buddhism, and is located in the context of technology innovation.

5.1 Structure-Agency-Action Paradigm

Knowledge is constructed and utilized by humans in organisations and societies. This observation convinces us that no generic model of knowledge and the management of it is complete without a conscious sociologist underpinning. It is in this spirit that we explore one for the *i*-System.

Proposed in Nakamori [22], the *i*-System has undergone some refinements, but so far been presented in a form of systems engineering, as a methodology, attached with conventional input, output, throughput connotations (Fig.3). However, with its spiritual roots in the *Shinayakana approach*, e.g., the principles of systems multiplicity (the ontological), nonlinear reductionism (the methodological), integrated assessments (the epistemological) and expending-deepening insights into the system (the moral) (Nakamori and Sawaragi [21], Sawaragi and Nakamori [31]), the *i*-System appears sufficiently sophisticated and inherently open for embracing sociologist elaborations.

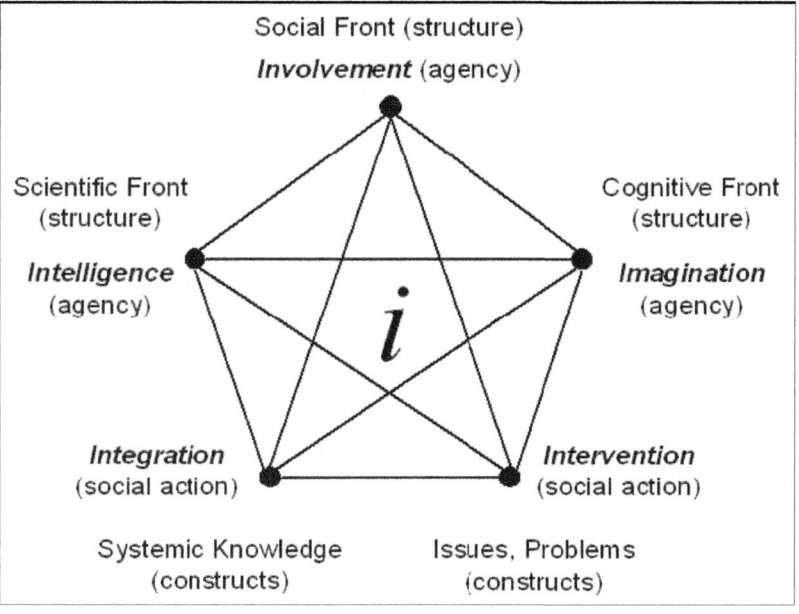

Fig. 4. i-System: a sociologist view

We want to make our assumptions transparent at the outset. First, in seeking for a sociologist underpinning for the *i*-System, we will draw mainly upon the *structure-agency-action* paradigm[1]. We are aware that there are many other useful sociologist paradigms which possess potentials to enrich the *i*-System and the wider "knowledge movement", and we intend to participate and invite plural and contesting explorations. Second, while open to the paradigm, our appropriation of the theories within it is selective albeit inclusive. This is not only because, whereas each provides us with significant source, none of the theories on its own appears sufficient for our task, but also because we have disagreements with and questions toward each and all of them. Further, we have no claim to being universal, culture- or interest-free. The appropriation is meant to be localised and purposive.

Nakamori and Zhu [24] introduced the *structure-agency-action paradigm*, followed by an exploration of the complexity of structures, agency and action respectively. In addition, they presented practical and policy implications as well as directions for further research.

5.2 An Intercultural View of Knowledge Construction

We unpack the structure, agency and action black boxes, discussing their internal complexity as well as that implicated in the relationships between them (see Fig.4). We now summarise the *i*-System view of knowledge construction. For this, we draw from, in addition toWestern social theories as well as Taoism and Buddhism, the realist Cheng-Zhu and the idealist Lu-Wang schools of neo-Confucianism (see Zhu [38][39][40]). Our key propositions are:

- Both knowledge-as-construct (the realist Confucianism) and knowing-in-practice (the idealist Confucianism) are indispensable for knowledge construction. Knowledge, stablised in structure and agency at focal empirical moments, provides actors material, intellectual as well as social capacities and contexts to conduct social action, whereas knowing as that action transforms knowledge, for the better or the worse, which is embodied "back" into structure and agency, over time.
- Both knowledge and ignorance are necessary for effective human action. No destruction, no creation; no forgetting, no knowing; no ignorance, no knowledge. Each contains the seed of becoming the opposite (Zhu [38]). The danger is not knowledge or ignorance per se, but the one-sided searching for simplistic answers for complex problems. Our current education and socialisation programmes have limits, not because of being inefficient, but single-minded. Ignorance, forgetting, innocence and emotion should be in knowledge agendas.
- "Construction" is meant to be practical, temporal and relational. As Wang Yang-ming, the 14th-century Confucianist contends, knowledge and action are but one, for purpose, and with consequences (Zhu [40]). Knowledge is not

---

[1] In the broad sense of the word 'paradigm', while being aware that Thomas Kuhn defined the meaning of this word more narrowly as an exemplary theory.

"created" if creation means, as it does in popular "knowledge creation" models, well-ordered, linearly progressive, interest-free, politically neutral and intellectually beyond dispute. Rather, knowledge is better seen as always and constantly messy, contextual, provisional, contestable, negotiated, agreed upon, in-forming, informing, constituting and legitimating.

- The *i*-System brings "the heart" back in knowledge agendas, rather than shy away from it or take it for granted. While knowledge enhances material wellbeing and spiritual sophistication, at least for some on the globe, it also grants humans awesome power to do all the ugly things to Nature and among human ourselves. Are knowledge, technology and innovation necessarily a good thing? How and who to manage it for good, good for Nature and all, not just the few? These are, to the *i*-System, legitimate and relevant questions in "knowledge management" that is not equivalent to knowledge comodification.
- Rooted in systems sciences, *i*-System intends to be integrative in spirit. A system to us is a set of components connected such that properties emerging from which cannot be found in components. Yin and yang never melt down into a "synthesis", the lost of opposites means death. Hence, integration is about openness, tolerance, interdisciplinary and intercultural, is an interactive and reciprocal process of perspective-making and -taking (Boland and Tenkasi [30]) and, we shall add, -sharing and -enriching, not of programming heterogeneity into homogeneity by the magic hand of "system experts".

Based on the explored *i*-System underpinning, we offer some practical and policy implications in the form of questions. To researchers: how to search for broad and balanced agency while at the same time materialise my/our distinct advantage in a particular agency cluster? How to adjust between temporal orientations of action as situational contingency unfolds? To managers: how to sensitise researchers toward structure-agency-action complexity? How to recruit and train for various kinds of agency and nurture different relational-temporal contexts so as to stimulate and support robust actions? To policy-makers: how to reform social institutions and practices, e.g., education, in order to restructure the agency of citizens? How to innovate suitable policies/systems for different industries/sectors which may demand different combinations of agency as well as contexts? The key guidance for considering these questions is: there can be no simple solutions to complex issues.

In advancing our exploration, we have noted several limitations in our approach, with which we wish to invite further research. First, we have concentrated primarily on disentangling the internal structures of structure, agency and action, therefore under-presented the simultaneous and mutual-penetrating effects within and between these internal structures. For example, when submitting that innovation demands inertial, projective and practical-evaluative actions, we stressed their different temporal orientations toward the past, the future and the present, we did not stress with the same weight that "all three of these constitutive dimensions are to be found, in varying degree, within any concrete empirical instance of action" (Emribayer and Mische [7]).

When we signified constitutive components in each of the structure fronts, agency clusters and action dimensions, we did not argue with equal force that each of the components be conceived to possess its own internal multiplicity. Social capital is an obvious example. We located social capital within the involvement cluster of agency, but did not elaborate in any detail that social capital itself can be meaningfully analyzed along a structural, a cognitive and a relational dimension (see Nahapiet and Ghoshal [19]).

Furthermore, in applying the *Institutional Theory*[12], *Structuration Theory*[8] and *Critical Realism*[4] notion of "stratified reality", we stressed the distinction between structure, agency and action. We should have stressed at the same time that these are merely mental constructs (knowledge!) for making sense of social reality in a particular, perhaps convenient, way. In the empirical world, there are no such clear-cut things "out there" as structure, agency or action. Does "structuredness" of mentality, for example, belongs to the macro (societal, sectional, industrial and organisational) structure only, or is it also a micro property of individual cognition, and hence agency? In other words, is "structured mentality" part of structure, of agency, or of both? If both, where is the line between structure and agency? If there need not be a line, then how interactions "between" them is to be meaningful and understood? (for a critique see Sztompka [33]). After all, Zhuang Zi's thesis of "great artifice" and "synthesised ignorance" should better be consciously applied onto our own constructs.

6   Application to Fresh Food Management

Demand forecasting is an important management skill, especially at grocery supermarkets which deal with perishable foods. Demand forecasting closely relates to sales rate, and demand forecasting errors directly influence the management performance of the company. Because perishable foods generally have short shelf life and are difficult to preserve, errors in demand forecasting result in excess product orders or production, that lead to added preservation/freshness management and personnel costs and losses due to waste and forced discounting. In addition, demand in excess of stock results in lost opportunity and customer trust. Therefore, demand forecasting is an important management skill at supermarkets, and minimizing the loss due to waste, forced discounting, and lost opportunity through effective demand forecasting plays an important role in the management activities.

Studies on demand forecasting developed in various fields such as system engineering and information science, based mainly on the results of research utilizing mathematic and statistical models (e.g. moving average model, simple linear regression analysis, and multiple linear regression analysis). In such research, researchers narrow down the objects to forecast more specifically and approach demand forecasting problems in various fields such as retail business, production business, mail-order business, textile/apparel business, electricity demand, and water demand. In addition, the spread of information systems such as POS (Point Of Sales) and FSP (Frequent Shoppers Program) has increased the data, in addition to sales data, that can be manipulated and research on demand forecasting in the retail business has been progressing.

Because current approaches fail to provide adequate solutions to these problems, new approaches are required. Research on demand forecasting has developed mainly in the scientific and technological fields. Recently, however, attempts have been made to reconsider demand forecasting from the management perspective [37], an approach that may yield potential solutions to the problems that have plagued the traditional approach. With this in mind, this study assumes the necessity of constructing a demand forecasting system that combines a traditional system engineering approach, one that forecasts demand from past sales data, with a knowledge management approach in order to develop solutions to demand forecasting problems.

This study examines the issue of demand forecasting in fresh food management based on a methodology for knowledge integration and creation called the *i*-System. More specifically, we divide the domain of the study into "managerial knowledge," "purchase behavior," and "demand forecasting model/system," and endeavor to integrate the findings of each area of the study. Finally, we propose a fresh food management system based on the findings.

6.1   Use of the i-System

This study employs the *i*-System to combine a system engineering type of approach with a knowledge management type of approach to address demand forecasting problems. The i-System is a "system theory that integrates and creates knowledge" combining Western structure - ability paradigm and Eastern dialectic thought. With the assumption that this structure is comprised of the scientific-actual front, the socialrelational front, and the cognitive-mental front, and that the abilities of the actors under each structure are the intelligence ability, the involvement ability, and the imagination ability, this methodology develops the union of theory and practice, in which the integration power of knowledge and the intervention ability of the leaders and analysts in relation to the structure and abilities listed above become inseparable.

First, the problem and the result desired as a goal are set:

- *Problem Setting*: For demand forecasting problems, a new approach combining a system engineering approach with a knowledge management approach is needed.
- *Knowledge*: Construct a fresh food management system.

The problem is divided into the below-listed three fronts and approaches are tested. That is, knowledge regarding scientific truth, relations with society, and individual awareness is collected for each front and integrated:

- *Cognitive-mental front*: Survey and analyze issues that are considered when the amount and kinds of products to be produced are decided by the manager, who has the authority to decide such, and the management method related to daily sales.
- *Social-relational front*: Collect and analyze issues that consumers consider when purchasing products and consumer opinion that is not reflected in POS data.

- *Scientific-actual front*: Just as in past research approaches, construct a demand forecasting model that forecasts the sales amount under certain conditions based on past sales data and a fresh food management system. Note that for this front, a system is proposed based on the outcome of the cognitivemental front and the social-relational front.

Using outcomes from the three above-listed fronts, we attempt to construct a demand forecasting management system that possesses the expertise of a system engineering approach as well as the expertise of a knowledge management approach.

6.2   Managerial Knowledge

In order to acquire managerial knowledge regarding prepared food department operation, such as decision making regarding the amount and types of prepared food to be produced and daily sales methods, we conducted interviews twice with managers responsible for decisions regarding the types and amount of prepared food to be produced.

The first survey was administered to ten managers working in Tokyo area supermarkets who have the power of decision regarding the types and amount of prepared food to be produced, and included a wide variety of items designed to elicit information concerning basic matters in the prepared food department, including issues to be considered when deciding on the types and amount of prepared food to be produced and measures taken to reduce lost opportunity and loss from waste. The period of research was from March 2nd, 2005 to March 23rd, 2005. The interview time was approximately one hour per person. The second survey was a follow-up interview of 3 managers who had participated in the initial survey. Follow-up questions concerned detail regarding prepared food department operation and were based on the results of the first survey. The survey period was from November 22nd, 2005 to November 24th, 2005, and the interview time was approximately 90 minutes per person.

We used the Semi-Structured Interview Method [10] from the Interview Guide. The Semi-Structured Interview Method is a surveying method wherein open ended question topics regarding the content that the researcher wishes to research are prepared in advance and the researcher actively asks questions in concordance with those question topics. However, it is also a survey method wherein the order of the questions and topics may be changed based on the conditions and atmosphere of the interview, allowing specific follow-up questions to be added on the spot in the course of conversation.

After making a transcript of the interview, information from the interview, such as considerations in deciding of the amount of prepared food products to produce and the types of prepared food products to produce and the daily sales method, were extracted and coded. The coded data was then organized, analyzed, and structured via the KJ Method [14], and the management methods of the prepared food managers were converted into diagram form. The diagramed management method of the prepared food managers was evaluated at the time of the second interview and amendments were added.

The results of analysis utilizing the KJ Method show that the categories of information which form the foundation for the management of prepared food product production and sales are as follows: "decisions regarding prepared food product type and amount," "prepared food sales," "the time period from close to closing to closing time," and "tasks after closing."

6.3   Consumer Purchasing Behavior

In order to ascertain matters which consumers consider when deciding on prepared food purchases and consumer opinion which is not reflected in POS data, we implemented a web questionnaire related to prepared food purchasing. We conducted a web survey of 1,000 males and females from 16 to 69 years of age living in the 23 Special Wards of Tokyo who make prepared food purchases two or more times per week at a supermarket. The survey elicited responses to questions concerning matters considered when making prepared food purchases and preferences concerning prepared food purchasing. The survey period was from November 11th, 2005 to November 15th, 2005. In order to more accurately grasp actual consumer tendencies, we corrected the distribution of respondents for each question by age group in line with the distribution of actual Tokyo population by age group based on the FY 2000 national census issued by the Ministry of Internal Affairs and Communications.

We created survey items based on the results of interviews with prepared food managers. The survey was structured to begin with basic questions such as survey participant profile (age, gender, region, and family structure), frequency of prepared food purchase per one-week period, and names of prepared foods that the participant frequently makes purchases, and divided matters which the consumer considers in making prepared food purchases into items evaluated on a 5-point Likert scale from "very important consideration" to "not a consideration at all" and items which the respondent could comment freely about, such as times when prepared food purchases are made impulsively and preference concerning prepared food purchases.

When comparing qualitatively the survey results of managerial knowledge and consumer purchasing behavior, we evaluate the validity of managerial knowledge. Regarding "weather and climate," "in-store events," "yearly and regional events," and "television," though the individuals involved in sales consider these factors to affect the production amount and produced type, consumers do not seem to give much consideration to these factors when making prepared food purchases according to the purchasing factor results. Because of differences in opinion between managers and consumers, confirmation via objective data such as POS is required in the future. Regarding the "day of the week," though it was not a major consideration for prepared food purchases, we found a trend for more prepared food purchases during the weekend period as compared to weekdays. Thus, the opinion on this matter is the same for both managers and consumers.

6.4   A Fresh Food Management System

Based on the results of the study on the managerial knowledge of prepared food departments and the study on consumer purchasing behavior pertaining to prepared food purchasing, we have developed a fresh food management system. As for a model which forecasts demand from past data, we used K-representatives [27], which is one form of clustering in which the concept of fuzziness is introduced into the traditional clustering technique. Specifically, we grouped data possessing the same conditions, estimated the distribution from the past sales amount data under those conditions, and forecasted the sales amount (For example, see Fig.5).

Via the results of the study on the managerial knowledge of prepared food departments and the study on consumer purchasing behavior pertaining to prepared food purchasing, it is thought that several important explanatory variables that increase the accuracy of demand forecasting results have been identified. However, it is not always possible to obtain data on these variables, a reason cited above for the low performance of demand forecasting in the real world. In order to respond to this problem, we designed the management system for this study, based on the experience and knowledge of fresh food product managers, in which the distribution calculated by a demand forecasting model could be altered freely, and constructed it so that the risk relationship of waste loss vs. lost opportunity would be indicated in line with the alteration (see Fig.6).

For example, as seen in Fig.5, if the forecast results for the sales amount under certain conditions are in the range from 1.9504 to 12.707, then the forecast range for those results (minimum production amount and maximum production amount) can be altered freely via the knowledge of the manager. After the alteration of forecast range, the post alteration distribution curves of lost opportunity and waste loss for the production amount between the minimum and maximum are displayed, as shown in Fig.6, and the point where both distribution curves cross is calculated as the optimum production amount. Moreover, it is possible to use the management system with the knowledge gained from the managerial knowledge study and consumer purchasing behavior study. By using the diagramed prepared food department management method and confirming the factors that impact production amount, and then altering the forecast range calculated from the management system, fresh food department management combining managerial knowledge and system engineering is possible.

For future work, the most important feature to be added is to implement the system as a network service that can be used by authorized managers and other personnel of supermarkets.

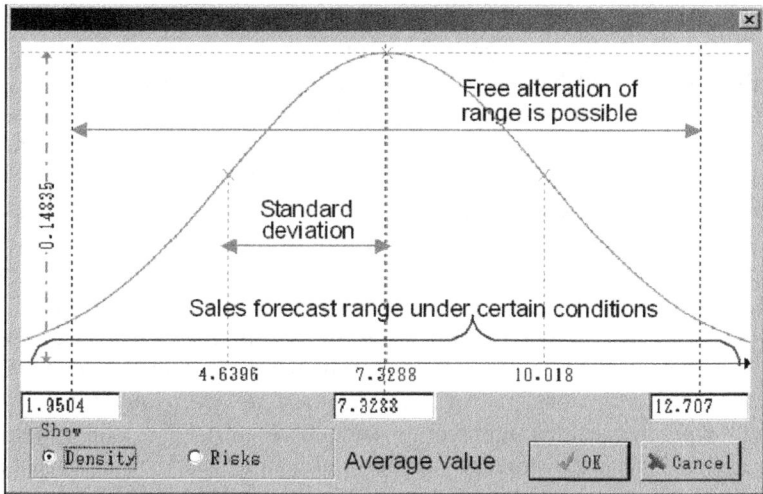

Fig. 5. Example of output screen of demand forecast result

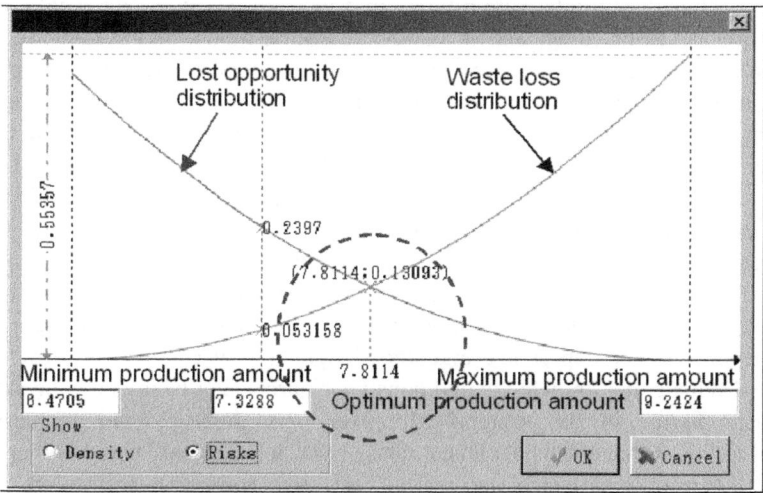

Fig. 6. Example of risk management screen

7   Summary and Future Outlook

This paper reviewed the Knowledge Pentagram System or the *i*-System for knowledge integration and creation and its relation to the new concept of the Creative Space. The five ontological elements of Pentagram System are *Intelligence*, *Involvement*, *Imagination*, *Intervention*, and *Integration* correspond to five diverse dimensions of the Creative Space. We discussed the meanings and functions of these dimensions in knowledge integration and creation. We also discussed the relation of the *i*-System to Far East philosophy and to *Shinayakana Systems Approach*.

The *i*-System can be called a knowledge creating system. The system integrates statistical data and individual persons' fragmentary knowledge, and then creates new knowledge nobody had before. Such knowledge must be tacit, otherwise someone including the system had it; this is a contradiction. Therefore, the system should have a process to convert tacit knowledge into explicit knowledge. This means that the members of the project or relevant people constitute a part of the system. For this characteristics, the *i*-System can be used for constructing technological roadmaps.

We explored the *i*-System as a (re-)structurationist model for knowledge management. Viewed through the *i*-System, knowledge is (re-)constructed by actors, who are constrained and enabled by structures that consist of a *scientific-actual*, a *cognitive-mental* and a *social-relational* front, mobilise and realise the agency of themselves and of others that can be differentiated as *intelligence*, *imagination* and *involvement* clusters, engage in *rational-inertial*, *postrational-projective* and *arational-evaluative* actions in pursuing sectional interests. The exploration intended particularly to unpack the structure, agency and action "black boxes", investigate the complexity, ambiguity and emergent properties internal to each of them, as well as those implicated in the relationships between them.

In order to develop a new fresh food management system, this study employed the *i*-System. The study fronts were divided into managerial knowledge study, consumer purchasing behavior study, and demand forecasting model and system study. In the managerial knowledge study, we administered an interview survey to prepared food department managers and gathered managerial knowledge for the prepared food department. In the consumer purchasing behavior study, we administered a questionnaire survey to consumers, surveyed the purchasing factors for prepared foods, and then qualitatively compared managerial knowledge and consumer purchasing behavior. In the demand forecasting model and system study, we constructed a system which is able to actively reflect the knowledge of human beings, unlike the way of thinking in traditional demand forecasting models and systems.

However, because the system constructed in this study exhibits a high degree of dependence on user experience and knowledge, it is necessary to allow the study results of managerial knowledge and consumer purchasing behavior to be reflected to a greater degree in the system. Moreover, regarding demand forecasting, the validation of forecasting accuracy and consideration of using other demand forecasting models are also necessary. The most important feature to be added, however, is to implement the system as a network service that can be used by authorized managers and other personnel of supermarkets. Thus, the models of knowledge creation and management presented in this chapter should be seen as prototypes of network services supporting knowledge management and generally creativity.

References

1. Ackoff, R.L.: Redesigning the future. Wiley, New York (1974)
2. Ackoff, R.L.: The art of problem solving. Wiley, New York (1978)
3. Ackoff, R.L.: Creating the corporate future. Wiley, New York (1981)

4. Bahskar, R.: The possibility of naturalism. Hemel Hempstead, Harvester (1989)
5. Boland, R.J., Tenkasi, R.V.: Perspective making and perspective taking in communities of knowing. Organisation Science 6, 350–372 (1995)
6. Checkland, P.B.: From optimizing to learning: a development of systems thinking for the 1990s. Journal of the Operational Research Society 36, 757–767 (1985)
7. Emirbayer, M., Mische, A.: What is agency? American Journal of Sociology 103/4, 962–1023 (1998)
8. Giddens, A.: Central problems in social theory: action, structure and contradiction in social analysis. Macmilian, London (1979)
9. Gu, J., Tang, X.: Meta-synthesis approach to complex system modeling. European Journal of Operational Research 166/3, 597–614 (2005)
10. Ito, T., et al. (eds.): Knowing while moving, thinking while involving - practice of qualitative research in psychology. Nacanishiya Publication Ltd. (2005) (in Japanese)
11. Jackson, M.C.: Systems approaches to management. Kluwer Academic - Plenum Publishers, New York (2000)
12. Jarzabkowski, P.: Strategy as practice: recursiveness, adaptation, and practices-in-use. Organisation Studies 25/4, 529–560 (2004)
13. Kant, I.: Kritik der praktischen Vernunft. (1911), E.Wende&Co, Warsaw (1788)
14. Kawakita, J.: Conception method - for the creativity development. Chuokoron-sha (2003) (in Japanese)
15. Kikuchi, T., Nakamori, Y.: Evaluation of Research Capabilities and Environments in Academia Based on a Knowledge Creation Model. International Journal of Knowledge and Systems Sciences 4/1, 14–24 (2007)
16. Kostoff, R.N., Boylan, R., Simons, G.R.: Disruptive technology roadmaps. Technological Forecasting and Social Change 71, 141–159 (2004)
17. Ma, T., Liu, S., Nakamori, Y.: Roadmapping as a way of knowledge management for supporting scientific research in academia. Systems Research and Behavioral Science 22, 1–13 (2005)
18. Motycka, A.: Science and unconscious. Leopoldinum, Wroclaw (1998) (in polish)
19. Nahapiet, J., Ghoshal, S.: Social capital, intellectual capital, and the organizational advantage. Academy of Management Review 23/2, 242–266 (1998)
20. Nakamori, Y., Sawaragi, Y.: Shinayakana systems approach in environmental management. In: Proc. of the 11th World Congress of International Federation of Automatic Control, Tallin, vol. 5, pp. 511–516. Pergamon Press (1990)
21. Nakamori, Y., Sawaragi, Y.: Shinayakana systems methodology and application to environmental problems. In: Wilby, J. (ed.) Systems Methodology: Possibilities for Cross-Cultural Learning and Integration, pp. 37–44. University of Hull, Centre for Systems Studies, Hull, UK (1996)
22. Nakamori, Y.: Knowledge management system toward sustainable society. In: Proc. of the 1st International Symposium on Knowledge and Systems Sciences, Ishikawa, Japan, September 25-27, pp. 57–64 (2000)
23. Nakamori, Y.: Systems methodology and mathematical models for knowledge management. Journal of Systems Science and Systems Engineering 12/1, 49–72 (2003)
24. Nakamori, Y., Zhu, Z.: Exploring a sociologist understanding for the *i*-System. International Journal of Knowledge and Systems Sciences 1/1, 1–8 (2004)
25. Nakano, M.: Consideration from demand forecast-management aspect as systematic knowledge creation. Osaka International University Bulletin 17, 147–162 (2003) (in Japanese)

26. Nonaka, I., Takeuchi, H.: The knowledge-creating company – How Japanese companies create the dynamics of innovation. Oxford University Press, New York (1995)
27. Ohn, M.S., Huynh, V.N., Nakamori, Y.: A clustering algorithm for mixed numeric and categorical data. Journal of Systems Science and Complexity 16, 562–571 (2003)
28. Phaal, R., Farrukh, C., Probert, D.: T-plan: fast start to technology roadmapping planning your route to success. Institute for Manufacturing, University of Cambridge (2001)
29. Popper, K.R.: Objective knowledge. Oxford University Press, Oxford (1972)
30. Saaty, T.L.: The analytical hierarchy process. McGraw-Hill (1980)
31. Sawaragi, Y., Nakamori, Y.: An interactive system for modeling and decision support: Shinayakana systems approach. In: Makawashi, M., Sawaragi, Y. (eds.) Advances in Methodology and Application of Decision Support Systems. International Institute for Applied Systems Analysis, Laxenburg (1991)
32. Sawaragi, Y., Nakamori, Y.: Shinayakana systems approach in modeling and decision support. In: Proc. of 10th Int. Conf. on Multiple Criteria Decision Making, Taipei, Taiwan, July 19-24, vol. I, pp. 77–86 (1992)
33. Sztompka, P.: Society in action: The theory of social becoming. Polity Press, Cambridge (1991)
34. Wierzbicki, A.P., Nakamori, Y.: Knowledge creation and integration: Creative space and creative environments. In: Proc. of the 38th Hawaii International Conference on System Sciences (HICSS-38), January 3-6. IEEE Computer Society, Hawaii (2005)
35. Wierzbicki, A.P., Nakamori, Y.: Creative space - Models of creative processes for the knowledge civilization age. Springer, Berlin (2006)
36. Wittgenstein, L.: Tractatus logico-philosophicus, Cambridge, UK (1922)
37. Yamashita, Y., Nakamori, Y.: Knowledge Integration Methodology for Designing a Knowledge Base of Technology Development in Traditional Craft Industry. In: Proc. of 2007 IEEE International Conference on Systems, Man, and Cybernetics (SMC 2007), Montreal, Canada, October 7-10, pp. 332–337 (2007)
38. Zhu, Z.: Conscious mind, forgetting mind: Two approaches in multimethodology. Systems Practice and Action Research 11/6, 669–690 (1998)
39. Zhu, Z.: The practice of multimodal approaches, the challenge of cross-cultural communication, and the search for responses. Human Relations 52/5, 579–607 (1999)
40. Zhu, Z.: Dealing with a differentiated whole: The philosophy of the WSR approach. Systemic Practice and Action Research 13/1, 21–57 (2000)

Ontology Construction and Its Applications in Local Research Communities

Hongtao Ren[1], Jing Tian[2], Andrzej P. Wierzbicki[3],
Yoshiteru Nakamori[2], and Edward Klimasara[3]

[1] International Institute for Applied Systems Analysis, Laxenburg, Austria
renh@iiasa.ac.at
[2] School of Knowledge Science, Japan Advanced Institute of Science and Technology (JAIST),
Asahidai 1-1, Nomi, Ishikawa 923-1292, Japan
{jtian,nakamori}@jaist.ac.jp
[3] National Institute of Telecommunications, Szachowa 1, 04-894 Warsaw, Poland
{A.Wierzbicki,E.Klimasara}@itl.waw.pl

Abstract. Ontological engineering has been widely used for diverse purposes in different communities and a number of approaches have been reported for developing ontologies; however, few works address issues of specific ontology construction for local communities, especially when taking into account the specificity of academic knowledge creation. This Chapter summarizes efforts done in two cooperating communities in Japan and in Poland, including attempts to clarify the concept and the field of knowledge science, to create an ontology characterizing a research program in this field, then to apply related results in another field – contemporary telecommunications. The distinctive approach to ontology creation is based on a combination of bottom-up and top-down approaches with the purpose of combining explicit knowledge with tacit, intuitive and experiential knowledge for constructing an ontology. Other possible views on constructing ontology are also presented and discussed; lessons from an ongoing application of this approach to a local research community working on contemporary telecommunication issues in Poland are also discussed. The combination of explicit and tacit, intuitive and experiential knowledge has led to a development of a software system named adaptive hermeneutic agent (AHA), a toolkit for documents gathering, keywords extracting, keywords clustering, and ontology visualization.

Keywords: ontology, knowledge science, knowledge engineering, software engineering.

1   Introduction

The word ontology was taken from philosophy, where it means a theory or a systematic explanation of being [10]. This word was borrowed by computer scientists in the middle of 1980s to express the meaning of an enhanced taxonomy – a structure of basic concepts together with their relations – of a given field of information and knowledge. A significant development of ontological engineering, corresponding

D. Dolk et al. (Eds.): Decision Support Modeling in Service Networks, LNBIP 42, pp. 279–317, 2012.
© Springer-Verlag Berlin Heidelberg 2012

tools and systems occurred in 1990s; later, the emergence of Semantic Web has marked an important step in the evolution of ontological engineering. Ontologies become regarded as means for a shared knowledge understanding and a way to represent real world domains. In the last decades, ontologies are expected to play a crucial role in the integration of data and applications at public and corporate level, for example, in the development of management information systems, organization of content in web sites, categorization of products in e-commerce, structured and comparative searches of digital content, standard vocabularies in expert domains, product configuration in manufacturing, among many others [3,11,15,22].

With all these developments, however, not all issues emerging during ontological engineering were sufficiently stressed. First issue is related to the character, reasons for, and possible explanations of the differences occurring during two distinctive approaches to ontological engineering: the *bottom-up approach,* constructing ontologies based on text repositories and data, and the *top-down approach,* constructing ontologies based on expert opinions. Because an ontology can be defined as a *formal specification of a shared layer of concepts* [9], its construction was originally approached as a purely *top-down approach,* a focused process organizing expert discussions and consensus opinions, see, e.g., [32]. However, other works, e.g. [6] point out that a *bottom-up approach* might be better, for diverse reasons, including the fact that knowledge creation proceeds all the time and thus ontologies must be dynamic, need continuous revisions that require automatic tools. While it is obvious that bottom-up approach is closer to automation and computer intelligence, whereas top-down represents human opinions, less attention was devoted to the fact that *this distinction corresponds also to the distinction of explicit knowledge versus tacit knowledge,* see, e.g, [34]. We believe in the superiority of an interplay between tacit and explicit knowledge, see [19], in all knowledge creation processes, thus we shall concentrate on *the ways of eliciting and using tacit knowledge in a combined bottom-up-top-down approach;* this is the essential aspect of novelty in our paper.

Second issue is related to the distinction between universal versus local character of a given ontology. There are experts who believe that any ontology can have only local character, be valid only locally (*"there is no universe, only a multiverse"[1]*). However, ontologies might be at least re-used in changed circumstances; thus, the question of "external validity" (understood not only as the possibility of external use, but also as consistency with external sources of knowledge) of an ontology has been raised , see, e.g, [1]. On the other hand, a technologist always assumes at least some external validity of the tools he creates. Therefore, from technological perspective it appears obvious that an ontology, to be useful, must be to some degree universal and to some degree local, the question is *how to define the degree and the character of universality and locality of a given ontology.* This, in particular, relates to ontologies characterizing local research communities, concentrating on a given field and a specific tradition of research.

---

[1] We shall not discuss in detail this philosophical issue here, recall only the hard wall test proposed in [34]: if somebody believes that there is only a multiverse, let him position himself against a hard wall, close his eyes and try to convince himself that the wall is not hard. If he cannot convince himself, the reality apparently has some universal aspects, hence there is not only a multiverse. If he can convince himself, he can try to falsify his convictions by running ahead with closed eyes ...

Third issue is related to the fact that *the needs of a local research community might be different than the needs of an industrial or market organisation,* since the character of academic knowledge creation is essentially different than that of organisational knowledge creation, see also [35]; however, we shall not concentrate on the third issue here and stress mostly aspects related to the first and second issues.

This Chapter presents two attempts to create an ontology for a local research community. First was characterizing a research program "Technology Creation Based on Knowledge Science" at Japan Advanced Institute of Science and Technology (JAIST) in its School of Knowledge Science, thus from a specific knowledge science perspective. Knowledge science is a new academic field which relates to the philosophy, methodology and techniques for creating knowledge, modelling knowledge creation processes and conducting research on knowledge engineering and knowledge management. The School of Knowledge Science at JAIST is the first school established in the world to make knowledge creation as the core of its scientific research. From the second half of 2003, the 21st-century COE (Center of Excellence) Program "Technology Creation Based on Knowledge Science" of JAIST sponsored by the Ministry of Education, Culture, Sports, Science and Technology (MEXT, Japan) has been initiated. This program aims to establish an interdisciplinary research field focusing on research and education exploring issues related to "knowledge science," including how to 1) create knowledge that can help spark innovation in a variety of situations, 2) develop individuals capable of coordinating knowledge creation processes, and 3) ensure ethical behaviour in a knowledge-based society. In order to combine theoretical research and practical research, a series of projects have been promoted at the Center of Strategic Development of Science and Technology of JAIST.

In this research, we tried to construct (see [25]) an ontology for COE program at JAIST with a new understanding of knowledge science and make explicit (at least, as much as possible) assumptions about this concept that are often tacitly made and never defined well. This work also will help the development of some projects of this program, clarify basic concepts for COE program itself, and help researchers in this program with vocabularies of keywords, with literature searches, etc.

There are many methods for developing ontologies, sometimes classified as those i) from scratch, ii) by reuse or iii) with the help of (automatic, thus bottom up) knowledge acquisition techniques [15]. In our case, we combined (as indicated above) the bottom-up classification and specification and the top-down reflection on concept of knowledge science to build the ontology from scratch. This approach emphasizes one of the most difficult aspects of constructing ontologies, namely, combining explicit knowledge, which typically used in bottom-up approaches, with tacit, intuitive and experiential knowledge, which typically used in top-down approaches. Some knowledge acquisition techniques were also taken into account in this work.

The second attempt to create an ontology for a local research community concerns recent publications of the National Institute of Telecommunications in Warsaw, Poland. An attempt of such ontology construction was undertaken as a part of preparations for building a knowledge management system in the Institute. The approach developed in the School of Knowledge Science at JAIST was used and tested in comparison with several generally available tools of ontological engineering, while generally concentrating on testing the effectiveness of bottom-up approach and on the issues of combining bottom-up and top-down approaches and of defining the degree of locality of the ontology. While this research is still in progress, some of the results obtained are interesting and show how the concentration on purely local data and automatic bottom-up ontology generation, while to some degree necessary, can nevertheless lead to rather limited results.

Based on a combination of a bottom-up and top-down approaches to ontology creation, an example of application of this ontology, related to an adaptive hermeneutic agent (AHA), was designed and implemented in COE program at JAIST. There are two purposes of implementation of such software tool: support for ontology construction as well as a local support (supplementing typical web-based tools) for a most basic process of scientific knowledge creation related to hermeneutics (gathering scientific information and knowledge from literature, the web, and other sources, interpreting, and reflecting on these materials).

The rest of this Chapter is organized as follows. Section 2 introduces our research goals and methods. Section 3 and Section 4 respectively explain the bottom-up keywords analysis and top-down reflection in the field of knowledge science. Detailed description of the ontology we built for COE program in JAIST is given in Section 5. Other possible views on ontology construction are discussed in Section 6, together with an indication of several ontological engineering tools available on the market. Section 7 describes the advancement of works on constructing an ontology for the National Institute of Telecommunications, together with some critical reflection. Section 8 presents an example of application of the ontology constructed at JAIST, related to an adaptive hermeneutic agent (AHA); and Section 9 summarizes this Chapter.

2   The Goals and Ways of Constructing Ontology of the COE Program

In addition to the philosophical origin, the term ontology has today diverse other meanings. In contemporary computer science, ontology is defined as a formal language-like specification of a domain knowledge – actually equivalent to a taxonomy of concepts in a given field of knowledge, enhanced by a structure of hierarchical dependences and other links between concepts constituting the taxonomy [4]. Ideally, an ontology should provide [6]:

1. a common vocabulary,
2. explication of what has been often left implicit,
3. systematization of knowledge,
4. standardization of terms,
5. meta-model functionality (providing a metalanguage for specific models in the domain).

Actually, these goals are not attainable: in order to have a formal meta-model [12], we need a meta-meta-model and so on, therefore we have to stop at some level of explication of basic assumptions and rely on an *hermeneutical horizon* – an intuitive perception what concepts and assumptions are basic and true and how we understand them. Thus, any ontology will achieve the ideal goals mentioned above only to a certain degree. Note, however, that this implies that any ontology can be re-engineered, corrected according to changes in the hermeneutical horizon.

We have tried to construct the ontology of 21st Century COE Program Technology Creation Based on Knowledge Science at JAIST as a case study, with the following goals:

> (A) To clarify the use of the concept of Knowledge Science in this Program and make explicit (at least, as much as possible) assumptions about this concept that are often tacitly made (ideal goals 2, 5);
> (B) To represent a vocabulary of terms used in this COE Program, together with a systematization of terms used (ideal goals 1, 3);
> (C) To help in the development of a software system designed to support hermeneutic search of literature, and possibly in other projects related to the COE Program.
> (D) To examine diverse ways in which a synthesis of top-down, tacit expert knowledge can be combined with bottom-up explicit knowledge (in order to provide a novel view on the ideal goals 2, 5)

The ideal goal 4) – standardization – was addressed only to limited degree, because of the heterogeneity of the interdisciplinary projects in the COE Program. Thus, we designed ontology for COE program at JAIST not only for helping in the development of some projects of this program, but also make to clarify basic concepts for COE program itself.

Known ways of constructing ontologies can be treated not as absolute recipes, but hints how to proceed. The distinction of a top-down approach and the bottom-up approach we interpret that top-down approach starts with an intuitive perception of the basic concepts in a hermeneutical horizon and specifies them in detail subsequently, while bottom-up approach starts (if from scratch) from textual data aiming to find concepts actually used in a given field of knowledge and then attempts to interpret them and their structural relations. The top-down approach thus starts with issues related to meta-model functionality (ideal goals 2, 5); the bottom-up approach starts with issues related to systematization and standardization (ideal goals 3, 4). Obviously, we need a combination of both bottom-up and top-down approaches in order to construct a useful ontology. This is expressed by many current writings on ontology construction (see, e.g. [7]); a review of how current literature on ontological engineering treats this issue would be very interesting, but would require a separate paper. The novelty of our approach consists thus not in proposing a combination of bottom-up and top-down approaches, but in viewing such a combination as an interplay of tacit and explicit knowledge and using our other research on such interplays [34,35] to examine ways of organizing such an interplay.

In order to create ontology, we proceeded along several lines. First, we checked the terms and concepts used by the program leader in a paper presenting an introduction to the COE program, thus providing an outline of COE ontology. Then, we collected papers composed by COE project members, which have appeared either at an international conference or journal. We extracted the keywords from the papers and counted the frequency of keywords in the full paper by using a computer program. We chose the keywords with high frequency to supplement the outline of COE ontology. We chose also pairs of keywords occurring with non-zero frequency to make a simple QT clustering of them [11] and compared the ontology emergent bottom-up from such clustering with the top-down outline of COE ontology. Finally, we took into account a hermeneutic reflection on knowledge sciences [36] and used this reflection for corrections of the supplemented outline; this way, we finally created the ontology for COE program. Fig.1 shows the process of constructing Ontology of the COE Program which combines both top-down approach and bottom-up approach.

Some comments might be useful here. The introduction to the COE program gave some guidelines for ontology construction, but these guidelines were not quite sufficient. Thus, a deeper reflection on knowledge sciences was needed. This is actually a *hermeneutic process* of an interplay between tacit and explicit knowledge that that is known in philosophy as *the heremeneutic circle* (Gadamer 1960), but in academic knowledge construction can be described by the hermeneutic EAIR (Enlightenment-Analysis-Immersion-Reflection) Spiral, see [34,35]. The classical approaches to ontological engineering combine explicit and tacit knowledge rather by *a debate,* which can be interpreted as an EDIS (Enlightenment-Debate-Immersion-Selection) Spiral of academic knowledge creation. Both types of approaches are useful, but stressing the role of hermeneutic processes and deep reflection might enrich ontological engineering.

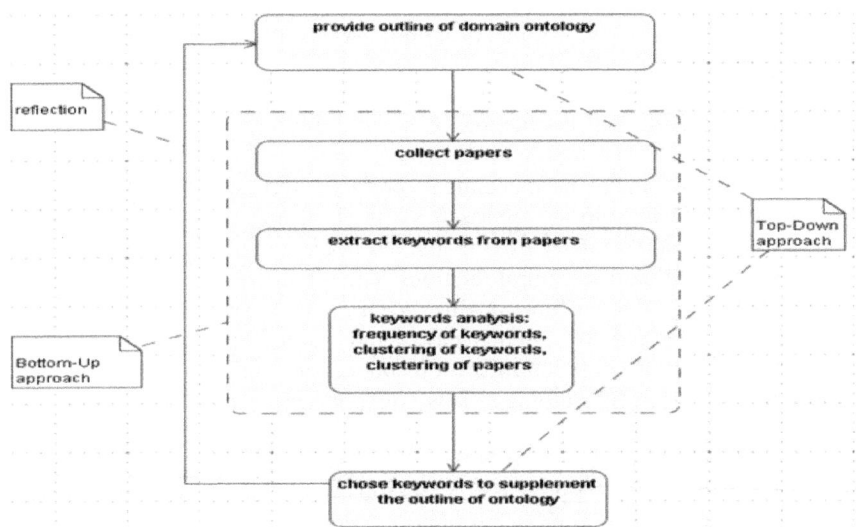

Fig. 1. A process of constructing ontology of the COE Program]

3   Bottom-Up Classification and Specification: Keyword Analysis

To build an outline of the ontology of COE program, we started with actually with a top-down like approach, although based only on a paper presenting an introduction to this program authored by the program leader [17]. After analyzing the purpose and sub-projects of the program, we selected the key terms and concepts mentioned in the paper and organized an ontology outline with three levels of branches. The first level included five main topics:

- Knowledge science
- Systems science and methodology
- Education in knowledge science
- Knowledge creation
- Management of technology

In addition, we also referred to the program reports presented by the program leader in later periods to check and revise the outline.

More detailed development of the ontology, however, was based on a bottom-up approach. We collected the papers authored by COE project members as many as were available. Since we had to limit this search to electronic files, we finally considered only 43 papers, which were either included in Proceedings of International Symposium on Knowledge and Systems Sciences (JAIST, 2004), or Proceedings of the First World Congress of the International Federation for Systems Research (Kobe, 2005), or in the International Journal of Knowledge and Systems Sciences (Issues 1 to 6). We extracted keywords (including keyphrases) from the full body of all papers; as the tool of ontological engineering, we used an especially developed software agent AHA (see Section 8).

3.1   Keyphrases Extractor

The keywords were specified by authors, but we thought they were not enough for our research to compare the contents of all papers. Thus, the additional keyphrase extraction was taken into account. This may increase the correlation and improve the clustering. Keyphrase extraction techniques for the English language have been well developed. Keyphrase frequency associated with keyphrase significations was proposed already in [13]. Based on the knowledge bases of "stop words", there are three steps to the keyphrases extractor:

> (1) Find Keyphrases: Extract keyphrases from the text file and make a list of all phrases. A phrase is defined as a sequence of one, two, or three words that appear consecutively in the text, with no intervening stop words or punctuation. In our case, phrases of four or more words are relatively rare.
> (2) Score Keyphrases: For each keyphrase, count how often the keyphrase appears in the text. Assign a score to each phrase. The score is the number of times the keyphrase appears in the file.
> (3) Final Output: We now have an ordered list of mixed-case phrases (upper and lower case, if appropriate). The list is ordered by the scores calculated in step 2.

We designed a small experiment by comparing machine-generated keyphrases with human-generated keyphrases. The performance is measured by the precision, where precision is defined the number of matches subdivided by a desired number of machine-generated phrases.

Table 1. Examples of the selected phrases for two papers from COE program

Paper 1:	KSS001.pdf
Keywords provided by authors	Scientific knowledge creation, knowledge management, knowledge management system, i-system
Top ten Keyphrases Given by Extractor	**knowledge management(31),** *knowledge creation(23),* **scientific knowledge creation(12),** research activities(11), knowledge sources(8), *explicit knowledge(5),* **knowledge management system(5),** *knowledge sharing(3),* knowledge creators(3) ,knowledge collaborator s(3)
Precision	**0.3**
Paper 2:	KSS002.pdf
Keywords provided by authors	knowledge management, knowledge management education, curriculum development, degree programs
Top ten Keyphrases Given by Extractor	**knowledge management (29), degree programs (18),** *content profile (10), information science (6),* organizational learning(5), **knowledge management education (4),** *knowledge managers(3), knowledge officers (3),* knowledge perspective (3), business perspective (3)
Precision	**0.3**

Table 1 shows the phrases selected by "Keyphrase Extractor" for two articles from the papers authored by COE project members. In these two examples, the desired number of phrases is set to ten. The phrases in bold match the author's phrases, while the phrases in italic are accaptable as keyphrases by other COE members.

It is not obvious whether a precision of, say, 0.3 for five phrases is good or bad. What we would really like to know is, what percentage of the keyphrases generated by the Extractor are acceptable to a human reader? We asked ten COE members; on average, about 84% of the keyphrases extracted by the Extrator were acceptable to them. Thus we believe the missed keyphrases are valuable for supplementing the outline of the ontology.

3.2 Keyphrases Clustering

Clustering methods are used to group the keyphrases based on their joint occurrence. There are various clustering algorithms, such as k-means algorithm, etc.; we selected for our purposes the simplest QT or quality threshold clustering algorithm [11], used originally for clustering genes. Quality of clustering is ensured by finding largest clusters with diameter not exceeding a given user-defined diameter threshold; the diameter can be also defined by a minimal treshold on the number of co-occurences of keyphrases. This is aimed at preventing dissimilar objects (genes in the original applications) from being forced into the same cluster and thus ensuring that only good quality clusters will be formed.

We extracted 128 keyphrases from 43 papers authored by COE project members. The matrix of co-occurrence of a pair of keyphrases should be a 128×128, because of space reasons, we show only a partial sample data (Table 2):

Table 2. Partial co-occurrence of a pair of keyphrases

Keyphrases	K1	K2	K3	K4	K5	K6	K7	K8
K1	47	9	1	0	0	0	0	1
K2	9	13	2	0	0	0	0	0
K3	1	2	11	0	0	0	0	0
K4	0	0	0	35	16	0	0	0
K5	0	0	0	16	26	0	0	0
K6	0	0	0	0	0	16	0	0
K7	0	0	0	0	0	0	6	1
K8	1	0	0	0	0	0	1	22
K1=data mining, K2=text mining, K3= information extraction, K4= Technology roadmapping, K5 = Roadmapping process, K6= adaptive agent, K7=knowledge integration, K8= Knowledge discovery								

It turned out that the joint occurrence of keyphrases is not common, most frequencies of such co-occurrence are zero, thus we set the parameter of the threshold as 1 (at the cost of quality of clusters, but with such small dimensions of data high quality clustering could not be expected). The algorithm determines all the clusters in the following steps:

1. For each keyphrase *K1, K2, ...,* determine a *candidate cluster* comprising given keyphrase and all other keyphrases with co-occurrence equal or exceeding assumed threshold.
2. Determine the biggest (in it's number of elements; in case of equal numbers choose either lexicographically or randomly) candidate cluster as the first actual cluster.
3. Remove keyphrases in the actual cluster from the overall list, repeat the procedure on the remaining shortened list until only single elements with no co-occurrence (unclassified) remain.

The result is a set of non-overlapping QT clusters:

- Cluster1:   {K1, K2, K3, K7, K8}
- Cluster2:   {K4, K5}
- Unclassified: K6

By this way, we actually generated 13 clusters from the entire data set. Because of the space limitations, we only list the outputs of following two clusters as examples.

Example of Keywords Clustering

```
Cluster1:
Papers:
{09_1_Minh.txt, 09_2_Nagai-kss04.txt, 12_2_phan.txt,
```

```
12_3_Tran.txt, 15_1_Zhang.txt, 15_2_huang-wei.txt,
20055.pdf.txt, 20057.pdf.txt, 20073.pdf.txt,
06_1_Hao.txt, 20177.pdf.txt}
   Keywords
{Data mining, Text mining, Information extraction,
Knowledge integration, Knowledge discovery, Text
summarization, Natural language processing, Association
rule mining, Anaphora resolution, Clustering algorithm,
Natural language processing, Clustering, Genetic
algorithm, K-means algorithm, Text clustering, Ant-based
Clustering, Semantic similarity measure, Ontology, Phrase
indexing, Sentence extraction, Ensemble learning, SVM
ensemble, Direct space method, Rough sets}
   Cluster2:
   Papers:
{05_1_ma.txt, 05_3_ JieYAN.txt, 20060.pdf.txt}
   Keywords:
{Technology roadmapping, Roadmapping process,
Transportation fuel cell forecast, Technology creation,
Technology forecasting, Roadmapping, Interactive
planning}
```

With respect to the proposal of COE ontology with three levels of concepts (see Section 5), the key phrases included in cluster one belong to the topic of "Knowledge Representation and Acquisition". The keyphrases included in cluster two belong to the topic of "Management of Technology". Additionally, we found that several other researchers than the authors of the papers classified were very interested in "Technology Roadmaps"; thus we have seen that even a simple bottom-up ontology construction is helpful in knowledge management. The clusters give us thus useful hints how to categorize the keywords; but matching all of them, particularly unclassified elements or small clusters, to the upper level ontology outline of COE Program turned out to be difficult. Therefore, we decided to start anew and consider a top-down reflection described in next section, using such top-down reflection for the enrichment of the original upper level ontology outline.

4   Top-Down Reflection on the Concept of Knowledge Science

Thus we turn back to a top-down approach, but enrich it by a hermeneutic reflection.

Knowledge science (KS) is often confused with or tacitly assumed to be subordinated to *knowledge management* (KM), thus we first reflect on the origins and meaning of the second term. Knowledge management has much popularity in management science, but its technological origins are often forgotten. It was first introduced by computer technology firms in early 1980-ies – first in IBM, then Digital Equipment Corporation who probably was the first to use the term *knowledge management* – as a computer software technology in order to record the current work on software projects. This started the tradition of treating knowledge management as a system of computer technologies. Later this term was adopted by management science, and made a big career. This has led to two opposite views how to interpret this term [5,37]:

- As *management of information relevant for knowledge-intensive activities*, with stress on information technology: databases, data warehouses, data mining, groupware, information systems, etc.
- As *management of knowledge related processes,* with stress on organizational theory, learning, types of knowledge and knowledge creation processes.

The first view is naturally represented by information technologists and hard scientists; the second by social scientists, philosophers, psychologists and is clearly dominating in management science. Representatives of the second view often accuse the first view of perceiving *knowledge to be an object* while it should be seen as *knowledge related to processes;* they stress that knowledge management should be *management of people.* For example, in an excellent book on the dangers of postponing action *The Knowing-Doing Gap* [20] say that "[an] article asserted that 'knowledge management starts with technology'. We believe that this is precisely wrong. …Dumping technology on a problem is rarely an effective solution."

However, while it is correct that knowledge management cannot be reduced to management of information; such a correct assessment tends to overlook both the complexity and the essence of the controversy. The complexity is that, historically, knowledge management has started with technology and cannot continue without technology; thus, both interpretations should be combined in adequate proportions. The essence of the controversy is that *management of people* should be also understood as *management of knowledge workers;* and knowledge workers are today often mostly information technologists, who should be well understood by managers. Thus, we believe that the two views listed above should be combined. Moreover, they incompletely describe what knowledge management is; there is a third, essential view, seeing knowledge management as the *management of human resources in knowledge civilization era,* concentrating on knowledge workers, their education and qualities, assuming a proper understanding of their diverse character, including a proper understanding of technologists and technology.

This is particularly visible concerning the concepts of *technology management* versus *knowledge management.* Management science specialists in knowledge management often tend to assume that *technology management* is just a branch of *knowledge management;* technologists specializing in *technology management* stress two aspects. First, an essential meaning of the word *technology* is *the art of designing and constructing tools or technological artefacts* (thus, *technology* does not mean *technological artefacts,* although such a meaning is often implied by a disdainful use of the word *technology*, e.g., in the quoted above phrase *dumping technology*). In this essential meaning sense, the term is used in the phrase *technology management*. Secondly, *technology management* might be counted as a kind of special *knowledge management,* but it is an older discipline, using well developed concepts and processes, such as *technology assessment, technology foresight* (Salo and Cuhls 2003) and *technology roadmapping* [21,38]. Only recently, some of these processes have been also adapted to knowledge management [14].

All the above discussion implies that we are observing now an emergence process of a new understanding of *knowledge sciences* – an interdisciplinary field that goes beyond the classical epistemology, includes also some aspects of *knowledge engineering* from information technology, some aspects of *knowledge management* from management and social science, some aspects of *interdisciplinary synthesis* and other techniques (such as decision analysis and support, multiple criteria analysis, etc.) from systems science. This emergence process is motivated primarily by the needs of an adequate education of *knowledge workers* and *knowledge managers and coordinators;* however, also the research on knowledge and technology management and creation needs such interdisciplinary support.

The classical understanding of the words *knowledge science* might imply that it is epistemology enhanced by elements of knowledge engineering, knowledge management and systems science. However, the strong disciplinary and historical focus of epistemology suggests an opposite interpretation: knowledge science must be interdisciplinary, thus it should not start with epistemology, although it must be enhanced by elements of epistemology. The field closest to knowledge science seems to be systems science – at least, if it adheres to its interdisciplinary origins and does not suffer too much from the unfortunate (but unavoidable today) disciplinary division into *soft* and *hard systems science.* The noticeable tension between *soft* and *hard* systems science is just an older version of the tension between understanding *knowledge management* either from the perspective of knowledge engineering, or from the perspective of social and management science, mentioned above.

To summarize, we should thus require that *knowledge sciences* gives home to several disciplines (quoted here in an alphabetic order):

- Epistemology and philosophy of science,
- Knowledge engineering,
- Management science and knowledge management,
- Sociological and soft systems science,
- Technological and hard systems science,

These disciplines should be treated on equal footing, with a requirement of mutual information and understanding; this basic classification should be also reflected in the proposed ontology of the COE Program.

To our knowledge, only one university in the world, the Japan Advanced Institute of Science and Technology, founded – already in 1998 – the School of Knowledge Science, while the field is understood similarly as described above. The university supports only graduate education, for master and doctoral degrees; in knowledge science, three types of graduates are typical:

- Specialists in management, with understanding of knowledge engineering and systems science;
- Specialists in systemic knowledge coordination, with understanding of knowledge engineering and management;
- Specialists in knowledge engineering, with understanding of management and systems science.

We can ask now the question: what has such a broad and deep reflection contribute to ontology construction? We could list the five disciplines above and the three types of educated specialists without such broad reflection, but the deep reflection underlines their importance in the upper layers of the corresponding ontology, allows us to understand better the underlying, often un-stated assumptions belonging actually to respective hermeneutical horizons. We see that a hermeneutic approach, relying on such broad and deep reflection, might be useful also in other applications when combining bottom-up and top-down ways of ontology construction.

The ontology of the COE Program might be also treated as a first step towards constructing an ontology for the School of Knowledge Science in JAIST, providing a better understanding of what is (or are) knowledge science (or sciences).

5   Final Proposal of the Ontology

Based both on the bottom-up classification and on the above reflection as a basis of top-down approach, the ontology of the COE Program can be proposed. It is organized as an inverted tree, with fourth-level branches corresponding to keywords found in the papers of COE Program members. The general category of the domain of Knowledge Science includes the following eight sub-domains as the first level of ontology of the COE Program:

- Knowledge Creation and Transformation
- Knowledge Representation, Systematization, Acquisition
- Knowledge Management
- Systems Science
- Education and Knowledge Science
- Management of Technology
- Technology Creation
- Diverse Related Themes

Each sub-domain consists of several topics (second level); these different topics include particular sub-topics (third level). All keywords was summarized as and categorized into the sub-topics (fourth level). In addition, the clustering of the keywords gave us the hints to find the relations between the subtopics and the further relations between topics as well as sub-domains. We list the proposed ontology in an Appendix. Our classification is naturally not absolute nor the ultimately final; it might be further enhanced and corrected as new data will become available. In Fig. 2 we can see a visualization of the current ontology of the COE Program (used as a part of the hermeneutic AHA agent described in Section 8).

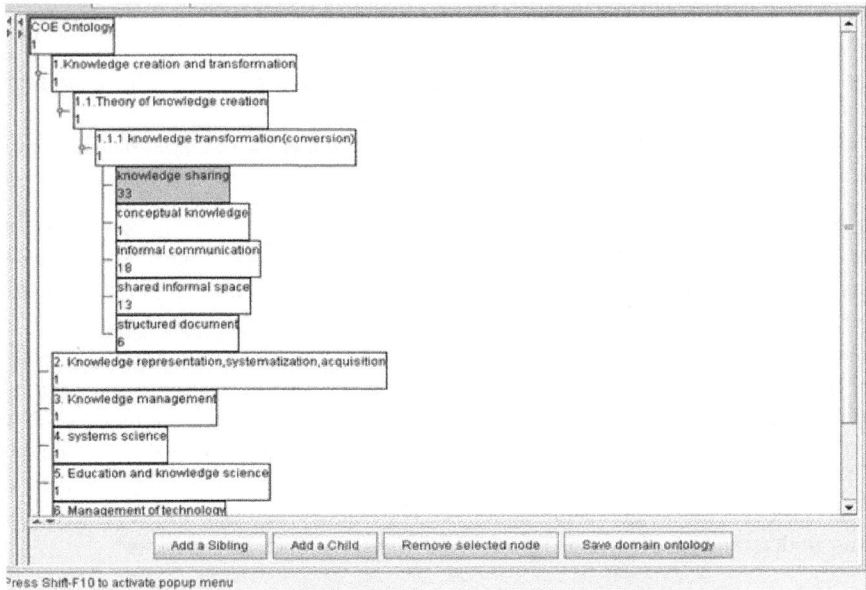

Fig. 2. Screenshot of AHA for construction COE ontology

6   Other Perspectives and Ontological Approaches

6.1   Other Approaches used in JAIST

Either before our work on COE ontology or at the same time, there are some related works in other perspectives for building an ontology or taxonomy, mostly in terms of knowledge management.

Dr. Totok H. Wibowo [30,31], a postdoctoral research fellow of COE Center, worked with other two colleagues to construct a Knowledge Map for the faculty members of School of Knowledge Science (KS) in order to provide a critical mechanism in creating a research network of professionals interested in knowledge creation and knowledge management. They conducted the survey and interview with the professors in KS School, and also referred many related journal papers, information from websites and other publications. However, their approach was only top-down and they concentrated on the perspective of knowledge management (KM) which, as discussed above, can be counted only as a part of knowledge sciences. Finally, they concluded with a taxonomy of knowledge management, which consists of eight disciplines: Business of KM, Technologies of KM, KM Processes, KM Systems, Sociology of KM, Creativity, Psychology of KM, and Philosophy of KM. This work was based on the classification of existing research fields and topics of KM by taxonomical method and it clearly represented a KM perspective.

In order to distinguish and describe KM technologies according to their support for strategy, [26] employed a top-dow ontology development method to describe the relations between technology, KM and strategy, and to categorize available KM technologies according to those relations. This study focused particularly on two sub-domains of the KM field: KM strategies and KM technologies. The processes of developing the ontology in this work included four steps:

- Definition of the domain and scope
- Identification of key terms and concepts, and their relationships
- Definition of the structure of the ontology as a hierarchy of categories
- Survey of KM technologies according to the ontology.

Another doctoral student of KS School, Kun Nie [18], is currently working towards a domain analysis of knowledge management as an organizational activity. He is trying to use domain analysis method to describe what KM really is and what is meant by KM. Domain analysis includes four main steps [2]:

- Step1: Collecting domain knowledge/expert knowledge;
- Step2: Simple data analysis and visualization of keyword relationships;
- Step3: Applying domain analysis (distribute the keywords in terms of the concepts of Entities, Events, Functions, Behaviours, Support Technology, Objectives, and Application);
- Step4: Results and conclusion;

This is an on-going work. All above researches concentrate on the filed of KM, try to develop a taxonomy of KM or describe the contents of KM in detail. Being aware of such research helped us in our endeavour, building an ontology for COE program, which is, however, based on the assumption that Knowledge Science (KS) has much more rich meaning than Knowledge Management (KM).

6.2   A Review of Ontological Engineering Tools

On the other hand, before applying experiences described above to the problem of local ontology construction in the National Institute of Telecommunications in Warsaw, Poland, we made also a search of ontological engineering tools existing on the market. A bottom-up construction of an ontology is usually based on an analysis of unstructured or diversely structured documents, thus an automatic or semi-automatic analysis of documents formulated in natural language. This might include various phases:

- A subdivision of the original text into sentences, phrases, tokens, words;
- An elimination of insignificant words (most frequently occurring but insignificant tags such as *and, or, a*, creating and using a stop-list of such words);
- Selection of significant words or phrases and a determination of their basic and derived forms (thematization and stemming). We can use either vocabularies or grammatical algorithms for this purpose;
- An automatic generation of keywords, clusterization of documents, ontology formation, thesaurus development etc.

This process depends on the language used in the texts and on the thematic field of interest. It is easier for English language, more difficult for languages with more complex grammar, such as Polish. Moreover, each discipline develops its own type of language: literary language differs from technical and from mathematical language; this involves not only a specific alphabet, such as the use of Greek letters in mathematics, but even preverbal assumptions of the hermeneutic horizon of a given field of knowledge that serve as the basis of interpretation of the text [12].

Moreover, there are several standards of the electronic text format: .txt, html, .doc or .pdf. When converting all of them to a unified standard, say, .txt, it might happen that more complex structures, such as mathematical or chemical formulae or specific alphabets are destroyed in the conversion; this requires the development of specific converters for a given class of documents.

Therefore, for text analysis there are diverse software tools. We can subdivide them into:

- *Simple text analysis tools* for creating basic statistics in texts, such as the frequency of occurrence or co-occurrence of a given word or phrase (e.g. TextSTAT);
- *Search engines* for indexing and finding required information in a large numbers of texts (such as Lucene, Windows Desktop Search, Google, Yahoo);
- *Advanced text analysis tools* including clusterization, visualization of results and the possibility of ontology creation, (such as SAS Text Miner , Oracle Text, OntoGen Text Garden).

A search in unstructured text documents (whole text analysis) uses a multi-dimensional space model. The original documents are supposed to determine (actually, a user intervention is necessary, as illustrated in next Section) a list of significant words, called *bag of words*. All original documents are characterized then by vectors $\boldsymbol{a}_k = (a_{ik} \ldots a_{ik} \ldots a_{nk})$, where n is the number of words in the bag, k is the index of the document, a_{ik} is the frequency of occurrence of the word number i in the document number k (*term-by-document frequency*). Then we can define a similarity measure $S(k,l)$ of two documents, say, k and l; most frequently the cosine of the vectors $\boldsymbol{a}_k$ and $\boldsymbol{a}_l$ is used for this purpose:

$$S(k,l) = \frac{\sum_i a_{ik} a_{il}}{\sqrt{\sum_i a_{ik}^2} \sqrt{\sum_i a_{il}^2}} \tag{1}$$

The *term-by-document frequencies* can be also arranged differently by combining the vectors $\boldsymbol{a}_k$ in a *term-by-document frequency matrix;* the dimension of such a matrix is determined by the number of documents and the number of words analyzed, hence an analysis of such a matrix can be quite expensive computationally. This is the reason why rather elementary statistical methods are typically used for such an analysis.

A frequently used approach is to select (arbitrarily, based on intuition resulting from experiments) a method of determining weighting coefficients w_{ik} that serve either instead or as multipliers to term-by document frequencies. If w_{ik} serve instead a_{ik}, they are called *weighted frequencies* and might be determined either binary ($w_{ik} = 1$ if the term occurs in the document, 0 otherwise), or logarithmic $w_{ik} = \log_2 (a_{ik}+1)$ in order to give a smaller weight to large frequencies, or uniform (simply $w_{ik} = a_{ik}$); we see that such transformations actually have the aim of simplifying the computations.

More complex are approaches when weights serve as multipliers, usually related to *term weights* w_k ($w_k a_{ik}$ is analyzed instead of a_{ik}). Term weights can be defined also in many ways, such as *entropy* (most weight for least frequent terms), *IDF (inverse document frequency)*, *GF-IDF (global frequency-inverse document frequency)*, *normal* (proportional to a_{ik}, actually equivalent to *none*, uniformly 1 or using a_{ik} without transformation), *chi-squared* (the value of the χ^2 test), *mutual information* (attempting to measure how the probability distribution of frequencies of using term i in all documents differs from the overall probability distribution of frequencies), *information gain* (attempting to measure entropy reduction due to a split of all documents based on the frequencies of the term i).

Another attempt of reducing the complexity of analyzing *term-by-document frequency matrix* is a theoretical possibility of reducing its dimension by *SVD (singular value decomposition)* and using an approximate term-by-document frequency matrix, which is reasonable if many entries in the original matrix are zeros; but then we can use also other techniques of analyzing sparse matrices.

All these possibilities, however, are more theoretical than practical, not sufficiently tested in actual applications; it is not clear, for example, why they should be superior to other methods of data analysis used, e.g., in data mining. Therefore, they should be used rather as a variety of tools that might work or not in a particular application. For further experimentation, we have chosen several advanced text analysis tools; before presenting the results of their application, however, we illustrate their capacities on the example of two of them: *SAS Text Miner* and *OntoGen Text Garden* .

A professional package SAS 9.1 dedicated to data analysis contains a subsystem Text Miner (a part of the module SAS Enterprise Miner) that can use both structured and unstructured documents, recognizing in particular such formats as .txt, .doc, .pdf. It analyses sets of documents (with the possibility of subdividing the set into several categories) and performs pattern searching on them. It is possible to analyse documents in many European languages (not yet in Polish; the language is too complex), in Chinese and Arabic. The system searches for the roots of words, recognises synonyms, recognizes phrases of words, standardises the use of some terms (such as dates, percents, currencies), recognises special terms such as titles, products, organisation units. The phases of use of the system contain an integration of all documents in a single text source, decomposition and suitable representation of the text, transformation and reduction of dimensions, analysis proper including grouping, classification, analysis of relations.

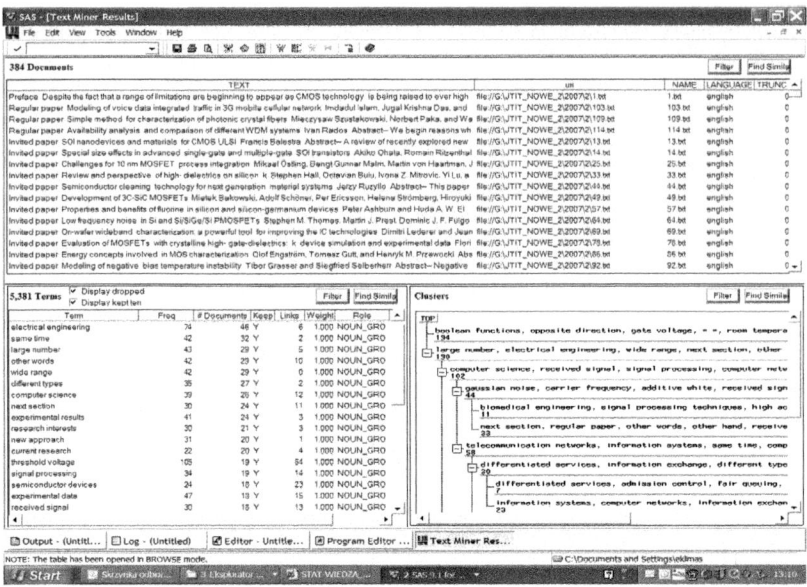

Fig. 3. An example of results of SAS Text Miner

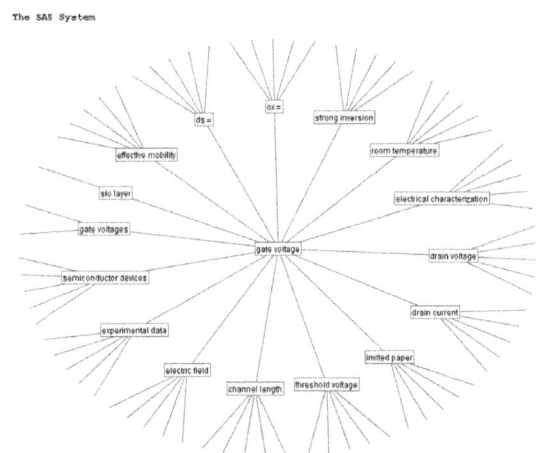

Fig. 4. An example of results visualisation in SAS Text Miner

The system for English language contains a standard stoplist of ca. 340 words with the possibility of modifications by the user. The system performs advanced stemming, it is also possible to ignore some other specified types of words (e.g., performing specified grammatical roles). A list of synonyms is also available and can be modified by the user. The analysis can use diverse statistical methods for the following tasks: grouping of documents (based on text similarity), clustering (with the possibility of hierarchical clustering and using diverse methods), creating a list of keywords and graphical representations including graphical interaction features. Examples are illustrated by Fig. 3, 4.The graphical interaction tools are truly effective, can produce, e.g., lists of documents related to a given concept, keywords for these documents, etc.

Another advanced system selected as an example is OntoGen TextGarden, developed by a consortium of a Framework Programme financed by the European Union. The consortium included many institutions (such as British Telecommunications, Empolis GmbH, Josef Stefan Institute, AIFB Institute of University of Karlsruhe, Department of Computer Science of University of Sheffield, Institute of Computer Science of University of Innsbruck, Intelligent Software Components S.A., Kea-pro GmbH, Ontoprise GmbH, Ontotext Laboratory of Sirma Group Corporation, Vrije Universiteit Amsterdam, Universitat Autonomia de Barcelona, Siemens Business Services GmbH & Co. OHG.). However, the leading role was played by the Josef Stefan Institute from Slovenia that supports now and further develops the system. The aim of the system is a semi-automatic ontology generation given a set of analysed documents (currently in English). In principle, the system performs many functions similar to SAS Text Miner, with diverse differences. There are several stoplists, not yet modified by the user. System accepts diverse formats of original texts. Terms are weighted according either to TF-IF method, or analysed using SVM (*Support Vector Machine*) algorithm. OntoGen performs a bottom-up analysis of texts, proposing first keywords on the lower level, then grouping them on further levels.

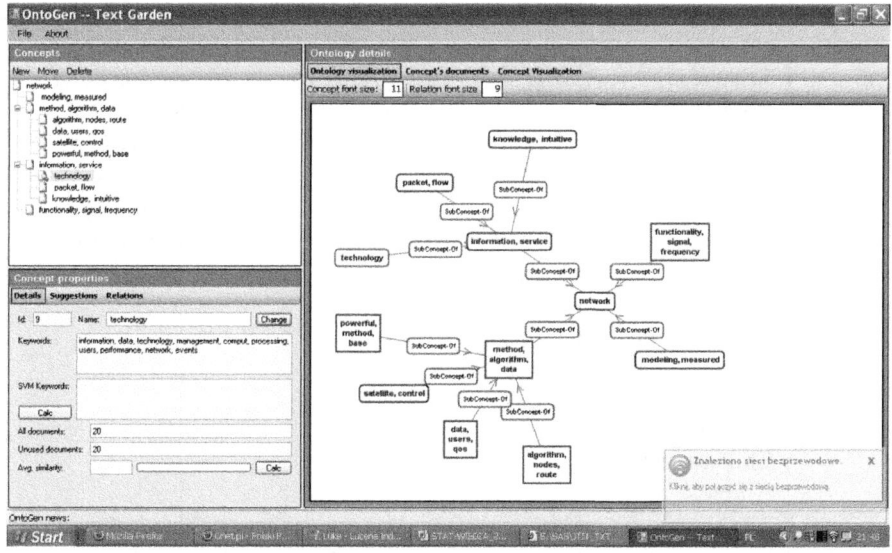

Fig. 5. An example of ontology constructed by with the help of OntoGen TextGarden

Great emphasis was given to the interaction with the user, according, however, to the classical paradigm of decision support: the system proposes, the user accepts or modifies. Therefore, two basic types of interaction are specified: semi-automatic (the user plays a limited role) or supervised (the user learns how to use the system); in both cases, however, the user is not fully sovereign, see further comments in Section 7. Fig. 5 illustrates an example of an ontology constructed with the help of OntoGen Text Garden. Diverse graphical representations are also supported by OntoGen Text Garden.

In the perspective of these two examples, we can compare several such systems presented in Table 3:

Table 3. Comparison of several tools of text analysis (see the last references in reference list)

Tool	Functions	Advantages	Weaknesses	Technology
TextST AT.7	Simple statistics and search functions.	Fast even for large data sets. Source version available. Works for several languages (not Polish). Accepts diverse formats.	No stoplist	Tcl, Python. Available for Windows, Linux, MacOS.
SAS Data Miner 9.1 Text Miner 4.3	Professional software. Diverse statistics of terms and phrases. Advanced stoplist, modified by the user., advanced stemming. Diverse clustering algorithms. Works for many languages (not Polish), including Chinese and Arabic.	Advanced clustering and other analysis tools. Advaced graphics.	Internal formats of data recording	Block and stream processing, paralel I/O operations, 4GL language procedures, graphical interface. Available for Unix and Windows.
Oracle Text 10g	Professional software with functionality similar to SAS, theoretically even supporting Polish language.	Own ontologies for diverse fields.	Cost increases with functionality	SQL, PL/SQL, Java, C. Available for Windows, Linux, Unix.

Table 3. (*continued*)

e: IAS 5.1	Professional software supporting also Polish language.	Professional stemming for Polish language	High purchase cost	Java, open JSP architecture, possible integration with ASP, .NET, CGI. Available for Unix, Linux, Windows.
Neuros oft Gram 2.3	Simple module for text analysis In Polish language, equipped with a stoplist and stemming. Can be used for preparing abstracts of documents.	Easy integration with other software tools.	Primitive stemming.	COM/DCOM Windows; CORBA for Linux and UNIX. Can be integrated with C++, Java, Python, JavaScript, C#.
Lucene 2.2	Search engine for indexing and finding documents. Internal stoplist and stemming. Support for composite logical questions (*and, or, not*). Ranking of answers. Export of results to HTML.	Source code accessible, integration with own extensions encouraged. Fast execution. Operates under WindowsMS	To extend the software, good working knowledge of Java needed	Java. Can function with Windows or Unix.
OntoGe n Text Garden 2.0	Advanced system for semi-automatic ontology creation. Languages: English, Slovenian. Advanced stoplists, stemming.	Fast execution. Advanced graphics for result presentation. Software under further development.	Stoplists currently not modifiable.	C+, C#. Operates under Windows XP.

7   Ontology Construction for National Institute of Telecommunications

7.1   Bottom-Up Ontology Formation Experiments

The bottom-up ontology construction was tested first by trying to classify 384 papers published in English in 2000-2007 in the Journal of Telecommunications and Information Technology (JTIT), published by the National Institute of Telecommunications (NIT) in Warsaw. The analysis concentrated on keywords provided by authors, abstracts prepared by authors, and full texts of papers. Papers were stored in .pdf format, hence they were converted into .txt format (obviously, no converter works ideally for complex documents, especially for mathematical formulae and text related to figures) and cleaned in cases of more significant conversion errors. The texts analysed are characterized by the basic statistics presented in Table 4.

Table 4. Statistics of publications in JTIT

Year	Issues	Number of papers	Selected phrases
2000	1-2	18	Optical fibre communications, lasers, material for optical communications, antenna.e
2000	3-4	11	Materials for mobile communications, transistor, power devices, microelectronic technology, radio propagations.
2001	1	15	Microelectronics.
2001	2	10	NIT, broadband radio Access systems, IP over optical transport network, microwave optical mixing.
2001	3	12	Filter, linear predictions, wireless communication, algorithms, material for telecommunications devices, optoelectronic switch.
2001	4	14	Radars, wireless communications.
2002	1	15	Integrated circuits, microwave generation, algorithms, e-learning.
2002	2	8	IP QoS, optical switching networks.
2002	3	11	Ambient intelligence, churn modeling, data mining, fraud management, teletraffic systems, machine learning, fuzzy control systems, decision makers, telecommunication networks, optimization problems, web cache management, network analysis.
2002	4	8	Security, cryptographic protocols.

Table 4. (*continued*)

2003	1	13	Microwave filters, microwave, digital networks, 3G network simulation,
2003	2	13	Optical multiplexing, filterbanks, GPS-based routing protocol, ad hoc networks, multi-path routing protocol, cellular networks, mobile networking, resource management, MPEG-7, metadata, image coding, wireless communication.
2003	3	19	Optimal decision, multiple criteria decision making, optimization, traffic management, dynamic routing, routing algorithms, network optimization, artificial neural networks, belief networks, data mining, decision support systems, data mining, cellular network planning.
2003	4	11	Digital radio communication systems, filters, IP QoS, traffic control, data interoperability; information exchange, Web services, firewall technologies; simulation war games, C2 systems, simulation, e-learning; dynamic channel assignment.
2004	1	15	Silicon, geochemical structure, silicon microelectronics, simulation, semiconductor devices, materials, optical crystal fibers, microwave devices.
2004	2	10	Traffic, routing, algorithms, MPLS, optimization, content delivery network, IP networks; services, wireless LAN, voice and data integration, HIPERLAN/2, QoS, MAC, wireless system, testing methodology, SMS Service, data transmission, transparent optical network.
2004	3	10	Optimization, simulation large computer networks, data mining, fault localization, geographic information systems, planning, decision-making, clustering, multi-criteria analysis, wireless systems, SLA, optical networking, ring network.
2004	4	15	NATO communications, Web devices, military, mathematical modeling, decision support, UMTS, mobile IP, cryptography, information technology, X.25, C4 systems, C2 systems, quality systems, ISO/IEC 17025 standard, IPSec; packet switching, simulation, communication protocols, radio monitoring.

Table 4. (*continued*)

2005	1	25	Materials, silicon, device integration, microelectronics, silicon micromechanics, nanostructures fabrication, traffic performance, mobile cellular network.
2005	2	15	Radar, signal processing, image processing, measurement, antennas.
2005	3	15	Knowledge theory, multi-criteria analysis, traffic control, optimization, computer networks; network design, data mining, event mining, satellite mobile systems, GPRS, mobile systems, microwave.
2005	4	18	Telemedicine, healthcare, medical education, biosignals, Decision support systems, structural modeling, e-commerce, e-shopping, micro payments.
2006	1	13	Image coding, testing, error protection, secure communication, QoS traffic, ad hoc networks, wireless system, algorithms, Internet, radio systems.
2006	2	11	Mobile knowledge management, European Document Exchange System, e-government, communication society, healthcare, e-learning, antenna wireless.
2006	3	10	Military communications.
2006	4	14	Decision support for telecommunication, information technology, network design, QoS, network simulation, optical materials.
2007	1	19	Microwave, antenna, satellite technology, network traffic QoS.
2007	2	16	Material of semiconductor industry, 3G mobile cellular network, photonic crystal fibers, WDM systems.

As it can be seen, texts analysed were broadly related to telecommunications and information technology, but rather diversified, often interdisciplinary, which is natural for a contemporary information technology. Thus, it would be rather difficult to extract from them an ontology characterizing the publisher – National Institute of Telecommunications. Nevertheless, text analysis was performed in order to test diverse tools available and to derive preliminary conclusions. Four tools were tested: TEXTSTAT, Lucene, SAS Text Miner and OntoGen Text Garden, using diverse subsets of documents, including sets of keywords, abstracts, full texts of papers, selected groups of phrases, etc.

TEXTSTAT was tested by preparing matrices of co-joint frequencies of phrases in selected groups. For example, phrases such as:

1. security,
2. cryptographic protocols,
3. authentication algorithms,
4. crypto,
5. digital signature ,
6. C2 systems,
7. Internet,
8. QoS,

resulted in the matrix of co-frequencies presented in Table 5.

Table 5. Co-frequencies of selected phrases

	1	2	3	4	5	6	7	8
1	854	155	47	58	16	6	192	84
2	62	68	0	211	157	3	391	81
3	3	0	4	2	1	0	3	0
4	58	0	1	61	17	0	32	2
5	16	1	2	5	20	0	14	0
6	6	0	0	0	0	13	0	0
7	192	10	8	30	14	2	546	154
8	84	0	0	3	2	0	258	452

Generally, TEXTSTAT worked fast and was reliable, but with limited functionality. Lucene has a stronger functionality, but produces similar results.

In turn, SAS Text Miner has even stronger functionality, particularly in graphical interaction and result representation. SAS Text Miner was tested on diverse subsets of documents, e.g., the set of all keywords of 384 papers. It resulted in 52 most frequently (from 62 to 7 occurrences) used keywords and the relations between them presented in Fig. 6.

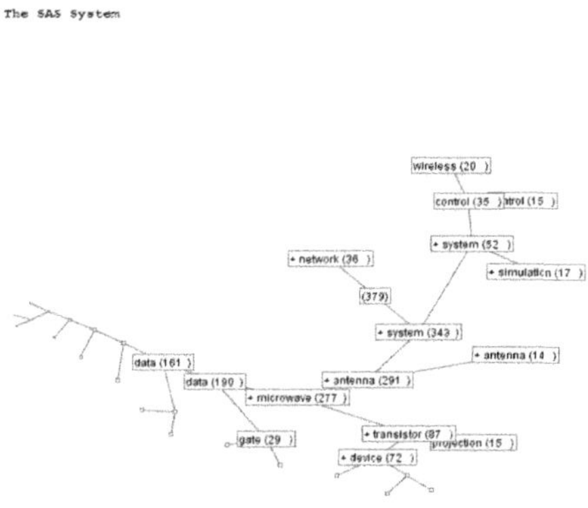

Fig. 6. Basic relations between concepts in the set of keywords for all documents

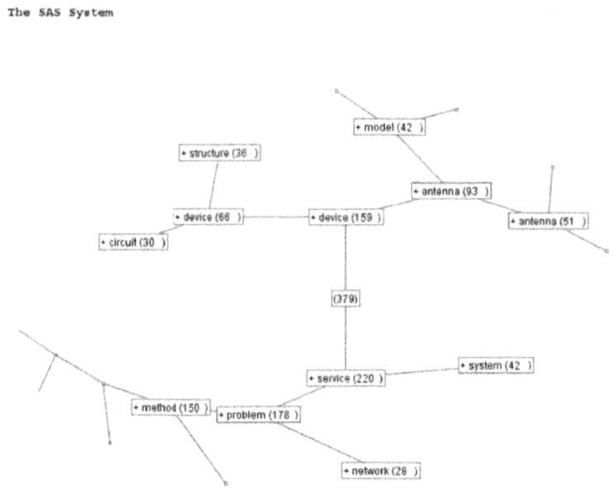

The SAS System

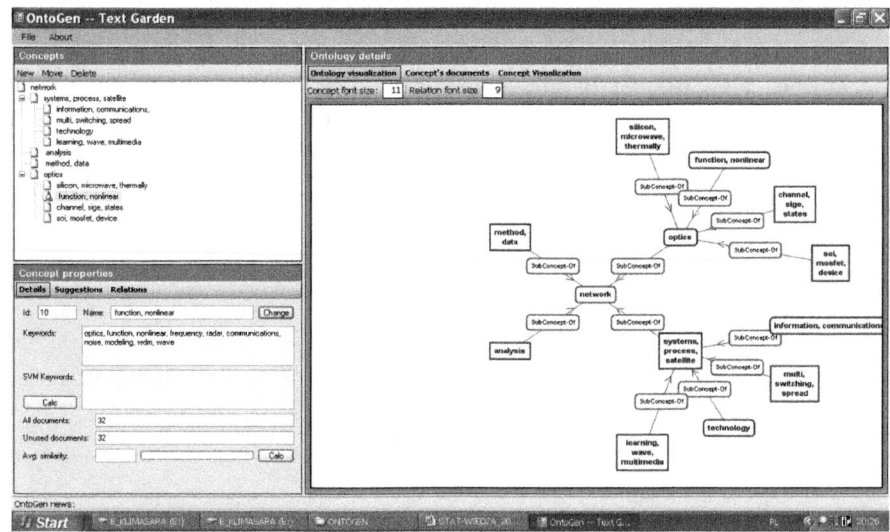

Fig. 7. Basic relations between concepts in the set of abstracts for all documents

SAS Text Miner works very reliably and gives excellent possibilities of diverse graphical analyses; e.g., we could select the concept network and display the relations of this concept to other keywords, etc. Similar results can be obtained when analysing, e.g., the set of all abstracts, see Fig. 7.

OntoGen Text Garden has a very well structured process of ontology construction, which results, in fact, in most adequate results. This is related to the interactive selection of key phrases; after such selection, the resulting ontology proposed by OntoGen is most rich between tested tools, see Fig. 8 illustrating the relations between concepts in the set of keywords of all papers.

Fig. 8. Ontology for the set of keywords of all papers proposed by OntoGen Text Garden

Thus, we can conclude that all tested tools work well and the more advanced between them produce interesting proposals of ontology. However, when it comes to an interpretation of these proposals by the user, the natural answer of any telecommunication specialist to the information structures presented, e.g., in Figures 6, 7, 8 is "so what is new?". In other words, the structures represents relations that are natural and logical to any specialist and have rather limited contribution to the specification of an ontology characterizing even the set of authors of the papers analysed, not to speak about characterizing the publisher of these papers.

There are diverse reasons for this fact, most of them related to the difference between tacit expert knowledge and explicit recorded knowledge, see, e.g., (Wierzbicki and Nakamori 2006, 2007). In other words, the concepts that are most important for an author creating a research paper are not necessarily used by her/him in the paper; contrariwise, s(he) might even avoid using explicitly concepts from her/his hermeneutical horizon (see Król 2007), the system of intuitive, unconscious beliefs what basic assumptions are fundaments of truth in a given field of research. Thus, listing concepts that are most important in characterizing a research institution might require special approaches, quite different from bottom-up methodology of ontological engineering. For example, the excellent tool OntoGen Text Garden assumes that the user, by dynamic interaction with the system, will convey her/his tacit, expert knowledge and thus contribute to relevant ontology formation. The experiments we performed suggest, contrariwise, that the user will not convey that what really matters, that the system is tacitly domineering the user who is thus not fully sovereign, and that different methods of eliciting most basic ontological concepts must be applied.

Tacit knowledge is mostly preverbal and difficult to formulate explicitly, hence it might seem that it is impossible to include tacit knowledge in ontology formation. Yet the example of the top-down ontology construction for JAIST COE Program presented in Section 5 proves other conclusion: not impossible, only we must take quite different approach to ontology formation. The top-down approach in JAIST was actually based on a hermeneutic reflection on a new field of research, knowledge sciences. For an established field of telecommunication and information technology, we must ask: how to reflect, what is essential for a given research institution, knowing generally its field of expertise?

Naturally, we could start with a general ontology of the field – or, if such an ontology does not exist, select texts characterizing this field published by an established and respected institution (such as ITU, International Telecommunication Union in our case) and attempt to create such an ontology. However, how should we adapt a general ontology of a field to generate a local ontology, characterizing a given research institution? A general ontology might again tacitly dominate the process, making more difficult the issue of characterizing a given institution and relevant local ontology formation.

7.2   Top-Down Ontology Formation and Reflection

A proposal of an answer to this question is illustrated by a top-down approach to the problem of creating an ontology for the National Institute of Telecommunications. We started with the question: what is characteristic for the Institute? This resulted in a list of diverse characterizations of NIT:

Activities: research and development, design, construction, implementation, technical services, equipment testing, measurement standards, education.

Research grouping (with examples of subgroupings given only in two cases):

- Radiocommunication:
  - Mobile services,
  - Satellite telecommunications
  - Digital television,
  - Electromagnetic compatibility,
  - Maritime communications
- Teleinformatics and convergent networks;
- Power supply systems in telecommunications;
- Advanced information technology:
  - Data mining,
  - Decision support,
  - Advanced logics,
  - Knowledge engineering,
  - Creativity support;
- Maritime communications;
- Applications of teleinformatics;
- Regulatory and socio-economic aspects of post and telecommunications;
- Teletransmission and optical techniques;
- Computer networks and scientific information service;
- Laboratory testing of telecommunication and teleinformatic equipment;
- Measurement standards and metrology for telecommunications.

Research environment: laboratories (research, testing, calibration), quality control system (procedures, quality service book, accreditation), computer network services, library, scientific information services, seminars, scientific conferences.

Types of services: general telecommunication, in this mobile, teleinformatics, convergent, etc. Testing quality of services.

Telecommunication devices: power supply systems; telecommunication hubs, servers, routers, switches; antenna and related equipment; fibre cables and related equipment; etc.

Telecommunication software: (very diverse, here examples): dedicated application systems, network protocols, network management systems; power supply management systems; decision support systems; knowledge management systems; electronic (distant) education systems.

Security in telecommunications: standards, security of systems, security of information, security of environment, electromagnetic compatibility.

Legal regulation in telecommunications: postal and telecommunication laws.

Socio-economic aspects of telecommunications: costs and pricing of telecommunication and postal services; diverse aspects of telecommunication and postal markets.

Standards in telecommunication and informatic services;

Products: publications (opinions, papers, doctoral dissertations, reports); implementations (designs, applications); standardisation documents; conferences; target-oriented education; etc.

Research financing: budgetary (long research programme; statutory activity; grants; dedicated programs; scientific investment); European Union (Framework Programme, Eureka; operational programmes, etc.); market customers; own funds.

From all above categories, most important for top-down ontology formation seems to be research grouping that in fact corresponds to the basic organisational subdivision of activities in NIT. In further work, we intend to develop top-down ontology starting with this grouping and obtaining interactive response from the management of NIT and research leaders. This in fact might be a universal rule for local research organisations: start with the organisational structure of an institution and convert it into a top-down ontology in an interactive learning process. An organisational structure, if accepted by its participants, seems to be a most powerful organizing principle and source of ontological concepts; if the structure is not fully accepted, the interactive learning process helps to improve it.

The work on an ontology for NIT is continued; we reported here only some general conclusions and do not list an example of the ontology, since it would take too much space while being only preliminary. We concentrated instead on the ways of eliciting tacit knowledge in top-down ontology formation, since combining top-down with bottom up results seems to be the most sensitive part of ontology construction.

8   An Application: Adaptive Hermeneutic Agent (AHA) and Network Services

As already indicated, a most basic process of scientific knowledge creation is *hermeneutics* – gathering scientific information and knowledge from literature (Gadamer 1960), the web, and other sources, interpreting, and reflecting on these materials. In its classical interpretation, the concept of *hermeneutics* as well as the related concept of a *hermeneutic circle* were restricted to humanities and even stressed in (Gadamer 1960) as defining features of humanistic research. However, *hermeneutics* is necessary in every knowledge creation, even in hard sciences or during technology creation. This was stressed in (Wierzbicki and Nakamori 2006), where the *hermeneutic circle* was represented as a spiral-like process of knowledge creation: the *EAIR Spiral* (Enlightenment – Analysis – Immersion - Reflection), which is a part of the *Triple Helix Model* of academic knowledge creation, see also [35].

In order to understand what aspect of knowledge creation process we should consider first and particularly, we conducted a survey at JAIST. Some specific diverse requirements as well as important factors have been discovered through the survey study [16]. According to the survey results, one of important requirements for researchers is "plentiful information and knowledge resources for research". It also confirmed the importance of the basic process of scientific knowledge creation – *hermeneutics* – independently whether it concerns humanities, social sciences, hard sciences or technology creation, whether it occurs at academia or in organisational knowledge creation.

On the basis of requirements of users (researchers) and the phenomenon of *hermeneutics*, a software tool for information and knowledge retrieval was designed, in order to help researchers in gathering and interpreting relevant knowledge or research materials; this software tool is called *Adaptive Hermeneutic Agent (AHA)*.

The AHA is equipped with a simple and intuitive search interface and uses familiar search syntax, such as used by popular search engines (like Google, Yahoo). The search support can be extended to the definition of queries that will be automatically executed by the system with a fixed period of time. The definition of a query by the user is helped by ontological information; actually, the ontology described above is used in AHA as a basis of defining queries that can be selected from this ontology, supplemented or modified, for example, by adding new keywords that are relevant to the searched topic. After the query is executed, the AHA can also filter the obtained results by using a reinforcement learning approach that relies on a profile of the user's interests. The AHA could also use a visual interface for the clustering and graphical presentation of search results. Fig. 9 presents the modular structure of the AHA.

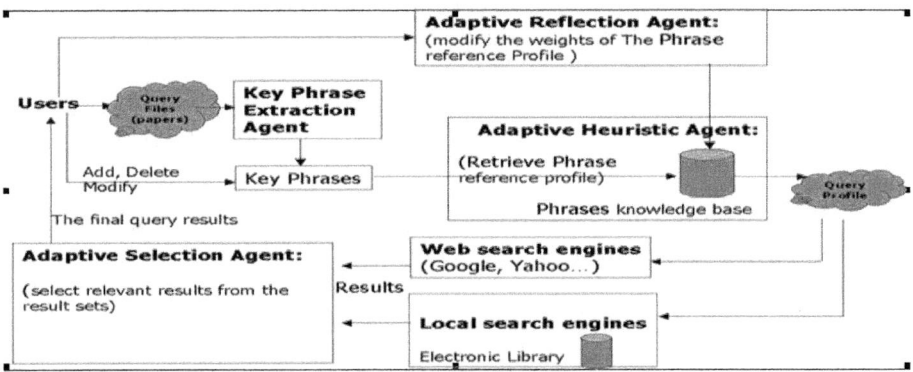

Fig. 9. The modular structure of the AHA

Therefore, the COE ontology as described earlier is an important element in developing the software tool of AHA. The general process of interplay with the AHA included four steps:

- *Construction of domain ontology* (as described earlier).
- *Creation of user profile*. The user, for example, a COE member, could extract the knowledge from COE ontology to formulate the outline of user profile, for example, select the domains (keywords) he are most interested in and give the weights for different keywords. Fig. 10 shows an interface of creating user profile based on a given ontology (e.g., that of COE Program).
- *Gathering of relevant knowledge*. The user could gather relevant knowledge and information based on his profile by using search engines connected to AHA. Fig. 11 shows the interface of the download agent, users can select search engines (Google, Yahoo, or both of them); select document types (PDF, Ms-word or both of them). Once the download process is done, the user can store the descriptions of the files into the local database. Fig. 12 shows the interface of management of the files, user can make the first round of selection: Open files from the files list; remove the files the user are not interested.

- *Adaptive selection*. The AHA will do adaptive selection automatically as following steps: text extraction (from MS-word file to text or from PDF file to text); keyword extraction and frequents calculation (extracting keywords from the search results by statistics method); measurement of the similarity of each file and user profile; giving a ranking list including top N results.

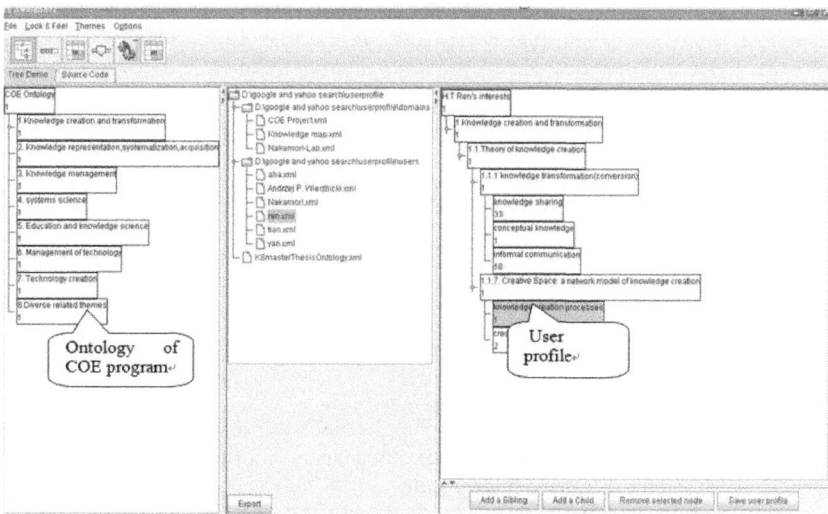

Fig. 10. The main interface of creating user profile based on a given ontology

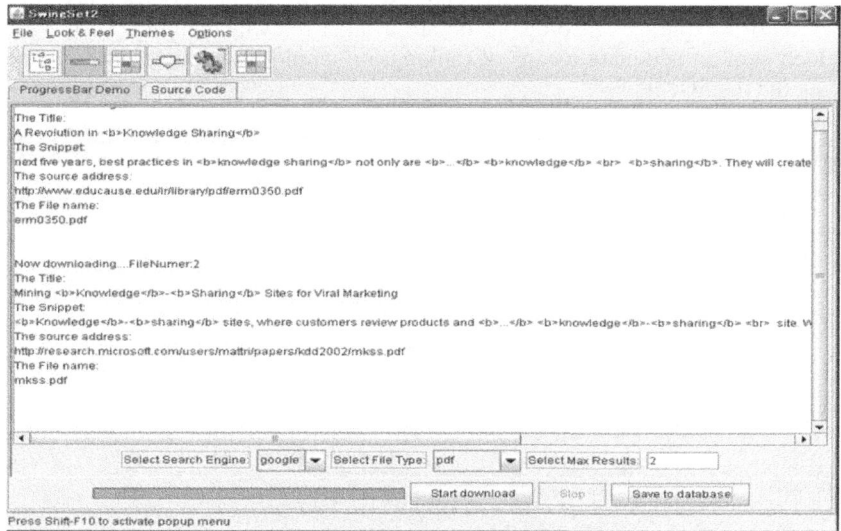

Fig. 11. The interface of the download agent

Fig. 13 shows the interface of text processing, Fig. 14 is graphical presentation of similarity of the document and the user profile, the group of blue bars shows the reference distribution, the group of red bars presents the keyphrases distribution of an exemplar of the document (TOMASSIN.txt). Fig. 15 gives a ranking list including top N results.

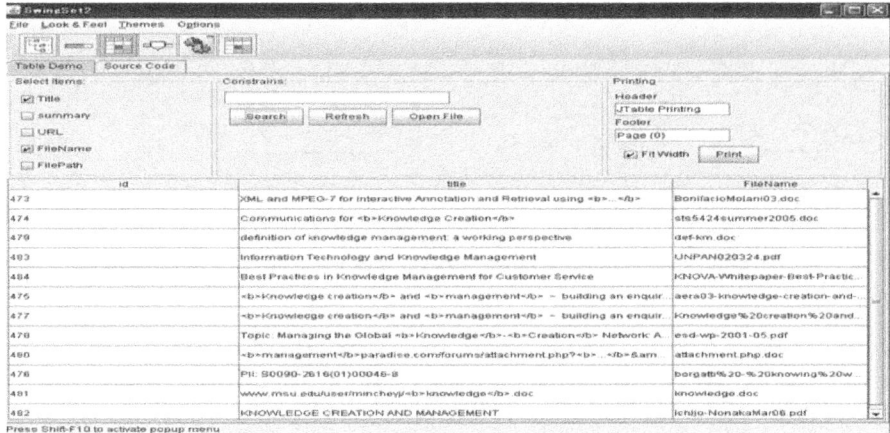

Fig. 12. The interface of management of files

The adaptive hermeneutic agent (AHA) is still being developed further. The crucial issues to be answered yet are: how to stimulate the user to specify most relevant keywords or keyphrases, knowing that her/his tacit knowledge is most important and difficult to elicit? How to modify and use the weighting coefficients for these keywords or keyphrases in order to obtain a most relevant ranking? Is the use of a weighted sum an adequate means of ranking, or should we include other methods of ranking the results; etc.?

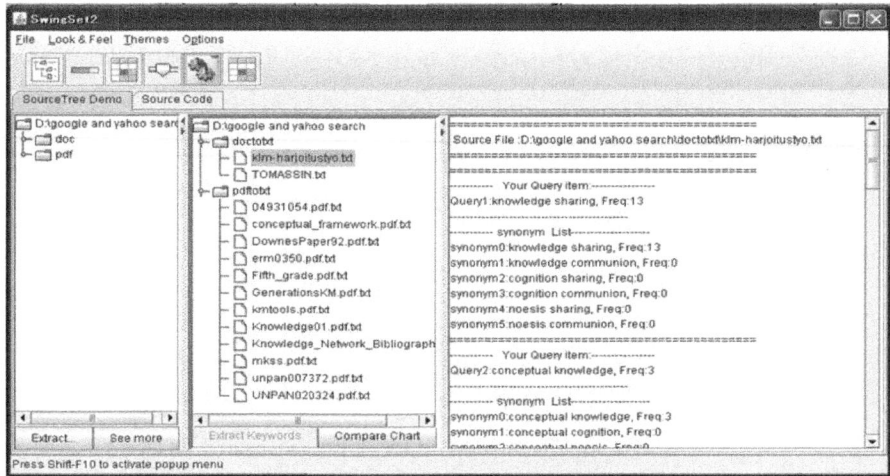

Fig. 13. The interface of text processing

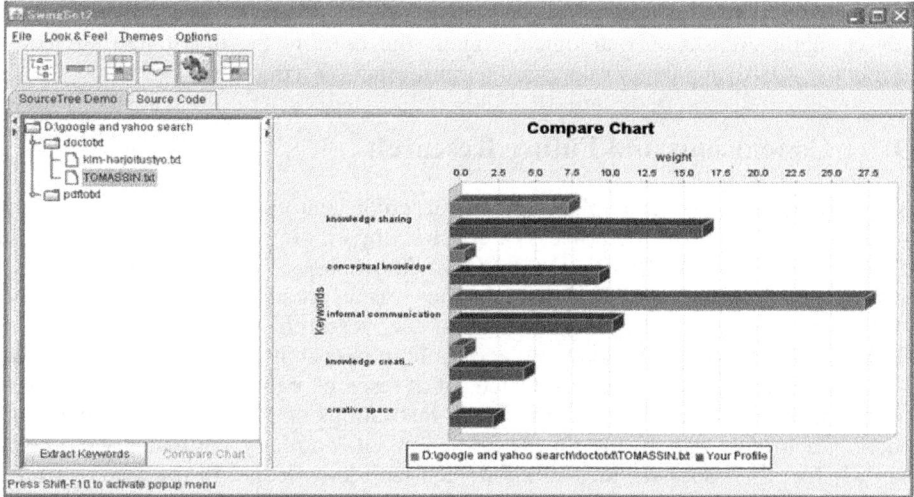

Fig. 14. Graphical presentation of similarity of documents and the user profile

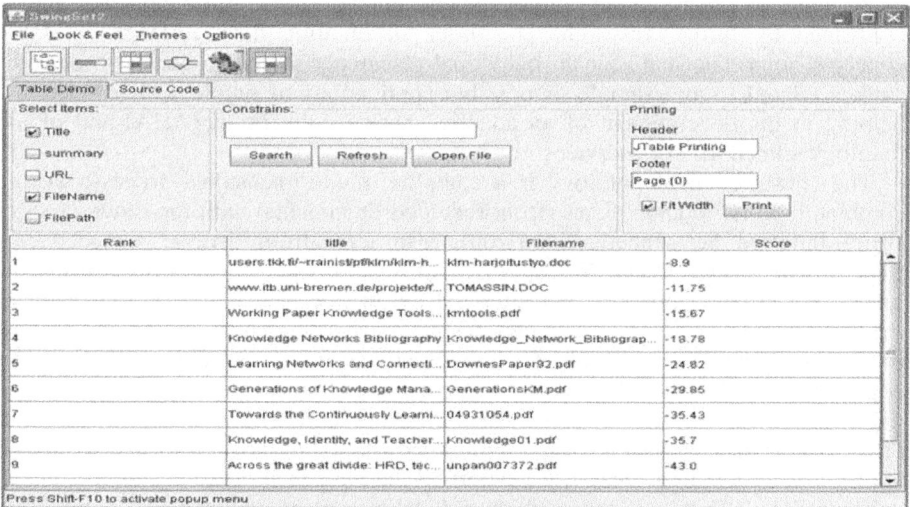

Fig. 15. A ranking list of the search results

Even if the results on the AHA are still tentative, we present them here because they can be used for developing network services in ontological engineering. The number of local, small universities or research institutions in the world will undoubtedly grow and not all of them will be able to develop ontological engineering services, while all of them will need support in local knowledge and creativity management. A solution might be to organize a network service: a server located, say, at a local (regional, etc.) university or research institution with strong capabilities in computer science, accessible as a network service by a distributed group of related small universities. The server might contain an ontological engine, the users at the distributed universities might use AHA support for scientific literature studies on the web.

9   Conclusions and Future Research

We presented two examples of constructing ontologies for local research organisations. One was the process of constructing ontology of the 21st Century COE Program *Technology Creation Based on Knowledge Science* in the School of Knowledge Science at JAIST, Japan; another was an attempt to use these experiences for constructing ontology characterizing the research of National Institute of Telecommunications in Warsaw, Poland. In both cases bottom-up ontology formation – starting with the analysis of a selected set of research papers – was essential but not sufficient for characterizing local research institutions or communities. In both cases more important was a top-down formation of ontology, utilizing expert tacit knowledge; the issue was how to elicit such tacit knowledge. In the case of COE at JAIST it was achieved with the help of a hermeneutic process based on reflection on the concept of knowledge science or sciences. In the case of NIT it seems that the most relevant results are derived by converting the organisational structure of the institution into a hierarchy of ontological concepts; this conclusion, however, must be confirmed by further research. This issue of eliciting most relevant ontological concepts, important, e.g., for an individual researcher, is also a question for further studies related to an example of possible applications of ontological engineering – helping in the development of an adaptive hermeneutic agent (AHA) and of local ontology related network services.

The construction of ontology is a complex, multidimensional process; we must combine bottom-up approaches (from recorded documents) with top-down processes (from intuitive hermeneutical horizon), also look from diverse perspectives to improve the final product. We stress in this paper that this process is actually a knowledge creation process, characterized by an interplay between using tacit and explicit knowledge, and all known results concerning such knowledge creation processes might be applicable for the combination of top-down and bottom-up approaches. Such a novel perception might enrich the methodology of ontological engineering. No matter, however, what methodological approaches are used, the effort spent on ontology construction is profitable in terms of diverse possible applications, including creativity support by helping in a creative illumination and enlightenment. Thus we foresee further development of applications of ontological engineering in diverse tasks of knowledge management, including a development of localized network services in ontological engineering.

Acknowledgement. The research was supported partly by 21st COE (Center of Excellence) Program "Study of Scientific Knowledge Creation" of JAIST, a fund by Ministry of Education, Culture, Sports, Science and Technology (MEXT, Japan), and partly by a grant of Polish Ministry of Science and High Education PBZ – MNiSW – 02/II/2007 entitled "Teleinformatic services and networks of next generation – aspects of technology, applications and market orientation". The authors would like also to thank an unnamed reviewer for helpful critical comments that helped to improve the manuscript.

Appendix: An Ontology of the COE Program at JAIST

General Category: Knowledge Science(s)

1. Knowledge creation and transformation
    1.1. Theory of knowledge creation
        1.1.1.   Knowledge transformation (conversion)
            knowledge sharing (40), conceptual knowledge (32), informal communication (19), shared informal space (10), cross-language text summarization (6), structured document (4), individual knowledge model (3), processes and spirals of knowledge (1), interdisciplinary communication, communication skill
        1.1.2.   Environments to support knowledge creation (Ba)
            creative environment (1), Ba
        1.1.3.   Organizational knowledge creation
            organizational knowledge creation(17), ensemble learning (1),
        1.1.4.   Academic and scientific knowledge creation
            scientific knowledge creation (32), academic knowledge creation (14), a shortage of researchers (1), research planning (7), research philosophy
        1.1.5.   I^5-System: a pentagram of knowledge creation
            I-system (1),
        1.1.6.   Theory of knowledge expression and integration
            clustering (68), feature extraction (64), text summarization (44), text clustering (36), sentence extraction (23), Knowledge discovery (22), semantic similarity measure (17), knowledge integration (6),
        1.1.7.   Creative space: a network model of knowledge creation
            knowledge creation processes (17), creative space (44)
        1.1.8. Innovation
            social innovation, regional innovation, regional revitalization system theory, methodology of regional revitalization, innovation in mature industries, pattern of innovation
    1.2. Creativity and knowledge
        1.2.1.   Tacit knowledge and creativity
            tacit knowledge (35), explicit knowledge (26), knowledge reconstruction (23)
        1.2.2.   The power and methods of stimulation of intuition in creative processes
        1.2.3.   The role of emotions in creative processes
        1.2.4.   Hermeneutics and creativity
            knowledge reconstruction (23), adaptive agent (16),
        1.2.5.   Debate and creativity
        1.2.6.   Experiments and creativity
        1.2.7.   Imagination and knowledge integration for creativity

1.3. Philosophy of knowledge

    1.3.1 Episteme of diverse cultural spheres

        knowledge civilization era (17), industrial civilization (26),

    1.3.2 Emergence of new concepts in science and technology

    1.3.3 Hermeneutics, ontology and hermeneutical horizons

2. Knowledge representation, systematization, acquisition

    2.1 knowledge representation and integration

    2.2 Knowledge systematization

        2.1.1.   Ontology of knowledge creation and management

            ontology (34),

        2.1.2.   International networking and knowledge mapping

        2.1.3.   Knowledge interest profiles, methods of web search

    2.3 knowledge acquisition (data and text mining)

        data mining (47), text mining (13), information extraction (11),

        natural language processing (1), association rule mining (20),

3. Knowledge management

    3.1 knowledge management in business and industry

    3.2 knowledge management in academia

        laboratory knowledge management (7)

    3.3 Information infrastructure for knowledge management

        information retrieval (20), knowledge management system (8),

        electronic library, information science (33), information technology

        (31),

    3.4 Development and practice of knowledge management

4   Systems science

    4.1 Hard (technological, mathematical) systems science

        4.1.1 Mathematical complexity theory

        Systems engineering (11)

        4.1.2 Hierarchical systems

        4.1.3 Systems of computerized decision support

        4.1.4 Multivalued logic (fuzzy and rough sets)

        rough sets (10)

    4.2 Soft (sociological, managerial) systems science and methodologies

        4.2.1 Systems thinking and soft systems methodologies

        systems thinking (19); systems approach (18); systems concepts

        (10); soft system methodology (3); systemic thinking (2);

        4.2.2 Integration of social information in knowledge

        informational revolution (8)

5   Education and knowledge science

    5.1 Education in knowledge sciences

        5.1.1 Knowledge creators

        5.1.2 Knowledge coordinators

        coordinator (1),

The above classification is naturally not absolute nor the ultimately final; it might be further enhanced and corrected as new data will become available.

References

1. Akkermans, H., Gordijn, J.: Ontology Engineering, Scientific Method and the Research Agenda. In: Staab, S., Svátek, V. (eds.) EKAW 2006. LNCS (LNAI), vol. 4248, pp. 112–125. Springer, Heidelberg (2006)
2. Bjørner, D.: Software Engineering: Domains, Requirements, and Software Design. Springer, Heidelberg (2006)
3. Simperl, E.P.B., Tempich, C.: Ontology Engineering: A Reality Check. In: Meersman, R., Tari, Z. (eds.) OTM 2006. LNCS, vol. 4275, pp. 836–854. Springer, Heidelberg (2006)

4. Corcho, O., Fernández-López, M., Gómez-Pérez, A.: Methodologies, Tools and Languages for Building Ontologies: Where is their meeting Point? Data & Knowledge Engineering 46, 41–64 (2003)
5. Davenport, T., Prusak, L.: Working knowledge: how organizations manage what they know. Harvard Business School Press, Boston Ma (1998)
6. Dieng, R., Corby, O.: Knowledge Engineering and Knowledge Management: Methods, Models and Tools. Springer, Heidelberg (2000)
7. Ding, Y., Foo, S.: Ontology Research and Development. Part I – A Review of Ontology Generation. Journal of Information Science 28(2), 123–136 (2002)
8. Gadamer, H-G.: Warheit und Methode. Grundzüge einer philosophishen Hermeneutik.J.B.C. Mohr (Siebeck), Tübingen (1960)
9. Gruber, T.R.: A Translation Approach to Portable Ontology Specifications. Knowledge Acquisitions 2(5), 199–220 (1993)
10. Heidegger, M.: Sein und Zeit, Niemayer, Halle (1927)
11. Heyer, L.J., Kruglyak, S., Yooseph, S.: Exploring Expression Data: Identification and Analysis of Coexpressed Genes. Genome Res. 9, 1106–1115 (1999)
12. Król, Z.: The Emergence of New Concepts in Science. In: Wierzbicki, A.P., Nakamori, Y. (eds.) Creative Environments, op.cit (2007)
13. Luhn, H.P.: The Automatic Creation of Literature Abstracts. I.B.M. Journal of Research and Development 2(2), 159–165 (1958)
14. Ma, T., Liu, S., Nakamori, Y.: Roadmapping for Supporting Scientific Research. In: 17th International Conference on Multiple Criteria Decision Making, Whistler, Canada (2004)
15. McGuinness, D.L.: Ontologies Come of Age. In: Fensel, D., Hendler, J., Lieberman, H., Wahlster, W. (eds.) Spinning the Semantic Web: Bringing the World Wide Web to its Full Potential, pp. 171–192. MIT Press, Cambridge (2002)
16. Mizoguchi, R., Kozaki, K., Sano, T., Kitamura, Y.: Construction and Deployment of a Plant Ontology. In: Dieng, R., Corby, O. (eds.) EKAW 2000. LNCS (LNAI), vol. 1937, pp. 113–128. Springer, Heidelberg (2000)
17. Nakamori, Y.: Introduction to a COE Program at JAIST. In: Proceedings of International Forum Technology Creation Based on Knowledge Science: Theory and Practice, JAIST, Japan, November 10-12, pp. 1–4 (2004)
18. Nie, K.: Towards a Domain Analysis of Knowledge Management as an Organizational Activity. Presentation in Group Seminar at COE Center of JAIST (2007)
19. Nonaka, I., Takeuchi, H.: The knowledge-creating company – How Japanese companies create the dynamics of innovation. Oxford University Press, New York (1995)
20. Pfeffer, J., Sutton, R.I.: The knowing – doing gap: how smart companies turn knowledge into action. Harvard Business School Press, Boston (2000)
21. Phaal, R., Farrukh, C., Probert, D.: Technology Roadmapping a Planning Framework for Evolution and Revolution. Technological Forecasting and Social Change 71, 5–26 (2004)
22. Pinto, H.S., Martins, J.P.: Ontologies: How can They be Built? Knowledge and Information Systems 6, 441–464 (2004)
23. Ren, H., Wierzbicki, A.P.: Implementing Creative Environments for Scientifc Research. Journal of Information and Decision Science (2008)
24. Ren, H., Tian, J., Nakamori, Y.M., Wierzbicki, A.P.: Electronic Support for Knowledge Creation in a Research Institute. Journal of Systems Science and Systems Engineering 16(2) (2007)
25. Ren, H., Tian, J., Wierzbicki, A.P., Nakamori, Y.: Ontology Construction and Its Applications to a Research Program. To appear in Journal of Integrated Computer Aided Engineering (2008)

26. Saito, A., Umemoto, K., Ikeda, M.: A Strategy-based Ontology of Knowledge Management Technologies. Journal of Knowledge Management 11(1), 97–114 (2007)
27. Salo, A., Cuhls, K.: Technology Foresight – Past and Future. Journal of Forecasting 22(2-3), 79–82 (2003)
28. Tian, J., Nakamori, Y.: Knowledge Management in Scientific Laboratories: A Survey-based Study of a Research Institute. In: The Second International Symposium on Knowledge Management for Strategic Creation of Technology, Kobe, Japan, pp. 19–26 (2005)
29. Tian, J., Wierzbicki, A.P., Ren, H., Nakamori, Y.: A Study of Knowledge Creation Support in a Japanese Research Institute. International Journal of Knowledge and System Science 3(1), 7–17 (2006)
30. Totok, H.W.: Towards Knowledge Mapping of Advanced Education in Knowledge Creation. Presentation in Group Seminar at COE Center of JAIST (2006)
31. Totok, H.W., Nie, K., Ji, Z.: An Implementation of Knowledge Maps for Sharing Explicit Knowledge. Presentation in Group Seminar at COE Center of JAIST (2006)
32. Uschold, M., Grüninger, M.: Ontologies Principles Methods and Applications. Knowledge Engineering Review 11(2) (1996)
33. http://www.upv.es/sma/teoria/sma/onto/96-ker-intro-ontologies.pdf
34. Wierzbicki, A.P., Nakamori, Y.: Creative Space: Models of Creative Processes for the Knowledge Civilization Age. Springer, Heidelberg (2006)
35. Wierzbicki, A.P., Nakamori, Y.: Creative Environments: Issues of Creativity Support for the Knowledge Civilization Age. Springer, Heidelberg (2007)
36. Wierzbicki, A.P., Nakamori, Y.: Knowledge Sciences – Some New Developments. Zeitschrift für Betriebswirtschaft 77(3), 271–296 (2007a)
37. Wiig, K.M.: Knowledge Management: an Introduction and Perspective. Journal of Knowledge Management 1(1), 145–156 (1997)
38. Willyard, C.H., McClees, C.W.: Motorola's Technology Roadmap Process. Research Management 30(5), 13–19 (1987)
39. http://www.niederlandistik.fu-berlin.de/textstat/software-en.html
40. http://www.neurosoft.pl
41. http://www.lucene.apache.org
42. http://www.empolis.com
43. http://www.oracle.com
44. Ontogeny.ijs.si
45. SAS 9.1documentation

Author Index